THE PURCHASE
OF INTIMACY

The Purchase
of Intimacy

Viviana A. Zelizer

PRINCETON UNIVERSITY PRESS

PRINCETON AND OXFORD

ISBN-13: 978-0-691-12408-7
ISBN-10: 0-691-12408-6

Library of Congress Cataloging-in-Publication Data

Zelizer, Viviana A. Rotman.
The purchase of intimacy / Viviana A. Zelizer.
p.   cm.
Includes bibliographical references and index.
ISBN 0-691-12408-6 (hardcover : alk. paper)
1. Couples—Finance, Personal. 2. Interpersonal relations—Economic aspects.
3. Financial security. I. Title.
HG179.Z45   2005
332.024′01′0865—dc22   2005007983

British Library Cataloging-in-Publication Data is available

This book has been composed in Janson Text with Copperplate Display

Printed on acid-free paper. ∞

pup.princeton.edu

Printed in the United States of America

10 9 8 7 6 5 4 3 2 1

To Jerry

CONTENTS

ACKNOWLEDGMENTS

This book took ten years to mature. During that time, I found myself increasingly involved in the emerging field of economic sociology. Whether we have agreed or disagreed, I have learned a great deal from dialogue with colleagues in that field as well as in economics and law. I have built many of the lessons I have learned into the book. Despite nineteenth-century origins with such greats as Karl Marx, Georg Simmel, and Max Weber, more recently changes in economic sociology have emerged from an uneven dialogue between sociology and economics. Economic sociologists have characteristically sought to criticize, extend, improve, or contextualize economists' own analyses of economic behavior. My own approach has been somewhat different. While dealing cordially and respectfully with my colleagues in economics, I have sought—in company with a number of other scholars—to analyze the interpersonal processes that actually go into what economists usually abstract into production, consumption, distribution, and transfer of assets.

My writings on economic sociology and my teaching of the subject at Princeton University have both reinforced my conviction that a distinct program of theory and research awaits those who are willing to work outside the shadow of neoclassical economics. To my agreeable surprise, this has meant that a number of innovative currents in contemporary economics—for example, behavioral economics, institutional economics, and feminist economics—are arriving at complementary definitions of the problems to be analyzed. The book draws repeatedly on contributions from these innovative fields.

While preparing this book, I have accumulated a great debt to American legal scholars. They have been surprisingly welcoming to a non-lawyer who has repeatedly called on them for information and advice. My helpful informants and advisers include Ariela Dubler, Hendrik Hartog, Barbara Hauser, Marjorie Kornhauser, Mark Momjian, Claire Priest, Carol Sanger, Reva Siegel, Rebecca Tushnet, Joan Williams, and John Witt. Dirk Hartog scrutinized the text knowledgeably for uncertainties and ambiguities in legal history and found quite a few; I am grateful to Dirk for his caring attention.

Outside the legal profession, a wide range of scholars have helped me along. They include Bernard Barber, Sara Curran, Paul DiMaggio, Mitchell Duneier, Marion Fourcade, Susan Gal, Michael Katz, Daniel Miller, Julie Nelson, Charles Tilly, Florence Weber, and Eviatar Zerubavel. Throughout the book's writing, Chuck Tilly gave me the benefit of his legendary help and criticism. A talented group of research assistants have also collaborated in this project: Nicole Esparza, Alexandra Kalev, and Anna Zajacova. At the last minute, Alexis Cocco hunted down precise citations for a number of the legal cases. Access to cases on Westlaw comes compliments of Thomson-West.

For helpful reactions and criticism, I am grateful to audiences at Columbia Law School; Harvard Law School; University of Miami Law School; Yale Law School; the annual meetings of the American Anthropological Association; the Center for Working Families, University of California at Berkeley; the École Normale Supérieure, Paris; the IX European Amalfi Prize Meeting; the Feminist Legal Theory Workshop; MIT's Sloan School of Management; the Radcliffe Institute; the Gender and Society Workshop, University of Chicago; and the departments of sociology at Rutgers University, Princeton University, Yale University, University of Pennsylvania, State University of New York at Albany, and University of California, Los Angeles.

The National Endowment for the Humanities at the Institute for Advanced Study, the John Simon Guggenheim Memorial Foundation, and Princeton University supported leave time for me to work on my research. Beth Gianfagna brought her elegant expertise to bear on editing my text. Deborah Tegarden of Princeton University Press took over the management of the manuscript masterfully. Throughout, virtuoso editor Peter Dougherty buoyed my spirits with his enthusiasm for the manuscript and his commitment to making the book widely available. And, finally, for moral support as I pursued this long inquiry, I am grateful to my families in Argentina and the United States.

Some passages in this book adapt materials from my previous publications: "Payments and Social Ties," *Sociological Forum* 11 (September 1996): 481–95; "Intimate Transactions," in Mauro F. Guillén, Randall Collins, Paula England, and Marshall Meyer, eds., *The New Economic Sociology: Developments in an Emerging Field* (New York: Russell Sage Foundation, 2002), 274–300 (French translation appeared as "Transactions intimes," *Genèses* 42 [March 2001]: 121–44); "Circuits of Commerce," in Jeffrey C. Alexander, Gary T. Marx, and Christine Williams, eds., *Self, Social Structure, and Beliefs: Explorations in Sociology* (Berkeley: University of California Press, 2004), 122–44; "Kids and Commerce," *Childhood* 4 (November 2002): 375–96; "The Purchase of Intimacy," *Law & Social Inquiry* 25 (Summer 2000): 817–48; "How Care Counts," *Contemporary Sociology* 31 (March 2002): 115–19; "Culture and Consumption," in Neil Smelser and Richard Swedberg, eds., *Handbook of Economic Sociology*, 2nd ed. (Princeton, NJ: Princeton University Press and New York: Russell Sage Foundation, 2005, pp. 331–54); and "The Priceless Child Revisited," forthcoming in Jens Qvortrup, ed., *Studies in Modern Childhood: Society, Agency and Culture* (London: Palgrave, 2005).

PROLOGUE

All of us sometimes gobble up the details of a famous couple's divorce settlement, worry about whether certain children are suffering from their parents' profligate spending, become indignant when someone close to us fails to meet important economic obligations, or complain about proposals to cut funding for day-care centers. When any of those things happens, we enter the territory in which economic activity and intimacy meet. In that territory, many people feel that two incompatible forces clash and wound each other: economic activity—especially the use of money—degrades intimate relationships, while interpersonal intimacy makes economic activity inefficient.

In these regards routine social life makes us all experts in the purchase of intimacy. Nevertheless, this book shows that the territory includes many a surprising corner. American law, for example, employs significantly different pictures of intimate social life from those that prevail in everyday American practices. One of this book's major objectives, indeed, consists of analyzing the relationship between everyday practices and legal disputes when it comes to intimate economic interactions. More generally, *The Purchase of Intimacy* deals with how people and the law manage the mingling of what sometimes seem to be incompatible activities: the maintenance of intimate personal relations and the conduct of economic activity. Taboos against romantic affairs in the workplace and against sex for hire both rest on the twinned beliefs that intimacy corrupts the economy and the economy corrupts intimacy. Yet, as this book shows, people often mingle economic activity with intimacy. The two often sustain each other. You will find the coexistence of economy and intimacy hard to understand if you think that economic self-interest determines all social relations, if you imagine that the world splits sharply into separate spheres of rationality and sentiment, or if you suppose that intimacy is a delicate plant that can only survive in a thick-windowed greenhouse. This book untangles those misunderstandings, replacing them with a clearer view of the conditions under which intimacy and economic activity complement each other.

Yet the book doesn't simply dismiss people's concerns about intimacy. A valuable by-product of this inquiry is fresh insight into how and why people worry so much about mixing intimacy and economic activity, for example, by fearing that introducing money into friendship, marriage, or parent-child relations will corrupt them. That is why *The Purchase of Intimacy* has a title with a double meaning: purchase in the sense of paying for intimacy, but also purchase in the sense of grasp—how the powerful grip of intimacy affects the ways we organize economic life. The book shows that people lead connected lives, and that plenty of economic activity goes into creating, defining, and sustaining social ties.

In 1994, I published a book called *The Social Meaning of Money.* In some ways, that book set the stage for this new inquiry. It documented, for example, the widespread employment of money in a large number of interpersonal relations and posed the question of how people manage the conjunction. Yet if you had asked me to predict in 1994 the subject and contents of my next book, I never would have expected it to take its present form. *The Social Meaning of Money* explored changes in U.S. social practices resulting from the expansion of monetary transactions. It showed that monetization did indeed present Americans with new challenges. But it also documented that instead of turning away from money or letting their social relations wither in the headlong pursuit of lucre, Americans actually incorporated money into their construction of new social ties and transformed its meaning as they did so. While still drawing on historical knowledge, the present book, in contrast, concentrates on the processes by which people negotiate coherent connections between intimacy and economic activity. Here economic activity includes uses of money, but goes far beyond money into production, consumption, distribution, and transfers of non-monetary assets.

That expansion of the problem leads to new understandings of the ways in which people actually construct viable interpersonal relations and ways of life. It provides unexpected insights into the moral discourse and practical distinctions that both ordinary people and legal specialists employ when dealing with disputed forms of interpersonal intimacy. So doing, it touches on a question that columnists, critics, philosophers, and politicians often ask: Does the penetration of an ever-expanding market threaten intimate social life? Many people have thought so. They have insisted that public policy must insulate household relations, personal care, and love itself from an invading, predatory, economic world. This book rejects such views. It analyzes how all of us use economic activity to create, maintain, and renegotiate important ties—especially intimate ties—to other people. It isn't easy. In everyday life, people invest intense effort and constant worry in finding the right match between economic relations and intimate ties: shared responsibility for housework, spending of household income, care for children and old people, gifts that send the right message, provision of adequate housing for loved ones, and much more. Furthermore, when these matters become the subjects of legal disputes, new distinctions, new rules, and new definitions of proper behavior in different social relations come into play. *The Purchase of Intimacy* shows how these crucial processes work.

Here are some very general questions the book raises and tries to answer:

- What explains the fears and taboos that surround the mixing of economic activity and intimate social relations?
- Given the delicacy of mixing economic activity and intimacy, how do people manage it?
- How do people balance the short-term economic requirements of intimate relations (for example, a cohabiting couple's food, rent, and transportation) with their long-term ac-

cumulation of rights, obligations, and shared means of survival?

- What happens when the mixing becomes a matter of legal dispute, for example, in contested divorces and claims of undue influence over a will?
- How well do existing explanations of these matters hold up, and how must we change them?
- What implications do correct answers to these questions have for policy on such matters as professional ethics and payment for personal care?

The Purchase of Intimacy offers answers to all these questions. More specific problems arise from these general issues. Consider the following, for example:

- How do ordinary people and courts distinguish between legitimate and illegitimate transfers of money between sexual partners?
- Is paid care for children fundamentally inferior to unpaid care provided by family members?
- Under what conditions does a divorced parent have a legal obligation to pay for a child's college education?
- When kin help each other with household responsibilities, what moral and legal claims do they acquire on each other's estates?
- How do courts go about assigning value to such household services when they become matters of legal dispute?

In this book, I work out answers to these questions through stories of how intimate transactions actually play themselves out, notably in the realms of coupling, caring relations, and household life. I draw many of my stories from law and the courts, which must often deal with situations in which people's intimate transactions degenerate. There we see clearly the gap between time-honored conventions and evolving social practices. The cases show both remarkable parallels and fascinating differences between everyday practices and the law. They also show how the law adjusts to evolving social rules and emerging social forms such as unmarried partnerships. Contests within the law lead to more general issues of public policy, such as obligations of divorced couples to their children, responsibility for care of the ill and the aged, rights of same-sex couples, and proper compensation for household caregiving. Although this book does not lay out a general program of social reform, it sheds light on why and how these issues matter.

The book draws especially on the work of social scientists, policy specialists, and legal scholars. But it also uses a wide range of other material, for example, reports on compensation to survivors of 9/11 victims, Web sites on financial management, and advice books for same-sex couples. It presents a number of legal cases in which plaintiffs, defendants, lawyers, judges, and juries fought over questions of intimacy. Despite their legal language, its case materials overflow with life. They also add up to a new story about intimate relations, one quite different from the idea of intimacy as a fragile flower that withers on contact with money and economic self-interest.

Although it analyzes extensive legal materials, this book is not, however, a legal treatise on intimate relations. As will soon become very clear, legal scholars energetically and fruitfully take up a number of issues that arise here, but from different perspectives than this study employs. My intention is not either to provide surveys of the history of law concerning intimacy and economic activity or to analyze the major competing schools of thought within contemporary legal scholarship, much less to resolve existing controversies in that contentious field. Nor do I say much about how and why legal treatments of intimacy have changed over time. Yet lawyers and legal scholars should find the book interesting simply because it looks hard at the relationship between everyday practices and legal proceedings. Any reader who has ever become involved in a legal wrangle over an inheritance, a broken engagement, a divorce, child care, obligations to aging parents, or compensation for loss of a loved one also has something to learn from looking at the legal arena in this book's light.

As a result, you can choose between two different ways of reading the book. You can read it chapter by chapter as I have written it, starting with general questions about intimacy and economic activity, moving on to legal treatments of intimacy, then proceeding through closer inspections of intimate couples, of caring relationships, and of households to general conclusions, including policy implications. Or you can turn directly to the topics that interest you most, for example, by starting with the chapter on households, which looks hard at household production, consumption, distribution, transfers of assets, and their connections with intimate relations before analyzing how household relations become matters of legal dispute. Either way, I promise you fresh insights into topics on which we all imagine ourselves to be experts from our own repeated encounters with intimacy.

CHAPTER 1

ENCOUNTERS OF INTIMACY AND ECONOMY

In the parish of Catahoula, Louisiana, during the 1840s Samuel Miller lived on his plantation with Patsy, his mulatto slave and sexual partner. In 1843, as Miller fell ill with dropsy, he sold the land and his slaves to Hugh Lucas, settling for nine promissory notes of $3,000 each, to be paid yearly. In April 1844, Miller, who was in declining health, left Louisiana with Patsy for St. Louis, Missouri. Before leaving, Miller gave the promissory notes to William Kirk, asking him to "keep them for Patsy's benefit" since "he intended to have her emancipated, and that he wanted the notes to enure to her benefit" (*Cole v. Lucas*, 2 La. Ann. 1946, 1948 (1847)).[1] The previous year, Miller had granted Kirk power of attorney, authorizing him to emancipate Patsy.

Later in 1844, Kirk brought the promissory notes to Missouri and returned them to Miller. Patsy received her emancipation in Madison City, Indiana, in May 1844. Back in Missouri, Miller gave

---

[1] All legal citations appear parenthetically in the text only; they are not repeated in the reference list. Most follow this format: (Name v. Name, Volume Reporter Opening page number (Court Year)). Depending on the reporter, some case citations don't require the court's name before the date. Occasionally, opinions are "unreported" by the official reporters but are available on Westlaw or Lexis anyway. In those instances, an asterisk precedes the page number. In order to make reading easier, I have departed from legal convention in one regard: where legal sources

her the notes. He died a week or so later, on May 21. Patsy and Miller were apparently living in modest circumstances; the inventory of his possessions conducted in January 1845 listed these items: "One man slave and four children, and one woman who had run away in October previous, and not since been heard of, a book-account of $500 against William Kirk, one dinner table, two breakfast tables, one feather bed and bedstead, one small bedstead or lounge and one gun" (949–50). After Miller's death, Cole, Miller's former neighbor in Catahoula, traveled to Missouri and bought the promissory notes from Patsy.

We know of these events and people because the court in Catahoula heard a suit by Cole against Lucas, the debtor in the notes. Cole, as owner of the notes, demanded that Lucas pay him the annual installments. As the suit proceeded, however, a certain Griffin, representing Miller's heirs, intervened, claiming ownership of the promissory notes. Yet the jury hearing this trial ruled against Griffin and in favor of Cole, confirming Cole as the notes' rightful owner.

On what grounds could the heirs intervene? Up to this point, after all, the transactions seemed straightforward. While acknowledging that Miller gave Patsy the promissory notes and that she sold them to Cole, the family claimed that Patsy had no legal or moral right to the notes. If the family's claim was correct, Cole himself therefore did not have legal ownership of the notes. The case pivoted on the relationship between Miller and Patsy: was she Miller's slave? Was she his concubine? Or were they essentially man and wife? If a slave, under Louisiana law she could legally receive no gifts at all. As a concubine, she could only receive the equivalent of one-tenth of the value of her lover's estate in movables, but no immovables. If his wife, she could receive any gift whatsoever. The Catahoula jury ruled that the gift was legal because Patsy was already free at the time she received the promissory notes. They also accepted Cole's claim that the more liberal laws of Missouri applied to her legal status and to the transfer itself.

---

that repeat a citation typically use the form "(*Id.* at 85)," I have simply reported the page number in parentheses: "(85)."

But the heirs did not give up; they appealed the Catahoula decision to the Supreme Court of Louisiana. The court accepted the heirs' arguments that Miller's move to Missouri had circumvented Louisiana law and that Miller's friends had provided no evidence of Patsy's having received the notes after her emancipation. Again, notice what is happening: except for some questions about dates, no one was disputing that Miller and Patsy had lived together or that Miller had given her the notes. The critical question was what relationship they had in the law's eyes at the time of the gift. The appeals court that reversed the initial jury verdict was anxious to defend the Louisiana law: "We have already stated our opinions of the relations subsisting between the parties to this donation. The disabilities under which the law places persons who have lived in this condition, are created for the maintenance of good morals, of public order, and for the preservation of the best interests of society" (952). Thus, the court inserted a condemnation of interracial concubinage into a judgment concerning domicile.

To twenty-first-century eyes, the whole case is astonishing. Here is a court overturning the efforts of a dying man, who clearly knew what he was doing, to protect his long-term companion's financial welfare. The couple had lived together for some time, and trusted friends knew of their connection. In fact, the court described their relationship as "open and notorious." Yet the appeals court decided that the legal standing of the relationship invalidated Miller's gift: Patsy had been his slave and his concubine. The court chose to interpret those relationships as applying to the moment of transfer. The issues raised by Patsy's 1847 case did not disappear with the coming of the twentieth century. They remain with us today. Courts still judge bitter disputes about economic rights and obligations established by competing personal relationships. They often pit two different intimate relations against each other: competing claims of siblings on their parents' estates, lovers versus estranged spouses, relatives against close friends, and more. Under the law, which relations imply what economic rights and obligations?

Settlements for victims of Al-Qaeda's 2001 suicide attacks on the World Trade Center and the Pentagon raised a surprising range of legal questions in exactly this vein. Seeking to head off the massive lawsuits against airlines and other organizations that survivors and families threatened to initiate, the U.S. Congress set up a Victim Compensation Fund for claimants who could prove their losses and who would forgo lawsuits. Experienced lawyer Kenneth Feinberg became the fund's master, adjudicating thousands of compensation claims. Feinberg settled most claims with substantial payments based on formulas assessing present and future financial losses due to deaths, injuries, and property damage. Yet in numerous cases more than one person claimed compensation for the same person's death. At times, spouses, parents, children, siblings, and lovers all claimed to be the fund's rightful beneficiaries.

These claims became especially contentious in the cases of unmarried but cohabiting couples, estranged spouses, and same-sex households. Fifty-year-old Patricia McAneney, for example, worked at an insurance company on the 94th floor of 1 World Trade Center, where she also served as her floor's fire marshal. She died in the 9/11 disaster. McAneney and her lesbian partner, Margaret Cruz, had lived together for almost twenty years. New York State, as a way of dealing with the 9/11 tragedy, recognized such domestic partnerships; along with New York's Crime Victim Board, the Red Cross and other organizations awarded Cruz $80,000. The federal fund, in contrast, generally appointed a spouse or relative as the victim's single official representative. In McAneney's case, her brother James claimed and received compensation for his sister's death. Cruz bitterly contested the Victim Compensation Fund's award exclusively to James.

Cruz submitted her own statement to Feinberg, detailing the couple's relationship. As a result, Feinberg doubled the original award on behalf of McAneney to about half a million dollars, basing his new estimate on a two-person household. But the fund still paid the additional money to James, as his sister's official representative. James refused to release any of the money to Cruz. At that point, Cruz filed a lawsuit against James, claiming that at least $253,000 of the award belonged to her. James rejected that claim on the grounds that under New York State law, Cruz had no legal rights to

any of his sister's property: the two women had no legally recognizable bond, they had never registered as domestic partners, and Patricia had died without leaving a will. Cruz replied, however, that

> her status as the domestic partner of the victim is authenticated
> by the fact that they lived together since 1985; that they re-
> cently occupied the same house in Pomona, NY; that they both
> paid the mortgage and shared basic household expenses; that
> they shared joint credit cards and joint AAA membership; and
> they owned a joint mutual fund, naming each other as the bene-
> ficiaries of their respective life insurance policies. In addition,
> Ms. Cruz notes that both the NYS World Trade Center Relief
> Fund and the NYS Crime Victims Board treated her as a surviv-
> ing spouse, awarding her the same benefit that she would have
> received had she and Ms. McAneney been legally married. (*New
> York Law Journal* 2004: 2)

New York Supreme Court Justice Yvonne Lewis supported Cruz's
claim. She turned down James McAneney's request to dismiss
Cruz's motion and ruled that Cruz was indeed entitled to at least a
portion of the award. The justice explained that "in light of the
plaintiff's relationship with the deceased, it would seem equitable
that she should receive a portion of any 9/11 fund" (Eaton 2004;
Leonard 2004). Nevertheless, Justice Lewis deferred her final decision, pending further information from Feinberg concerning the
basis for his increase of the award to McAneney. As recently as July
2004, American courts were still deciding bitter contests over the
legal and economic rights attached to intimate relationships.

Cases argued before the Louisiana Supreme Court in 1847 and
the New York State Supreme Court in 2004 set two major themes
for this book. First, the mingling of economic transactions and intimate relations regularly perplexes participants and observers, and it
does not perplex them because it happens rarely. On the contrary,
people are constantly mixing their intimate relations with economic
transactions. That mixing perplexes observers because of a common
belief that economic rationality and intimate ties contradict each
other, because each such intersection raises delicate questions about

the nature of relationships between those involved, and because shared economic activities establish strong rights and obligations among the participants. Second, the legal interpretation of intimate economic relations causes further perplexity. American law has trouble with those relations because it harbors some of the same suspicions concerning the compatibility of economic calculations with interpersonal solidarity and because cases that come before the law usually spring from serious disputes among intimates over who owes what to whom.

This book takes up these issues by asking three sets of questions.

1. Under what conditions, how, and with what consequences do people combine economic transactions with intimate relations?
2. Why and how do they erect complicated stories and practices for different situations that mingle economic transactions and intimacy?
3. How does the American legal system—attorneys, courts, judges, juries, and legal theorists—negotiate the coexistence of economic claims and intimate relations?

The book pursues its three questions by looking both at a wide variety of actual social practices as well as an array of court cases and legal disputes concerning intimacy and economic transactions. It thus explores the purchase of intimacy. I mean purchase in two senses: first, the frequent supposition that people use money to buy intimate relations and, second, the grip—the purchase—of intimacy on the forms and meanings of economic transactions.

The evidence shows, on one side, that over a wide variety of circumstances people do in fact negotiate the coexistence of economic interchange and intimate social relations. On the other side, however, it shows that maintaining their coexistence calls up a series of distinctions, defenses, and beliefs exerting substantial social power. Confronted with the mingling of intimacy and economic activity, participants, observers, legal authorities, and social scientists introduce powerful stories concerning the mutual effects of economic transactions and intimate social relations. They also introduce crucial distinctions among different combinations of relations, transactions, and payment media; defend those distinctions with moral practices; and put pressure on participants to respect relevant moral and legal codes. These stories and distinctions shape both social behavior and legal decisions.

The Catahoula case depended heavily on the proper definition of Patsy and Miller's relationship at the time of Miller's handing of the promissory notes to Patsy. If the Louisiana appeals court had recognized them as man and wife, the heirs would have had no claims whatsoever on the disputed notes; under Louisiana law, married couples had every right to own and transfer such media as commercial paper. Instead, the appeals court chose to interpret the relationship as slave to master, with the heirs benefiting as a consequence. Thus, at issue were definitions of Patsy and Miller's relationship, specification of the rights and duties belonging to that relationship, questions about the propriety of economic transfers within the relationship, plus a penumbra of concern about cohabitation between white men and black women (see Davis 1999; Pascoe 1999; Romano 2003; Van Tassel 1995).

For all its embedding in the histories of Louisiana, Missouri, slavery, race relations, and laws of property, the Catahoula legal dispute does not single out a rare, exceptional, now irrelevant set of circumstances. The mingling of economy and intimacy continues to pose challenges for social practices, judicial doctrines, and sociological explanation. As recently as 2004, 9/11 cases presented similar challenges, just as urgent for their participants. Within the range of American history since the 1840s, this book examines a wide variety of intersections between economic transactions and multiple forms of intimacy. Economic transactions include all social interactions involving consumption, production, and distribution of goods, services, or the means of acquiring them—for example, when one sibling buys a car from another, an immigrant father supervises his daughter's work in the family's store, a salesman spreads free samples among his close friends, or parents lend their children money for purchase of a home.

More often than not, the analyses that follow involve transfers of money. Money ultimately consists not of dollar bills but of accounting systems—those systems that produce equivalence among goods, services, and titles to them, plus the media used to represent value within the systems. For practical purposes, however, here we can call the media themselves money. Media range from very specific tokens, such as merchandise coupons, to extremely general devices, such as electronic currency transfers. The media used in the economic transactions that are the focus of this study most often consist of legal tender and its close equivalents, such as checks, credit cards, and commercial paper. I single out money-based transactions for three reasons: first, because they leave obvious traces in available records; second, because they dramatize questions of valuation that arise throughout this zone of mingled intimacy and economic transactions; and third, because many people (including social scientists) consider monetization an extreme and threatening form of economic rationalization (Zelizer 2001).

What about intimacy?[2] Like most value-laden terms, intimacy scintillates with multiple meanings, ranging from cool, close observation to hot involvement. The *Oxford English Dictionary* offers these main definitions: "1. (a) the state of being personally intimate; intimate friendship or acquaintance; familiar intercourse; close familiarity. (b) euphemism for sexual intercourse. (c) closeness of observation, knowledge, or the like. 2. Intimate or close connection or union."

Following the *OED*'s lead, let us think of relations as intimate to the extent that interactions within them depend on particularized knowledge received, and attention provided by, at least one person—knowledge and attention that are not widely available to third parties. The knowledge involved includes such elements as shared secrets, interpersonal rituals, bodily information, awareness of personal vulnerability, and shared memory of embarrassing situations. The attention involved includes such elements as terms of endearment, bodily services, private languages, emotional support,

[2] Bawin and Dandurand 2003; Cancian 1987; J. Cohen 2002; Collins 2004; Davis 1973; Giddens 1992; Hochschild 2003; Neiburg 2003; Simmel 1988; Swidler 2001.

and correction of embarrassing defects. Intimate social relations thus defined depend on various degrees of trust. Positively, trust means that the parties willingly share such knowledge and attention in the face of risky situations and their possible outcomes. Negatively, trust gives one person knowledge of, or attention to, the other, which if made widely available would damage the second person's social standing. Trust in either sense is often asymmetrical— for example, a young child trusts its parent more than the parent trusts the child—but fully intimate relations involve some degree of mutual trust.[3]

This broad definition of intimacy covers a range of personal relations, including sexually tinged ties of the type illustrated by Patsy and Miller, but also those between parent-child, godparent-godchild, siblings, and close friends. It also extends to the varying degrees and types of intimacy involved in the relations between psychiatrist-patient, lawyer-client, priest-parishioner, servant-employer, prostitute-customer, spy–object of espionage, bodyguard-tycoon, child-care worker–parent, boss-secretary, janitor-tenant, personal trainer–trainee, and hairdresser-customer. In all these social relationships at least one person is committing trust, and at least one person has access to information or attention that, if made widely available, would damage the other. All these relations, moreover, generate their own forms of economic transfers.

Legal scholars have sometimes recognized these varieties of intimacy, including both wide-ranging personal relations and specialized aspects of professional services. Kenneth Karst, for example, introduces a distinction between two types of intimacy. The first involves transfer of possibly damaging private information from one party to the other, information not typically available to third parties. The second entails close enduring relations between two people. Karst points out that legally the second typically entails the first. He goes on to comment: "Personal information disclosed only to a counselor or doctor may be intimate facts; similarly, even a casual sexual relationship involves intimacy in the sense of selective disclo-

---

[3] For a survey and synthesis of trust's place in social structure, see Barber 1983; for a contrasting view, Weitman 1998.

sures of intimate information" (Karst 1980: 634n.48). This book deals with both kinds of intimacy—transfer of personal information and wide-ranging long-term relations—showing how they connect and overlap.

In fact, intimate relations come in many more than two varieties. They vary in kind and degree: the amount and quality of information available to spouses certainly differs from that of child-care worker and parent, or priest and parishioner. The extent of trust likewise varies accordingly. Because we are dealing with a continuum, exactly where we set the limit between intimate and impersonal relations remains arbitrary. But it is important to see that in some respects even the apartment janitor who knows what a household discards day after day gains access to information with some of the same properties as the information flowing in more obviously intimate relations. The variety of intimate relations could complicate this book without clarifying its arguments. I have simplified things through two steps. First, I have concentrated my attention on longer-term, wider-ranging, more intense relations in which at least one party gains access to intimate information. Second, within that range, I have deliberately included and compared different *kinds* of intimacy: physical, informational, and emotional. The comparison will serve us well, for it counters the widespread suspicion that some sorts of intimacy are necessarily deeper, more crucial, or more authentic than others.

ESCAPING CONFUSION

Isn't intimacy a good in itself, a bundle of warm emotions that promote caring attention? Drawing a continuum from impersonal to intimate helps us avoid some common, morally tinged confusions in these regards: intimacy as emotion, intimacy as caring attention, intimacy as authenticity, and intimacy as an intrinsic good. Many analysts are tempted to define intimacy by the emotions it typically evokes, such as intense, warm feelings. This is a mistake. Intimate relations, from gynecologist-patient to husband-wife, vary systematically in how they express or inhibit emotions. Nor (as most doctors and most spouses know well) does intimacy exclude anger, despair, or shame. The word *intimacy* also often calls up caring attention. Many intimate relations include a measure of care: sustained attention that enhances the welfare of its recipients. But in other intimate relationships the parties remain indifferent to each other or even inflict damage on one another. Abusive sexual relations, for example, are certainly intimate, but not caring. Such relationships supply risky information to at least one party and thus entail trust of a sort, yet do not include caring attention. Intimacy and care do often complement each other, but they have no necessary connection.

What of authenticity? Analysts of interpersonal relations frequently distinguish between real and simulated feelings, disparaging simulation with such terms as *pseudo-intimacy* and *emotion management*. They often draw on the idea that routinization of emotional expression in such jobs as waitress, flight attendant, or store clerk deprives the social relations in question of their meaning and damages the inner lives of the people involved. In such a view, truly intimate relationships rest on authentic expressions of feeling (see, for example, Chayko 2002; Hochschild 1983).[4] The closer we look at intimacy, however, the more we discover two flaws in this reasoning. First, no single "real" person exists within a given body; feelings and meanings vary significantly, understandably, and properly from one interpersonal relationship to another. In fact, the feelings and meanings that well up regularly in mother-child relationships can seriously hinder relationships between lovers. Second, simulation of feelings and meanings sometimes becomes an obligation, or at least a service, in some sorts of relationships. Just consider intimate relations between adult children and their aging parents, or between nurses and their terminally ill patients.

Intimacy, finally, often looks like a good in itself, especially to social critics who deplore the loss of intimacy in an impersonal

---

[4] For more general discussion of emotions in social life, see Collins 2004; Hochschild 2003; Katz 1999; Kemper 1990; for the place of emotions in law, see Kahan and Nussbaum 1996.

world. Yet a little reflection on undesirable uses of intimacy—date rape, blackmail, malicious gossip, and more—underlines two more facts about intimacy. First, it ranges from damaging to sustaining, from threatening to satisfying, from thin to thick. Second, it matters sufficiently to its participants and to third parties that people constantly draw moral boundaries between proper and improper uses of intimacy. Yes, intimacy bears a moral charge, but precisely because different sorts of intimacy vary in their moral qualities. When people distinguish between "true" and "false" intimacy, treating the "true" kind as a good in itself, they are making just such distinctions.

In all intimate relationships, accordingly, participants and observers take great care to distinguish them from other relationships that share some properties with them. As we will see, relations of sexual intimacy frequently include transfers of money. Those involved, however, are careful to establish whether the relationship is a marriage, courtship, prostitution, or some other different sort of social tie. In the absence of sexual intimacy, people also establish fine distinctions, for example, among caring services provided by physicians, nurses, spouses, children, neighbors, or live-in servants. In each case, participants and observers frequently engage in fierce debates about the propriety of different forms and levels of compensation for the caring attention involved. They often ban certain combinations of relations, transactions, and media as utterly improper. Later chapters of this book will provide innumerable examples of variation and moral boundary drawing. They will even propose explanations for variation and moral boundary drawing in intimate social relations.

Take the case of psychotherapy. This sort of relationship is necessarily delicate, since effective treatment depends on the quality of the relationship itself. A semiofficial American guide to legal issues in psychotherapy makes the following recommendations concerning payment systems appropriate for a therapeutic relation:

> "Special" billing arrangements make the patient "different" and are associated with an increased opportunity for misunderstanding (real, displaced, or projected) and, when countertransference rears its head, improper or substandard care (cf.

treating VIP patients). Barter arrangements can be specially problematic. Money is a very consistent medium of exchange, and patients' reactions to it are reasonably predictable and understandable by the psychotherapist (and judge or jury, if it comes to that). Trading clinical services for other items, such as goods or services, although not illegal or necessarily unethical, complicates treatment and increases the probability of boundary and transference-countertransference problems. The same applies to free or discounted care. (Reid 1999: 60)

The guide delineates which media (legal tender, no "special billing") and transfers (compensation, not barter or gifts) correspond to the therapist-patient relationship.

In addition, the manual explicitly differentiates between permissible and impermissible therapist-patient relationships. It specifically calls attention to markers for the boundaries between permissible and impermissible relations. When it comes to sexual relations, some "red flags" symbolizing improper "boundary violations" include the following:

- Avoiding documentation of incidents or parts of the treatment that reasonable therapists would be expected to note in the chart (for example, not mentioning gifts, telephone calls to or from the patient, or sexual material, or the clinical discussion they should generate).
- Seeing patients of the opposite sex alone in a deserted clinic or office, especially during odd or evening hours.
- Changing session hours or meeting circumstances to such a setting without documenting a good reason.
- Seeing patients alone in their homes, or yours.
- Avoiding supervision, consultation, or documentation with one or two female patients when such activities are routine for other patients.
- Locking the office door during therapy sessions. (83–84)

The guide also delineates nonsexual therapist-patient "boundary violations," including accepting substantial gifts or compensation beyond the routine fee from a patient or profiting from a patient's "inside information" on an investment. "Your usefulness to patients," it declares, "lies in your clinical skills and your separation of your professional role from other roles better found elsewhere in their lives" (89–90).

In Ontario, a comparable Canadian text for therapy-providing psychologists goes even further. It provides an actual matrix of what the authors identify as problematic "dual relationships." Dual relationships, according to the manual, not only threaten the therapeutic bond but also bring therapists the risk of legal penalties. Table 1.1 presents excerpts from that elaborate matrix. Although one might have thought that sexual predation would constitute the major risk in such relations, the matrix has two striking features: first, it warns against a wide variety of nonsexual relations as risky, and second, sometimes the risk to the therapeutic bond arises from previously existing relationships rather than the other way round. As in other professional-client relationships, psychotherapists and practicing psychologists establish a complex but relatively clear set of distinctions among appropriate and inappropriate matchings among relations, media, and transactions.

What explains the proliferation of distinctions, practices, stories, and moral injunctions concerning the interplay of economic transactions and intimacy? Why do participants, critics, moralists, jurists, and observers worry so much about finding the "right" sort of compensation for their various intimate relations? What sorts of social effects are participants and observers producing, or at least trying to produce?

SEPARATE SPHERES? HOSTILE WORLDS?

Social critics and scholars have divided among three clusters of answers to these questions. A first group, the most numerous, have long proposed the twin ideas of "separate spheres and hostile worlds": distinct arenas for economic activity and intimate relations,

TABLE 1.1.
Risky Dual Relationships for Practicing Psychologists

Prime Professional Relationship	Other Relationship	Example
Therapist/Counselor	Political	A client asks you to join a local constituency organization and to support a client whom the client is working to elect. The client is also soliciting funds for this purpose.
Therapist/Counselor	Sexual	You have been treating a client for some time. You find the client attractive; you begin to dress to please the client; you schedule late sessions that tend to run long into the evening. The client has begun to express a desire to have sex with you.
Therapist/Counselor	Business	A lawyer, who is one of your best referral sources, approaches you requesting your professional involvement concerning personal problems.
Educational	Therapist	A student in your class approaches you about personal problems and asks you for help because you are seen as competent and trustworthy. A variant of this is a request on behalf of a family member or significant other.
Advocate	Therapist	You are a member of the advocacy committee of your collegial body and a local politician becomes your client.

Adapted from Evans and Hearn 1997: 55–57.

with inevitable contamination and disorder resulting when the two spheres come into contact with each other. A second, smaller group has answered "nothing-but": far from constituting an encounter between two contradictory principles, the mingling of economic activity and intimacy, properly seen, is nothing but another version of normal market activity, nothing but a form of cultural expression, or nothing but an exercise of power. A far smaller third cluster—to which I belong—has replied that both of the first two positions are wrong, that people who blend intimacy and economic activity are actively engaged in constructing and negotiating "Connected Lives."[5]

How does the first view work? An old, influential tradition asserts the existence of separate spheres and hostile worlds. In this account, a sharp divide exists between intimate social relations and economic transactions. On one side, we discover a sphere of sentiment and solidarity; on the other, a sphere of calculation and efficiency. Left to itself, goes the doctrine, each works more or less automatically and well. But the two spheres remain hostile to each other. Contact between them produces moral contamination. Monetization of personal care, to take an important example we will revisit later on, corrupts that care into self-interested sale of services. The doctrine of hostile worlds rests (sometimes invisibly) on the doctrine of separate spheres. Intimacy only thrives, accordingly, if people erect effective barriers around it. Thus emerges a view of the separate spheres as dangerously hostile worlds, properly segregated domains whose sanitary management requires well-maintained boundaries. Parties to intimate relations often speak the language of hostile worlds and separate spheres, insisting that the introduction of economic calculations into intimate relations would corrupt them. Critics and analysts often follow their lead.

In a normative version, the hostile worlds view places rigid moral boundaries between market and intimate domains. It condemns any intersection of money and intimacy as dangerously corrupting. Love and sex, Michael Walzer tells us, belong prominently among those "blocked exchanges": spheres of life where monetary exchanges are "blocked, banned, resented, conventionally deplored" (Walzer 1983: 97). In the context of our "shared morality and sensibility," he explains, "men and women marry for money, but this is not a 'marriage of true minds.' " Sex is for sale, but the sale does not make

---

[5] Earlier statements of my arguments (e.g., Zelizer 2004) used the terms *differentiated ties*, *bridges*, and *crossroads* to identify the alternative view. All of these terms catch some of the reality, but *connected lives* points more directly to the interaction and interdependence I want to signal here.

for 'a meaningful relationship' " (103). Or, as Fred Hirsch more pungently warns: "orgasm as a consumer's right rather rules it out as an ethereal experience" (Hirsch 1976: 101). This view springs from widespread popular concerns. Murray Davis puts it thus:

> Sex for money . . . muddles the distinction between our society's sexual system and its economic system. Every transaction between prostitute and customer is an overlap point at which each social system exchanges characteristics: sex becomes commercialized while commerce becomes sexualized. Our society's attempt to avoid this cross-system contamination helps explain why it forbids us to sell our bodies but not our time, energy, thought, and behavior—even though most people identify with the latter at least as much as with the former. (Davis 1983: 274 n.9)

In fact, the feared contamination runs in both directions: according to the hostile worlds view, intimacy can also contaminate rational economic behavior (see Saguy 2003; Salzinger 2003; Schultz 1998; Williams, Giuffre, and Dellinger 1999). Workplaces, as James Woods has shown, are typically constructed as asexual spheres where sexuality looms as "an external threat to an organization . . . something that must be regulated, prohibited, or otherwise held at the company gates" (Woods 1993: 33). What he calls the "asexual imperative" goes beyond protecting vulnerable workers, typically women, from sexual harassment. It supports organizational prohibitions against the use of sexuality to determine matters of workers' hire, pay, promotion, or dismissal. One of the worst aspersions one can cast against a rising company official is that he or she slept their way to the top. (Equally damning is the accusation of having put a lover on the company payroll.) Corruption thus runs in both directions. Better to keep the separate spheres far apart.

Such worries about the incompatibility, incommensurability, or contradiction between intimate and impersonal relations are long-standing and persistent. Since the nineteenth century social analysts have repeatedly assumed that the social world organizes around competing, incompatible principles: *Gemeinschaft* and *Gesellschaft*, ascription and achievement, sentiment and rationality, solidarity and self-interest. Their mixing, goes the theory, contaminates both; invasion of the sentimental world by instrumental rationality desiccates that world, while introduction of sentiment into rational transactions produces inefficiency, favoritism, cronyism, and other forms of corruption. Only markets cleansed of sentiment can generate true efficiency.

The theory gained force with reactions to nineteenth-century industrial capitalism. Although earlier theorists had often allowed for the coexistence of solidarity and self-interest, both advocates and critics of industrial capitalism adopted the assumption that industrial rationality was expelling solidarity, sentiment, and intimacy from markets, firms, and national economies (Hirschman 1977; Tilly 1984). Whether they deplored capitalism's advance, celebrated it, or treated it as a necessary evil, they commonly agreed on an idea of contamination: sentiment within the economic sphere generates favoritism and inefficiency, while rationality within the sentimental sphere destroys solidarity. Thus strong segregation of the spheres served both of them. The nineteenth-century ideology of domesticity provided further, powerful justification for the separate spheres doctrine. Despite some feminists' critiques, social theorists upheld separate spheres and hostile worlds views as essential for preserving the sacredness of the family. In this deeply gendered scheme, households, women, and children needed protection from the dangerously encroaching and aggressively masculine market (Boydston 1990; Cott 1977; Welter 1966).

The theory reappeared in camouflage as organizational analysts noticed new forms of capitalism emerging after World War II. Where firms, markets, friendships, families, governments, and associations had seemed to be differentiating ever more sharply as capitalism advanced, now new organizational forms called forth such terms as flexible production, hybrid firm, and network forms. Paul DiMaggio points out that:

> for all their diversity, the firms to which researchers called attention shared several notable features: greater suppleness than their more traditionally bureaucratic counterparts, a greater

willingness to trust employees and business partners, a preference for long-term "relational contracting" over short-term
market exchange for many transactions, a commitment to ongoing technological improvement—and an apparent renuncia-
tion of central features of Weber's model [of bureaucratiza-
tion]. (DiMaggio 2001: 19)

Given dichotomous theories of sentiment and rationality, the new
organizational forms presented an acute puzzle: wouldn't such new
ways of doing business eventually suffer inefficiency, cronyism, and
corruption precisely because they breached boundaries between rationality and sentiment? For the most part, analysts of economic
change clung to the idea of incompatible separate spheres.

Professional students of economic processes have commonly incorporated more sophisticated versions of the same doctrine into
their analyses of globalization, commodification, and rationalization. They have thought that market expansion inexorably eroded
intimate social ties and narrowed the number of settings in which
intimacy could prosper, while increasing contrasts between such settings and the cold world of economic rationality. They have therefore often joined social critics in supposing that twenty-first-century
globalization will undercut caring activity, deplete the richness of
social life, and thus threaten social solidarity. Consider as one instance of this perspective Robert Kuttner's provocative analysis of
contemporary markets. "As the market vogue has gained force,"
worries Kuttner in *Everything for Sale*, "realms that used to be tem-
pered by extra-market norms and institutions are being marketized
with accelerating force" (Kuttner 1997: 55). This "relentless en-
croachment of the market and its values" he claims, "turns the shal-
low picture of economic man into a self-fulfilling prophecy" (57).

As if to bid up Kuttner's already extreme position, activist-critic
Jeremy Rifkin argues that the world of "hypercapitalism," with its
instantaneous transfers of money and information, is accelerating
and aggravating the substitution of market transactions for genuine
human relationships. "When most relationships become commercial relationships," he asks, "what is left for relationships of a noncommercial nature . . . ? [When] one's life becomes little more than

an ongoing series of commercial transactions held together by contracts and financial instruments, what happens to the kinds of traditional reciprocal relationships that are born of affection, love, and devotion?" (Rifkin 2000: 112). Rifkin's implied answer: nothing is left but cold instrumental rationality.

Jean Bethke Elshtain agrees: while "it used to be that some things, whole areas of life, were not up for grabs as part of the world of buying and selling," today, she laments, "nothing is holy, sacred, or off-limits in a world in which everything is for sale" (Elshtain 2000:47). Hostile worlds doctrines are alive and well in the twenty-first century. They continue to treat the widespread mingling of intimacy and economic transactions as a dangerous anomaly, one that calls forth protective measures against contamination in both directions.

MONEY AND INTIMACY

Take the special case of money. Many social critics concede that peasant households, craft workshops, and fishing villages inevitably mingled economic activity and intimate relations, but somehow escaped the curse of hostile worlds. Elshtain and others reserve their fears and condemnations for monetized social relations, which they see as invading intimate spheres as markets expanded across the globe. Surely the quintessential impersonal medium, goes the reasoning, draws people into thin, fragile, calculating relations with others.

By now, however, the idea that money acts as a universalizing, standardizing medium has taken hard blows. Social scientists, social critics, and ordinary economic actors all recognize as a practical matter—if not necessarily as a matter of principle—that food stamps, subway tokens, local currencies, and commercial paper all qualify somehow as varieties of money but circulate within restricted circuits rather than merging into a single homogeneous medium. Within the zone of money, separate spheres and hostile worlds ideas figure even more prominently than elsewhere in economic analysis.

A closely related idea dies hard: that money and intimacy represent contradictory principles whose intersection generates conflict, confusion, and corruption. Thus people debate passionately the propriety of compensated egg donations, sale of blood and human organs, purchase of child care or elder care, and wages for housewives.

The surprising thing about such debates is their usual failure to recognize how regularly intimate social transactions coexist with monetary transactions: parents pay nannies or child-care workers to tend their children, adoptive parents pay money to obtain babies, divorced spouses pay or receive alimony and child support payments, and parents give their children allowances, subsidize their college educations, help them with their first mortgage, and offer them substantial bequests in their wills. Friends and relatives send gifts of money as wedding presents, and friends loan each other money. Meanwhile, immigrants support their families back home with regular transmission of remittances.

Collectively, such intimate transactions are not trivial. They have large macroeconomic consequences, for example, in generating large flows of cash from rich countries to poor countries and in transmitting wealth from one generation to the next. As intergenerational transmission of wealth illustrates, moreover, intimate transactions also create or sustain large-scale inequalities by class, race, ethnicity, and even gender. For participants, the secret is to match the right sort of monetary payment with the social transaction at hand. That matching depends strongly on the definition of more general ties among the parties. Indeed, the meanings and consequences of ostensibly similar monetary transfers such as allowances, remittances, fees, bribes, tips, repayments, charity, and occasional gifts emerge only from identification of the social ties in question. All these payments, and more, commonly occur in the company of intimate transactions, take their meanings from the longer-term social ties within which those transactions occur, and vary in consequences as a function of those longer-term ties—the limiting and exceptional case being the tie defined as no more than momentary.

My arguments concerning money, then, constitute no more than a special case of this book's general argument. I argue, first, that people engage routinely in the process of differentiating meaningful social relations, including their most intimate ties. They undertake relational work. Among other markers, they use different payment systems—media—to create, define, affirm, challenge, or overturn such distinctions. When people struggle over payments, of course they often quarrel over the amount of money due, but it is impressive how often they argue over the form of payment and its appropriateness for the relation in question. They argue, for example, over distinctions among payments as compensation, entitlements, or gifts. When you handed me that hundred-dollar bill, were you paying me for my services, giving me my weekly allowance, or displaying your generosity?

Second, I argue that such distinctions apply to intimate social relations. People regularly differentiate forms of monetary transfers in correspondence with their definitions of the sort of relationship that obtains between the parties. They adopt symbols, rituals, practices, and physically distinguishable forms of money to mark distinct social relations. Precisely because of the trust and risk involved, relational work becomes even more delicate and consequential when intimacy comes into play. Although hostile worlds doctrines lead to the expectation that monetary transactions will corrupt such relations and eventually transform them into impersonal mutual exploitation, close studies of such relations invariably yield a contrary conclusion: across a wide range of intimate relations, people manage to integrate monetary transfers into larger webs of mutual obligations without destroying the social ties involved. Money cohabits regularly with intimacy, and even sustains it.

So are hostile worlds pure inventions? Examined carefully, hostile worlds arguments cannot simply be dismissed as fantasies. In their strong advocacy of separate spheres, people are surely doing some kind of significant work. As we will see in detail later, in fact, people regularly invoke hostile worlds doctrines when they are trying to establish or maintain boundaries between intimate relations that might easily be confused, for example, when a father employs a daughter in his firm, or when a lawyer handles his old friend's divorce. In such circumstances, participants often employ hostile worlds *practices*, using forms of speech, body language, clothing, uniforms, and spatial locations to signify whether the relationship between this man and this woman is boss-secretary, husband-wife, patron-prostitute, lover-mistress, father-daughter, customer-waitress, or something else. They thus prevent confusion with the "wrong" relationship. One of this book's main aims is to examine when, where, how, why, and with what effects people involved in intimate relationships invoke the ideas and practices that segregate ostensibly hostile worlds from each other.

NOTHING-BUT?

If prevailing analyses of intimacy and economic activity get causes and effects wrong, but still point to problems real people face, how can we improve on the faulty arguments of separate spheres and hostile worlds? One possibility is that some simpler principle—economic, cultural, or political—actually explains what is going on; that is the nothing-but line of argument. The second possibility is that we need a better account of how people construct and negotiate their social relations: the connected lives alternative. Let us review the strengths and weaknesses of nothing-but before going on to this book's own account of connected lives.

Impatient with stark dualisms, critics have sometimes countered separate spheres and hostile worlds accounts with reductionist nothing but arguments: the ostensibly separate world of intimate social relations, they argue, is nothing-but a special case of some general principle. Nothing-but advocates divide among three principles: nothing but economic rationality, nothing but culture, and nothing but politics. Thus, for economic reductionists caring, friendship, sexuality, and parent-child relations become special cases of advantage-seeking individual choice under conditions of constraint—in short, of economic rationality. For cultural reductionists, intimate relations become expressions of distinct beliefs or ideological scripts, regardless of what economic connection they may entail. Others insist on the political, coercive, and exploitative bases of the same phenomena. Occasionally, participants in intimate relations themselves insist on nothing-but: We must run this relationship rationally; your behavior offends our religion; or "If you don't ——, I'll hurt you." Social critics and social scientists often follow one or another of these leads.

Across social science as a whole, economic reductionism has provided the most coherent and powerful challenge to separate spheres and hostile worlds views. That category is exemplified by Richard Posner, who in the tradition of Gary Becker, claims the equivalence of all transfers as rational quid pro quo exchanges. Posner has championed the influential "law and economics" paradigm and pioneered its extension to sexuality. Take away any cultural camouflage, such nothing-but theorists maintain, and we will find that intimate transfers—be they of sex, babies, or blood—operate according to identical principles governing transfers of stock shares or used cars. Consider how Posner justifies the "feasibility and fruitfulness of an economic approach to [sexuality]":

> The effort may seem quixotic, for it is a commonplace that sexual passion belongs to the domain of the irrational; but it is a false commonplace. One does not will sexual appetite—but one does not will hunger either. The former fact no more excludes the possibility of an economics of sexuality than the latter excludes the possibility of an economics of agriculture. (Posner [1992] 1997: 4–5)

Similarly, David Friedman, another "law and economics" enthusiast, explains why long-term contracts work as efficiently for marriage as for business:

> Once a couple has been married for a while, they have made a lot of relationship-specific investments, borne costs that will produce a return only if they remain together. Each has become, at considerable cost, an expert on how to get along with the other. Both have invested, materially and emotionally, in their joint children. Although they started out on a competitive

market, they are now locked into a bilateral monopoly with associated bargaining costs. (Friedman 2000: 172)

"Law and economics" analysts argue that markets provide efficient solutions. Efficient solutions, they tell us, exhaust the legal problems posed by intimacy. Intimate relations, in this view, pose the same problems of choice within constraints as ordinary market transactions.

Nothing-but cultural theorists, in contrast, replace efficiency, rationality, and exchange with meaning, discourse, and symbolism. In its extreme position this view sees cultural representations as determining both the character of intimacy and the place of economic transfers. Take for instance Noah Zatz's analysis of the prostitution exchange as "a site of powerful sexual pluralism, capable of contesting hegemonic constructions of sexuality that at first seem far removed: the movement from anatomical sex to sexuality to identity and the maintenance of the public/private distinction through the isolation of sexuality and intimacy from productive work and commercial exchange" (Zatz 1997: 306). While nodding to institutional features, on his way to this conclusion Zatz argues that prostitution has no necessary connection to genitalia or to sexual gratification: "constructivist theories of sexuality need to consider," he tells us, "both that sexuality may be nongenital and that genitalia may be nonsexual" (281).[6]

A third influential nothing-but analysis holds that intimate relations are nothing but the result of coercive, and more specifically patriarchal, power structures. Kathleen Barry's analysis of the "prostitution of sexuality," for instance, derives women's sexual subordination from "gender relations of sexual power" (Barry 1995: 78). Commercialized sex, as in prostitution, from this perspective is no different from unpaid sex in rape, dating, or marriage. The problem here is not commodification but men's coercion of women.

---

[6] For another example of a culturalist approach, see Laqueur 1990. For an excellent review of prostitution studies, including culturalist analyses, see Gilfoyle 1999. An influential culturalist account appears in Butler 1990, 1993.

Common interpretations of the intersection between economic interchange and intimate relations, as we see, range from the moral concerns of hostile worlds theorists to the pragmatism of nothing-but economic views, the constructivism of nothing-but culturalists, and the political critique of nothing-but power analysts. In the case of separate spheres and hostile worlds arguments, the spheres of economic transactions and intimacy remain both morally unbridgeable and practically antagonistic; in the case of nothing-but views, only one sphere matters.

In some respects, nothing-but accounts improve on hostile worlds formulations. Taken together, at least they point out that economic activity, power, and culture all play significant parts in intimate relations. Relations tinged by intimacy often do figure crucially in economic activity, for example, in remittances within migrant families and in household production. At times, only an understanding of cultural distinctions permits us to explain the patterns of connection between economic activity and intimacy, such as in the payment of dowry. Sometimes, finally, intimate relations raise serious questions of power, as when managers seek sexual favors from their employees. However, none of the nothing-but alternatives by itself provides a plausible set of explanations for widely observed variation in combinations of economic transactions and intimate relations. In everyday life, how do people negotiate intersections of economic activity with intimate social relations?

CONNECTED LIVES

In the broadest terms, people create connected lives by differentiating their multiple social ties from each other, marking boundaries between those different ties by means of everyday practices, sustaining those ties through joint activities (including economic activities), but constantly negotiating the exact content of important social ties. In order to understand these complicated processes, we must begin with three facts that we all experience as human beings but have trouble talking about.

First, we construct the most coherent set of social worlds we can by negotiating and adopting meaningful ties to other people, but differentiating sharply among the rights, obligations, transactions, and meanings that belong to different ties. Second, we mark differences between ties with distinctive names, symbols, practices, and media of exchange; despite some similarities in emotional intensities and significance to our lives, we establish sharp distinctions among our personal ties to physicians, parents, friends, siblings, children, spouses, lovers, and close collaborators. Third, economic activities of production, consumption, distribution, and asset transfers play significant parts in most such relations. Interpersonal relations within households provide the obvious example: no household lasts long without extensive economic interaction among its members.

A fourth fact is less obvious, but no less important. In any particular social setting—not only households, but also workplaces, schools, churches, and clubs—multiple ties of different kinds coexist and often extend across the setting's boundary into other settings. Ties themselves vary from intimate to impersonal and from durable to fleeting. But almost all social settings contain mixtures of ties that differ in these regards. Participants in intimate relations often signal their connections to others indirectly, in two ways. They do so by insisting on the special characteristics of their relations, for example, mother-daughter bonds or relationships with one's gynecologist. They also adopt economic practices—forms of payment, routines for shared work, joint participation in shopping, and so on—that conform to their understandings of the relationships at hand. These four facts add up to a picture of connected lives.

My analysis of intersections between intimacy and economic transactions stems from a more general view of interpersonal relations. As I see it, all ongoing social relations (intimate or not) include at least a minimum of shared meanings, operating rules, and boundaries separating one relation from another. As a matter of common sense, for instance, people within a given culture recognize differences in shared meanings, operating rules, and boundaries between the relations of store clerk and customer and those of nurse and patient. In most such relations, institutional supports, widely shared definitions, and coaching by third parties reduce uncertainty and negotiation concerning meanings, rules, and boundaries; few people, for example, have much trouble working out how to behave as student and teacher.

Nevertheless, when relations resemble others that have significantly different consequences for the parties, people put extra effort into distinguishing the relations, marking their boundaries, and negotiating agreements on their definitions. As we will see later, even if they engage in sexual intercourse, courting couples commonly take great care to establish that their relationship is not that of prostitute and client. More precisely, to the extent that two relations are easily confused, weighty in their consequences for participants, and/or significantly different in their implications for third parties, participants and third parties devote exceptional effort to marking what the relationship is and is not; distinctions among birth children, adopted children, foster children, and children taken in for day care, for instance, come to matter greatly for adult-child relations, not to mention relations to the children's other kin.

Why, then, does it make any difference how economic activity intersects with interpersonal relations? Including economic transactions in social relations generally magnifies the effort that people invest in defining and disciplining their relations. It does so because the coordination of consumption, distribution, production, and asset transfers with their consequences now become integral to the relations. When spouses and lovers succeed in sustaining each other's lives, they don't do it with love alone, but with concrete contributions to their joint material welfare. Still, people vary significantly in how widely and easily they maintain intimate relations. As a result of a number of circumstances past and present—including childhood socialization, cultural location, status differences between the parties, and current availability of other intimate relations—people vary dramatically in the extent to which and the means by which they seek to expand or contract the degree of intimacy prevailing in relations that are not already deeply intimate.

Another major point follows directly. People devote significant effort to negotiating meanings of social relations and marking their boundaries. They do so especially when those relations involve both intimacy and economic transactions. They engage in *relational work* of two important kinds. First, they create differentiated ties that distinguish the relations at hand from others with which they might become confused, with deleterious consequences for one party, both parties, or third parties. Second, they sustain, repair, and renegotiate those ties as new opportunities, threats, and problems arise. Relational work includes the establishment of differentiated social ties, their maintenance, their reshaping, their distinction from other relations, and sometimes their termination. Differentiated ties form in all arenas of social life, including schools, armies, churches, corporations, and voluntary associations. Patron-client relations operate within firms, for example, just as friendship networks often organize a great deal of inequality within schools. Because hostile worlds and nothing-but formulations have most often caused confusion in the analysis of intimate transactions, I concentrate here on issues raised by caring, friendship, sexuality, or parent-child relations.

PURCHASES OF INTIMACY

Where does the connected lives perspective take us? Stated compactly, the argument pivots on three main points:

1. For each meaningfully distinct category of social relations, people erect a boundary, mark the boundary by means of names and practices, establish a set of distinctive understandings and practices that operate within that boundary, designate certain sorts of economic transactions as appropriate for the relation, bar other transactions as inappropriate, and adopt certain media for reckoning and facilitating economic transactions within the relation. All these efforts belong to relational work.
2. Within the legal arena, a parallel but stylized matching of social relations, understandings, practices, transactions, and media occurs. Despite that stylization, legal negotia-

tions over appropriate transactions by type of relation draw on prevailing social relations outside the legal arena, but also influence how people deal with each other in routine social life.

3. Hostile worlds ideas and practices emerge from the effort to mark and defend boundaries between categories of relations that contain some common elements, could be confused, and would threaten existing relations of trust if confused.

How do intimate relations and economic activities interact? Maintaining any sort of durable social relations depends on creating culturally meaningful institutional supports. Consider what husband-wife relations take for granted: among other things, an income tax code distinguishing between single and married people; businesses that provide special perquisites for spouses; and couples' memberships in health clubs. Those same sorts of culturally meaningful institutional supports underlie all intimate social relations. In fact, such relations only survive with institutional supports. This is also true for various forms of market relations. These relations likewise depend on extensive, meaningful institutional supports, but of a different sort. Consider for instance auctions, which economists often proclaim as the purest type of impersonal process, efficiently matching individual preferences of buyers and sellers. Charles Smith's observations (1989) of actual auctions have shown that a vast set of institutional connections and conventions come into play and actually undergird the price making.[7]

We need not deny the distinction between intimacy and impersonality. One dimension of variation in social relations does run from intimate to impersonal. The quality of transactions within those relations does vary significantly. But relations also vary in terms of their durability, scope, predominant activity, and risk. Here we concentrate on the continuum from intimate to impersonal, only occasionally examining the other dimensions. Within all such di-

---

[7] On other sorts of markets, see Abolafia 2001; Hochschild 2003: esp. 30–44; Ingram and Roberts 2000; Keister 2002; Knorr Cetina and Bruegger 2002; Uzzi and Lancaster 2004; Velthuis 2003; White 2001.

mensions, people take care to establish boundaries between significantly different relations, marking those boundaries by means of labels and symbolically potent practices. Those boundaries emerge from interpersonal negotiation. The boundaries change incrementally as people interact within and across them. For example, people establish, negotiate, and rework boundaries among friends, relatives, and neighbors.

We are, then, dealing with connections among four elements: relations, transactions, media, and boundaries. Relations consist of durable, named sets of understandings, practices, rights, and obligations that link two or more persons. Transactions consist of bounded, short-term interactions between persons. Media consist of accounting systems and their tokens. Boundaries consist, in this case, of known perimeters drawn around distinctive combinations of relations, transactions, and media. Relational work involves creating viable matches among relations, transactions, media, and boundaries.

When it comes to economic activity—transactions involving production, distribution, and consumption of valuable goods and services—people mark relevant boundaries by identifying acceptable matches of relations, transactions, and media. (The same reasoning applies to transfers of titles to goods and services, such as inheritance). They distinguish different sorts of social relations, establish which sorts of transactions belong appropriately to each relation, employ appropriate media for those transactions, and mark off the combination by means of names, symbols, and practices. Following an old American tradition, for example, a boss sometimes awards a gold watch to a retiring employee. Media often include properly marked money, but they also range across various forms of barter, multiple systems of credit accounting, and tokens that bear only distant connections with legal tender.

Media and transactions often appear to transform relations. The spread of commercialized child care, in this view, necessarily reduces the quality of care, as compared with the attention previously provided by relatives. This view gets things backwards. In fact, as they choose certain media and transactions, people actually choose relations. Take the obvious symbolism of an unmarried man's placing of a newly bought diamond ring on the third finger, left hand, of an unmarried woman. From that moment, in contemporary American culture, the couple become engaged to marry. The diamond does not cause the couple's relationship to change. Instead, the couple announce their changed relationship by means of the diamond. Nevertheless, autonomous changes in media and transactions do sometimes affect the terms by which people conduct social relations. When governments impose legal tender, for example, gifts of money and government securities to intimates become more common. Similarly, when certain kinds of transactions become much more prevalent, they too transform relations by challenging previous distinctions. For instance, widespread adoption through commercial services, expansion of commercial child care, and placement of foster children by public agencies alter prevailing definitions of parenthood. In such cases, people actually begin to renegotiate markers, boundaries, and relationships. They elaborate new distinctions among birth children, clients' children, adopted children, foster children, children from previous relationships, and so on.

HOW INTIMACY WORKS

How and why? It will take the rest of this book to answer that question adequately. But some preliminary answers deserve attention now. Over all of history, authorities have built their own templates of social relations and their boundaries into enforceable obligations and rights. Over most of history, however, valuation and compensation have occurred in nonmonetary forms, for example, by awarding title to land, services, symbols, or persons. That is still true in some branches of law, notably criminal law, where valuation, retribution, and compensation commonly concern life, honor, and freedom. In cases of disaster, accident, and lethal malfeasance, families reckon justice in terms of retribution, responsibility, and recognition of personal suffering as well as financial loss.

Nevertheless, with the expansion of monetized markets, Western legal systems did shift increasingly to monetary valuation, retribution, and compensation. Thus the legal arena frequently matches monetary transactions with social relations, employing standards of propriety that depend implicitly on templates derived largely from nonlegal social patterns, as translated into law by lawyers and judges. The two influence each other: participants in litigation draw on implicit catalogs of social relations that depend heavily on routine social interaction (and, at least in systems of case law and precedent, commonly lag behind current practice), but legal decisions (for example, conditions of eligibility for public welfare) also influence routine social relations and distinctions among them.

However confusedly, then, critics of commodification are pointing to some changes that actually occurred. Within the law, monetary standards of loss and gain have become increasingly prominent. As a consequence, such questions as whether an adult wage earner's death deserves greater compensation than that of a dependent child or an aged person have weighed more heavily in legal disputes. More generally, across the Western world the range of goods and services available for money has expanded enormously during the last two centuries; widespread commodification really has happened. Commodification, moreover, means that differences in human welfare depend increasingly on market position.

Where people produce most goods and services outside of organized market economies, their variable monetary incomes and access to monetary capital do not necessarily determine whether they thrive or suffer. In extensively monetized economies, however, variation in human welfare depends heavily on differences between high wages, low wages, and no wages; between generous and stingy public benefits; between extensive, meager, and no inherited wealth. Furthermore, as wage, benefit, and wealth inequality increase, so do inequalities in human welfare. In this fundamental regard, commercialization of markets for labor, goods, services, and capital heightens the moral dilemmas faced by courts and citizens alike. Monetization does not in itself corrupt moral life. But it moves moral questions increasingly into the arena of cash and carry.

In all these regards, it helps to separate normative arguments from the statements of fact, possibility, and cause-effect relations that ordinarily accompany them in any program for change. We must recognize that hostile worlds disputes frequently involve questions of justice, inequality, power, and exploitation. Simply "letting the market do its work" rarely produces equity. Existing markets often generate inequitable outcomes. This happens for two main reasons. First, as a result of social experiences over which they have little or no control, people bring unequal resources into markets. Second, markets themselves regularly incorporate categorical inequalities, such as highly unequal rewards for similar work depending on whether the worker is male or female, employed in a big firm or toiling at home, providing services to the wealthy or the poor. Even if (as some economists proclaim) the overall operation of such markets produces efficiency in the sense of greater output per capita for equivalent inputs, whole categories of people walk away with lesser qualities of life. Reformers and radicals often respond to these circumstances with a hostile worlds conclusion: markets corrupt.

In order to arrive at clearer, more equitable, and more effective policies, however, we must get past the simple opposition of sustaining intimacy and corrupting markets. Any normative program such as wage equality for women involves not only a statement of preferences (it would be better if women received equal wages for equal work) but also statements of fact (where we stand now), statements of possibility (how equity would actually work), statements of cause and effect (what it would take to get from here to there). To understand fact, possibility, and cause-effect relations, we have no choice but to unpack existing relations between various forms of intimacy and economic transactions. Clearer descriptions and explanations will therefore facilitate the development of normatively superior programs. The idea of connected lives promotes clearer descriptions and explanations of what happens when intimacy and economic activity coincide.

The twenty-first century may well bring terrifying changes in social life, but they will not occur because commodification in itself generally destroys intimacy. This book challenges the widespread assumption that markets ipso facto undercut solidarity-sustaining personal relations. It offers an alternative to the conventional account of interplay between market transactions and personal relations. Its analysis of connected lives shows that across a wide range of intimate relations, in the provision of personal care, and in the complexities of household life, people manage the mingling of economic activity and intimacy by creating, enforcing, and renegotiating extensive differentiation among social ties, their boundaries, and their appropriate matching with commercial media and transactions of production, consumption, and distribution.

INTIMACY, LAW, AND ECONOMIC ACTIVITY

The following chapters draw extensively on American legal disputes. Scrutiny of such disputes shows, among other things, that relational work takes distinctive forms in the legal arena. The law, for example, defines spouses' mutual rights and obligations somewhat differently from spouses' own definitions of those relations. This book's treatment of American law cases may, however, strike professional legal scholars as odd, or even dangerous. Nowhere does the book offer a general description for American law's treatment of intimacy, much less an explanation of how intimacy came to occupy its peculiar position in the law. Sometimes it offers historical sketches of significant changes in the legal treatment of issues bearing on intimacy, such as women's compensation for loss of their husbands' caring attention. But those sketches never reconstruct in detail the legal process that produced the changes or deal systematically with their implications for legal procedures.

Overall, I have chosen the most general legal doctrines and practices as I understand them. Two features of the American system make my approach risky and perhaps even offensive to legal specialists. The first is the considerable variation among courts and areas of law—especially of state courts—with regard to the precise doctrines and practices employed when it comes to intimacy and economic transactions. We have already seen how discrepancies between the laws of Louisiana and Missouri shaped the 1840s *Cole v. Lucas* case. The second feature is the constantly changing and contested character of existing laws. American law operates through adversary proceedings and competition among arguments. The laws that deprived Patsy of her inheritance in 1847 have disappeared, but the laws that govern claims of 9/11 survivors for compensation live despite intense contestation today. Legal contestation means that at any given point in time, contradictory doctrines, practices, and rulings prevail in one segment or another of the American legal system. Instead of noting these variations and discrepancies each time they come up I have opted for points of convergence.

Specific legal cases often appear in the book to make points concerning how lawyers, judges, and legal scholars handle the delicate distinctions that almost always arise in disputes over the intersection of economic transactions and intimate personal relations. After an extensive search of law review articles, treatises, and casebooks, complemented by consultation with specialists in the field, I located several hundred cases. From those I selected a set of exceptionally well-documented cases that illustrate the range of variation in disputes conjoining contested economic transactions and intimate relations. I make no claim whatsoever to have assembled a representative sample of all such cases.

While respecting the best legal scholarship on the subject, furthermore, I do not offer my own survey, synthesis, or critique of the present state of the relevant law, much less lay out or endorse programs of legal reform. Readers will find me taking normative positions from time to time, notably when it comes to inequalities in the legal treatment of intimacy by gender, class, or race. Still, the book's value does not pivot on its evaluations, implicit or explicit, of American law's present condition. Instead, *The Purchase of Intimacy* concentrates on demonstrating parallels and contrasts between the treatment of intimate economies in everyday life and in the legal arena. Each serves to illuminate the other, as we witness how regularly participants on both sides must deal with the incessant mingling of economic and intimate relations, yet try repeatedly to treat economic and intimate relations as though they were independent, even antagonistic, essences.

The following chapter examines how legal doctrine and practice approach the conjunction of intimacy and economic transactions. When, why, and how does the American legal system contemplate the economic valuation of intimacy? I then turn to three chapters dealing with different arenas of intimacy—coupling, caring, and household life—in each one comparing and connecting routine social practices and legal approaches. The book concludes by returning to the general issues of this chapter.

APPENDIX:
A NOTE ON INTIMACY IN ECONOMIC SOCIOLOGY

Within the social sciences, sociologists and anthropologists have taken the major responsibility for describing and explaining intimate relations. My analyses will frequently refer to anthropological studies, but will draw especially on sociology. This appendix provides a brief overview of relevant discussions in economic sociology for those who have a special interest in the field.

Sociologists have long wavered between hostile worlds and nothing-but accounts of economic processes. The hostile worlds view rested on the separate spheres idea: a sharp division between economy and society, with the one embodying impersonal rationality and the other intimate sentimentality. Such theorists as Talcott Parsons saw society as providing the normative and social context for markets, but assumed economic and personal spheres were highly differentiated from each other and operated on the basis of contradictory principles. While attempting to specify the articulation of family and market, Parsons drew on conventional polarities: "the prototypical institution of the modern economy is the market, but inside the family anything too much like market relationships, especially competitive ones, are, if not totally excluded, very significantly limited" (Parsons 1978: 15).

As economic sociology grew into a self-defined specialty, it implicitly accepted such divisions between a market sphere and a noneconomic sphere. However, economic sociologists began to consider the social structure that underlies what they continued to regard as a semiautonomous economic sphere. This led people into a variety of nothing-but explanations. Although studies of consumption and household economies have often adopted cultural and political reductionism, within self-defined economic sociology, economic reductionism has been most common. Nothing-but economic arguments often come into play when economic sociologists interpret a wide variety of social processes in ways that resemble the neoclassical paradigm of individual choice within constraints. In such views, religion, warfare, sport, and various forms of intimacy look much like market operations.

More recently, economic sociologists have worked hard to move beyond hostile worlds and nothing-but economic reductionism. They do so by treating economic processes and behavioral assumptions—such as markets, rationality, or self-interest—as products of underlying social processes. As Harrison White puts it, market activity is "intensely social—as social as kinship networks or feudal armies" (White 1988: 232; see also White 2001). Yet, current economic sociology has not yet fully relinquished its hostile worlds tradition. The field repeatedly focuses on firms and corporations—allegedly "true markets"—while relegating other forms of economic activity (such as gift transfers, informal economies, households, and consumption) to a nonmarket world.

Scholars developing alternative views nevertheless provide more radical departures from standard treatments of intimate economies; first, by expanding the definition of work; second, by shifting the emphasis to recognition of differentiated social ties; third, by looking at the actual content of transactions among economic actors, and fourth, by locating cultural content within those very transactions instead of treating culture as external constraint. They map the crossroads of interpersonal relations and economic activity. Chris Tilly and Charles Tilly, for instance, define work in ways that directly challenge the separate spheres/hostile worlds split vision: "Work," they emphatically declare, "includes any human effort adding use value to goods and services. Only a prejudice bred by Western capitalism and its industrial labor markets fixes on strenuous effort expended for money payment outside the home as 'real work,' relegating other efforts to amusement, crime, and mere housekeeping" (Tilly and Tilly 1998: 22). Work's many worlds, therefore, include employment for wages but also unpaid domestic labor, barter, petty commodity production, and volunteer work.

Paul DiMaggio and Hugh Louch's analysis (1998) of consumer behavior illustrates the second shift toward recognizing differentiated social ties. As they survey preexisting noncommercial ties between buyers and sellers in consumer transactions involving the purchase of cars and homes, as well as legal and home repair services, DiMaggio and Louch find a remarkably high incidence of what they call within-network exchanges. A substantial number of such transactions take place not through impersonal markets but among kin, friends, or acquaintances. Noting that this pattern applies primarily to risky one-shot transactions involving high uncertainty about quality and performance, they conclude that consumers will be more likely to rely on such noncommercial ties when they are unsure about the outcome.

Looking at the actual content of transactions among economic actors, Nicole Woolsey Biggart observes the operation of intimate ties within direct selling organizations. Companies such as Amway, Tupperware, or Mary Kay Cosmetics, far from introducing narrow professionalized relations, rely on intimate social networks for merchandising their products. Close relatives—spouses, mothers, daughters, sisters, brothers, cousins, or nephews—sponsor each other into the organization. Moreover, direct selling is perceived as strengthening marriage and family bonds. Because blue-collar women, Biggart observes, often define direct selling "as a sideline and not a 'real job,' they can have the happy combination of making money and being an 'at home' mother." She reports a revealing statement by a Tupperware dealer:

> I was driving my son and four friends to a birthday party, and
> I heard them talking in the back about their moms working.
> And one of the kids says, "Say, does your mommy work?" And
> he goes, "No." That's what I want. I don't want them to think
> I work. They don't even think that I have a job because I'm not
> gone from eight to five. (Biggart 1989: 82)

As they describe their reality, ironically, participants themselves re-create the ideas and practices of separate spheres and hostile worlds.

What about cultural content? My own earlier analyses of monetary transfers located cultural content within social ties rather than seeing culture as external to those ties. For example, the crucial distinctions among gifts, compensation, and entitlements show how people differentiate forms of payments in correspondence with their definitions of the sort of relationship that exists between the parties. They adopt symbols, rituals, practices, and physically distinguishable forms of money to mark distinct social relations and forms of monetary transfers (Zelizer 1994).

Economic sociologists studying intersections of economic interchange and intimate ties, in short, long hesitated between hostile worlds and nothing-but formulations. They never arrived at a satisfactory adjudication among such views because the social reality in question requires not a choice between the two, but their transcendence. Recognition of differentiated ties, each involving distinctive forms of economic transaction, offers an exit from the impasse. The connected lives conception promotes superior explanations.

CHAPTER 2

INTIMACY IN LAW

We return to Louisiana more than a century later. In 1958, super-market entrepreneur John G. Schwegmann Jr. began dating, and bedding, sixteen-year-old Mary Ann Blackledge. They continued to have sexual relations when they started living together in May 1966. At that point, according to Blackledge, the middle-aged, twice divorced Schwegmann offered to "share everything" with her, and she said "okay." They cohabited for twelve years, until May 1978. During that time, they continued to share bed and board. Schwegmann supported Blackledge, paying her dental and medical bills, clothing, entertainment, and travel expenses, as well as providing her with a monthly allowance check. Meanwhile, she served as his companion, housekeeper, cook, and chauffeur. She also cared for Schwegmann's daughter Melba Margaret, and for Schwegmann himself after he had a stroke. Blackledge further collaborated as business adviser, political assistant, and confidante to Schwegmann and the corporations he controlled; for example, she helped compose newspaper ads and offered investment advice. Although Blackledge moved out in 1978, their sexual relations continued thereafter when she visited Schwegmann at his house. So did his monthly allowance checks. According to Blackledge, "John and I made all the commitments and agreements to each other that anyone would take when they got married," including sexual fidelity.

Once again, we know about this couple's history because it later came to trial. Blackledge sued Schwegmann, his two children, and his corporate holdings for substantial compensation beyond the monthly check she had been receiving (*Schwegmann v. Schwegmann*, 441 So. 2d 316 (La. Ct. App. 19833)). In her suit, Blackledge alleged multiple breaches of contract—of an explicit oral agreement to split the returns from their efforts evenly, an implicit agreement to compensate her for multiple contributions to the relationship, and de facto establishment of a universal partnership, giving her claim to all of Schwegmann's property.

Both the trial court and the court of appeals emphatically rejected all of Blackledge's claims but one: compensation for her services to Schwegmann's businesses. Unlike husbands and wives, concubines and their paramours, declared both courts, have no rights in each other's property. As the appeals court noted, "The law could scarce be plainer: a sharing of bed and table, for a night or for a lifetime, does not by itself constitute marriage" (323). Nor could Blackledge collect for her domestic services, as they were "inextricably interwoven with sexual services" (324), and therefore part of unlawful concubinage. Faced with Blackledge's claims that in this modern age, her relationship to Schwegmann should establish the same rights as a legally certified marriage, the court replied, "To equate the non-marital relationship of concubinage to a marital relationship is to do violence to the very structure of our civilized society" (326). Louisiana courts still justified judgments by their contribution to the defense of civilization. Yet both courts allowed compensation for Blackledge's business services to the defendants, including Schwegmann. As long as "the commercial enterprise is independent of the illegal cohabitation," the appeals court stated, "each party may assert his rights in the common endeavor" (325). In their view, Mary Ann Blackledge's previously uncompensated business ties to the defendants were distinct from the concubinage relationship to Schwegmann.

The Blackledge-Schwegmann dispute sets the problem for this chapter: how does American law deal with intersections between intimacy and economic transactions? How do legislators, lawyers, judges, juries, and legal scholars create or transform the doctrines, distinctions, and practices that apply when participants in routine (or, for that matter, not so routine) social relations bring their disputes to court? In what ways does the law's relational work differ from that of everyday practice? The chapter documents the presence of separate spheres and hostile worlds arguments in the law and then examines how legal doctrine and practice treat the intersection of intimate relations and economic transactions. From then, it moves on to contest and change over these legal practices, using the doctrines of coverture and consortium as prime examples. Its final sections deal with competing legal theories, including feminist theories, concerning the proper relationship between intimacy and economic transactions.

Warning: this book is not a guide to American law concerning intimate relations. Lawyers, judges, juries, and legal scholars usually get involved in such cases in one of two ways. In the first version, a dispute between two parties to an intimate relation generates legal proceedings, and legal specialists search for applicable statutes, principles, and precedents. In the second version, advocates of a change in existing law affecting intimate relations argue for the application of some legal principle to a certain body of cases, actual or potential. This book, however, steps back to look at similarities and differences between the ways that ordinary people manage the mingling of economic activity with intimate relations and how the legal system approaches the same sorts of intersections between intimacy and economic activity. I have chosen cases not to survey all legal principles that bear somehow on intimacy, much less to survey a representative sample of all such cases that come before the courts, but instead to clarify similarities and differences between everyday practices and legal contests over those practices.

Courts perform a distinctive variety of relational work. They adopt a fascinating procedure in dealing with intimate relations and economic transactions, calling up a matrix of possible relationships (in this case, concubine-paramour, husband-wife, and business partners) and implicitly distinguishing these relations from others, such as prostitute-customer, professional-client, friend-friend, or brother-sister. They then match economic transactions and ties connecting the pair under examination to that matrix. Indeed, they match different transactions to different sets of ties within the matrix. As participant in concubine-paramour relations, the court found Blackledge had already received the economic benefits of cohabitation. As Schwegmann's business partner, however, she was entitled to more compensation than she had yet received. The court drew on standard doctrines of marital obligations and contract in reaching these decisions.

In their reasoning, courts strongly invoke separate spheres and hostile worlds arguments. They claim to protect the sacredness of marriage both against illicit sexual relationships and against the intrusion of improper economic considerations. Essentially, courts defend the principle that business should not mix with pleasure, since contamination runs in both directions. Concubinage as well as marriage provide their own rewards and should not be treated as ordinary business transactions, whereas business equally needs defense from sexually tinged sentiment. The courts' hostile worlds reasoning does not simply draw a sanitary perimeter around the sacred zone of traditional marriage. Instead, it distinguishes a range of intimate relations from each other.

For a surprising variation on the same theme, consider the 1980 suit by Leonard Wilson Trimmer against Catherine Bryer Van Bomel (*Trimmer v. Van Bomel*, 434 N.Y.S.2d 82 (N.Y. Sup. Ct. 1980)). When Trimmer was a fifty-five-year-old travel operator, he met Van Bomel on one of his tours. She was a sixty-three-year old widow with assets of some $40 million. Trimmer left his $8,900-a-year job to become her full-time companion. With her subsidy, his life was transformed: "He moved to larger quarters and modified his wardrobe to suit her tastes. He accompanied her to lunch and dinner, escorted her to the theatre and parties, and traveled with her on her trips to Europe. . . . He also acted as her confidante, and her friends became his friends" (83) Over the next five years, Mrs. Van Bomel spent an estimated $300,000 on Trimmer's personal expenses. Her payments covered not only rent and travel expenses, but Italian and British handmade suits, two Pontiacs and a Jaguar, plus jewelry and a monthly stipend. They never became sexual partners.

When the relationship ended, so did Trimmer's perks. In a case that dragged through New York courts for eight years, Trimmer sued Van Bomel, demanding $1.5 million compensation for his past services as her companion and escort, and for violation of an oral agreement that Van Bomel would take care of "costs and expenses for sumptuous living and maintenance for the remainder of his life" (83). The New York County Supreme Court judge rejected Trimmer's claims for what the judge dubbed "companiomony." The judge had to work hard in matching this unusual relationship to the standard matrix. He said explicitly, for example, that since no sexual relationship was involved, "at best the plaintiff may be regarded as a companion and paid escort, and not as a substitute mate" (84). Surely Trimmer and Van Bomel's ties were not marital, nor were they paramour-concubine, or just ordinary friends. Was it perhaps a routine employer-employee relationship, or a peculiar form of unmarried cohabitation? With apparent discomfort, the judge's answer was some of each, but not enough to establish claims to further compensation.

Edward J. Greenfield, the judge in question, began his opinion on the case in a philosophical mood, reflecting that "The complex and varied relationships between men and women, when they come to an end, oft leave a bitter residue and a smoldering irritation for which the salve, often the only soothing balm, is cash. It is a poor substitute for love, affection or attention, but for many its satisfactions are longer lasting" (83). But soon Justice Greenfield reverted to the tried-and-true principles of hostile worlds, declaring:

> The claims of friendship, like the claims of kinship, may be many and varied. To imply an obligation by a wealthy friend to compensate a less wealthy companion for being together, dining together, talking together and accepting tokens of regard stretches the bond of friendship to the breaking point. The implied obligation to compensate arises from those things which, in normal society, we expect to pay for. An obligation to pay

> for friendship is not ordinarily to be implied—it is too crass.
> Friendship, like virtue, must be its own reward. (85–86)

By this reasoning, the court separated the anomalous relationship at hand from true friendship.

Note the parallels between the two decisions, *Schwegmann v. Schwegmann*, and *Trimmer v. Van Bomel*. Despite differences between Louisiana's civil law and the common law of New York, as well as striking contrasts in relations between the parties, interpretive principles in the two cases greatly resemble each other. Both courts voice vehement separate spheres rhetoric distinguishing intimate relations from economic transactions. Mary Ann Blackledge could collect for business services, not personal attention; Leonard Trimmer's contributions were deemed exclusively sentimental, and therefore not compensable.

If we take a closer look at these legal proceedings, however, we observe both the people involved and the judicial authorities constructing roads across the boundaries of intimacies and economic transactions. The Louisiana court acknowledged that Schwegmann paid Blackledge a monthly allowance check in addition to subsidizing her living and entertainment expenses. The New York court, while declaring Trimmer's relationship to Van Bomel sentimental in the eyes of the law, explicitly recognized the transfer of $300,000 in cash and kind from defendant to plaintiff. Thus, in practice, people and courts do not segregate spheres of intimacy and economic transactions but engage in a complex process of matching certain forms of intimacy to particular types of economic transactions. They discriminate sharply between appropriate and inappropriate matchings.

INTIMATE ECONOMIES AND THE LAW

More generally, the two cases illustrate important points concerning the law's intervention in intersections of intimacy and economic life. Intimate relations only become legal cases in rare circumstances;

most of the time intimately connected people work out their differences without litigation. However, when such private disputes turn into legal suits, courts regularly adopt hostile worlds language. Furthermore, they often pretend to judge intentions. So do people who bring cases to court. Trimmer argued, for example, that Van Bomel intended to provide for him after their breakup. This produces interesting, complex efforts at translation and mystification on both sides.

Courts and people actually do relational work. They both match appropriate relations, transactions, and media. Disputes, therefore, concern how those three elements are defined and matched. A divorcing couple contest, for example, whether an earlier purchase of an automobile from their pooled funds was a gift from spouse to spouse, a common investment in the household, or a business deal. Appropriate media and transactions vary systematically with relations. As relations change over time and vary across places, so do media and transactions. As long as slavery survived in the United States, the case of Patsy and Miller showed us in chapter 1, American law barred most transfers of wealth to an enslaved concubine regardless of the couple's domestic arrangements. That distinctive legal category and its attendant matchings of relations, transactions, and media disappeared with slavery's abolition.

Different branches of law treat relations and intentions differently. Contract law, as we have already seen, distinguishes a somewhat different array of relations from the laws of torts, testaments, and taxation. Judgments concerning which intimate relations actually exist and confer legally enforceable rights arise in a number of areas this book does not much discuss, including eligibility of partners and dependents for veterans' benefits or pensions, qualification for welfare payments, rights of children to enroll in local schools, and granting of legal immigration or work permits to spouses of citizens. These various branches of law, therefore, pose different problems of translation and application. The language of intention, for example, figures centrally in disputes over testaments and contracts, but more peripherally in disputes over taxation; tax courts care less about what the taxpayer (or tax evader) was trying to do than about whether that act conformed to the law.

Legal practice also creates embeddedness; the legal arena has a certain coherence and inertia, which means that legal practice commonly lags behind routine social practice and constitutes a realm of expertise requiring translation in both directions. Moreover, big changes in relations within routine social life affect legal definitions and practices. Thus, as unmarried cohabitation becomes more common, lawyers and courts begin creating new categories and doctrines (or modifying old ones) to regulate disputes concerning unmarried partners.

The idea that relations have legal standing recurred in nineteenth-century treatment of parent-child and husband-wife relations, and relational issues continued to concern legal scholars during the twentieth century. In 1934, legal theorist Leon Green clarified and codified one aspect of this process by defining what he called a "relational" interest. For Green, relational interests are "interests in relations with other persons. . . . They extend beyond the personality, and are not symbolized by any tangible thing which can legitimately be called property" (Green 1934: 462). He defines relational interests broadly, including family relations, trade relations, professional relations, and political relations. Green distinguishes a relational interest from interests of personality (persons' claims to their own individual integrity) and property interests (persons' claims to goods and services). "While in hurts to personality or property only two parties, plaintiff and defendant, are involved," Green notes, "in hurts to relational interests, three parties must always be involved" (462). He points out that courts had been uneasily granting relief for certain relational interests in tort and defamation cases. At the same time, they typically resisted making awards for such harms—treating them instead as property interests. Since Green's codification, legal theorists and courts have used the doctrine more widely.[1]

---

[1] See Foster 1962; Leslie 1999; Macneil 1980; Prosser 1971: 873; for an earlier statement, see Pound 1916.

In current legal practice, relational interests extend far beyond the zone of intimacy into commercial contracts; in that zone the related doctrine of "reliance interest" often comes into play. What then distinguishes relationships in which intimacy and economic transactions intersect? Any such relation involves four elements: first, ties between persons; second, sets of transactions; third, media for those transactions; and fourth, a boundary separating this relationship from others that resemble it in some regards. In the relationship between Trimmer and Van Bomel, we observe a (later disputed) tie of companionship, a series of purchases and exchanges of personal attention on the couple's part, and media ranging from cash to services to expensive durable goods. We also witness negotiation over the boundary separating close companionship from a paid escort service. Intimate ties characteristically include attention, information, trust, exclusiveness, and particularity. More concretely, they involve a set of intimate practices: personal care, sex, affection, housework, health care, advice, conversation, companionship. As a matter of fact, courts inspect relations for precisely these practices. Trimmer's services, the judge noted, included the "time and attention [devoted] to the defendant, to allow her wishes to prevail concerning his deportment, habits and associations," as well as being her confidante and companion.

When does the law engage intimacy? Parties to intimate relations typically resort to the law only when they cannot settle disputes over rights and obligations with the means available in their own personal settings (Ewick and Silbey 1998, 2003). Courts step in to enforce obligations or settle disputes in three rather different circumstances. The first involves *abuse* of intimacy, as when a psychotherapist seduces a patient. The second concerns *deprivation* of intimacy, as when an automobile accident kills a loving spouse. The third centers on *illegitimate* intimacy, as when the heirs of a deceased lover contest his bequest to his mistress. The law thus certainly intervenes directly in disputes among the participants in a contested intimate relation. But it also gets involved with third parties having direct connection to, and interest in, the disputed relationship, as well as with authorities interested in the whole category of relations. Mary Ann Blackledge, for instance, did not sue John Schwegmann alone, but also his two children and his firms. In class-action suits, courts often engage authorities; cases concerning the rights of same-sex couples, for instance, typically involve heads of corporations, public agencies, and advocacy groups. Again, after the devastating attacks on New York's World Trade Center in September 2001, survivors threatened to sue a wide range of organizations, including airlines, that they held responsible for the wrongful death of their loved ones.

LEGAL CATEGORIES

Let us look more closely at legal practices that regulate intersections of intimacy and economic transactions. Legal practice displays a degree of internal coherence and autonomy, but it does not evolve and exist in an entirely separate world. As a first approximation, it helps to distinguish three interacting social phenomena: relational packages, social categories, and legal categories. *Relational packages* consist of real-life combinations among (a) named interpersonal ties, (b) interpersonal transactions, and (c) media. Thus, persons X and Y call each other "sweetheart," engage in transfers of information, advice, gifts, financial aid, and occasional sex, using the telephone, Internet, and money as their media. *Social categories* classify widely recognized relationships within a certain population, again using names, transactions, and media. Here the relationship between X and Y might fit into the social category of friends or the category of lovers, each with its distinctive transactions and media. In fact, social categories distinguish relationships more sharply than real-life practices do. *Legal categories* parallel social categories in matching widely recognized relations, transactions, and media and making them subject to legal action—enforcement, compensation, and penalties. Thus, conceivably X and Y could appear before the law as partners to a contract; as concubine-paramour, prostitute-client, benefactor-beneficiary; or even as members of a common-law marriage. Legal categories always differ in some regards from social categories, for example, in accepting or rejecting distinctions among prostitution, concubinage, common-law marriage, and legally certified marriage.

A double matching process occurs. Within each of these sets—relational packages, social categories, and legal categories—participants match relations, transactions, and media. But the three sets also interact, such as when legal advocates of same-sex marriage propose extending the rights and obligations that the law currently recognizes for heterosexual spouses to same-sex spouses. Notice what happens with social and legal categories. In routine social life, people regularly distinguish among categories of relations that share important properties. For instance, they often take considerable care in differentiating rights and obligations attached to kinfolk, friends, and colleagues, even though the three categories often overlap both in persons and in behavior. Implicitly, people consult a grid of relationships arranged by their similarity or dissimilarity and mark boundaries between adjacent relations. Consider how many ways men and women differentiate among relations involving the fact or possibility of sexual intimacy:

Dating	Prostitution
"Hooking up"	Pedophilia
Engagement	Incest
Use of escort services	Marriage
Frequentation of strip clubs	Sexual surrogacy
Telephone sex	Acting in pornographic films
Cybersex	

When a male and a female engage in sex, how do we recognize which of these relations it is? Although their scripts overlap in some regards, each category of relationship names a somewhat different configuration. We mark distinctions with different names and rituals, as well as with special media and transactions. Notice, for instance, that all of these relations include distinctive economic transactions determining who pays, how, when, for what, at what time, how much, how often, for how long. Even within the world of prostitution we find differentiation: prostitutes distinguish their income by type of activity or by customer.

What about legal categories? Courts adopt a similar procedure, but their matrix has some distinctive properties. Consider what happens when personal disputes get into court. Our four couples—Patsy and Miller, Cruz and McAneney, Blackledge and Schwegmann, and Trimmer and Van Bomel—all had their own definitions of their relations, conflicts, and hardships, their own conceptions of justice or injustice. But when they went to court, their definitions and conceptions had to conform to existing legal criteria. Those criteria are remarkably diverse depending on the particular legal rubric under which courts and lawyers place a dispute. Indeed, in the case of *Schwegmann v. Schwegmann*, Mary Ann Blackledge, testified that "she was a wife" to Schwegmann, serving as his companion, housekeeper, and cook. Yet, as we saw earlier, the court would not tolerate any such reading of husband-wife obligations. The court registered the relationship as concubine-paramour. Blackledge's sole victory in court was as a business associate, not as a wife.

Although American courts recognize some of the sexually intimate relations in the list above, they have their own array of legally distinctive categories of relations and transactions. Following are some crucial definitions from *Black's Law Dictionary* (1999):

> *Criminal coversation*: A tort action for adultery, brought by a husband against a third party who engaged in sexual intercourse with his wife.

> *Alienation of affections*: A tort claim for willful or malicious interference with a marriage by a third party without justification or excuse.

> *Consortium*: The benefits that one person, especially a spouse, is entitled to receive from another, including companionship, cooperation, affection, aid, and (between spouses) sexual relations.

> *Breach of promise*: The violation of one's word or undertaking, especially a promise to marry.

> *Seduction*: The offense that occurs when a man entices a woman of previously chaste character to have unlawful intercourse with

him by means of persuasion, solicitation, promises, or bribes, or other means not involving force.

Marriage: The legal union of a man and woman as husband and wife.

Concubinage: The relationship of a man and woman who cohabit without the benefit of marriage.

Palimony: A court-ordered allowance paid by one member to the other of a couple, that though unmarried, formerly cohabited.

Marital rape: A husband's sexual intercourse with his wife by force or without her consent.

Prenuptial agreement: An agreement made before marriage usually to resolve issues of support and property division if the marriage ends in divorce or by the death of a spouse.

Meretricious (of a romantic relationship): Involving either unlawful sexual connection or lack of capacity on the part of one party (a meretricious marriage).

Each of these terms brings its own set of further understandings and legal practices. Take "meretricious," a hostile worlds concept par excellence. Lawyers working in the American legal system spend a great deal of time avoiding any arrangement that can be construed as legally binding compensation for sexual services. They therefore make distinctions that separate direct reward for sexual services from legitimate contracts. As *Schwegmann v. Schwegmann* illusrates, "severability" rules in cohabitation disputes distinguish meretricious or illicit sexual aspects of an unmarried couple's long-term relationship from their legitimate contractual arrangements, such as contracts for domestic services or business partnerships. Most famously, the controversial 1976 *Marvin v. Marvin* decision stated that "express agreements will be enforced unless they rest on an unlawful meretricious consideration" (557 P.2d 106, 122 (Cal. 1976)). The court distinguished sexual services from domestic labor and the sacrifice of a career. That distinction allowed Michelle Marvin compensation for a relinquished career.

Here, too, courts debate which relationships qualify for economic compensation, when, why, and how much. Legal categories do not recognize all social categories, and they often make distinctions that do not appear in everyday life. The authors of a well-known casebook in family law make this clear:

> The facts of a case, as they present themselves to the practicing lawyers, tend to be diffuse and complex. For example, in a particular case whether there was a marriage or not may be obscure. A judge is expected to come to a clear result, perhaps by attaching a fictitious intent to the parties or applying a presumption. It may be difficult, however, for the lawyer to say whether a set of facts constitutes an engagement, nonmarital cohabitation, marriage, business partnership, cotenancy, employment, or something else. Traditional legal theory provides little guidance to the practicing lawyers in determining which characterization to adopt because it is too often limited to artificially tidy classifications. Moreover, legal theory tends to focus upon pairs of conceptual opposites—such as marriage or no-marriage—to the exclusion of other possibilities. The skilled lawyer selects from an open-ended checklist of multiple choices those that are strategically most advantageous to the client. What may appear later in court as fact is only a reflection of reality as seen and presented by the lawyer for judicial decision. (Weyrauch, Katz, and Olsen 1994: v)

We begin to see that lawyers and courts are bringing three elements together, struggling over them, and in the process changing them. The first is the matrix of recognized relations. Within that matrix, distinctions and distances change; for example, legalization of same-sex marriage shifts the boundary of marriage and reduces the legal distance between homosexual and heterosexual relationships. The second element is a body of decided cases that serve as analogies and precedents for the case at hand. As this book proceeds, we will often see lawyers and judges using cases creatively, not matching the case at hand mechanically with already tried cases, but arguing that previous cases embodied a principle that no one had so far recognized, pressing for extension of a principle to an adjacent area of legal application, or claiming that precedents contradicted each other, hence that the court had an opportunity and obligation to make new law.

A third element binds together available precedents and the matrix of recognized relations. A body of legal doctrines incorporates categories of cases and rules for their interpretation. At the broadest level stand conventional distinctions among doctrines that distinguish tax law, the law of contracts, criminal law, and other specialized legal fields. Within each of these fields, further doctrines hold sway. Later in this chapter, for example, we will encounter the time-honored doctrines of coverture and consortium, which long affected the recognized legal rights of spouses in the United States. As we follow the intimacy of coupling, caring, and households into the legal arena, furthermore, we will eventually meet such exotic doctrines as undue influence, conditional gifts, and innocent spouse.

Take the legal doctrine of *consideration*. American law does not generally recognize a contract as binding unless the parties have exchanged something of value, a consideration, however nominal or unequal the exchange. What about the mutual commitments that intimate partners make without ever arriving at a formal agreement including conditions and terms of exchange? Especially after death, divorce, or separation, courts frequently find themselves forced to determine whether such commitments (for example, to provide lifetime care) are legally enforceable. As they do so, they regularly scrutinize the commitment's origins for evidence of considerations exchanged.

Through the intersection of legal struggles, legislation, and broad social change, all three elements—doctrines, exemplary cases, and matrices of recognized relations—change continuously, but mostly in small, inconspicuous increments. Typically, legal categories tend to lag behind the current everyday categories, as in the cases of same-sex marriages or cohabitation. On the whole, lawyers and courts respond cautiously to changes that have already gone quite far in the behavior of ordinary people. They negotiate matches, however uneasy, between everyday relationships and the existing legal matrix before they argue for changes in the matrix itself. Legal practice therefore only recognizes certain combinations of relations, transactions, and media as appropriate for its jurisdiction. For example, American law generally forbids litigation of spousal obligations such as food preparation, child care, and sexual intercourse. It also generally refuses to recognize distinctions household members have themselves established among various sources of income, such as windfall earnings committed to vacations and regular wages committed to food purchases.

Let us consider more precisely how legal practice treats interpersonal relations. Lawyers and courts match existing relational packages with established legal categories. From that matching they derive appropriate elements of intimacy, determining whether attention, information, advice, trust, exclusiveness, particularity, personal care, sexual relations, housework, feeding, health care, conversation, and/or companionship properly belong to that relationship. From that reasoning they then deduce rights and obligations binding the parties, including third parties. They also assign values to these various sorts of transactions, for example, deciding how much (if anything) advice given was worth. Finally, they adjudicate rewards, penalties, legal standings, and the propriety of transactions (such as bequests) on the basis of the legal category into which the relational package falls.

Closely observed, courts apply a simple questionnaire to connections between the parties involved. They ask the following:

1. What kind of relationship is this?
2. What rights, obligations, and interactions belong to that class of relationships? (Proper interactions are those that no third party has the right or obligation to interfere with; improper, those that at least one third party has a legal, enforceable right or obligation to challenge.)
3. Did one of the transactions violate those rights and obligations?
4. If so, what legal remedies apply?

To repeat, in applying these standards, courts and legal specialists implicitly invoke legal categories: a map of relationships, including boundaries, proximities, and appropriate bundles of rights, obligations, and interactions. They also typically adopt and rely on hostile worlds justifications of their boundary making. In *Schwegmann v. Schwegmann*, the court declared it not only legally incorrect to frame their relationship as marriage but morally perilous: "To equate the non-marital relationship of concubinage to a marital relationship is to do violence to the very structure of our civilized society."

In order to avoid just this kind of condemnation, lawyers advise their clients how to present their cohabiting relations. The American Bar Association provides specific practical advice to potential litigants. Unmarried, cohabiting couples, instructs its *Guide to Family Law*, may enter legally binding agreements about "how much each will pay for rent, mortgage, utilities, groceries, auto expenses." The authors warn, however, against "pillow-talk" agreements—the "don't worry, I love you. I'll take care of you. Everything will be okay" statements often made while "the couple may be in bed enjoying a moment of intimacy." Such agreements, cautions the guide, are rarely enforceable. Even more emphatically the guide discourages agreements that closely entwine sexual relations with other obligations, explaining that "if a court thinks an agreement amounts to providing financial support in exchange for sexual relations, the court will not enforce it. Such an agreement will be viewed as uncomfortably close to a contract for prostitution" (American Bar Association 1996: 6–8).

Lawyers, judges, and juries do relational work of a distinctive kind: they work hard to establish proper matching within legal categories. Consider the provision of health care. People provide treatment for each other's illness in a wide variety of relationships—parent-child, wife-husband, friends, physician-patient, nurse-patient, teacher-pupil, priest-parishioner, pharmacist-customer, servant-employer, nursing home attendant–inmate, and more. Courts repeatedly find themselves adjudicating the appropriateness and value of the treatment by placing the relationship within a legal category. For which categories of relations is this treatment permissible?

What responsibility do the parties bear for the consequences? What rewards, punishments, and constraints should the law therefore apply? Lawyers, judges, juries, and parties to disputes thus engage in the delicate work of translating from the language of everyday practices and social relations into the specialized idioms of the law (Felstiner, Abel, and Sarat 1980–81; Gal 1989; Rotman 1995).

In typical disputes, someone uses the available array of legal categories to allege a mismatch. A party, as we have seen, may propose straightforward matching of behavior to a location within the array. Another party may argue for excluding the relationship from legal jurisdiction, as in a wide variety of disputes between spouses. Doctrines and cases available as precedents come into play at precisely this point. Parties may engage in disputes concerning boundaries or contents of relations; in the case of a gay couple, for example, courts may have to decide whether they qualify as spouses for the purposes of taxation, whether they have the right to adopt children, or whether they acquire rights in each other's property. In such cases, especially where the proper classification of the relationship is under dispute, argument often proceeds by analogy and proximity to other legally established relationships. This is where the legal categories listed above come into play. Is this relation meretricious? Does it qualify as concubinage? Lawyers and courts often engineer change in precisely this way, by arguing new analogies and applications for existing categories. They fashion novel combinations of cases, doctrines, and relational categories.

CONTEST AND CHANGE

As a consequence of negotiation, the law changes incrementally through an incessant process of contestation. Lawyers specialize in introducing new distinctions, new analogies, new arguments, and new doctrines. What is more, courts respond, however slowly, to changes in social life at large. Legislatures also enact new statutes in response to gradual social changes and to pressure from mobilized constituencies. Amid these pressures, however, courts thread their own path, leaving precedents that influence subsequent decisions. As a consequence, the grid of legally available relations changes, as does the matching with media and transactions.

The American system involves the additional complexity of variation from state to state. Despite some influence of predominant law schools, doctrines, and national courts, plus a degree of convergence during the twentieth-century, individual states follow distinctive trajectories concerning laws governing intimacy. In his authoritative legal history of nineteenth-century American marriage, Hendrik Hartog documents extensive state variation in this regard. When it came to laws of marriage and divorce, he explains, "every state had a law of marriage. Every state had its legal peculiarities" (Hartog 2000: 12). Negotiation between everyday practices and legal practices therefore took place not only in terms of American legal culture but in terms of each state's laws.

Nevertheless, some overall trends did occur. Take the case of common-law marriage. Earlier we saw courts struggling over the propriety of various forms of heterosexual cohabitation and with the rights and obligations attached to them. In her legal history of "nonmarriage," Ariela Dubler traces remarkable changes in the legitimacy of such arrangements. Nineteenth-century state courts, for instance, increasingly endorsed the doctrine of common-law marriage, "by which courts could recognize unsolemnized, long-term, sexual unions as marriages" (Dubler 1998: 1886). Although some states rejected the doctrine, and states varied in their precise definition of common-law marriage, standard rules of thumb included cohabitation, sharing of bed and board, public self-representation, public recognition, and the absence of legal impediment (such as an existing marriage) to the union. By the late nineteenth century, Dubler reports, most American states treated such relations as legally permissible and binding. States typically distinguished common-law marriages from other forms of cohabitation, such as bigamy and temporary liaisons. While opponents decried what they saw as public endorsement of immoral relations, supporters justified their approval by defining marriage as foremost a private civil contract. The U.S. Supreme Court agreed, endorsing the validity of a long-term informal union in an 1877 decision (*Meister v. Moore* 96 U.S, 76 (1878); see Dubler 1998: 1889).

Around the 1930s, American law concerning intimate relationships underwent a major shift. Courts and legislatures moved to dislodge common-law marriage as a legally recognized relationship. They also withdrew recognition from engagement as a legally enforceable contract, denied actions against third parties for interference with a couple's affections, yet increased the power of married couples to collect from third parties for deaths or injuries depriving a spouse of affectionate companionship. Legislatures, lawyers, courts, and juries converged, in effect, on sharpening the boundary that separated relations of legal marriage from all other relations. During the 1970s, another partial shift occurred, as American law began to recognize analogies between the rights of legally married couples and other forms of companionship—never erasing the boundary between marriage and nonmarriage, but extending some rights across the boundary. Clearly, the array of relationships recognized, distinguished, prohibited, or defended by the law altered significantly over time. In each of these regards, courts did not merely name and distinguish relations, they matched them with appropriate transactions and media. We can see change more clearly by concentrating on rights and obligations of legally married couples. Consider two significant shifts that took place in the United States from the early nineteenth century to the recent past concerning coverture and consortium.

COVERTURE

The law of coverture was inherited from English common law and regulated legal transactions between husbands and wives. Most significantly, it established a sharp distinction between a legally independent unmarried woman and a married wife. Single women obviously did not enjoy full legal citizenship, for example, with respect to voting or jury duty. Nevertheless, they enjoyed almost all other legal and economic rights, including the right to direct economic enterprises in their own names. By marrying, however, a woman lost such entitlements. Although widows retained ownership of their personal effects and acquired rights to fixed shares (typically a third) of their husbands' estates, at the husband's death women lost their prior claims to the rest of the marital property (on dower, see Dubler 2003).

In its pristine form, coverture treated husband and wife as indistinguishable legal actors from the perspective of the outside world, but highly differentiated from the point of view of the marriage contract. This had some surprising consequences; under coverture, for instance, a wife could legally act as her husband's agent. The so-called law of necessaries specified and limited a wife's right in these regards. The law provided wives with some legal recourse by making a husband directly responsible to a merchant for the purchases made by his wife. Yet even this entitlement to pledge a husband's credit faced stringed limits. Necessaries were so ambiguously defined that merchants were reluctant to risk extending credit to a wife for goods which might fall outside that class. Moreover, husbands were entitled to determine where necessaries should be purchased and could terminate a wife's authority to pledge his credit by demonstrating that he had provided the necessaries or a sufficient allowance to obtain them. The law, in fact, was explicitly concerned with protecting husbands from the "mad" expenditures of "extravagant" wives.[2]

Within marriage, in its eighteenth- and early-nineteenth-century form, coverture therefore implied enormous economic inequality. By law, all personal property or real estate a wife owned, or any income she earned outside of the household, belonged to her husband. So did her domestic and sexual services. In exchange, husbands were legally responsible for supporting their wives. In fact, any legally binding transaction conducted by the wife passed through her husband. Coverture's legal implications, furthermore,

---

[2] On the concern about "extravagant wives," see *Ryon v. John Wanamaker, New York, Inc.*, 190 N.Y.S. 250 (N.Y. Sup. Ct. 1921); *Saks v. Huddleston*, 36 F.2d 537 (D.C. Cir. 1929); and W.A.S. 1922. See also Salmon 1986.

deprived wives of most legal recourse against wrongs inflicted upon them by their husbands. (In some circumstances, however, coverture provided separated women with claims on support from their estranged husbands [Hartog 2000: 125].)

Through legal and political struggle, however, American courts gradually chipped away at both aspects of coverture. First, husband and wife became increasingly capable of acting as legally independent agents, and second, within their marriages, wives gained greater economic autonomy. For instance, as it did for inventions by slaves, nineteenth-century patent law denied the husband—or master—the right to patent his wife's invention (Kahn 1996; Kahn and Sokoloff 2004: 395). Mid-nineteenth-century married women's property acts granted married women rights over the possessions they brought to the marriage or that they gained by inheritance. After the 1860s, a few state legislatures passed laws allowing women control over their earnings—so long as the income was obtained by labor outside of the household.

Linda Kerber (1998) has dramatically portrayed a series of legal and political struggles that produced changes in coverture. Kerber concentrates on legal relations between women and the American state. She shows, for example, how through conflicts over such matters as taxation, jury duty, and military service women acquired rights and obligations directly tying them to the state, rather than mediating all such rights and obligations through their husbands. The Nineteenth Amendment, granting women the vote, marked a major transformation in women's legal status. To be sure, these changes occurred very slowly. Kerber locates two major challenges to coverture as late as the 1990s: demands for recognition of same-sex marriages and the Supreme Court's Planned Parenthood decision of 1992. Both cases, Kerber observes, confirmed that marriage might confer legal rights on the spouses, but those rights then belonged to the individuals, not their partners. Once political rights no longer depended on marital status, coverture had virtually disappeared.[3]

---

[3] For reservations concerning the obliteration of coverture, see Hasday 2004.

The 1990s culminated a series of changes that had being going on for several decades. As Hartog observes in his legal history of American marriage, "We have lived through a striking transition in marital law and marital behavior . . . including the obliteration of legal language that once established and defined distinctive marital identities and the apparent triumph of an egalitarian and contractual conception of marriage" (Hartog 2000: 3). Thus, coverture in the United States virtually disappeared as a legal doctrine and practice during the waning twentieth century. Its transformation and eventual abolition systematically altered the correspondences among media, transactions, and relations with respect to marriage.

LOST CONSORTIUM

Coverture's decline, moreover, is linked to a second significant transformation in husbands' and wives' legal relationship to each other—focusing on what the law defines as marital consortium: the investment that husbands and wives acquire in each other's company. Consortium becomes a crucial doctrine in tort cases when third-party actions damage that investment, either intentionally or through negligence. The extreme case occurs when one of the spouses disappears or becomes incapacitated as a consequence of third-party action. In cases of third-party negligence causing injury or death to husband or wife, the spouse suffering the loss can sue third parties for loss of marital consortium (of course, courts and juries distinguish between the amounts and grounds of awards for injury and death, but those differences matter little for this discussion). Meanwhile, in so-called heart-balm actions, a wronged spouse could sue a third party for two types of intentional interference with the marriage relationship. First, in cases of adultery, the aggrieved spouse claimed damages from the third-party lover in a suit for criminal conversation, claiming, among other harms, loss of consortium. In the second category of heart-balm actions, alienation of affections, the plaintiff accused the defendant of injuring or breaking up the marriage.

No evidence of adulterous sexual relations was necessary for this second type of action, nor was adultery by itself sufficient to claim alienation of affections. In fact, such suits could be brought against relatives and friends not just for theft of affections, but more broadly for injuriously and unjustifiably meddling with the marital relationship. A 1934 review noted that "probably . . . more suits for alienation of affections are brought against parents and other very close relatives of the alienated spouse than against any other class of persons" (Brown 1934: 483). In contrast with the pecuniary emphasis of other nineteenth-century domestic jurisprudence, heart-balm cases often extended beyond immediate financial losses to compensation for such nonmonetary damages as loss of companionship. Yet plaintiffs often received large awards. (Clark 1968: 266).

As it happens, heart-balm actions also occurred outside of marriage. In cases of broken commitments to marriage, jilted fiancées could sue for breach of promise, while parents of a seduced woman claimed damages from the seducer. The reasoning was directly parallel to that applied for the disruption of a marital relationship: the investment that one party had in a relation to the other (Tushnet 1998; VanderVelde 1996). However, the relative significance of these two kinds of claims (intentional and negligent interference with marital consortium), the substance of the loss, and the gender symmetry of consortium rights, all changed substantially over time (see Brown 1934; Clark 1968; Fox 1999; Hartog 2000; Holbrook 1923; Keeton 1984; Korobkin 1998; Lippman 1930). As usual, change resulted from the convergence of three different causes: general alterations in social practice outside the law, political pressure, and internal developments within the legal field.

The relative importance of intentional and negligent actions involving loss of consortium claims seesawed throughout the nineteenth and twentieth centuries. Heart-balm actions boomed between the late nineteenth century and the 1930s, with successful plaintiffs receiving significant compensation. Between the 1930s and the 1950s, however, reformers successfully acted to reduce such claims. One of the major arguments was a hostile worlds complaint. Heart-balm actions, in the view of its reformers, put an unseemly monetary price on priceless companionship. Yet consortium claims did not disappear with these restrictions. Disputes over negligence had often figured in heart-balm cases, and as their numbers dwindled, negligence soon became the primary basis for consortium claims. In its two major forms, injury and wrongful death, spouses laid claims for harm to their marital relationship. In cases of both injury and death, the law recognized the surviving spouse's loss of some or all of the companion's contribution to the relation.

What losses were spouses suing for? The substance of consortium claims altered significantly over time. In cases of injury or death, nineteenth-century courts were very reluctant to make consortium awards for anything but material losses. They resisted assigning value to marital companionship as such. In close correspondence to coverture, early-nineteenth-century courts compensated husbands exclusively for the pecuniary loss of their wives' services. Later, however, courts moved increasingly toward recognizing companionship as a loss, in addition to material services. As they did so, they oscillated between treating companionship and service as indissolubly linked and treating them as legally separable.

Even in the 1930s, Leon Green complained that at least in death actions, courts "deny any substantial protection to the relational interest" of surviving spouses: "It would seem that both legislatures and courts have looked upon the death action more as a form of insurance, or as an emergency relief for the survivors against the poorhouse, rather than as a method of protecting the relational interest or as compensating for any injury done to such interest" (Green 1934: 472–73). By then, in fact, the law was already changing, however slowly. Indeed, at the beginning of the decade in a *Columbia Law Review* article on the "breakdown of consortium," Jacob Lippman, an influential opponent of separating material and relational interests, had noted that "courts have undertaken to break up consortium into two component parts, practical (service) and spiritual (affection, companionship, etc), completely overlooking the fact that in its inception and in its very nature consortium was and must be an indestructible entity" (Lippman 1930: 672–73).

By the 1960s, consortium awards regularly included compensation for lost companionship. Homer Clark's *Law of Domestic Relations* offers the following definition:

> Apart from support, consortium could be summed up as referring to the variety of intangible relationships prevailing between spouses living together in a going marriage. In earlier times there was more emphasis upon the wife's services than today when it is coming to be recognized that the parties' mutual affection, with all that that implies, is more important than the wife's household chores. (Clark 1968: 261)

After the 1930s, as courts ruled out heart-balm compensation, they became more generous in awards for related damages of injury and wrongful death.

In addition to shifts in the relative importance of intentional versus negligent actions and the substance of the claimed loss, the gender symmetry of legal claims noticeably changed as well. Who could sue? For the most part, since 1800 American law has defined consortium very asymmetrically. Husbands were the sole plaintiffs in early-nineteenth-century actions, suing for both intentional and negligent interference with their marital rights over a wife's services—much as a master was entitled to recover for loss of a servant's labor. After the mid-nineteenth-century enactment of wrongful death statutes by most states, and for most of the rest of that century, husbands generally lost their claims in connection with a wife's services. Meanwhile, wives could now bring wrongful death actions for loss of their husband's wages and support (Witt 2000, 2004).

By the late nineteenth century, wives also gained legal access to claims for intentional disruption of the marital relationship, as courts allowed them to sue for alienation of affection and criminal conversation. Yet women were still not permitted to claim damages when their husbands were injured. Why this persistent exclusion? Courts argued that because the husband recovered damages for his loss of earning capacity, he was therefore able to continue supporting his wife. In such cases, additional awards to the wife would entail either illegitimate double recovery for the same injury or provide inappropriate compensation for nonpecuniary loss. Only after the 1950 landmark case of *Hitaffer v. Argonne Co.* (183 F.2d 811 (D.C. Cir. 1950)), did states regularly start equalizing husbands and wives' entitlements for loss of consortium in cases of injury (on gender and loss of consortium actions, see Ridgeway 1989).

Notice the law's inconsistencies concerning who could legally claim loss of consortium and for what. During late-nineteenth- and early-twentieth-century cases, wives could not sue for loss of their husband's consortium if he was negligently injured, yet they could do so when another woman intentionally seduced him. Both men and women, meanwhile, were denied recovery for the sentimental aspects of consortium in death or injury cases but allowed such compensation in heart-balm suits.

How Consortium Changed

The following list outlines, in summary form, the changes that the doctrine of consortium has undergone:

- *Criminal conversation*: Only men can collect until the late nineteenth century, when women acquire rights to sue, but the doctrine itself simultaneously dwindles in importance at the same time.
- *Alienation of affections*: Only men can collect until the late nineteenth century, when women acquire rights to sue.
- *Wrongful death*: Only men can collect for loss of services by other household members until mid-nineteenth-century statutes intervene. After that, a remarkable change occurred: men could no longer recover damages. Women could now claim damages for pecuniary loss of support through disappearance of the male wage-earner. From that point on, nonpecuniary losses are only nominally recognized; during the twentieth century, slow movement is made toward compensation for nonpecuniary losses.

- *Injury*: Only men can collect, for loss of a wife's services. After the 1950s, gradually, women can collect for loss of marital companionship as a result of a husband's injury.

As legal discourse and practice with regard to consortium changed, so too did the use of separate spheres and hostile worlds distinctions. Throughout this history we have been reviewing, legal specialists invoked the image of two worlds, one of sentiment, the other of rational efficiency, operating according to distinctive rationales with very different consequences for their participants. They repeatedly warned that blurring the boundary between the worlds would contaminate both of them, by making sentimental relationships mercenary or introducing personal considerations into business dealings. They generally called up separate spheres imagery to mark boundaries whose moral value they prized. But the relevant moral values, the distinctions, and the justifications changed deeply over time.

For one thing, nineteenth-century legal developments increasingly distinguished the position of wife from that of servant and increasingly marked that boundary with rights distinctive to wives. By the 1930s, what had once seemed an unimportant legal boundary became paramount: a wife's practical services could no longer be distinguished from her sentimental attachment to her husband. Analysts thus shifted the application of hostile worlds reasoning. Jacob Lippman made this abundantly clear as he argued the case for joint compensation of sexual, sentimental, and practical services:

> It seems to me that if the right of *consortium* is to be recognized, there can be no distinction made between negligence actions and so-called intentional actions. The services of a wife cannot be said to include housekeeping and exclude affectionate care of the husband and children. *Consortium* which embraces all of these duties, must remain intact or else perish completely. (Lippman 1930: 668)

Thus, it was not simply a matter of justice but also a matter of preserving marriages from commercial contamination, by legally acknowledging their inextricable sentimental elements.

As the changing treatment of consortium suggests, American courts were doing relational work in three regards. First, they were deploying—and in the long term significantly modifying—the grid of relationships available for legal action and the distinctions among them. We see them, for example, increasingly distinguishing husband-wife relationships from those of master-servant and parent-child. Second, they were matching relations, transactions, and media, likewise altering legally acceptable definitions as they went along—eventually conceding the rights of women to collect for loss of consortium in cases of a husband's injury and also moving reluctantly toward compensation for nonpecuniary losses, such as companionship, affection, personal care, and sexual relations.[4]

Third, courts partially reversed their reasoning. In addition to deducing appropriate transactions and media from the publicly recognized relationship, they also reasoned from observed transactions to the relationship's quality. In cases of injury to a spouse we see the participants debating the character of interactions between spouses—how loving, how attentive, and so on—in assessing appropriate damages for loss of consortium. Among the evidence relevant to such cases, *American Jurisprudence* lists "the character and conduct of the spouses, the quality of the relationship between the spouses, any impairment of the sexual relationship, and the length of the marriage" (41 *Am. Jur.* 2d Husband and Wife § 264 (2004)). And a commentator in *American Law Reports* in the 1970s writes: "It has been held that in assessing the 'value' of a wife's loss of her husband's sexual relations, the jurors may consider not only frequency of such relations prior to the husband's injury, but also evidence of how important a role sex plays in the wife's life generally" (Litwin 1976).

---

[4] Later, courts in some states conceded the extension of consortium rights to parent-child relations and, in some cases, to cohabiting couples—see Korzenowski 1996; Mogill 1992; Soehnel 1985; Szarwark 2003. Meanwhile, whether consortium applied to same-sex couples stirred legal contestation; see Culhane 2000–2001; Markowitz 2000; Merin 2002: 209–17.

We find a similar relational rationale in alienation of affection cases.[5] In the South Dakota case of *Pankratz v. Miller* (401 N.W. 2d 543 (S.D. 1987)), the plaintiff, Duane C. Pankratz, a veterinarian, sued Winston Miller, a childhood friend, for alienation of his German-born wife Elke's affection. Duane and Elke had been married for twenty years and had five children. Miller entered the couple's life when after many years of absence, he returned to South Dakota as an insurance salesman. Elke's intimate relations with him began when she started commuting to attend summer school and spent one night away from home. In a 1986 decision the trial court awarded Duane $10,000 in actual damages and $10,000 in exemplary damages.

But a year later the Supreme Court of South Dakota reversed the judgment. Miller successfully argued that he had not been responsible for Duane's loss of his wife's affection. In fact, it was Elke who initiated their relationship: "The first time they were intimate, it was Elke who invited Winston up to her room. She sent him cards and gifts upon occasion; he did not reciprocate. They were not in love; Winston did not promise her any future relationship, nor did she make any such promises to him. Indeed, Elke was seeing another man at the time of trial" (547). Elke herself admitted that "our relationship [with Duane] was very strained by that time. . . . I lost my love and affection for my husband many years ago already" (546n.5). The court concluded that "the evidence shows that Elke's affections for Duane were alienated long before her involvement with Winston" (547). A standard torts manual reporting on this case comments: "There is no liability if all affection between the spouses has already terminated and there is no affection to alienate" (Dobbs et al. 1988: 129).

[5] A 1925 New York decision, *Buteau v. Naegeli*, 208 N.Y.S. 504 (N.Y. Sup. Ct. 1925), shows both relational strategies at work. In an alienation of affections suit, the court allowed a jury's nominal award of $1 in compensatory damages to the plaintiff wife, finding she had little affection for her husband. Yet the court also allowed $5,000 in punitive damages, endorsing the jury's intention to punish the defendant's "disregard of the marital relationship in its aspect of menace to the

Although they speak of it in other terms, American lawyers, judges, and juries regularly enact a standard procedure. They call up a relational matrix distinguishing different bundles of social ties, transactions, and media from each other. They match the relationship to its proper location within that matrix, reasoning from the public standing of the tie to appropriate transactions and media as well as from observed transactions to the tie's proper legal definition. They negotiate a match. As they do so, they frequently justify their actions by means of hostile worlds rhetoric and practice, carefully distinguishing the relation at hand from others with which it might wrongly—and banefully—be confused.

In the transformation of coverture and consortium, participants in American legal processes deeply altered correspondences of relational packages, social categories, and legal categories. On the whole, these shifts did not eliminate legal boundaries between supposedly sentimental and rational spheres; instead, they redefined the location and character of that boundary. Most often, furthermore, legal categories lagged behind relational packages and social categories. Nevertheless, alterations in legal categories wielded influence of their own. For example, married women acquired rights to dispose of their property and their earnings without their husband's authorization.

Within the legal arena, in fact, weighty struggles continue over the purchase of intimacy. Legislatures debate laws that govern marriage, cohabitation, parentage, inheritance, and sexual practices, not to mention such forms of intimacy as doctor-patient relations. Lawyers, judges, and juries respond to novel cases by negotiating new interpretations of existing law. Throughout these changes, furthermore, legal scholars formulate critiques, codifications, and doctrines that, if adopted by legislatures or courts, significantly shape subsequent legal practices. A selective review of recent debates among legal scholars will illustrate connections between current legal practices and arguments over fundamental principles.

---

community" (506). The appellate court later reduced the judgment to $1,218.76 (see Brown 1934: 501–2).

COMPETING LEGAL THEORIES

Attempts to reconcile economic transactions and intimacy have generally tried to strike some balance between the two, but have not surpassed either hostile worlds or nothing-but reductionisms. In the preceding chapter, we have already seen Richard Posner's attempt to get rid of a hostile worlds view by replacing it with a nothing-but economic alternative. According to Dan Kahan, this "law and economics" approach:

> presents a comprehensive theory of legal rules founded on the rational actor model. Descriptively, it posits individuals who react to legal incentives in a manner rationally calculated to maximize their material well-being. Normatively, it appraises legal rules according to their contribution to social wealth. And prescriptively, it presents a programmatic collection of maxims and algorithms designed to make the law efficient. (Kahan 1999)

In recent years, a number of legal scholars have reacted against this extraordinarily influential economic paradigm. In some cases, scholars have returned to a hostile worlds argument, insisting that there are some ranges of social behavior that commodification does corrupt after all. Others have moved toward cultural reductionism, by emphasizing social norms, meanings, and values as an alternative to economic rationality. Still others have begun to formulate more substantial institutional and relational accounts as competitors of the economic narrowness of the law and economic paradigm.

Let's proceed from minor revisions to major challenges. For a relatively minor revision of separate spheres and hostile worlds thinking, consider philosopher Elizabeth Anderson. At first reading, her arguments cling closely to a separate spheres view where intimate and market relationships occupy polar normative spaces. "Personal goods," she argues, "are undermined when market norms govern their circulation" (Anderson 1993: 152). More specifically, commodifying sexual relations "destroys the kind of reciprocity required to realize human sexuality as a shared good" (154). We see

Anderson delicately balancing the need to renegotiate gender power relations without making them into marketlike contracts. She endorses, for instance, marriage contracts designed to equalize couples' equality "provided that the spirit of a market transaction . . . does not dominate their interactions" (157). A critical task for modern societies, therefore, "is to reap the advantages of the market while keeping its activities confined to the goods proper to it" (167).

Along the way, however, Anderson qualifies her hostile worlds diagnosis by opening up the possibility of morally differentiated market practices. While declaring herself strongly against legalization of prostitution, she allows that under circumstances of dire economic deprivation, impoverished women should have the right to sell their sexual services. Invoking the possible scenario of professional sex therapy designed to free people from "perverse, patriarchal forms of sexuality," Anderson acknowledges that some commercial sexual services might have "a legitimate place in a just civil society" (156). Thus, she envisages the use of legal means to maintain the boundaries between separate spheres. But she leaves us with a theoretical dilemma: are markets inherently incompatible with intimacy, or are there some forms of market transactions that correspond to different forms of intimacy? Facing the same question, legal philosopher Margaret Jane Radin breaks with Anderson by offering a bold critique of both hostile worlds analyses and Posner-like "universal commodification" theories. Yet in the last instance Radin returns to a modified version of the hostile worlds view.

In *Contested Commodities*, Radin proposes a body of law that would regulate and distinguish the zone she calls incomplete commodification—where "the values of personhood and community pervasively interact with the market and alter many things from their pure free-market form" (Radin 1996: 114). As she clearly states, this zone includes instances of commodified sexual relations and parent-child ties. In her model, "payment in exchange for sexual intercourse" along with "payment in exchange for relinquishing a child for adoption" are "nodal cases of contested commodification" (131).

Sexual relations, Radin argues, "may have both market and non-market aspects: relationships may be entered into and sustained partly for economic reasons and partly for the interpersonal sharing that is part of our ideal of human flourishing" (134). However, despite her insistence on the interaction of culture and law, as well as her cogent objections to what she calls the "domino" theory of commodification, Radin implies that "complete commodification" would occur with monetization in the absence of institutional—especially legal—protections. In the case of prostitution, for instance, while she advocates the decriminalization of the sale of sexual services, she also insists that "in order to check the domino effect," the law should prohibit "the free-market entrepreneurship" that would tag along with decriminalization and "could operate to create an organized market in sexual services." Different forms of regulation—including a ban on advertising—are necessary, she concludes, "if we accept that extensive permeation of our discourse by commodification-talk would alter sexuality in a way that we are unwilling to countenance" (135–36).

When it comes to baby-markets, ranging from what she calls "commissioned adoptions" to "paid adoption of 'unwanted' children," and including surrogacy (136), Radin wavers even more visibly. Although baby giving may in fact constitute an act of "admirable altruism," both toward the baby's and the adoptive parents' welfare, baby selling would put that altruism in question. She concedes, however, that in principle babies could belong to a zone of "incomplete commodification," with "coexistent commodified and noncommodified internal rhetorical structures" allowing altruism along with sales (139). But, once again, as with prostitution, she fears the ultimate dominance of market discourse. "If a free-market baby industry were to come into being," Radin asks,

> how could any of us, even those who did not produce infants for sale, avoid measuring the dollar value of our children? How could our children avoid being preoccupied with measuring their own dollar value? This measurement makes our discourse about ourselves (when we are children) and about our children (when we are parents) like our discourse about cars. (138)

Even though Radin comes much closer than Anderson to rejecting the hostile worlds dichotomy, in the last instance she flinches.[6]

Similarly, Margaret Brinig recognizes the weaknesses of both hostile worlds and nothing-but formulations, yet hesitates to specify what lies beyond them. She directly confronts the standard legal treatment of intimate family relations. We cannot, she argues, transfer intact, commercially rooted concepts of market, firm, and contract to the sphere of family interactions. While conceding that a contract or market model may be usefully applied to the formative stage of family relationships, as in courtship and adoption, she contends that the model fails to accommodate ongoing family ties. Most notably, contract law "does not have the right concepts or language to treat love, trust, faithfulness, and sympathy, which more than any other terms describe the essentials of family" (Brinig 2000: 3). Struggling to move beyond an orthodox nothing-but economic view, Brinig often veers toward traditional hostile world polarities, declaring that

> marriages, or at least most marriages, are not like these contracts or Chicago School law and economics efficiency-seeking venturers. When marriages are good, they involve self-sacrifice, sharing, and other-regarding behavior, perhaps a more "feminine" view of the universe. They are relationships, not just relational contracts. . . . As a society we have tremendous incentives to promote the noncontractual, nonmarket view of marriage. (18)

Brinig moves cautiously however toward less dualistic or reductionist paradigms. To replace the monistic contract model, she dis-

---

[6] Similarly, Stephen Schulhofer, in his concern with establishing protections for sexual autonomy, dismisses economic reductionism as an explanatory model. He likewise moves away from a hostile worlds view, but not completely. Recognizing that "we cannot automatically condemn every exchange of sex for money, regardless of context," he still worries that "sexual relationships founded on economic motives seldom seem admirable, and we often regard them as degrading." The challenge, he says, "is in knowing when, if ever, a person can *legitimately* link sexual intimacy with economic support" (Schulhofer 1998: 161).

tinguishes between contracts and covenants; the first restricted to "legally enforceable agreements," the latter, "agreements enforced not by law so much as by individuals and their social organizations" (1). Covenant, she further specifies, "is a compact or promise that cannot easily be broken even if one side does not perform fully or satisfactorily. It thus has durability beyond that of many firms and far beyond the time horizon of the market, where a transaction may be entirely episodic or discrete" (6). Such covenants—especially applicable to husband-wife and parent-child ongoing relations—imply not only "unconditional love and permanence," but third-party involvement, such as God, the community, or both.

Brinig never quite specifies the differences in relations or transactions that characterize what she calls contracts and covenants. She declares:

> Although the classical theory of the firm gives us some valuable insights into marriage, it falls short in part because of the special characteristics of marriages, primarily intimacy and privacy. It may tell us why a continual stream of contracts will not work in the context of marriage, and even why people marry, but not why in the most successful of marriages each spouse will gladly contribute without "counting the cost." Here the new institutional economics does far better. Through stressing transaction costs, the new institutional economics approaches the idea of covenant and the broader community concerns about marriage. (109)

Extended only slightly, however, Brinig's covenant and contract distinction conveys not just polarities but appropriate ways of representing social relations.

Like Radin and Brinig, legal theorist Cass Sunstein is trying to find a superior analytic position somewhere between hostile worlds and nothing-but conceptions. Searching for ways out of the economic reductionism dominant in legal scholarship, Sunstein and other proponents of what Lawrence Lessig (1998) calls the "New Chicago School" of law, are paying close attention to social meanings and norms (see also Lessig 1995, 1996). More specifically, in his *Free Markets and Social Justice*, Sunstein insists: "We should agree that social norms play a part in determining choices, that people's choices are a function of their particular social role; and that the social or expressive meaning of acts is an ingredient in choice" (Sunstein 1997: 36). Noting that economics "at least as it is used in the conventional economic analysis of law—often works with tools that, while illuminating, may be crude or lead to important errors," he challenges economistic accounts of human motivation and valuation (4). In particular, sharply critical of "monistic" legal theories of value, Sunstein makes a compelling argument for the multiplicity and incommensurability of human values, such as the distinction between instrumental and intrinsic values attached to goods or activities.

When it comes to the economic valuation of intimacy, including sexual relations, Sunstein's notion of norm-determined incommensurability marks a sharp cultural divide between financial and sexual exchanges. He notes that "if someone asks an attractive person (or a spouse) for sexual relations in return for cash" the offer would be insulting, as it reflects "an improper conception of what the relationship is" (75). He goes on to explain that

> the objection to commodification should be seen as a special case of the general problem of diverse kinds of valuation. The claim is that we ought not to trade . . . sexuality or reproductive capacities on markets because economic valuation of these "things" is inconsistent with and may even undermine their appropriate kind (not level) of valuation. (76)

Yet Sunstein opens a significant wedge in his analysis. While on the one hand endorsing the view that some kinds of transactions, including sexual ones, are utterly incompatible with the market, hence with monetary transactions, he also acknowledges that markets and monetary transactions can accommodate multiple systems of valuation. Markets, he points out, "are filled with agreements to transfer goods that are not valued simply for use. People . . . buy human care for their children. . . . They purchase pets for whom they feel affection or even love." Therefore,

the objection to the use of markets in certain areas must depend
on the view that markets will have adverse effects on existing
kinds of valuation, and it is not a simple matter to show when
and why this will be the case. For all these reasons, opposition
to commensurability, and insistence on diverse kinds of valuation, do not by themselves amount to opposition to market exchange, which is pervaded by choice among goods that participants value in diverse ways. (98; for a more general discussion
of commensuration, see Espeland and Stevens 1998)

In the same way, Sunstein agrees that money, rather than necessarily
flattening goods and relations, is itself socially differentiated: "Social
norms make for qualitative differences among human goods, and
these qualitative differences are matched by ingenious mental operations involving qualitative differences among different 'kinds' of
money" (41). While at first Sunstein seems to have responded to
the nothing-but "law and economics" with a nothing-but culture
alternative, he moves on to a much more sophisticated analysis of
social relations.

More impatient than Sunstein with uncritical adherence to hostile
worlds views, philosopher Martha Nussbaum sets out to debunk the
widespread presupposition that "taking money or entering into contracts in connection with the use of one's sexual or reproductive
capacities is genuinely bad" (Nussbaum 1998: 695; for a more general exposition of Nussbaum's ideas, see Nussbaum 1999). Nussbaum points out how much revulsion against payment for bodily
performance has proceeded from class prejudices. Using the case of
prostitution to deconstruct sexual commodification more broadly,
Nussbaum asks us to reassess rigorously "all our social views about
money making and alleged commodification" (Nussbaum 1998:
699). Notice, she tells us, how most cultures mingle sexual relations
and forms of payment, and establish differentiated continua of such
relations—ranging from prostitution to marriage for money and including "going on an expensive date where it is evident that sexual
favors are expected at the other end" (700). Nussbaum goes farther:
she documents the wide range of paid occupations in which women

accept money for "bodily services," from factory workers and domestic servants to nightclub singers, masseuses, and even the professor of philosophy who "takes money for thinking and writing about what she thinks—about morality, emotion . . . all parts of a human being's intimate search for understanding of the world and self-understanding" (704).[7]

Yet despite sharing many features with these other forms of "bodily services," only prostitutes are stigmatized. Step by step, Nussbaum dismantles standard explanations of what makes prostitution unique, such as its immorality or its support of gender hierarchies. Along the way, she provides persuasive philosophical arguments against hostile world doctrines, in particular the assumption of money's incompatibility with intimacy. Not true, she argues, that a prostitute "alienates her sexuality just on the grounds that she provides sexual services to a client for a fee" (714). Accepting money in exchange for services, even intimate services, is not intrinsically degrading. After all, Nussbaum reminds us, musicians laboring under contract and salaried professors still produce honorable and spiritual works. In the same way, she insists, "there is no reason to think that a prostitute's acceptance of money for her services necessarily involves a baneful conversion of an intimate act into a commodity" (716). Nor does prostitution, despite hostile worlds concerns, contaminate noncommercial sexual relations; different types of relationships can and have always coexisted.

Instead of debating the morality of commercial sex, insists Nussbaum, we should be concentrating on expanding women's limited labor opportunities by means of education, skills training, and creation of jobs. Criminalizing prostitution, Nussbaum argues, will not correct an unequal labor market but further limit poor women's employment alternatives. She does, however, draw the line at nonconsensual, coerced prostitution and child prostitution. Thus, short of that limit, Nussbaum provides a strong case against the hostile worlds argument and for the equivalence of a wide variety of connections between payment and intimacy. That equivalence, how-

[7] For a male equivalent of bodily services, see Wacquant 1998 on boxing.

ever, fails to recognize sufficiently that in practice payment systems and social ties differentiate and that people attach great importance to those differentiations.

Legal scholars Linda Hirschman and Jane Larson propose a still more radical overhaul of hostile worlds views. Although at first reading their alternative resembles a Posner-like nothing-but economistic script, on close analysis it puts us on quite a different, more political ground, Applying a feminist-sensitive bargaining theory to heterosexual relations, they advocate a new sexual order of what they call "hard bargains" where "men and women can recognize the age-old political nature of their negotiations over sexual access as well as their more recent commitment to equality and begin to develop workable processes for resolving their differences and making a fair division of the goods of their sexual cooperation" (Hirschman and Larson 1998: 3).

Dismissing the hostile-worlds paradigm, Larson and Hirschman insist that sexual bargaining goes on "despite the cultural association of male-female sex with unreasoning romance and passion" (27). Because heterosexual bargaining "takes place between naturally and socially unequal players" (267), they propose legal intervention to redress unequal bargaining outcomes. "Structured bargaining" is possible, they argue, precisely because "eroticism and emotions are [not] exempt from the ordinary rules of human behavior" (268). More concretely, their policy proposals to achieve more equitable sexual bargains directly challenge notions of separate spheres. Instead they distinguish four sexual regimes, each involving distinct relations between the parties and distinctive payment systems—except for rape, where they propose to criminalize the relationship entirely. The four are marriage (as seen from the viewpoint of adultery), concubinage (or in their terms, fornication), prostitution, and rape. Let us take them up each in turn.

When it comes to extramarital sex, Hirschman and Larson envision a radically transformed negotiation between spouses. Arguing that marriage should include "a nonnegotiable duty of sexual exclusivity" (285), they recommend civil compensation for the personal injury of adultery: either as a "bonus" when dividing marital property after divorce or death, or by an even more revolutionary "tort

action for money damages available during the ongoing marriage or
after divorce" (285). Hirschman and Larson acknowledge that in the
context of a "sharing model of marriage" (286) their proposed tort
of adultery involving compensatory monetary transactions within
legally intact marriages might appear incongruous. Yet they strongly
justify their proposal as a much-needed legal strategy for redressing
spouses' bargaining power.

In the case of nonmarital long-term cohabitants, Hirschman and
Larson's emphatic "concubinage proposal" (282) argues in favor of
contractual obligations between unmarried sexual partners. Significantly, they recommend doing away with the legal fiction underlying the landmark *Marvin v. Marvin* palimony decision, which distinguishes meretricious or illicit (sexual) aspects of an unmarried
couple's long-term relationship from their legitimate contractual
agreements, such as contracts for domestic services or business partnerships. This is quite a reversal, because, as we saw earlier, courts
have worked hard to construct such "severability" rules as a way to
distinguish legitimate marital ties from prostitution.[8] Arguing that
"we see no reason why sex should be ruled out as motivation for
an exchange between intimates," Hirschman and Larson support
nonmarital sexual bargains as "fair trades" (280–81). They do not,
however, propose to abolish relational distinctions. Instead, they
seek to redraw the boundaries among relationships, matching types
of entitlements to those relationships. Their proposed regulatory
statute, for instance, applies to couples who "have been sexually involved for a specified duration of time" (280), not to short-term
sexual partners. Therefore, they explain, the differentiation between

---

[8] On how courts have moved away from the more severe "meretricious spouse"
rules toward a more flexible contractual approach to cohabitation arrangements,
see Hunter 1978. The controversial 1976 *Marvin v. Marvin* decision dramatized
the new reach of the severability rule. Stating that "express agreements will be
enforced unless they rest on an unlawful meretricious consideration," the court
distinguished sexual services from domestic labor and the sacrifice of a career,
allowing Michelle Marvin recovery for the latter. Ironically, by allowing recovery
for domestic services, the court, as Hunter points out, grants "meretricious partners" greater economic latitude than married couples, who cannot contract for domestic services (Hunter 1978: 1,092–94).

prostitutes and concubines "remains a morally meaningful distinction" (282). The regulation of concubinage, furthermore, offers couples choices "from a graduated series of relational obligations, with marriage as the most comprehensive" (285).

Meanwhile, note Hirschman and Larson, prostitution appears to be the "purest of bargained-for sex" (6). Yet it is often a bad bargain involving unequal power, frequently bordering on coercion. That does not however make selling sex—especially adult consensual exchanges—a criminal activity. Instead of criminalizing prostitution, they propose the regulation of the sex business via existing labor laws, thereby redefining the kind of relationship among prostitutes, patrons, and pimps by assimilating them to a different widely recognized relational category of employer-worker.

Hirschman and Larson's clear-headed mapping of relational distinctions does not however lead them to blankly endorse all sexual relationships. In direct parallel to Nussbaum, when it comes to nonconsensual intercourse or, regardless of consent, sexual relations between adults and children, they recommend criminal penalties. In that way, they are not so much denying the boundary between legitimate and illegitimate sexual relations as displaying and fortifying that boundary. By proposing to legitimize new forms of monetary compensation for unmarried and married couples and by treating prostitution as labor rather than crime, Hirschman and Larson undercut hostile worlds views in fundamental ways. Nor, regardless of their hard-nosed economistic vocabulary, are they forwarding a nothing-but market alternative. Like advocates of comparable worth in employment, they promote legal intervention to reorganize inequitable markets and to ban unacceptable contracts.

FEMINISTS ATTACK GENDER INEQUALITY

A different radical challenge to hostile worlds and separate spheres legal principles comes from a cluster of feminist legal scholars who claim that separation of spheres fundamentally undermines women's interests.[9] Turning traditional women's work exclusively into a matter of sentiment dangerously obscures its economic value. American courts, these scholars argue, have long collaborated in such disentitlement.

Carol Rose for instance, has offered a powerful critique of separate spheres reasoning in the legal arena. Pointing out that property transfers occur extensively within households and that property relations outside of households rest on elaborate social connections, Rose rejects conventional boundaries: "There is no 'In-Here' of family and 'Out There' of work. . . . These spheres interact incessantly" (Rose 1994: 2417). The traditional "rhetoric of sharing and nurturance," she warns, builds the illusion that "property questions stop at the homestead door. They don't" (2414). Only by addressing such questions, can gender equality be achieved both during marriage and after divorce: "When we see the unspoken property within arrangements that masquerade as 'sharing,' we can also see their injustice and hypocrisy. It is only when we neglect the property aspects of marriage that we dub as 'equal' relationships that may be profoundly hierarchical" (2415). Courts, however, Rose points out, strongly resist treating family disputes as matters of property, typically ignoring, for instance, the economic contributions of women's household labor.

Indeed, as Reva Siegel amply documents, splitting family and market spheres took painstaking legal effort. Focusing on nineteenth-century debates over the valuation of household labor, she shows how courts carefully segregated that labor as a nonmarket exchange. As earning statutes increasingly gave wives a right to income from their "personal labor" for third parties, they consistently excluded the household labor performed for their husbands or families (see also Cott 2000; Stanley 1998). Courts, Siegel reports, "refused to enforce interspousal contracts for household labor, reasoning that such contracts would transform the marriage relationship

[9] See Chamallas 1998; Dubler 2003; Fellows 1998; Finley 1989; Goodman et al. 1991; Jones 1988; Kornhauser 1996; McCaffery 1997; Schlanger 1998; Schultz 2000; Silbaugh 1996; Tushnet 1998.

into a market relationship" (Seigel 1994: 2139–40). Thus, courts assumed and defended both separate spheres and hostile worlds. Their strategy worked. More than a century later, Siegel notes:

> We live in a world in which unwaged labor in the home stands as an anomaly lacking explanation but not requiring one either. In this world it takes an act of critical scrutiny to discern that market relations have been systematically delimited and that labor vital to their support is, with equal systematicity, expropriated from women on an ongoing basis. (2210)

Similarly unmasking what she calls "commodification anxiety," Joan Williams argues that "the fear of a world sullied by commodification of intimate relationships feeds opposition to granting wives' entitlements based on household work." More radically departing from hostile worlds views than does Margaret Jane Radin, Williams notes that, along with other legal experts in commodification, Radin ignores that "women's key problem has been too little commodification, not too much" (Williams 2000: 118).

Williams calls attention to the arbitrary gendering of commodification that goes on in divorce settlements. As a result of what she calls the "he-who-earns-it-owns-it" rule, husbands typically are awarded a greater share of marital property. The prevailing separate spheres assumption that "family work is an expression of love" (120), she remarks, disregards that family work is also labor. Williams then turns to the crucial example of "degree cases," in which a wife claims compensation at divorce for having financed her husband's professional degree. She reports courts' hostility to such requests, in ways that directly parallel the nineteenth-century decisions cited by Siegel. In one 1988 West Virginia case, the court declared that "characterizing spousal contributions as an investment in each other as human assets, demeans the concept of marriage" (quoted in Williams 2000: 117). Determined to undo such prejudicial sentimentality, Williams puts forth remedial policies to achieve just compensation for women. For instance, her joint property proposal would recognize family work as economically valuable, justifying income sharing by spouses after divorce. It would thereby undermine courts' and legislatures' assumption that "men's claims give rise to entitlements while women's claims are treated as charity" (131).

At times, Williams' hard-nosed critique of hostile worlds, like Brinig's, edges toward nothing-but economistic reductionism. Nevertheless, she is careful to distinguish her income-sharing proposals from others that rely on what she sees as "strained analogies to commercial partnership law" (126). In so doing, she begins to recognize differentiation of social ties among such settings as families, firms, markets, and organizations. At the same time, however, she wants a reading of the law in which such relations cast legal shadows that are financially equivalent.

Martha Ertman joins the feminist effort toward a revised, more equitable, economics of intimacy. She offers legal remedies that specifically bridge the divide between intimacy and economic transactions, without reducing one to the other. Drawing on the flexibility and acceptability of business law, Ertman intends to open wedges for the legal defense of intimate relations as enforceable private contracts (see also J. Cohen 2002). She outlines three arguments for that strategy: first, since family law doctrine already endorses privatization, judges and legislators will be receptive to applying business models to domestic matters; second, the flexibility of business law will accommodate the increasing variations in intimate relationships; and finally, business models are well suited to deal with legal interventions in the financial aspects intimacy, such as the division of assets after divorce.

The analogies that Ertman proposes include "an understanding of marriage as akin to corporations, cohabitation as akin to partnerships, and polyamory as akin to limited liability companies" (Ertman 2001: 83). The unfamiliar term *polyamory* refers, in Ertman's analysis, to

> a wide variety of relationships that include more than one participant. For example, one man may affiliate with a number of women who are sexually involved with the man but not with one another. Such an arrangement, polygamy, has been associated with Mormons, and is still common in many nonindustri-

alized societies. . . . The term also includes arrangements with combinations of people who organize their intimate lives together, regardless of the extent of the arrangement's sexual elements. Thus, if a lesbian couple has a child by alternative insemination, using a gay man as a known donor to father the child, and the donor remains involved in the child's life, the arrangement is polyamorous. (124)

Fending off possible accusations of nothing-but economistic reductionism, Ertman explains that the comparison between business models and intimate arrangements "is not an equation: not every intimate interaction is akin to a business transaction, nor are all business relationships solely financial in character." Her aim is to find "new ways to think about the old problems rooted in naturalized understandings of intimacy" (98; see also Ertman 2003). For example, she has proposed "premarital security agreements" to ensure that women continue to get compensation for their household efforts after the breakup of a relationship (Ertman 1998). In short, Ertman makes explicit a widespread strategy in legal argument, drawing analogies with established law to alter existing forms of legal doctrines and practices.

INTIMACY AND THE ECONOMY REVISITED

All these recent efforts reorient discussions of the intersection between intimacy and monetary payments in fundamental ways. They reject separate spheres–hostile worlds dichotomies as well as nothing-but reductionisms. What's more, in one way or the other, each critic discussed recognizes the presence of differentiated social ties and corresponding variations in payment systems. They begin to appreciate the prevalence and complexity of relational work. Thus, they move closer to adopting a view of connected lives.

This book joins their effort. It examines how people and courts alike actually negotiate the overlap of intimate social ties with economic transactions. It does so by concentrating on three highly contested areas of intersection between them. The first, chapter 3, is coupling, the whole range of social relations in which one significant present or future possibility is sustained intimacy, including sexual intimacy. The second, chapter 4, deals with caring, the provision of personal attention and services, running from professional to domestic. Chapter 5 takes up households, broadly defined as all forms of durable cohabitation; in households we see strong overlaps among coupling, caring, and cohabitation. After these close examinations, the book closes with a more general reconsideration of intimacy's purchase.

CHAPTER 3

COUPLING

On June 23, 1997, the Kansas Board for Discipline of Attorneys convened to consider the conduct of Jerry L. Berg, a Wichita, Kansas, divorce lawyer. In separate complaints, six of Berg's female clients accused him of improper sexual behavior. After considering the evidence, the panel recommended disbarment. Although no specific prohibition exists in Kansas banning attorney-client sexual relations, the board condemned "exploitation of the attorney-client relationship to the detriment of the client" (*In re Berg*, 955 P.2d 1240, 1247 (Kan. 1998)).

In one of the six complaints, R. M. reported consulting Berg about her divorce in August 1993, after her first lawyer had made no progress with her case. Berg and R. M. had first met during her parents' divorce some three or four years earlier, and Berg had discussed with the then fourteen- or fifteen-year-old R. M. her alcohol and drug addiction problems. R. M., "stressed, confused, suicidal and seeing a counselor" (1244), now worried about losing custody of her one-year-old child to her husband, as well as ensuring his child support payments. On October 14, 1993, the night before her divorce was final, R. M. went to Berg's office between six and seven o'clock to sign a property settlement agreement. Although she was below the legal drinking age, Berg invited her out, ordering several alcoholic drinks, including one called "sex on the beach."

After discussing sexual matters, they returned to his office to sign further papers.

It was then, R. M. testified, that Berg "grabbed" and kissed her, and she performed oral sex on him. Although acknowledging that the sex was not forced, she reported being scared and worried that if she resisted, Berg would not represent her in court the next day. After the divorce was granted, R. M. endorsed an income tax refund as payment to Berg. Although she was still short by $200, Berg marked it "paid in full." R. M. testified, "I felt like a whore because I felt like I had paid for my services the night before." Berg did not send her any further bills. Their sexual relationship continued, as R. M. still consulted Berg on other legal matters. It ended abruptly on June 14, 1994, when Berg, seeking consolation after losing an important case, visited R. M. at her apartment. Recovering from a miscarriage, she refused to have sex, but he insisted. Two days later, she sent Berg a letter terminating his services as her attorney. Until then, R. M. stated, she considered Berg to be her lawyer.

In his defense, Berg contended that his sexual relations with R. M. did not start until October 15, 1993, after her divorce settlement. At that point, in his view, she was no longer his client. If the attorney-client relationship did not exist, Berg argued, the sexual relationship was legitimate. To bolster his defense, Berg brought in a psychologist who had been treating him as a sexaholic. Berg also stated he had been attending weekly Sexaholics Anonymous, Bible study, and Promise Keepers meetings, and finally that he was reconciling with his wife.

Berg appealed his disbarment. On March 6, 1998, however, the Supreme Court of Kansas concurred with the Board of Discipline's decision to disbar Berg. Among other issues, the court determined that R. M. continued to be Berg's client through June 16, 1994. In any case, the court declared:

> It is no more persuasive to attempt to justify one's conduct by arguing a scenario of scarcely letting the ink on the divorce decree become dry, extracting all available funds from the client

(an income tax refund), and then writing off the balance of the bill with the stroke of a pen and immediately beginning to seduce with alcoholic drinks an under the drinking age and vulnerable client. (1255)

The Berg case reports spectacular mingling of intimacy, economic transactions, and professional relations. In such cases, lawyers and legal scholars constantly dispute exactly where to draw the line between proper and improper relations (see, for example, Bohmer 2000; Larson 1993; Mischler 1996, 2000; Schulhofer 1998). The discipline panel and the Kansas Supreme Court finally decided to treat Berg as a lawyer who had abused his relationship with a client.

In so doing, they denied that the couple were lovers or, for that matter, a prostitute and client. The parties hardly disputed what had happened, or even the participants' intentions. At issue was whether the combination of relationships, transactions, and media was morally and professionally acceptable. The board and the State Supreme Court said no. They were defending a well-marked professional boundary from corruption in two opposite directions. On one side, they defended against the possibility that licensed practitioners would use their authority to gain illicit intimate attentions, thus bringing external dishonor and distrust on the profession. On the other, they defended against the possibility that intimate relations would lead practitioners to violate established understandings, practices, and relations, thus disrupting the profession's carefully rationalized internal organization.

Consider another case that came to trial in Wisconsin six years before the Berg judgment. David Kritzik, a wealthy widower, "partial to the company of young women," had over the course of at least six years given Leigh Ann Conley and Lynnette Harris, twin sisters, more than half a million dollars, in kind and cash: he regularly left a check at his office, which Conley picked up every week to ten days, either from Kritzik himself or from his secretary (*United States v. Harris* 942 F.2d 1125, 1128 (7th Cir. 1991)).

The case raises the issue of the taxability of monetary transfers to a mistress in long-term relationships.[1] Were those transfers gifts or compensation? If gifts, Kritzik had to pay gift tax on the money; if compensation, the sisters had to pay income tax. The United States claimed that the money was compensation. As part of its evidence, the government argued that the form of transfer, a regular check, was that of an employee picking up wages. Sisters Harris and Conley were convicted of evading income tax obligations and sent to jail. After Kritzik's death, however, their attorneys appealed the case. Although the government insisted that the form of monetary transfer identified it as compensation, the appeal pointed out that it could have been an entitlement: "this form of payment . . . could just as easily be that of a dependent picking up regular support checks" (1129). The district court, furthermore, rejected an affidavit presented by Kritzik to Internal Revenue Service investigators before his death, in which he stated that both Harris and Conley were prostitutes. The court dismissed his claim as a likely lie to protect himself from civil or criminal penalties for his failure to pay gift taxes.

The court finally agreed that Kritzik's payments were gifts. Invoking legal precedent, the appellants' counsel successfully argued that "a person is entitled to treat cash and property received from a lover as gifts, as long as the relationship consists of something more than specific payments for specific sessions of sex" (1133–34). A number of Kritzik's letters to Harris entered the trial record as evidence of his continuing affection and trust. He wrote, for instance, that "so far as the things I give you are concerned—let me say that I get as great if not even greater pleasure in giving than you get in receiving," adding, "I love giving things to you and to see you happy and enjoying them" (1130). In another letter, he told Harris, "I . . . love you very much and will do all that I can to make you happy" (1130), adding that he would take care of Harris's financial security.

---

[1] On this issue, see Bittker 1983: chap. 3, pp. 11–12; McDaniel, Ault, McMahon Jr., and Simmons 1994: 149; Klein and Bankman 1994: 150–51. *United States v. Harris*, a criminal prosecution, is of course an exception to the usual pursuit of such cases in civil courts.

What was appellants' counsel doing? The appeal challenged the idea that economic transactions speak for themselves, as well as the effort to deduce relations from transactions alone. Indeed the judges in the case negotiated over exactly where to place the boundary of commercial and loving relationships. Judge Flaum, while concurring in the reversal of the sisters' convictions, worried about the breadth of the principle that his fellow judges invoked: "I part company with the majority when it distills from our gift/income jurisprudence a rule that would tax only the most base type of cash-for-sex exchange and categorically exempt from tax liability all other transfers of money and property to so-called mistresses or companions" (1135).

Regardless of their philosophical differences, members of the court agreed that distinctions between categories of payment, in this case between a gift and compensation, hinge on the type of relationship between the parties involved: lover-mistress versus patron-prostitute. Courts had no choice but to examine the matching of relation, media, and transactions in order to identify the transactions' legal standing. In fact, tax courts defined superficially similar relationships in other cases as prostitute-client, charging the woman income tax on her payments (see, for example, *Jones v. Comm'r*, 36 T.C.M. (CCH) 1323 1977)). Of course, if Kritzik and Harris had been husband and wife rather than lover and mistress, their transfers of money would likely have been tax-free domestic transactions.

By now, no reader should be surprised to see what the Kansas and federal courts were doing. Although they speak a language of intention and morality, courts do the legal version of relational work. They consult a matrix of possible relations among the parties involved, locate the relationship at hand within that matrix, establish distinctions from other relationships, and within the relationship insist on the proper matching of relation, transaction, and media. Exact boundaries within the matrix themselves become objects of contestation, as interested parties negotiate the line separating proper and improper forms of intimacy. With Berg and R. M., both the discipline panel and the Supreme Court of Kansas defined the contested relationship as attorney-client, setting it apart from ordinary lovers or prostitute-patron. They thereby declared Berg's sexual interaction with R. M. and his billing procedures illegitimate. Ironically, they also agreed implicitly that if the relationship between the couple *had* been that of lovers, rather than attorney and client, precisely the same transactions would have been acceptable, or at least legal. The court drew a moral boundary, separating the proper relations of lawyer and client from those of lovers.

Boundaries between intimate relationships have some remarkable characteristics. Although participants, observers, and third parties commonly mark such distinctions with moral discourse and moral practice, rarely are the defining interactions on one side of a boundary or the other universally acceptable or unacceptable in themselves; they depend on context. Sexual intercourse, for example, becomes an enforceable obligation for spouses, an option for lovers, and a forbidden transgression for lawyer-client pairs. Similarly, expensive gifts become obligations in some relations, options in others, and forbidden transgressions in still others. The matching of relation, transaction, and medium matters crucially. Such boundaries also include temporal limits, so that questions arise concerning what relation a couple occupied at the time of a certain transaction: were they *then* a married couple, engaged to be married, unmarried lovers, spouses of other persons, business partners, lawyer and client, patron and prostitute, or acquaintances on a date? All these relations have fairly clear beginnings and endings. Between those temporal limits, participants, observers, third parties, and boards of discipline work to match relations, transactions, and media. When it involves intimacy, relational work takes plenty of effort.

Surprising features of intimacy do not end there. Counterintuitively, intimate relations rarely involve two persons alone. Third parties acquire strong investments in a pair's intimacy and often act to channel, inhibit, alter, or even initiate the transactions and media a couple employ. The Berg and Kritzik cases have shown us the interest that professional associations and government agencies (in the Kritzik case, the Internal Revenue Service) exert over intimate relations. Parents, kin, friends, and fellow members of religious congregations often intervene to promote some versions of courtship and to discourage others. When it comes to provision of advice, bodily care, confidential information, or emotional support, third parties frequently act very effectively to insure that the recipient of these services gets them from the right persons, under the proper definition, in an acceptable form, with appropriate compensation to the provider. Within intimate relations, the parties negotiate the particular forms and meanings of their relationship. But third parties almost always stand close at hand, defending the boundaries.

Outside the legal arena, in ordinary, everyday practice, people engage in a similar sorting of couples. They do not employ precisely the same distinctions as lawyers or invoke exactly the same moral evaluations of different kinds of relations. But they sort across the whole range of relations that involve the possibility of intimacy, from lawyer-client or doctor-patient to friends, neighbors, work-mates, and kin. Legal and ordinary categories interact, further-more; legal proceedings affect how people couple, whereas routine practices affect how the law works; we saw judges in both the Berg and Kritzik cases referring to current practices as they made their decisions.

ANALYZING INTIMATE PAIRS

This chapter concentrates on paired relations that—like those of Berg with R. M. and Kritzik with Harris—involve the possibility of extensive intimacy. In both these cases, the intimacy was sexual, but similar principles apply to a wide range of intimacy. Sharing of se-crets, handling confidential files, providing advice, giving insider economic information, offering solace, and administering bodily care all involve different sorts of intimacy, but commonly occur in the absence of sexual relations. Whether sexual or otherwise, as Randall Collins has argued, paired intimate relations hold out the promise—and threat—of emotional interaction more intense and consequential than everyday social relations (Collins 2004, esp. chap. 6). They all require relational work: establishment of differentiated social ties, their maintenance, their reshaping, their distinction from other relations, and sometimes their termination.

Such intimate transactions occur over a wide range of pairs: friends, partners, neighbors, coworkers, employer-employee, professional-client, parents-children. In all of them, economic transactions frequently mingle with intimacy. As we shall see, in such pairs participants and third parties regularly match the relationship at hand with a matrix of possible relations between the two people, distinguish it clearly from nearby relations with which it might become confused, mark the boundary by means of concerted effort, and within the pair negotiate appropriate matches of relation, transactions, and media. They often invoke separate spheres and hostile worlds ideas and practices as they fend off inappropriate matches. Third parties obviously play important parts in shaping paired relationships: mutual friends introduce likely couples, parents try to block unfortunate matches, police monitor illegal transactions, couples themselves go to authoritative advisers for adjudication or support. This chapter will feature a great deal of third-party intervention—including legal intervention—in paired relations. But its analysis focuses on how interaction between the two principals works, and why. At first, I look at couples' relationships in routine social practices. Later, I take up a parallel analysis of legal practices.

I begin with the pair as the most elementary setting for intimacy, giving special attention to courtship and sexual relations. The narrow focus will allow us to see the process of matching and boundary drawing more clearly. Chapter 4 will move on to caring relationships, those in which at least one party provides sustained and/or intensive life-enhancing attention to another. Caring relationships often involve more than two people, and therefore take us beyond the scope of the present chapter. But caring does not exhaust intimate relations between couples, since intimacy includes some forms of secret sharing, advice giving, personal scrutiny, and forceful intervention—for example, rape—that are by no means life-enhancing. Chapter 5, on households, will take up a setting in which intimate pairs and caring often coincide, but not always; cohabitation sometimes takes place with a minimum of intimacy and caring. The book as a whole therefore looks at the intersection of intimacy and economic transactions through three different, and increasingly complex, lenses.

Given an interacting pair of people, the first lens consists of a series of questions:

- What is the name of this relationship?
- Where does it fit in the array of similar relationships?
- What marks its boundaries from the closest similar relationships?
- What combinations of names, transactions, and media are appropriate for this category?
- How do participants and third parties negotiate the definition?
- How do they negotiate the matching of definition, transaction, and media?
- What happens when one of the parties rejects the current matching as inappropriate?
- How do the parties negotiate transitions across boundaries into adjacent relationships?

How, in short, do couples and third parties do their relational work? In ordinary practice and in legal disputes, we can apply these questions to the whole range of intimate couples. The remainder of this chapter first surveys ordinary practice, then moves on to legal disputes.

In order to discipline the argument, I have omitted a number of fascinating topics in both practices and law, including marriage brokers (whether it is legal or proper for a broker to arrange a marriage), premarital agreements (under what conditions, if any, they constitute binding contracts), insurable interest (whether one party can properly take out insurance on another's life), loss of consortium for engaged couples (whether one engaged party can sue for loss of the other's companionship and services), gifts to employees (under what conditions and under what form are they forbidden, tolerated, or required), and finally, defensible reasons for breaking engagements.

When it comes to hostile worlds ideas, the chapter spends more time on the dangers that intimacy will corrupt professional, commercial, and bureaucratic relations than that such relations will corrupt intimacy. In contrast, the next chapter (on caring) devotes much more attention to the possible corruption of intimate relations by commercialism.

DIFFERENTIATED INTIMACY

Many professions build in stringent boundaries separating appropriate from inappropriate relations between practitioners and clients. The boundary protects against abuse by the professional and inappropriate demands by the client. Remember the clinician's guide for psychotherapists. In addition to the practices mentioned in chapter 1, it warns sternly against providing patients with falsified diagnoses that qualify the patient for reimbursement or disability payments, and against testifying for a patient in a legal dispute. Besides being illegal and unethical, the guide warns, such practices go beyond "the clinician-patient relationship to become a 'special favor' " (Reid 1999: 87). Clinicians are similarly cautioned not to make disability assessments for patients applying for insurance or government benefits. Furthermore, and even more strongly, the guide stigmatizes the disclosure of confidential patient information except in cases of lawful subpoenas, or patient-authorized release to payers, such as insurers.

Clinician and patient relations, moreover, should never slip into financial adviser–investor exchanges:

> For example, if a patient who is a company executive divulges some business matter during therapy that might affect the price of a stock, buying or selling the stock could be considered a breach of privilege, an action in other than the patient's interest, or insider trading. The same applies to help or "tips" you might give the patient.... Do not suggest, recommend, or even inform the patient concerning such things as investments,

and be cautious about direct advice on such topics as employment and relationships. There is a difference between eliciting
thoughts and feelings to encourage good decision making and
inappropriately influencing those decisions. (Reid 1999: 89–90)

The guide also counsels against seeing patients after hours or making the clinician's home telephone available to them. Psychotherapists center their professional expertise on a certain kind of intimacy.
Yet they also impose a sharply bounded definition of proper and
improper intimate transactions between therapist and patient.

Not only psychotherapists, but many other medical specialists,
run the risk of damaging intimacy. They, too, commonly set up ethical barriers against the possibility that intimate relations will com-
promise the effectiveness of their treatment—and the reputation of
their profession. A widely used manual on medical interviewing,
written for students, presents this cautionary tale:

> When I was an intern, I remember spending a great deal of
> time with a young woman diabetic patient who had taken an
> insulin overdose after an argument with her boyfriend. I offered
> her empathy and understanding, talked to her about the impor-
> tance of getting counseling, and explored ways that she could
> improve her social situation and respond more appropriately to
> stress. The Sunday after her discharge, she paged me and asked
> if she could see me in the hospital lobby. Though I was having
> a busy on-call day, I met with her, listened to her latest prob-
> lems with her boyfriend, and held her hand as she cried. She
> asked if we could have lunch the next day. I agreed.
>
> I realized that meeting her for lunch was inappropriate, but
> had felt that doctors needed to be available for their patients
> and should be able to "go the extra mile" to help them. I had
> been flattered that she found me so helpful and enjoyed feeling
> competent in my counseling skills, at a time when my feelings
> of competence were being otherwise challenged by the sick and
> dying patients on my service. I probably was also attracted to
> her, and enjoyed the intimacy of our conversations. I realized,
> though, that responding to my own needs was undermining

my ability to help her. At lunch the next day, I told her of my discomfort and discussed the need for setting appropriate professional boundaries if I were to continue caring for her in the outpatient clinic. (Cole and Bird 2000: 242–43)

"Appropriate professional boundaries" prevent the corruption of medical treatment by the wrong kind of personal intimacy. The professionals differentiate sharply between interpersonal transactions that are appropriate or inappropriate for different sorts of intimate relations.

INTIMACY AMONG HOUSEHOLDS

Similar differentiation occurs with very different consequences in relations among friends, neighbors, and kin.[2] Margaret Nelson and Joan Smith's study of interhousehold exchanges among Coolidge County, Vermont, working-class residents captures some of this variation. Examining economic survival strategies in this rural community, Nelson and Smith found extensive differentiation of the services that neighbors, friends, and kin rendered to each other. Different transactions and media applied to different social relations. One resident couple, Bruce and Nancy Sharp, for instance, reported Bruce's varied fee schedule for his snowplowing services in the community, which he did as a side business. When he said that his rates varied depending on the time spent on the job, Nancy soon revealed her husband's more complex tariff schedule. Although Bruce charged an hourly or contracted rate for the town store, he expected only a token, reduced rate from an elderly couple and exclusively in-kind reciprocity from his friends: a six-pack of beer or some Friendly's ice cream, for example, from his friend Ted. When the interviewers asked if he had expected money from Ted, Bruce was emphatic: "No, not for friends." His reduced rate for the elderly

[2] See Adams and Allan 1998; Allan 1989; Boase and Wellman 2004; Di Leonardo 1987; Hansen 1994; Kendall 2002; Litwak 1969; Menjívar 2000; Pahl and Pahl 2000; Rubin 1985; Silver 1990, 2003; Stack 1997.

couple, explained Nancy, was "because they want to pay something. You don't make a killing on that." He did it, Bruce explained, "to give me extra soda money, cigarette money." Nancy again qualified her husband's answer, adding, "you did it a lot of times as a favor; . . . you just did it to be nice different times. He does one for the apartment house [in return for which] Stuart brought you a load of corn" (Nelson and Smith 1999: 11–12).

Gender differences also figured importantly in the local economy of favors. Women's provision of goods and services to kin and friends, for instance, were more likely to be treated as giftlike trading or swapping, while men were "allowed" to collect fees, even from friends and relatives. Thus, women referred to their exchanges of babysitting as trading or swapping, never as barter. The same was true with women's sewing and knitting; they offered these products as gifts, rarely bartering them one for another. One of the study's respondents, Barbara Lattrell, whose side job involved sewing, explained why she made all her niece's wedding dresses for free: "That was her wedding present. Many hours of hand sewing" (128).

The system as a whole had an ironic consequence: those for whom the interhousehold exchanges were most valuable actually incurred fewer obligations. Households with higher, more stable income readily took on long-term commitments to barter goods and services; people in lower-income households, however, were reluctant to take on extensive commitments because of the risk that calls for reciprocity would come when they had few resources to offer. For instance, two other respondents, Ellen and Charles Rivers, who had been deeply involved in the community, withdrew after their economic troubles began. When asked, "What do you think people owe their families?" Ellen responded, "I don't feel I have any obligation to anybody, really. When my sister has her baby in September, yuh she's watched my kids a lot for me, for no pay or anything. Yes, I will return the favor to her. . . . But as far as owing anybody anything—no." The same strategy applied to neighbors and friends: "Both Charles and I feel the same way about this—we don't really like to owe anybody anything including favors because they can always come back on you in a negative way. So, whenever things are done it's usually been an exchange for pay" (111–12).

Thus, differentiation occurred at three different levels, among kin and acquaintances, between men and women, and according to income and job stability. Among other things, the differentiation involved a remarkable elaboration not only of transactions, but also of payment media. As in professional-client relations, bartering of goods and services among kin and acquaintances exemplifies the main point of this chapter. On one side, participants unquestionably mingle intimacy and economic transactions; on the other side, however, they do not do so indiscriminately. On the contrary, they make fine differentiations and mark significant boundaries between relations, and within each set, they carefully match transactions and media with those relations.

COURTSHIP

A surprisingly similar dynamic operates in the very different world of courtship and sexual relations. Clearly, in both cases, participants regularly mingle economic transactions with strong intimacy. Although moralists and participants often invoke hostile worlds concerns when sexual relations are at risk, in fact the differentiation of relations, the marking of boundaries, and the matching of relations with transactions and media go on intensively in the overlapping worlds of courtship and sexual relations. Conventional forms of courtship that frequently lead to marriage operate somewhat differently from relations that might produce intense sexuality but are unlikely to end with marriage (Laumann et al. 2004). They also call up contrasting sorts of moral concerns. At one end we have the specter of a woman's ruined virtue, at the other, the specter of crass prostitution.

Consider courtship first. Defined broadly, courtship includes all the relationships that have some significant chance of leading to long-term public cohabitation—the whole range from flirtation to the verge of marriage. Courtship necessarily involves economic transactions in a number of ways:

- The couple frequently undertake immediate mutual expenditures, such as shared entertainment, meals, and gifts.
- Courting couples mark transitions in their relationships with costly ceremonies, festivities, investments, and gifts; in recent years, for example, U.S. expenditures on the costliest such events of all—weddings—range from $40 billion to $130 billion a year (Holson 2003: 1; Howard 2000; Mead 2003: 78; Otnes and Pleck 2003).
- Courting couples often anticipate and prepare for their future economic household collaboration by such devices as establishing a trousseau or saving for a house. During an average month, engaged couples spend about $250 million on furniture, the same amount on tableware, and a little under $200 million on housewares (Mead 2003: 86).
- Couples regularly connect their families to each other, often depending on their families' economic support.
- Over the long run, the families themselves often develop an interest in the economic return from those who marry in.
- Often families incorporate newcomers into family farms, businesses, or housing.

From dating to the brink of marriage, therefore, the mingling of courtship and economic transactions occurs continuously.

ENGAGEMENTS

Courtship practices, meanings, and relations, to be sure, vary dramatically from one setting to another. Take the case of engagement; the transition from courtship to engagement still marks an important moment in American young people's lives. For many couples, it involves substantial expenditures. Indeed, a recent study shows they spend an estimated annual $9 billion in engagement rings and wedding bands (Tannenbaum 2003). According to another study, for 70 percent of all U.S. brides and 75 percent of first-time brides, the diamond ring is a couple's first wedding-related purchase (Ingraham 1999: 51). But engagement has evolved substantially over time.

Westerners have employed various forms of betrothal—public announcement of a couples' intention to marry—for centuries. Under such regimes, a marriage-bound couple commonly took on formal obligations to churches and families in addition to their mutual commitments. Indeed, churches and families often enjoyed rights to impose sanctions on young people who flaunted those obligations, for example, by eloping or by withdrawing from the commitment to marry after a period of intimacy. In the United States, however, the custom known as engagement only became common during the nineteenth century (Rothman 1984: 157–68). Less a church and family announcement than a couple's own declaration of intentions, engagement consisted of a pair's designating each other publicly as committed to marrying. As a consequence, relations to other parties—former lovers, friends, and family—changed significantly.

Engagement stood between informal courtship and marriage. It involved sexual exclusivity, greater intimacy, and a distinctive set of economic transactions. Couples withdrew from more general courtship activities with others, not carrying on the usual conventions of flirtation, and commonly appearing together on social occasions. Despite significant class and ethnic differences, in all cases engagement also involved greater physical and emotional intimacy than less-committed forms of companionship. In 1926, famous feminist and birth control advocate Margaret Sanger strongly endorsed the special intimacies of engagement:

> One indispensable truth the engaged girl must remember: The fiancé's breath, odor, touch, embrace, and kiss must be pleasing to her. If they are not, if there is an impulsive or instinctive emotional and physical recoil, then under no circumstances should the engagement be prolonged. . . . The intimacies permitted during the engagement, the legitimate intimacies of

> kisses and caresses, in the protecting atmosphere of poetic ro-
> mance, thus fulfills a distinct and all-important function—the
> deepening of desire and the commingling of the spiritual and
> the physical. (Sanger [1926] 1993: 74–75)

Legitimate sexual intimacies between the engaged couple escalated.
At about the time Sanger was writing, engaged couples were increasingly likely to have sexual relations before marriage (see Fass 1977:
289; Modell 1989; Rothman 1984: 297).

The engaged couple further marked their relationship with a variety of economic transactions. The most dramatically public was the
engagement ring. Beginning in the 1840s, couples announced their
new relationship with a mutual exchange of rings. Only later did the
ring become a female token (Rothman 1984: 161–62). But a wide
range of other joint economic transactions followed from the fact
of engagement. They included the trousseau, acquisition of goods
and housing for the prospective cohabiting couple, and exchange of
personal gifts. In fact, the trousseau often accomplished both of the
first two, outfitting both the bride and the home.

Nineteenth-century trousseaus turned into a formidable economic venture, as future brides sewed and shopped for increasingly
elaborate sets of clothing, linens, and various other household
furnishings. Men, meanwhile, were typically saving money for housing. In addition to a couples' own economic preparation for marriage, engagement frequently changed other relations within families. For example, interviewing retired Amoskeag mill workers in
New Hampshire in the 1970s, Tamara Hareven and Randolph
Langenbach report the recollections of seventy-one-year-old Anna
Douville, the last to marry out of twelve children in her family.
While she still lived at home, Anna turned her entire pay over to
her mother, unlike her siblings, who only contributed board. When
Anna met her future husband, the mother reciprocated:

> She got me started on my hope chest. After the week's shopping
> was done and the bills were paid, we would take all the money
> that she had left to the store and buy me sheets and pillowcases.
> She bought me a dishpan, all my pots and pans, knives, and

dishes. When I got married [in 1933] we didn't have to buy a damn thing for years because I had all the things I needed. My mother thought I deserved it because I gave her all my pay to the last week that I worked. She never did that for the others, and they got jealous about it. They were on their own when they got married and had to buy all the stuff they needed themselves. (Hareven and Langenbach 1978: 289)

Besides the engagement ring and the trousseau, engaged couples entered a distinct informal gift economy. Etiquette manuals were emphatic: expensive presents "unless it be the engagement ring" were "not in the best taste." Nor was wearing apparel, especially not the wedding dress. Even if the bride was "as poor as a church mouse," advised experts, a very plain trousseau was preferable to "the elaborate outfittings towards the purchase of which the groom-expectant has largely contributed" (Cooke 1896: 124; Cushing 1926: 110). The first edition of Emily Post's noted *Etiquette*, which came out in 1922, while somewhat less strict about a "bridegroom-elect's" gifts to his future bride, still insisted that any item considered "maintenance"—such as wearing apparel, a motor car, a house, or furniture —was off-limits. Post was quite specific: "It is perfectly suitable for her to drive his car, or ride his horse. . . . But, if she would keep her self-respect, the car must not become hers. . . . He may give her all the jewels he can afford, he may give her a fur scarf, but not a fur coat." While the scarf was an "ornament," Post explained, the coat was "wearing apparel" and thus an unfit gift for a bride (Post 1922: 311).

Etiquette writers thus struggled to draw a line defining proper and improper gifts between engaged parties. Their boundary drawing excluded gifts that would be appropriate between husbands and wives on one side, and from a prostitute's clients on the other. The wrong gift, warned Emily Post, could cast the bride "in a category with women of another class" (311), meaning a prostitute or a kept woman. That is why courtship gifts were supposed to express affection or admiration without suggesting payment or support. The gift economy changed radically when the bride became a man's wife;

her husband's gifts and his money then turned into household trans-fers, subject to a different set of rules and expectations. Etiquette manuals reminded brides of the distinction between engagement and marriage transfers: "until the fateful words are spoken that make the twain one flesh" instructed one etiquette writer, the bride "has no claim whatever on the purse of her future husband." As she approached marriage, however, the bride was advised to start treating her husband's money with wifely concern and discourage, as Post put it, any "charming, but wasteful, presents." Unless the fiancé was very wealthy, noted Ethel Frey Cushing's *Culture and Good Manners*, "a young girl prefers to have [her fiancé] save his money for the home and its furnishings" (Cooke 1896: 143; Post 1922: 310; Cushing 1926: 110).

For all their period charm, these concerns about proper engagement etiquette have not disappeared today. A late 1990s edition of *Emily Post's Etiquette* declares, for example, that

> the engagement ring is worn for the first time in public on the day of the announcement. In the United States it is worn on the fourth finger (next to the little finger) of the left hand. In some foreign countries it is worn on the right hand. It is removed during the marriage ceremony and replaced immediately afterward, outside the wedding ring.
>
> *An engagement ring is not essential to the validity of the betrothal.* Some people confuse the engagement ring with the wedding ring and believe the former is as indispensable as the latter. This is not the case. The wedding ring is a requirement of the marriage service. The engagement ring is simply evidence that the couple definitely plan to marry. A man may give his fiancée a ring no matter how many times he has been married before. (Post 1997: 666)

The same manual devotes eleven full pages (672–82) to enumerating items that belong in a proper bride's trousseau.

Similar issues become acute in the case of broken engagements. If an engaged couple have acquired common property, pooled their funds, started shared economic enterprises, received support from families, or exchanged substantial gifts, the status of those economic transactions after an engagement ends frequently becomes a matter of rancorous dispute. Engagement rings provide an obvious case in point: typically expensive and closely tied to the public announcement of a commitment to marry, rings raise the question of ownership when the engagement ends. The 1990s *Emily Post* manual states the rule unequivocally:

> In the unfortunate event of a broken engagement, the ring and all other gifts of value must be returned to the former fiancé. Gifts received from relatives or friends should also be returned with a short note of explanation:
>
> *Dear Nancy,*
> *I'm sorry to have to tell you that Mitch and I have broken our engagement. Therefore I am returning the towels that you were so sweet to send me.*
> *Love, Elizabeth*
>
> A notice reading, "The engagement of Ms. Caroline Muller and Mr. John Ryan has been broken by mutual consent," may be sent to the newspapers that announced the engagement, although this is not at all necessary and it is seldom done.
>
> If the man should die before the wedding, his fiancé may keep her engagement ring. However, if it happens to be an old family heirloom and she knows that his parents would like to have it remain in the family, she would be considerate to offer to return it. She may keep any gifts that were given her by friends.
>
> If the bride-to-be should die, her family should return the engagement ring to the groom and any gifts received to the donors (Post 1997: 672).

A bride whose wedding the New York Times reported in 2003 "proudly noted" that on the occasion of two previous broken engagements "she'd returned *all* of the gifts" (McKinley 2003: ST11). Thus the matching of economic transactions to relations continues in force. The purveyors of etiquette spell out practices that represent a very general set of understandings about engagement: that it is a distinct form of relationship rather than a weak form of marriage; that the man and woman involved retain control over their own property, and yet, that a proper engagement involves preparations for the married stage of their lives.

DATING, TREATING, AND GOING STEADY

Engagement takes its place in a wide range of courtship relations. From the early twentieth century to the 1950s, for example, middle-class Americans distinguished a whole series of possible relations between unmarried couples other than engagement, most notably dating and going steady (for eighteenth-century practices, see Godbeer 2002). Originating as a working-class practice, among the middle class, dating replaced the older custom of calling (Bailey 1988: 17; see also Modell 1989; Schrum 2004). By the mid-1920s, Beth Bailey tells us in her history of American courtship, "going somewhere"—to restaurants, theater, dance halls—had displaced the earlier system of young men "calling" at a girl's home or "keeping company" under the watchful eyes of her family.

What defined the date? It meant that when a couple "went out," the man spent money on their entertainment. Thus, Bailey concludes, "money—men's money—became the basis of the dating system, and thus, of courtship" (Bailey 1988: 13). Observers watched with frightened fascination the increasingly competitive streak in dating, which Willard Waller, in his 1937 study of Pennsylvania State University, dubbed the "dating and rating" system—the establishment of a strict hierarchy of desirability, hence of prestige, among companions for public occasions such as dances and sports events (Waller 1937; see also Horowitz 1987; Whyte 1990). For the next few decades, dating continued to pivot on the man's payment for most of the entertainment expenses (see for example Holland and Eisenhart 1990; Illouz 1997: 66–76; Komarovsky 1985: 231–33; McComb 1998).

The new relations of dating thus involved a distinct intimate economy. After World War II, although young people continued to date, they created a new form of relationship halfway between engagement and dating. They called it "going steady," a more exclusive, longer-term, and often more sexually intimate relationship than dating. Sometimes, going steady subdivided into more than one category. Among University of Kansas college students of the 1950s, for example, Beth Bailey reports: "A whole new set of 'official' statuses emerged to designate the seriousness of relationships: going steady, lavaliered, pinned, engaged. Each of these was more serious than the last, and each step allowed greater sexual intimacy. Necking with a 'steady' was one thing, necking with a casual date something else entirely" (Bailey 1999: 77). Going steady created its own characteristic matching of relations, transactions, and media. In general, the couple involved pooled resources far more than dating couples, typically planning their expenditures to assure their appearance at major social occasions. Among high school students, who rapidly adopted the practice, boys and girls, for instance, exchanged class rings, wore matching "steady jackets," or boys gave the girl a letter sweater (Bailey 1988: 50–51; see also Palladino 1996: 112).

Thus an elaborate system of courtship with multiple forms of relations prevailed in U.S. schools at the mid-twentieth century. Today, of course, single men still invite single women out for meals or entertainment, pick up the tab, and expect a degree of intimacy to prevail during the encounter. They still sometimes call this arrangement dating. However, since the mid-1950s, a whole new array of courtship relations has evolved in the United States, including such pairings as hooking up, friends with benefits, going out, or hanging out. In a preliminary survey of women on eleven college campuses, for example, Norval Glenn and Elizabeth Marquardt (2001) found that college undergraduates divided their heterosexual encounters into five rough categories: first, interactions involving sex without commitment, including "hooking up" or what some of the women called "friends with benefits"; second, rapidly established committed relationships involving sexual activity, sometimes referred to as "joined at the hip"; third, less intense, slower moving, committed relationships that might or might not involve sexual activity. "Hanging out" was the fourth—and the most common—type of relationship; it means going out or spending time with one or more partners (see also Brooks 2002; Wolfe 2000; for teen-age practices, Schneider and Stevenson 1999: 190–91). Finally, dating in the old sense of the word accounted for only a small minority of those encounters. When it came to men's payment for shared entertainment, these college women only rarely and ambivalently took part in such arrangements.

Despite the new terminology and practices, some residues of the old system remain. The *Fabulous Girl's Guide to Decorum*, touted as the "etiquette guide for the new millennium," offers the following advice on "proper date behavior" to young women:

> Some women feel it's not a date unless the guy pays the bill. But . . . an FG [Fabulous Girl] is a modern woman and does not hold to these old-fashioned principles. Usually. Who picks up the tab on those early dates can be tricky. If your suitor makes it clear that he'd like to take you out to dinner, then you can let him pay for the meal. When a man asks a FG out for an afternoon coffee or cocktails, it is not wrong to assume that he will pay for her. Nonetheless, an FG always carries some cash in case he's cheap. . . . If you do not intend to see this guy again, then you should definitely pay for your half of the bill. Of course, *you* know that paying for a meal doesn't mean anyone is obliged to offer themselves for dessert later, but he might not. (Izzo and Marsh 2001: 145–46)

Thus, who pays continues to be a crucial question symbolizing the nature of the relationship.

Will the Internet change all that? From the 1990s onward, electronic chat rooms, instant messaging, and computer-mediated dating services certainly introduced new practices into the old world of courtship (Constable 2003). According to a *New York Times* report, more than 45 million Americans visited dating Web sites in a single month of 2003. The same report projected that in 2003 they would spend about $33 million a month on electronic dating services (Harmon 2003) New combinations of intimacy and economic activity will surely emerge over decades to come. None of them, however, will eliminate the work of matching relations, media, and economic transactions, much less the effort to mark the boundaries between the relations at hand and others with which they might easily and banefully be confused.

These past and current urban middle-class customs do not, of course, exhaust the great variety of courtship that has existed in the United States. Courtship has always differed by ethnicity, race, class, and religion.[3] Among urban working-class Americans who had left school, for example, a new form of relationship called "treating" emerged in the twentieth century. Treating was a popular arrangement by which young working-class women obtained financial help, gifts, and access to entertainment from a fiancé or a "steady" but also from casual acquaintances, in exchange for a variety of sexual favors, from flirting to intercourse. Young working women earning low wages and obligated to contribute to their families' income, had little spending money left over for their own clothes or entertainment. So they relied on men friends to "treat" them to dancing, drinks, theater, or dinner. As Kathy Peiss (1983; 1986) reports, working-class informal etiquette allowed a much broader range of respectable indirect payments to women than did that of the middle class; working girls accepted not only recreation and food from a man but gifts of clothing or even a vacation trip.

People distinguished treating not only from the much more sexually restricted relationship of middle-class dating but also from the sexually explicit bargain of prostitution. They invested considerable effort, indeed, in marking the boundary between acceptable treating and unacceptable whoredom. As long as she did not receive cash payment from men at the time of sexual relations, the treating (or "charity") girl did not become a prostitute. Surveying the practice of treating in New York City between 1900 and 1932, Elizabeth Clement reports that "the young women exchanged sexual favors

[3] See D'Emilio and Freedman 1988; Holland and Eisenhart 1990; Joselit 1994; Modell 1989; Stansell 1986.

for dinner and the night's expenses, or more tangibly for stockings, shoes, and other consumer goods" (Clement 1998a: 68). These women, she notes, used treating "to gain entry into the expensive world of urban amusements and to distinguish themselves from the prostitutes who lived and worked in the bars alongside them." In contrast to prostitutes, treating women and their companions established a sort of gift economy. Clement explains: "Not only did they not accept cash, but they did not really exchange services for material goods. Instead, they received presents from their friends" (120).[4]

As in any gift economy, not all presents were equally acceptable. Reporting on the same custom in Chicago, Randy McBee (2000: 108) quotes Rose Kaiser, a young Jewish woman. Kaiser rejected certain gifts from men, such as silk stockings, "because they'd want to put them on [me]." Treating girls and their companions thus worked out a complex round of exchanges far different from the conventions of dating and prostitution.[5] Yet working-class treating paralleled middle-class dating in four important regards. First, it permitted a degree of interpersonal intimacy the parties would not ordinarily engage in outside of the arrangement. Second, it remained temporary: once entered, a treat did not imply either party's right or obligation to continue the relationship. (Hence many a negotiation over whether a couple *were* treating.) Third, through known transitions and agreements it could lead into adjacent relationships—certainly prostitution on one side, but even clearly longer-term monogamous commitments on the other. Finally, treating was in itself no more a paid occupation than was dating. Despite the woman's receipt of valuable gifts and services, treating did not qualify a woman as a sex worker, identify her male companion as her client, or for that matter keep her from gaining her livelihood through nonsexual forms of work.

[4] See also Clement 1998a on club hostesses and female vaudeville performers as new forms of commercial heterosexual interaction after the 1920s.
[5] On treating, see also Gilfoyle 1992: 56, 288, 311. Gilfoyle suggests that the adoption of treating was related to the decline in commercial sex. On Jewish courtship and treating, see Heinze 1990.

SEX WORK

Nevertheless, many American women—and some men—have at one time or another earned their livings through the sale of explicitly sexual services. For pay, they have participated in interactions that regularly produce sexual arousal in their purchasers. Informal estimates place the American commercial sex industry in the vicinity of $8 billion to $10 billion a year (Weitzer 2000; Schlosser 2003: 61). Those occupations have only occasionally and contingently overlapped with courtship. Let us call the entire array of specialized sex-providing occupations "sex work." Such occupations include telephone sex, production of pornography, peep shows, some forms of massage, escort services, and a wide variety of prostitution. They vary enormously in duration of encounters, extent and character of physical contact, range of intimacy, setting, and overall style. We need not survey the entire range of sex work, however, to make this chapter's main points: in this zone of intimacy as in others (both sexual and otherwise), couples mingle economic transactions with intimate attentions; implicitly consult available matrices to define their relations; mark the boundaries of those relations emphatically; match relations, transactions, and media according to established conventions; yet within those limits negotiate their own versions of intimacy. Meanwhile, third parties generally act to defend the boundaries, as observers invoke separate spheres/hostile worlds ideas and practices to draw the line between acceptable and unacceptable relations. Comparison of two frequent forms of sex work—taxi dancing and prostitution—will underline these points.

Let us begin with taxi dancing, an occupation that moral critics of the 1920s and 1930s often lumped with treating and prostitution. In early-twentieth-century American cities, dance halls became increasingly important sites for encounters between single men and women. In fact, treating women often met their companions in popular dance halls. These ranged from social club dances to public, commercial establishments (McBee 2000). The taxi-dance hall, typically restricted to male patrons, was a remarkable setting for social encounters. The men paid an entrance fee and then purchased tencent tickets for sixty to ninety seconds of dancing with a young woman. The taxi dancers worked on a fifty-fifty commission arrangement, with half of the money going to the dance hall owner.

At first glance, taxi dancing seems like a peculiar form of sex work: a fleeting, flirting contact between man and woman akin to telephone sex or a peep show. On closer examination, however, it turns out to contain a whole differentiated world of intimacy. Within its commercial framework, men and women formed friendships, paired off for liaisons outside the dance hall, initiated courtship, and created a complex economy of favors, gifts, tips, and obligations. From one perspective, the taxi dance hall operated as a crass commercial establishment. From another, it served as a remarkably sophisticated and effective matchmaker.

Speaking of the 1930s, Leo Rosten, chronicler of American immigrant and working-class life, recalled a Saturday night tour of three New York taxi dance ballrooms and his encounters with the women who made their living by dancing with paying customers (Mona, Jean, Honey, and others). At Seventh Avenue's Honeymoon Lane Danceland, Mona led him to the dance floor letting "her body, all marshmallow, flow against mine . . . and murmured a voluptuous 'Mmmm-mmh!' " After dancing for a moment "approaching ecstasy," a buzzer loudly "honked." Mona quickly "disengaged her clutch" instructing him to get more dance tickets. When Rosten protested that he thought his ticket was for a whole dance, Mona announced that "a dance is every time the buzzer buzzes." Which was every minute.

After Rosten promptly returned with ten more tickets, Mona was once again "warm and yielding in my arms—until the buzzer finished its tenth pecuniary decree." Jean later explained that the dancers kept half of the price of their tickets, plus "you have to add the *presents* . . . like nice lingerie, a bracelet, a purse, a piece of jewelry, maybe an evening gown." Or sometimes cash. At the Majestic Danceland, Honey told Rosten about a St. Louis real-estate dealer who dated her: once "he leaned over in the cab he was taking me to some scrumptious Chinese food in, and without one single word he leaned over and kissed me—nothing rough or forcing, just a real

sweet little kiss. Then he handed me ten dollars without a peep"
(Rosten 1970: 289–91, 297). Clearly more was happening in and
around the dance hall than the simple exchange of dimes for dances.

Sociologist Paul Cressey provided a systematic account of Chicago taxi dance halls in the 1920s. He started out as a case worker
and investigator for Chicago's Juvenile Protective Association, but
later reported his findings under the supervision of the great University of Chicago urban sociologist Ernest W. Burgess. Analyzing
the phenomenon, he invoked classic hostile worlds reasoning. First
he worried about the "mercenary and silent world" of taxi dancing,
where "feminine society is for sale, and at a neat price" (Cressey
1932: 11). As a result, "the impersonal attitudes of the market place
very soon supersede the romantic impulses which normally might
develop." Still worse, romanticism "becomes merely another acceptable method for the commercial exploitation of men" (39–40).
But then Cressey noted how the "romantic impulse" often undermined the rational economic order of the taxi dance hall preferred
by its proprietors. Indeed, as we'll see, dancers often made private
arrangements that cut into the owners' profits, for example, by offering free dances to favored customers. Owners acknowledged their
repeated failure to restrict intimate relations between their dancers
and patrons. As one proprietor noted, "As long as boys are boys and
girls are girls they're going to get together somehow" (quoted in
Cressey 1932: 50).

Despite his moral qualms, Cressey provided dramatic, careful observations of what actually went on. Here he describes the standard
encounter:

> As soon as the girl receives a ticket from the patron, she tears
> it in half, gives one part to the ubiquitous ticket-collectors,
> and the other half she blandly stores with other receipts under
> the hem of her silk stocking—where before the evening is
> over the accumulation appears as a large and oddly placed
> tumor. She volunteers no conversation, as the music begins, she
> nonchalantly turns toward her new patron ready for the dance
> with him. (6)

The dance lasted ninety seconds and shrank to sixty seconds near closing hour. After closing time—between midnight and 3 a.m.—those men who had not already made arrangements to meet women after the dance often stood outside the dance hall waiting for the women to emerge, pairing off with them if possible (McBee 2000: 109).

In the course of his description, Cressey actually distinguished five different relationships that sometimes existed between taxi dance girls and their patrons, each with its own rules of payment: (1) the standard dance session; (2) "free dances" for more "favored suitors"; (3) "mistress" arrangements, an "alliance" in which for a few months a man paid for the dancer's rent or groceries; (4) the "plural alliance," where the girl "enters an understanding by which she agrees to be faithful to a certain three or four men," who through "separate arrangements" meet her "financial requirements" of rent, groceries, or clothes; and (5) dates, running from a shared drink or show to what Cressey called "overnight dates," which according to him, "quickly take on the character of clandestine prostitution" (48–50). In some cases, a sixth relationship emerged from one of the first five: the dancer and the patron married (see, for example, Cressey 1932: 115–17; Vedder 1947: 155–58).

Although a standard dance session usually initiated acquaintance between a man and a woman who later went on to more extensive companionship, the date provided a crucial pivot among these relationships. From a date the couple might move on to longer-term cohabitation, exclusive or shared. But they might also simply return to the occasional dance session. Preoccupied to some extent with his moral conceptions, Cressey understated the extent to which the taxi dance hall was operating as a local social center. In fact, his descriptions document a wide range of flirtation, friendships, and matchmaking. In a later study of Los Angeles, Chicago, and Detroit taxi dance halls, Clyde Vedder—who worked as pianist in several dance halls—revealed a broad scope of social relations between patrons and dancers, matched with a striking variety of payments. Besides gifts and generous tips, the remunerations included the following possibilities, each of which clearly entailed far more than quid pro quo for dances and sexual services:

- Redeeming a dancer's pawned items
- Assistance in building and furnishing a dancer's home: labor and materials (cement for foundation, roof, electrical wiring)
- Cosigning a dancer's charge account at various stores
- Down payments on major purchases
- During World War II, ration coupons, including gas coupons, and rationed products such as butter, toilet paper, nylons, Kleenex, butter, cigarettes, and gasoline (Vedder 1947: 136–40)

Thus, despite Cressey's misgivings, none of the various patron-dancer relationships equated with prostitution, the straightforward sale of sexual services. Indeed, Cressey himself acknowledged the distinction. Patrons eager to obtain an after-dance date with one of the girls, he observed, were "polite and courteous":

> Since the girl's society outside the dance hall—so much sought after by many of the patrons—can be secured only through the dubious process of courtship rather than the more dependable method of bargaining, the popular taxi dancer has a favorable status . . . which seems to arise in part from the very uncertainty of her favors. (37–38)

One patron explained his courting strategies:

> I've found that the main thing to remember in trying to interest these girls is that they are not hard-boiled prostitutes. They don't want to make money that way. But they do like presents, and—most of all—attention. . . . They are great on expecting presents. But I soon found that an inexpensive present would do just as well as an expensive one. What they are interested in is its sentimental value. They want presents, not for their money value, but as keepsakes to remind them of their good times and their men friends. (Quoted in Cressey 1932: 141)

Clearly, taxi dancers and their patrons were negotiating individualized relationships within the limits of available conventions. Far from a pathetic imitation of courtship or a furtive neighbor of prostitution, the world of the taxi dance reveals a terrain of differentiated ties, each with its own matching of relation, transactions, and media.[6]

PROSTITUTION

In a largely forgotten but still telling article first published in 1952, C. Wright Mills vented his famous indignation on rich men who condemned street prostitutes but maintained high-priced mistresses, frequented call girls, purchased sexual services for their customers, and thus lured young women into vice; "American salesmanship and plutocratic demand," he argued, offered irresistible lures: "In fact, wherever attractive, ambitious girls meet men with the money or power to realize their ambitions, sex will be available at a price" (Mills 1963: 329). For all his radical populism, Mills resorted to a standard hostile worlds conclusion: money corrupts intimacy.

Despite popular awareness of differentiation among types of prostitution, the relation between prostitute and patron looms as the ultimate triumph of commercialism over sentiment. Hostile worlds theorists continue to warn that the introduction of economic transactions into sexual life pushes it toward the corrupt calculating world of the market. Yet the realm of prostitution and other sex work shows us a differentiated social landscape, with its own well-marked boundaries and its own distinctive matching of relation, transactions, and media. Prostitution has of course undergone enormous mutations as American social life has altered. Changes include the rise and fall of the brothel, emergence of the call girl, and the expansion of electronic contacts. The word *prostitution*, furthermore, covers a wide range of activities, such as brothel prostitution, streetwalking, call girls and more. Here I concentrate on women

---

[6] For race relations in dance halls, see Moran 2001. Taxi dancing continues, with modifications, to this day: see Meckel 1995.

who offer their sexual services more or less publicly in American urban areas.[7]

During the nineteenth century, brothel prostitution, running from sordid to sumptuous, played a significant part in American public life (see Cohen 1998; Gilfoyle 1992). In the later heyday of taxi dancing and treating, prostitution persisted as a quite separate professional activity. Ruth Rosen studied American prostitutes— women who regularly offered to perform sexual intercourse or closely related services for a fee—between 1900 and 1918. Her historical survey covers the range from low-paid streetwalkers to expensive kept women. She shows that prostitutes made two kinds of distinctions: between different kinds of prostitution and between themselves and other women. Higher-ranking prostitutes, for instance, distanced themselves very clearly from the unladylike "low women" (Rosen 1982: 107). Prostitutes also contrasted their professionalism with the gullibility of nonprofessionals. As Rosen reports, "They joked about the 'charity girls' who freely gave away sexual favors, and they derided the 'respectable' wives of their customers. . . . They expressed contempt for the 'respectable' domestic and factory workers who worked for subsistence pay . . . and often had to submit to sexual harassment by their bosses" (102).

Similar divisions persist to our own time. Contemporary variants on prostitution in the United States include streetwalkers, call girls, escorts, and brothel prostitutes, as well as male and transgendered prostitution. Within each of these we find further differentiation and hierarchies of prestige, power, and wealth. Although in the extreme, the narrow exchange of sexual services for money does indeed occur, even within the world of prostitution we find differentiation as prostitutes distinguish their income by type of activity or by customer.[8] Streetwalkers, for instance, report differences between what Elizabeth Bernstein (1999) calls "career prostitutes"

[7] The literature on sexual payments among men is very thin. For preliminary indications, see Aggleton 1999; Boag 2003; Chauncey 1985, 1994; Humphreys 1975; Reiss 1961.

[8] See Wood Hill 1993. For a graphic description of prostitutes' negotiation over the category of sexual relationship and associated monetary transfers, see Sanchez

who exchange sex for cash, and the lower-ranked "crack or heroin prostitutes" who barter sex for drugs. Meanwhile, call girls' income and prestige are not only higher than that of streetwalkers but also outdo escorts, brothel, or massage parlor workers (Weitzer 2000: 4; see also Heyl 1979; Miller 1986).

Let us look more closely at differences among streetwalkers, call girls, and brothel prostitutes. It would be easy to reduce those differences to degrees of economic complexity; streetwalkers are nothing but the equivalent of street vendors, while call girls are boutique experts, and brothel prostitutes, supermarket salesgirls. It would be equally easy to assume that lurking behind such structural differences, hides a homogeneous moral world of commercial degradation. For all prostitutes, in this view, the ever-present price for sex eliminates any possibility of intimacy. There is, to be sure, some truth in these ideas. In some cases, precisely because of the money to be made in sexual services, these are occupations at great risk of exploitation, degradation, and violence. Furthermore, there are indeed striking differences in the working conditions of different kinds of prostitutes. Nevertheless, all three variants of prostitution exhibit a complex economic organization, and in all three the providers establish a set of contingently negotiated relations, some fleeting but others quite durable, with their clients.

Streetwalkers, who reportedly constitute a minority of prostitutes (Weitzer 2000: 4), typically pick up their dates in public settings for brief sexual encounters in hotels or "car dates." Bernstein describes three distinct sites within a ten-block radius in San Francisco: the "upper-class" women of Geary and Mason; the "middle-class" women of Leavenworth and Geary, and the "lower-class" women of O'Farrell between Taylor and Jones, each category of women distinguished by race and physical appearance. The largely white, Asian, and light-skinned black women—who stand alone or in all-female groups—at the Geary-Mason stroll, she notes, "are young, slim and expensively dressed; their tightly fitted suits, sweater sets

---

1997. For the adjacent world of female dancers in strip clubs, see Frank 1998, 2002. On prostitution, see also Stinchcombe 1994.

and fur or leather coats code them for a relatively upscale market"
(Bernstein 1999: 103). Their prices start at $100, while only a
few blocks away, African-American streetwalkers, more shabbily
dressed, get between $20 and $100. On two other sites (Hyde Street
in the Tenderloin and on Capp Street in the Mission) the usually
older, homeless "crack prostitutes" exchange sex for either $20 or a
vial of drugs.

Bernstein's geographic divisions represent distinct categories of
streetwalkers. Within each category, the women establish their own
negotiation with clients, for instance, by discriminating among preferred, acceptable, and rejected partners. Indeed, as Janet Lever and
Deanne Dolnick (2000) report, street prostitutes often have regular
clients, sometimes long-standing ones. Some clients offer prostitutes gifts of food, cigarettes, alcohol, and occasionally, jewelry or
flowers. Street prostitutes further mark the boundary of their relationships with customers by restricting the forms of physical contact
they permit, for example, by negotiating which sexual acts they will
perform, withholding orgasm, and refusing such contact as mouth-
to-mouth kissing (see Bernstein 1999: 105; Brewis and Linstead
2000: 214–21; Lever and Dolnick 2000: 97).

Call girls establish quite different relations with their clients.
They contract individually with customers in advance for a rendez-
vous that typically takes place on the woman's own premises or in
the client's home. Lever and Dolnick surveyed Los Angeles streetwalkers and call girls in the late 1990s. Compared with streetwalkers, call girls charged significantly higher prices (a median of $200
versus the $30 median for streetwalkers), spent much longer periods
of time with the client, and were more likely to have an ongoing
relationship with him. Call girls also engaged in a wider range of
social interaction with the clients. Interactions included an occasional lunch or dinner, "sleepovers," conversation, caresses, nonsexual massage, and even kissing. From clients they often received
jewelry, perfume, flowers, and champagne. Call girls also formed
particular attachments to some of their long-standing clients. One
woman explained: "You cannot know someone that long without it
being a real relationship" (Lever and Dolnick 2000: 97–98).

What is more, call girls develop distinctive strategies for attracting long-term clients, although those strategies sometimes backfire. One sex worker that Bernstein talked to explained why she no longer offered her favorite clients free sex or cheaper rates:

> They pretend to be flattered, but they never come back! . . . There was one client I had who was so sexy, a tai-chi practitioner, and really fun to fuck. Since good sex is a rare thing, I told him I'd see him for $20 (my normal rate is $250). Another guy, he was so sexy, I told him "come for free." Both of them freaked out and never returned. . . . They don't believe they can have no-strings-attached sex, which is why they pay. They'd rather pay than get it for free. (Quoted in Bernstein 2001: 203–4)

For a much more bureaucratized version of prostitution than either streetwalking or the call girl business, we can turn to high-priced contemporary brothels. Legal brothels bring the state of Nevada a yearly income of $40 million. Take the Moonlite Bunnyranch, one of Nevada's thirty-five licensed brothels (Mead 2001; see also Hausbeck and Brents 2000). At the Bunnyranch, the customer picks one of the twelve to twenty girls lined up at the parlor, or else the girls approach him at the bar, for a "tour." This involves going to a bedroom for negotiation of a service, including length of time and price. Each girl sets her own price, ranging from $150 to many thousands for "fantasy parties." Once a deal is made, the customers pays the office manager in cash or credit card. Bunnyranch workers receive cash and free food. Dennis Hof, the brothel's owner, also rewards top earners with special gifts, photo frames, or CD cases. As independent contractors, the women must pay taxes and are supposed to split their earnings fifty-fifty. They must also purchase their own condoms and pay for maids' services, use of the house's tanning-bed, adult movies, sex toys, and their weekly medical exams.

Brothel management sets very serious restrictions on client-prostitute interactions: bedroom price negotiations are closely monitored from the office via intercom to avoid cheating, and kitchen timers are used by the office manager to regulate the agreed number of minutes couples spend together. Newly recruited workers must

learn the brothel's printed rules, while the more experienced workers train younger women in negotiating skills. Both the management
and workers pride themselves on giving exceptional service. Air
Force Amy, one of Bunnyranch's top earners explained to a reporter:

> A thousand bucks is a hell of a lot of money. . . . But half of
> what you spend here has nothing to do with sex. It goes to the
> house for providing a nice, safe environment. No one here is
> going to take your wallet; the police aren't going to come and
> raid the place; your name is not going in the paper. I am not
> calling you in the morning saying, "I thought you loved me, I
> think I'm pregnant." (Quoted in Mead 2001: 79)

To be sure, many American brothels have operated under much
more dangerous and oppressive conditions (see Clement 1998b;
Gilfoyle 1992; Rosen 1982), but in general brothels have organized
the provision of intimacy quite differently from other forms of sex
work.

Taxi dancing and prostitution are only two cases of commercial
sex work. Other varieties include lap dancers, strip dancers, porn
stars, telephone sex workers, and masseuses.[9] Clearly, sex work differentiates at least as much as courtship. Throughout the world of
commercial sex, we find the distinction of different, well-bounded
intimate relations, the matching of relation, transactions, and media,
heavy involvement of third parties in enforcing those boundaries,
and further negotiation of meanings by the parties. We see participants engaging in delicate, consequential relational work.

COUPLING IN THE LAW

Both criminal and civil law intervene in intimate relations, sometimes to enforce certain rules of intimacy, sometimes to prevent
certain forms of intimacy. Criminal law covers such offenses as prostitution, incest, rape, pedophilia, sexual harassment, and pornogra-

---

[9] See Flowers 1998; Frank 1998; Garb 1995; Lewis 2000; Rasmussen 1979; Rich
and Guidroz 2000.

phy. Civil law likewise deals with intimacy but in a rather different manner, sometimes enforcing obligations, sometimes protecting rights, sometimes barring certain transactions, and sometimes determining the standing of transactions on the basis of relations between the parties. Thus, civil law provides compensation for lost consortium, enacts divorce and child support settlements, determines whether gifts between lovers are recoverable if they break up, and decides whether bequests from friend to friend are legal. (As we will see later, a third body of legal doctrines—tax law—also applies to intimate relations when government authorities claim that sexual or other services constitute taxable commercial transactions.)

When the law intervenes in intimate relations, it establishes a partly independent realm from everyday practices; a realm involving its own legal matrix of relations, and therefore of boundaries for appropriate transactions. This legal realm and the realm of practices necessarily interact, since all participants (notably plaintiffs and defendants) are also pursuing real-life agendas. So, we find incessant problems of translation between legal and practical realms, a process that runs in both directions. Thus, a longtime companion must contend with a court's ruling that his late lover had no right to bequeath him the house they shared. In the opposite direction, a jury puzzles over whether the law allows them to compensate a girlfriend for her domestic services to an ex-boyfriend. A good deal of legal work thus goes into (a) matching intimate relations with appropriate economic transactions, (b) distinguishing similar but morally and practically different relations from each other, (c) justifying such distinctions by invoking general doctrines. Hostile worlds is the most powerful of such doctrines.

In the forms of intimacy already discussed in this chapter—from courtship to sex work—the law intervenes repeatedly in all these different ways. Let's begin with courtship. To what extent, and under what conditions does the law recognize courting couples as legally existing parties? What rights and obligations follow from that standing? What happens when one party defaults or terminates the relationship? When couples are involved, how does American law do its relational work?

LEGAL ENGAGEMENTS

Recall our earlier discussion of the engagement as a changing set of practices. In general, American law currently treats engagement as a quasi contract to marry. It intervenes when the contract is fraudulent, when one party breaks the engagement improperly, or, most commonly, to settle disputes over property when an engagement ends contentiously. To do so, courts must first determine the relationship between the parties; were they actually engaged? Or was the couple simply courting, cohabiting, carrying on a commercial relationship, maintaining a common-law marriage or actually occupying a legal marriage? The law marks boundaries among the rights and obligations attached to each of these relations. Therefore, the stakes in defining the relationship properly are serious.

Determining the legitimacy of an engagement matters because often the couple have acquired property, invested in wedding preparations, paid for a trousseau, exchanged valuable gifts, taken up joint economic activity, established obligations to third parties, including families, left jobs, or changed their line of work. When something interrupts their agreement to marry, all of these economic commitments turn into contested transactions. How they are resolved depends on determining the nature of the couple's relationship.

Exactly what legal rights and obligations attached to engaged couples and what distinguished an engagement from ordinary courtship, marriage, or other intimate relations has changed significantly over time. In the largest arc, engagement went from being a public agreement that linked families, and therefore obligated third parties, to a private agreement undertaken by a couple. For courts and legal experts, however, the breaking of engagements posed the most enduring and acute legal questions. When and why should the law intervene at all in the private affairs of couples? And when it did, whose rights was the law expected to protect, and which rights? What about the rights of third parties—relatives and friends of the engaged couple?

Defining an engagement, however, posed special challenges for American courts. Without official certification that the couple was indeed engaged, courts searched for other evidence to prove the nature of their relationship. In general, they sought signs that the couple had committed themselves to marry. Homer Clark's influential text on domestic relations, for instance, noted that courts had often relied on "evidence that the parties spent much time together, that they often expressed affection for each other or that preparations for the wedding were made" (Clark 1968: 3–4). In some circumstances, courts accepted testimony of third parties who witnessed a couple's promises to marry, as well as evidence of sexual intimacy between the couple as proof of their engagement.

The kinds of evidence that were available for engagement understandably changed as engagement practices changed. Broadly speaking, engagement went from a public (and often religious) declaration of intentions that clearly involved a couple's families to a private agreement between two persons that might or might not include announcements and obligations to third parties. Moreover, as we saw in chapter 2, as long as coverture existed, marriage itself entailed a woman's considerable loss of legal, economic, and political autonomy. Under such circumstances, engagement constituted a distinctive, relatively privileged but temporary position for women. As coverture declined, the transition to marriage changed in character.

As time went on, the sorts of evidence for engagement that courts honored therefore changed significantly. Michael Grossberg sums it up:

> The privacy of courtship was the initial obstacle facing judges determined to supervise nuptial selection. Especially after the decline of the banns (posted declarations of marriage required by traditional nuptial statutes), lovers rarely plighted their troth before a coterie of witnesses or in sealed agreements; often an exchange of promises never took place. To surmount the secrecy of espousals courts applied liberal evidentiary rules built on Lord Holt's 1704 ruling in *Hutton v. Mansell* that mutual promises of marriage need not be proven by direct evidence but could be authenticated by circumstantial proof. This freed courtship from a number of limitations usually applied to contracts, and highlighted the unique contractual nature of nup-

tials and the willingness of American judges to deviate from contractual uniformity when a larger goal—in this case protecting deserted brides—demanded it. . . . Judicial laxity in admitting evidence of nuptial promises, and a refusal to demand strict corroboration of circumstantial evidence, imposed serious nuptial liabilities on men. (Grossberg 1985: 39–40)

Later in the nineteenth century, indeed, men's complaints about those liabilities drove courts to narrow the range of evidence they would accept as evidence of nuptial agreements (Grossberg 1985: 56–58).

Far more changed, however, than rules of evidence. A series of broad transformations occurred in the way courts treated engagement, distinguished it from adjacent relationships, and dealt with the economic transactions of engaged couples. Speaking very approximately, from the mid-nineteenth century to the early twentieth century, American courts increasingly handled engagement as an asymmetrical quasi contract in which a woman put her reputation at risk more so than did her fiancé. A woman whose engagement ended short of marriage, reasoned the courts, lost some of her appeal as a marriage partner, especially if she and her fiancé had consummated sexual relations. During this period, courts became increasingly disposed to compensate jilted women not only for material losses but also for pain and suffering.

During the 1920s and 1930s, a reaction against asymmetrical compensation for broken engagements set in, with much hostile worlds talk of gold diggers who enticed men into nuptial agreements for mercenary purposes. From the 1930s onward, American law moved toward a sharper distinction between (1) economic transactions of engaged couples that depended on their commitment to marry and therefore became reversible if a marriage did not occur and (2) other transactions between the same people that did not constitute part of the commitment to marry. Although courts continued to examine whether the relationship between a woman and a man qualified as engagement, courtship, marriage, prostitution, business partnership, friendship, or something else, they thus began to rule that only a relatively narrow range of a couple's economic transactions belonged to the engagement as such.

BREACH OF PROMISE

Suits for breach of promise reflected this evolution. American states have always varied widely in their treatment of such suits, but on the whole, state courts became more receptive to large settlements for breach of promise as the nineteenth century wore on, then reversed direction during the twentieth century. Breach of promise suits, a mixture of contract and tort law, initially focused on monetary compensation for the financial injuries of a broken engagement, including the loss of virginity. Plaintiffs—typically female—increasingly claimed a wider range of damages, including loss of reputation, injury to health and feelings, and mental suffering.[10] During the early twentieth century signs of division arose between judges and juries on this very issue. While juries continued to make large awards for emotional and reputational damage, lawyers and judges began to look askance at these forms of compensation.

Evelyn Garmong eventually lost her suit for breach of promise against John B. Henderson as a consequence of such a shift (*Garmong v. Henderson*, 99 A. 177 (Me. 1916)). Garmong dropped out of medical school in 1908, when she was in her late twenties, and began working as a nurse in Washington, D.C. She met thirty-nine-year-old Henderson, a wealthy widower, in 1909. Over the following year, the two went out for automobile rides, dined together, and had sexual relations in Washington; Philadelphia; Bar Harbor, Maine; and elsewhere. In July 1910, Garmong, now living in her hometown of Des Moines, Iowa, resumed relations with a former lover, Roscoe D. Smith, to whom she was engaged. Three months

---

[10] For a telling analysis of changing legal treatments in breach of promise suits and premarital law more generally, see Tushnet 1998. See also Brinig 2000: 40–42; Ludington 1960. In a separate action for seduction, fathers had the right to sue their daughters' errant lovers. Juries often awarded large monetary compensation for the loss of fathers' material welfare or honor caused by sexual injury to their daughters. As fathers' financial interests in their daughters' marriagability lost standing in American law, the women themselves acquired the legal right to sue their seducers (VanderVelde 1996). In breach of promise cases, however, seduction did not constitute a separate cause for action, but served to increase damages (Clark 1968: 13).

later, she unsuccessfully sued Smith for seduction, then for breach of promise, aggravated by her pregnancy. Abandoning the effort to coerce Smith in October of that year, she returned to Washington, where her child was born. She now charged Henderson with paternity. Henderson visited her, sent her fruits and flowers, and over the next five months gave her about $900 "to buy his peace" (179).

After Henderson refused any further contact, Garmong instituted and lost a bastardy suit against him. Then, in October 1913, she sued Henderson for breach of promise, alleging that in March of 1910 he had promised her marriage. Claiming that they were "affianced husband and wife," Garmong asked for $250,000 in damages. Henderson countered that they were never engaged to be married but "merely friends." In January 1915, a jury in Penobscot County, Maine, awarded Garmong $116,000, a huge sum at that time. After the verdict was set aside by the Law Court—claiming that the jury was "influenced by sympathy, passion, or prejudice"—a second jury in April 1916 awarded Garmong $75,000 (177, 180). Once again, a review court sent the case back to trial. Finally, on November 27, 1916, the Supreme Judicial Court of Maine ruled in favor of Henderson, the defendant in Garmong's suit.

The case pivoted on Evelyn Garmong's claim that she and Henderson had been legally engaged, making her eligible for compensation. She testified to that effect. In conformity with the increasing rigor of courts, J. Cornish, one of the presiding judges, rebutted her testimony with a series of observations, including the following:

- John P. Garmong, Evelyn's brother and her sole new witness, could only report that Henderson had once spoken to him about her with "the highest respect." The conversation was found to bear "no resemblance to the expected conversation between prospective brothers in law" (179). Nor did John report that conversation to other members of the family.
- No engagement was announced publicly.
- No one provided evidence that any friend or relative knew about the engagement.
- There was no engagement ring.
- There were no presents "as one would expect a person of the wealth of the defendant to shower upon his affianced wife."

- There was "no public conduct from which an engagement could be inferred."
- There was no evidence that the "alleged engagement was ever referred to by the defendant or by any third person in his presence."
- Letters written by the defendant to the plaintiff were not those of "an affianced husband. They were infrequent in quantity and meaningless in quality." (179–80)

The judge concluded that Garmong and Henderson had maintained an "illicit relation" quite distinct from both a legal engagement and a mere friendship. The court therefore overturned the juries' initial generous awards.

In the 1930s, jilted women's claims came under even more severe and widespread attack. Critics argued that compensation for reputation and emotional distress commercialized couples' engagements and provided undue incentives for its exploitation by scheming women (Coombs 1989; McLaren 2002, chap. 7; Tushnet 1998). They thus once again invoked hostile worlds doctrines against an unwanted practice. The attack succeeded. Starting in 1935, a number of states passed the so-called heart-balm acts—statutes abolishing breach of promise suits, along with the related torts of seduction, criminal conversation, and alienation of affections. (The trend continued; by 2003, thirty-nine states had abolished the alienation of affections tort).

ENGAGEMENT TODAY

Courts did not, however, withdraw from legal regulation of engagements. Instead, the broader breach of promise action was restricted to legal adjudication of property transactions between the engaged couple. Within this narrower focus, legal issues continue to pivot on such questions as: Was this relation an engagement? What economic transactions belong to an engaged couple? And what rights does each of the parties have? While most American states today do not allow breach of promise suits (and few cases exist even when the plea is legally available), courts intervene regularly in formerly engaged couples' property disputes (see Perovich 1972; Tomko 1996). Indeed, Philadelphia attorney Mark Momjian notes that during the 1990s family lawyers became increasingly involved in broken engagement cases, which "can be as litigious as those involving long-term marriages" (Momjian 1997: 1).

More specifically, current engagement law relies on a no-fault theory of conditional gifts. Twentieth-century American jurisprudence applied this doctrine precisely to distinguish engagement from other forms of relationships. In this theory, people undertake certain gifts and economic transactions on the expectation that marriage will result (Tomko 1996). The failure of a marriage to occur breaks the contract and poses the problem of restoring property acquired under that contract to its rightful owners. In principle, neither party bears the legal blame for an engagement's termination, but courts must still decide what claims on joint or transferred property the ruptured contract entails. Whether an engagement terminates through mutual consent, the defection of one of the parties, or a death, the problem of adjudicating ownership of such property becomes acute. One engaged party, both engaged parties, or even third parties such as family members may have claims over the property remaining after a disrupted engagement.

Courts must therefore decide which sorts of transfers and joint acquisitions of property belong to the engagement as such, and which do not. Those that are contingent on marriage belong to the engagement contract, and differ from the rest. Courts thus commit themselves to identifying "gifts in contemplation of marriage." But there lies the legal problem: How do engagement transfers differ from courtship transfers? And to what extent are joint purchases, joint savings, or jointly operated economic enterprises themselves part of the property attached to the engagement? Courts therefore have to resolve four related sets of issues: First, are the couple engaged or courting? Second, if engaged, what transfers and joint property belong to the engagement and which do not? Third, what rights do the parties in a broken engagement have to the property?

Finally, are the couple actually eligible for engagement? I will take up each of these questions in turn.

Are the couple engaged or courting? Legal manuals explicitly provide a rule that courtship refers to "the pre-engagement period, and it is deemed ended when the parties expressly or impliedly agree to marry" (Martin 1952: 582; see also Tomko 1996: 60). Engagement therefore typically begins with some public manifestation of the agreement to marry. Without such public manifestation, courts remain uncertain about the couple's status until the parties supply further information about their behavior to each other or their declarations to third parties. A courting couple who have broken up have almost no legal rights with respect to property they have exchanged.

In a 1969 Louisiana case (*Fortenberry v. Ellis*, 217 So. 2d 792 (La Ct. App. 1969)), Earl C. Fortenberry was denied recovery of a Magnavox stereo-phonograph set he had given Barbara Ellis precisely because he could not prove that the couple had been engaged. Fortenberry purchased the $650 stereo on December 23, 1965, Ellis's birthday. He testified that a month earlier the couple had become engaged, agreeing at that time to substitute the stereo for the conventional engagement ring as their official engagement gift. But Ellis, the defendant, countered that while she and Fortenberry had indeed dated for quite some time and shared two joint savings accounts, no engagement ever took place. The stereo therefore was not an engagement gift, but a combined birthday and Christmas present.

In an effort to prove his case, Fortenberry called on his mother, his sister, and his cousin to testify that he had informed them of the couple's engagement. The three witnesses, however, failed to confirm the 1965 agreement to marry. Worse still, Fortenberry admitted under cross-examination that after the alleged engagement day, both he and Ellis had dated other partners and that he was the defendant in another woman's paternity suit. He further acknowledged that he and Ellis had never announced their engagement publicly: there had been no party or newspaper release. Nor had the couple taken out a marriage license. On the basis of the evidence, the trial judge ruled that Fortenberry and Ellis had never been engaged. As a result, the stereo was not a gift in contemplation of marriage and therefore remained Ellis's legitimate property. On January 6, 1969, an appellate court affirmed the initial ruling.

If the couple are engaged, which transfers and joint property correspond to the engagement, and which do not? Judges and lawyers commonly make the distinction between absolute and conditional gifts; the crucial difference being that conditional gifts are those that depend explicitly on a commitment to marry. Courts are actually adjudicating among three categories: first, property belonging to courtship but not part of an engagement (such as that in the *Fortenberry v. Ellis* case); second, property belonging to the engagement; and finally property exchanged during the engagement but not qualifying as conditional gifts. One legal commentator further differentiates the engagement gift economy. Besides the engagement ring, he identifies three other types: those "casual gifts such as affectionately disposed persons might be expected to give from time to time"; "gifts between engaged persons at Christmas and on holidays, all intended for the donee's sole enjoyment"; and "gifts, or transfers having the form of gifts, intended in one way or another to promote the marital economy, such as household furnishings and homes" (Martin 1952: 601–2).

In an ironic way, courts thus become gift counselors. It is not always an easy task, since drawing boundaries around the different categories of gift transfers may turn into a contested legal struggle. Consider for instance, Philip I. Lewis's and Rochelle Permut's claims against each other (*Lewis v. Permut*, 320 N.Y.S.2d 408 (N.Y. Civ. Ct. 1971)). After their four-month engagement ended on February 17, 1970, Lewis went to court demanding recovery of the $1,350 diamond engagement ring; six other pieces of jewelry he had given Permut during their courtship; eight wedding gifts the couple received from Lewis' parents, relatives, and friends; plus one-half of a joint savings account in which the couple had deposited savings and cash gifts. Permut in turn demanded that Lewis return a gold pocket watch and chain she had given him as an engagement gift, plus a Hitachi FM-AM stereo radio and receiver with two speakers that she had loaned him.

Despite New York's no-fault rules, Judge Nat H. Hentel assigned responsibility for the couple's breakup to Lewis, the plaintiff, and on that ground allowed Permut to keep the engagement ring. Nevertheless, for the remainder of the transfers and joint property, Judge Hentel relied on conditional gift doctrine quite consistently. He tried accordingly to discern which transfers and acquisitions of property the couple had made in expectation of their marriage. Thus, Permut was instructed to return her garnet-set gold wedding band to Lewis, since regardless of who had broken off the engagement "such a gift was predicated upon the parties entering into marriage. . . . The Court cannot see any logic in allowing the defendant to retain such unhappy souvenirs of an event which was never consummated" (410). She also had to return the contested wedding gifts.

But Permut was allowed to keep the other items of jewelry claimed by Lewis, as they were "delivered by plaintiff to defendant as gifts on her birthday or for other holiday or representative occasions" (410). Thus, these qualified as friendship, not engagement gifts. Using a similar rationale, the Court ruled that Lewis was not obliged to return the gold pocket watch and chain Permut had given him: "If defendant gave to plaintiff a gold watch and chain to express her happiness at her engagement and her love for and esteem of her fiancé, it was a completed gift with no 'strings attached' " (411). On the other hand, the court agreed that Lewis should return the Hitachi FM-AM stereo and receiver, because the transfer was not a gift, but a temporary loan. What's more, the judge divided the couple's joint savings bank account according to the sums deposited by each party. When it came to a $350 deposit for a bedroom set that had been paid by, and credited to, Lewis' parents, the judge turned down, for lack of evidence, Permut's claim that she had contributed $175 for the deposit.

What property rights do couples have after a broken engagement? As Judge Hentel's complex allocation of resources in the *Lewis v. Permut* case indicates, courts are not merely organizing equitable distribution of property but deciding item by item what rights and obligations are in play. The most obvious and common cases concern the ultimate conditional gift, the engagement ring. The issue figures clearly in the case of *McIntire v. Raukhorst* (585 N.E.2d 456 (Ohio Ct. App. 1989)). The couple began dating in October 1986. In January 1988, after Teresa Raukhorst accepted his marriage proposal, Craig McIntire gave her a $440 diamond solitaire ring. The bride-to-be chose her wedding dress and put down a deposit on a hall for the wedding reception, in addition to other expenses in preparation for their marriage. About a month after his proposal, McIntire terminated the engagement and requested the ring back. When Raukhorst refused, he went to court, then appealed the first decision allowing Raukhorst to keep her ring. An appellate court reversed that initial decision, declaring that regardless of who breaks the engagement, "the gift of an engagement ring, given in contemplation of marriage, is a conditional gift which, absent an agreement to the contrary, must be returned to the donor if the condition of marriage is not fulfilled" (467). The disappointed bride-to-be lost twice: not only her engagement ring but also the money she had spent in preparation for her wedding.[11]

Brides to be, however, do not always lose. In a 2003 case pitting Virginia DeFina as plaintiff against Stephen Scott as defendant (*DeFina v. Scott*, 755 N.Y.S.2d 587 (N.Y. Sup. Ct. 2003)), a court awarded substantial damages in compensation for the money DeFina had spent in preparation for her wedding to Scott. DeFina, a nurse practitioner, and Scott, a twice-divorced attorney, became engaged in 2000. The couple registered at luxury stores and planned a wedding at St. Patrick's Cathedral and a reception at the United Nations Plaza Hotel. Scott purchased an expensive engagement ring at Tiffany's for DeFina. The couple agreed that DeFina would pay for all wedding-related expenses. For his part, Scott transferred to DeFina one-half interest in his condominium apartment. In March 2001, the couple split up "in a flurry of heated actions" (589), and by April they went to court. At issue were not only wedding expenses, but also the engagement ring, the apartment, and third-party gifts.

---

[11] For a discussion of gender bias in legal treatment of broken engagements, see Tushnet 1998.

Although DeFina claimed that the ring had been a Valentine's Day gift, the court ruled that, since it remained covered by Scott's homeowner's policy, it remained his property. But because the ring had vanished from DeFina's lower Manhattan apartment soon after September 11, 2001, Scott was instead able to keep insurance proceeds that covered the loss. When it came to the apartment, however, the court rejected Scott's claim that DeFina return her half-interest. Instead, the court, citing DeFina's almost $16,000 pre-wedding expenses (which included half the cost of Scott's bachelor party), granted her a lien on the condominium, leaving title to Scott. Scott was also ordered to compensate DeFina for the five engagement gifts he had kept, despite the couple's agreement that all gifts should be returned to their respective donors. Judge Diane A. Lebedeff said of the case:

> The distinguishing feature of this case—that both parties were well-established professional adults who embarked upon preparations for a formal wedding paid for from their own funds, primarily acting upon clear plans regarding their engagement and the establishment of their eventual economic union—calls for application of contract-based theories to the maximum extent possible, a legally novel approach, but one particularly suited to couples of this type and to contemporary society. (588–89)

Once again, property rights depended simultaneously on a definition of the couple's relationship and on the legal interpretation of the contract attached to that relationship.

Are the couple actually eligible for engagement? In the cases considered so far, both parties had the legal right to contract an engagement. However, several impediments can exist to that right—notably, fraud, present marriage by either party, or the condition of one or both parties being underage (Tomko 1996). In any of these cases, the usual transactions that an engaged couple can legally undertake become invalid. Consider the case of Guy A. Armitage against Ann Tracy Hogan (*Armitage v. Hogan*, 171 P.2d 830 (Wash. 1946); see also Martin 1952: 595). In 1942, Armitage, a traveling shoe salesman in his early fifties, and Hogan, a known prostitute, met in Seattle during one of his business trips. She recalled the encounter as follows: "Well, I was walking on Pike Street, and I ran into him, and I spoke to him. . . . And he said he was lonesome and invited me to come to the hotel, and I went, and he paid me for my entertainment, and I stayed, and I got ready to leave. He didn't want me to go, so I remained overnight, and he give me money" (833).

Their meetings continued each time Armitage traveled to Seattle; he regularly gave her expensive presents, such as a fur coat and money, including $500 to buy a massage parlor and $375 to aid her sick sister. Several times, he gave her $200 to $300 when she asked for cash. In July 1944, Armitage allegedly proposed marriage to Hogan, although no definitive time was set for the ceremony. He then put down $2,500 as down payment for the purchase of a hotel Hogan was to operate. In September of that year, Armitage gave Hogan a $2,000 diamond ring. Two months later, Hogan married Joe Ennette, a "colored man."

Armitage went to court claiming that Hogan had broken her agreement to marry him and therefore should return the diamond ring—or its cash equivalent—and the down payment for the hotel. Both gifts, he argued, were given in consideration of their intended marriage. He expected no compensation for his earlier courtship gifts. He declared that Hogan "always presented herself in a ladylike manner, and that he had no idea she was a prostitute." She had therefore defrauded Armitage of his money, intending all along to marry Ennette, not him. When asked, "Was there any reason why you should give her this money and these gifts than what you have already testified?" Armitage responded, "No, nothing other than the marriage agreement which was inducement for me to make these loans and gifts" (833, 835–36). If Armitage's story was correct and if Hogan had fraudulently agreed to marry him without any intention of doing so, the gifts were indeed conditional on their marriage. He was therefore entitled to recover those expenses.

But Hogan denied Armitage's claims. She testified that "from the first time she entertained him at his hotel" (833), Armitage was aware of her occupation. He had never proposed. His gifts therefore were offered only in exchange for her affections. For instance, when it came to the hotel down payment, Hogan recounted, "He said, 'Well what will you do for me if I pay this other $2,500?' I said, 'I would be nice to you like I have always been. Haven't I been nice?' Shortly afterwards I received a letter after he left telling how nice I had been with him" (834). As for the engagement ring, Hogan testified as follows:

> That morning we were lying in bed in the Drexel Hotel, and I told him, "Let's get up early," and wanted him to go and buy me something. So we went to Dootson's for breakfast . . . [and went] to the jewelry store. I said, "Here it is, " and so we asked to show the ring I had looked at, and they showed it. . . . He bought it . . . and [we] were waiting for the red light at Fifth and Pike. He said, "I should have waited a little while and bought this for your Christmas gift." I said, "That's fine. We'll call it a Christmas gift anyway." He said, "Would you?" and I said, "Yes." (835)

Asked if "there was any talk about being an engagement ring at any time," Hogan declared, "Never" (835).

In October 1945, the court dismissed Armitage's suit; the following year, the Supreme Court of Washington affirmed that judgment. There had been, both courts agreed, no valid agreement to marry between the parties. Two features of the situation wrecked Armitage's claims; first the court established that Hogan was a known prostitute and concluded that Armitage must have been aware of this. In fact the court stated:

> [W]e are convinced that appellant was induced to give respondent the presents which he did, and to furnish her the money for financing the hotel deal, by his desire to have the illegal and immoral association with respondent continued; that he never asked for or expected a return of the ring or money, but the

only payment appellant ever expected to receive from respondent was the pleasure he apparently enjoyed and expected to enjoy from such association. (836)

The court's second finding was even more devastating. It turned out that Armitage was still married to another woman. He and his wife had separated some years before, but Armitage had taken no legal steps toward divorcing her. Armitage and Hogan were thus doubly ineligible to marry. The doctrine of conditional gift could not possibly apply to any of Armitage's generosity toward Hogan. All his gifts were hers to keep (see also Martin 1952: 595).

Jeffers, one of the appellate judges, spoke emphatically:

> As I have listened to this testimony now for more than two days, I am satisfied that this is a case solely of a scheming woman who is engaged in prostitution . . . having met the plaintiff and peddled her wares, and apparently Mr. Armitage, a married man, became infatuated with her and gave her considerable money over a period of several years. To put it in the vernacular, I am satisfied that he was just a plain sucker, and that she played him for all that he was worth. . . . [W]hile I regret that she is permitted to retain these funds, I must conclude that the funds were given to her. (836)

In essence, the judge reluctantly decided that Armitage was simply paying a very high price for sexual services. Hostile worlds had clashed once more.

Here again, the outcome of the case depended first of all on the court's assessment of the relationship between the parties. Under other circumstances, exactly the same transactions would have led to recovery by Armitage. Despite what happened in the *Armitage v. Hogan* case, generally speaking, courts treat engagement rings as quintessential conditional gifts, returnable to the donor almost regardless of the circumstances that ended the engagement. In contrast, wedding rings fall under a different regime, since courts do not require their return after a divorce, even in the case of a short-lived marriage (Tushnet 1998: 2603).

BETWEEN COURTSHIP AND SEX WORK

Across this complex, fascinating terrain, American courts continue to follow the strategy of relational work outlined earlier: They match intimate relations with appropriate economic transactions and media, they distinguish similar relations from each other, and they often justify their distinctions by invoking hostile worlds doctrines. Although they maintain a distinctive legal classification of intimate relations and of valid evidence for those relations, they alter the rules in response both to changes in ordinary practices and to the rise or fall of more general legal doctrines.

Some legal disputes lie halfway between the law of engagement and the law governing commercial sex. Courts have difficulties with these cases, because they again must decide what relationship applies to the couple. A case in point is Deborah Vandevelde's $3.5 million breach of contract suit against Thomas Colucci. According to forty-one-year-old Vandevelde, the two first met in 1999 when fifty-three-year-old Colucci, a wealthy Long Island businessman, approached her in a Madison Avenue café, offered her a ride home in his golden Mercedes, and sent her flowers the next day. After the relationship began, Colucci treated Vandevelde—then employed by Christie's auction galleries—with an array of expensive gifts: Bergdorf Goodman furs, designer clothing, a Mercedes CL500, a penthouse apartment on Central Park South, and another luxury forty-eighth-floor apartment on Fifth Avenue, next to St. Patrick's Cathedral.

Vandevelde further claimed that Colucci asked her to sign a $100,000 a year contract offering her employment in one of his companies. The contract stated that Colucci owed her $492,000 for past "business services." Their agreement, however, went far beyond business into a form of courtship, bordering on commercial sexual services. In a television interview, Vandevelde stated that she and Colucci, still married and the father of two teenage children, were engaged. He had promised to divorce his wife and had bought Vandevelde a Vera Wang wedding dress and an engagement ring at Graff. Vandevelde added that while their relationship lasted, Colucci "enjoyed unrestricted sex . . . while promising her financial security." Colucci's "appetite for sex" noted Vandevelde, "was insatiable" (*Abrams Report* 2002; Maull 2002). Two years later Colucci broke up with Vandevelde, accusing her of betraying him with another boyfriend. He stopped paying her rent. At that point, he denied Vandevelde's account of their relationship. The two met, according to his testimony, through an escort service: "Ms. Vandevelde," claimed Colucci in an affidavit filed in Manhattan Supreme Court, "was the girl whom the escort service sent to my room." He compensated her "affections and loyalty" with lavish gifts. Colucci further argued that their contract was an agreement to facilitate adultery, and therefore illegal (Maull 2002; *New York Daily News* 2002).

The judge in this case, Manhattan State Supreme Court Justice Leland DeGrasse, struck a delicate balance between commercial and moral considerations. First, he separated Vandevelde's breach of contract suit from a different suit for unpaid rent by the owners of the building in which Vandevelde lived. In the latter case, he ruled against Colucci, ordering him to pay more than $50,000 in back rent. Once again, we find courts making fine distinctions on the way to placing a couple's relationship in its proper location within an available matrix.

SEX WORK IN THE LAW

In the Vandevelde-Colucci case, much of the dispute hinged on whether their relationship qualified as commercial sex work. Plenty of disputes arise, however, in cases where there is little question that part of what was going on was the commercial provision of sexual services. As we have seen, sex work covers a wide range of relationships including involvement of customers with lap dancers, telephone sex workers, escort services, pornography, adult Web sites, various forms of prostitution, and much more. In addition to prosecuting certain forms of sex work, the law, however reluctantly, gets involved in adjudicating whether certain relations constitute sex work and, if so, determining their legal standing.

Laws against prostitution form the foundation of a wide range of actions concerning sex work. Despite the specter of prostitution as the end-point of any commodification in sexual relations, however, in practice courts and judges have not maintained a simple dichotomy of legitimate, nonmonetary sexual relations versus illegal monetized prostitution. Most American states make prostitution illegal, usually declaring it a misdemeanor. In general, American laws pinpoint the exchange of money for sexual services as the defining element of prostitution. Thus, for example, Florida defines prostitution as "offering to give or receive or giving or receiving the body for sexual activity for hire," while for the Illinois statute, prostitution consists of: "offering or agreeing to perform or performing any act of sexual penetration or touching of genitals for money or anything of value. A person patronizes a prostitute by engaging in sexual penetration with a prostitute who is not that person's spouse" (Posner and Silbaugh 1996: 161, 164–65).

The Illinois law has two remarkable features: it self-consciously distinguishes a spouse's (legal) provision of sexual services from a prostitute's (illegal) provision of the same services, and it explicitly stigmatizes the provider rather than the recipient of the services. As in other cases, legal practitioners implicitly construct a matrix of relations, one of which is prostitution. They then distinguish prostitution from adjacent relations such as marriage, they mark boundaries, and they specify the proper correspondence among the relations, transactions, and media for those transactions.

Thus, lawyers, judges, and juries are often deciding whether a given relationship is that of married couple, lovers, engaged parties, prostitute and client, or something else. They make weighty legal decisions depending on where they place the relevant relationship. Not that all parties always agree on this matter. The matrix itself and its boundaries frequently come under sharp contest, as opposing lawyers and outside advocates disagree over the propriety or impropriety of different relationships, transactions, and media. What's more, different types of law employ somewhat different matrices, for example, tax law focuses on whether a relationship generated earned and taxable income, while the law of engagement, as we have seen, focuses on the conditional promise to marry.

A dramatic example comes from a 1992 tax dispute (*Toms v. Comm'r*, 63 T.C.M. (CCH) 2, 243 (1992)). During the early 1980s, Frances Mary Granato Toms ran a freelance escort service and a house of prostitution in New Jersey. She employed five female prostitutes as well as three male escorts and advertised widely in local newspapers. She favored "customers who were financially generous older men" (*4). Toms's fees ranged from $35 to $125 per service; she paid $30 to the employee and pocketed the balance. Between 1965 and 1974, Toms had been involved with Sam Celona, a gas station attendant thirty-four years her senior. In 1974, she met and married Paul Toms, thirty years older than herself; he died four years later, in 1978. That year, Toms advertised for a millionaire who would support her, and apparently received over two thousand responses. In 1980, she met Samuel Cohen, a retired IRS employee, who was despondent following a recent separation from his wife of twenty-five years. On their first date, Toms and Cohen went to dinner, the movies, and back to his home in Philadelphia to listen to music and talk. That evening, Cohen paid Toms $200, and for the next few years, continued paying $200 for each of her biweekly four-to-five hour visits. They did not, he later declared, have sexual relations. Each time, nevertheless, he gave her the money as she left his home.

In 1982, Toms met Joseph DeFelice when she arranged sexual services for him with Michelle Barns, one of her employees, for $125. On a second visit, DeFelice paid $50 for sexual intercourse with Beth, another employee. After that, between 1982 and 1983, DeFelice met with Toms several times a week, paying her for each encounter. Frances Toms's legal troubles began during those years. After five years of surveillance by a sergeant-detective, she pleaded guilty and was convicted of prostitution in 1985. At about the same time, a special agent from the IRS began investigating Toms's tax reports. By 1988, she was convicted of willful evasion of income tax for profits from her prostitution business.

She appealed, claiming that a large portion of her accumulated savings and investments were gifts from the two men she called her "sugar daddies," Samuel Cohen and Joseph DeFelice. Cohen's payments, she declared, were expressions of "love and affection." DeFelice, meanwhile, testified that his relationship to Toms "had blossomed into a love affair," and "he showered [her] with more money than he conceivably had" (*35–37). If gifts, the payments were not taxable income. The Tax Court disagreed, finding "unpersuasive" the evidence that either of the men's transfers were gifts. In Cohen's case, the presiding judge explained:

> Whether a transfer of funds is a gift is based upon an objective inquiry into the facts. . . . Mr. Cohen testified that he has not had sexual relations with petitioner. That is immaterial to our decision. Mr. Cohen paid petitioner for the first evening she spent with him and paid her most nights she saw him. This suggests a paid escort relationship, not gifts to a friend.
>
> While we do not question the importance Mr. Cohen places on his companionship with petitioner, we believe that his regular payments to her were not out of [affection]. . . . Instead, we believe the payments were for services rendered, and therefore not gifts. (*37–38)

As compensation for prostitution and escort services, the payments became taxable income. The court rejected Toms's appeal.

In order to make its judgment, the Tax Court thus got involved in delicate questions about the nature of Toms's intimate relationships, specifically whether or not her ties to Cohen and DeFelice were that of lovers or participants in a commercial sexual arrangement. It is a crucial distinction. Recall what happened in the case of Kritzik and the twin sisters. Originally, both Leigh Ann Conley and Lynnette Harris went to jail for failing to pay income tax on the more than half a million dollars the old widower had given them over several years in exchange for their sexual services. After Kritzik's death, however, the appeals court reversed the conviction precisely by affirming the women's claims that the relationship was not that of prostitute-client, but lovers. The money payments thereby became nontaxable gifts. The Tax Court ruled that these two cases were different. But why? In both episodes unmarried persons maintained intimate relations over a long period of time, and the men gave the women money. Yet the courts found that in the first case the monetary transfers qualified as compensation for services while in the second they qualified as gifts.

EXOTIC DANCING

Legal efforts to classify varying forms of sex-for-money relationships go farther than criminal prostitution or income tax evasion. The case of lap dancing, for instance, has created a great deal of controversy precisely as a result of its uncertain legal status. Uncertainty begins with the entertainment's very name. Professionals prefer to call the practice exotic dancing. Some observers and participants speak of topless dancing. But legislation and court decisions often refer to lap dancing. In a narrow sense, lap dancing includes gyrations by a nearly nude woman on a customer's lap. Somewhat more broadly, the practice includes erotic motions in close proximity to male customers, who often reciprocate by placing money in whatever receptacle the dancer makes available. In either the narrow or the broader sense, courts often assimilate lap dancing to prostitution by declaring it in violation of statutes forbidding sexual conduct for a fee (see *Obscenity Law Bulletin* 2000: 1; and for graphic testimony, see *Steinbach v. Texas*, 979 S.W.2d 836 (Tex. App. 1998)).

Still, in most other aspects, the law distinguishes the lap dancer–spectator relationship from the prostitute–client tie. It does so through setting precise legal rules about what the parties may or may not do. For instance, so-called buffer zone laws prohibit touching between patron and dancer by establishing legally enforceable spatial constraints. Specifically, dancers must remain anywhere from three feet to ten feet away from the nearest patron, often on a raised platform. In many cases, direct payment by patron to dancer is likewise avoided by prohibiting tips. A 1986 decision upholding these restrictions concluded that buffer zone regulations did not challenge First Amendment rights: "While the dancer's erotic message may be slightly less effective from ten feet, the ability to engage in the protected expression is not significantly impaired. Erotic dancers still have reasonable access to their market" (*Kev, Inc. v. Kitsap County*, 793 F.2d 1053, 1061 (9th Cir. 1986)). Nevertheless, local jurisdictions vary greatly in where they draw the line between proper and improper lap dance behavior. For instance, while the city of Las Vegas allows touching and tipping, in 2002, adjacent Clark County imposed stricter rules. In Clark County, lap dancers were allowed to touch or dance on a customer's legs, but prohibited from touching the customer's genital area. Stuffing money in the women's G-strings was likewise banned (Wagner 2002).

Thus, lap dancing law makes a double distinction, separating relations between dancer and client from prostitution and other forms of sex work, but also from the legal intimate relations of lovers and married couples. In the process, the law ironically draws perimeters around legally tolerable forms of sex work. Similarly, courts, lawyers, and juries intervene in a variety of other exchanges of sex for money—hostess dance halls, massage parlors, phone sex, and pornography. But in each case they draw the lines between acceptable and unacceptable behavior in slightly different ways.

In distinguishing legitimate from illegitimate forms of intimacy, American law faces some surprising choices. A bill (no. 469) introduced in the Ohio General Assembly 2001–2002 session includes the following provision:

> "Sexual encounter establishment" means a business or commercial establishment that, as one of its principal business purposes, offers for any form of consideration a place where two or more persons may congregate, associate, or consort for the purpose of specified sexual activities or when one or more of the persons is nude or seminude. An establishment where a medical practitioner, psychologist, psychiatrist, or similar professional person licensed by the state engages in medically approved and

recognized sexual therapy is not a "sexual encounter establish-ment" or an "adult entertainment establishment." (Ohio General Assembly 2002: 6)

Clearly Ohio legislators found that if they imposed too great a restriction on paid forms of intimacy, they would start ruling out intimate relations they actually wanted to protect, in this case, relations between licensed professionals and their clients.

PROFESSIONAL INTIMACY

American law does not, however, give professionals a free ride. On the contrary, it regulates intimate professional-client relations closely. As we saw in the lawyer–client–bar association case that opened this chapter, professional organizations, courts, and legislatures collaborate in protecting the boundary of professional practice against two kinds of violations. The first defends against forms of intimacy that will corrupt professional practice; the second, against forms of professional practice that promote unwanted or improper intimacy. Of course, as in the Berg case, sexual intimacy causes serious threats, but so does control over a client's private information. The kinds of information that various professionals acquire in the course of intimate but nonsexual relations with their clients often becomes germane to other crucial aspects of their clients' lives. Indeed, a considerable body of law governs the confidentiality of personal information that professionals acquire from their clients. Physicians, psychologists, lawyers, priests, and even teachers sometimes acquire intimate information that could damage their subjects if revealed to third parties. Yet sometimes professionals pass on such information. Sometimes they have the legal right or even the legal obligation to do so. Claims to such rights and obligations come into dispute repeatedly, however, in legal proceedings concerning the intersection of economic transactions and intimacy.

Consider three such contestations—the cases of Andrew Goldstein, Chari Lightman, and Antoinette Crescenzo. In 1997, Andrew

Goldstein killed Kendra Webdale by pushing her in front of an incoming Manhattan subway train. Goldstein had been treated at several mental health facilities, most recently the Bleuler Psychotherapy Center. The Department of Mental Health, Mental Retardation, and Alcoholism began an investigation of the case in order to improve the city's service for the mentally disabled. As part of its investigation, the department requested that the Bleuler Center turn over Goldstein's medical records. After the center refused, then failed to comply with a subpoena, claiming the confidentiality of medical records, the case went to court. On August 25, 1999, the Supreme Court of New York ordered the Bleuler Center to turn over Goldstein's records, stating that "the interests of justice outweigh any need for confidentiality" (*City of New York v. Bleuler Psychotherapy Center, Inc.*, 695 N.Y.S.2d 903, 906 (N.Y. Sup. Ct. 1999)).

In 1995, Chari Lightman, an Orthodox Jew, consulted two New York rabbis, Rabbi Tzvi Flaum and Rabbi Weinberger, seeking spiritual and religious guidance. In the course of the counseling sessions, she disclosed intimate information to both rabbis. A year later, when she initiated divorce proceedings against her husband, including seeking temporary custody of their four children, her husband contested her claims, using damaging confidential evidence revealed to him by both rabbis, including that she was "seeing a man in a social setting," and she had stopped fulfilling "religious purification laws." Chari Lightman sued both rabbis, claiming breach of fiduciary duty violating clergy-penitent privilege. After several appeals, on November 27, 2001, the New York Court of Appeals turned down Lightman's case, declaring that the statute creating clergy-penitent privilege, "does not give rise to a cause of action for breach of a fiduciary duty involving the disclosure of oral communications between a congregant and a cleric" (*Lightman v. Flaum*, 97 N.Y.2d 128, 131–32, 137 (2001)).

In 1992, Antoinette Crescenzo first consulted Walter D. Crane, a New Jersey physician for injuries caused by a car accident. She and her daughter continued under his care, and in 1997 Crane treated her for a head injury. At that time, Crescenzo confided in the doctor about her marital problems and related stress symptoms. He treated her depression with Prozac. In 1998, when Crescenzo's husband initiated divorce proceedings, Crane was asked to turn over his patient's medical records. He complied, and the records were used as evidence against Crescenzo in the divorce case, specifically as to her mental capacity to care for the couple's minor child, Dana Santora. Crescenzo's lawyer filed a complaint against the records' release, as a violation of patient-physician privilege. After the Superior Court, Law Division, Atlantic County dismissed the complaint, Crescenzo appealed. On February 26, 2002, the court reversed the decision and remanded the case (*Crescenzo v. Crane*, 796 A.2d. 283 (N.J. 2002)).

In a remarkable reversal of the direction of the information flow between professional and client invoked in these three cases, columnist Lauren Slater reports an unexpected variant:

> In early 2003, in his consulting room, a psychiatrist confessed to his patient he planned to kill six people, including a female patient who was also the doctor's lover. What's more, the doctor asked the patient for help finding chopped bait and a gun with a silencer. The doctor was later arrested at a Home Depot parking lot and charged with three counts of weapons possession by the Nassau County D.A.'s office. (Slater 2003)

More important than who revealed information is that the crucial intimacies across all four instances did not involve sexual relations, but communication of personal information. In parallel to their intervention in cases of contested sexual relations, American courts constantly get involved in adjudicating the propriety of other forms of intimacy: sharing of confidential information, offering of professional advice, provision of personal care, joint acquisition of domestic property, and transfers of valuable gifts. In doing so, they give priority to ascertaining the relationship between the parties before deciding whether the transactions they shared and the media they employed for those transactions pertained properly to that relationship.

COUPLING IN AND OUT OF THE LAW

Precisely because courts proceed in this way, a significant share of contestation between and about couples in American law turns less on what actually happened than on what relationship prevailed when it happened, and what separated that relationship from others it resembled in some regards. As we saw earlier, outside of the legal process couples and third parties to coupling regularly engage in practices that resemble legal practices without mimicking them precisely; they deploy somewhat different matrices, distinctions within those matrices, and doctrines to justify those distinctions. To put it another way (and a bit more accurately), American courts parallel ordinary practice as they guard the boundaries between proper and improper forms of intimacy. Their relational work interacts with that of everyday social life.

Formation of intimate couples, as we will soon see, poses fewer problems for American law than do caring and household interactions. The law has available the model of a two-party contract and frequently applies that model to intimate pairs. When caring connects pairs of people other than spouses or involves multiple parties, however, standard contract models fit less well, and legal practitioners must exercise greater ingenuity as they translate from everyday practices to legislatures and courtrooms. In practice, intimate couples often pose serious problems to people in adjacent social relations. Is this person an appropriate partner for our daughter? Can the profession tolerate these sorts of relations between its members and their clients? Will this office romance disrupt the firm? Coupling poses problems, paradoxically, precisely because it almost always has strong implications for third parties.

Some of the relationships we have examined under the rubric of coupling involve caring: sustained provision of life-enhancing attention by at least one of the parties. Shifting the focus to caring, however, raises questions this chapter has barely touched: who has the right or obligation to give life-enhancing care? To receive care? What compensation, if any, does the provision of care justify? Does commercialization of care inevitably corrupt it and the relationships within which it occurs? Such questions arise more or less equally in ordinary practice and in legal disputes. They call up some of the same social processes we have observed in coupling: boundary drawing, matching of relations and transactions with media, assignment of existing relations to morally charged categories, and claims of third parties to intervene. The following chapter enters the world of intimate care.

CHAPTER 4

CARING RELATIONS

Estimating her net worth at $2.4 billion, in 2001 *Forbes* magazine rated Barbara Piasecka Johnson among the world's twenty wealthiest women. Forty years earlier, the young, impoverished Barbara Piasecka had arrived in the United States from her native Poland and worked as a cook. In between, however, she had married medical and baby products heir J. Seward Johnson and nursed him through his final illness. She then fought a fierce legal battle against her six stepchildren to retain the fortune Johnson had willed her. In his detailed analysis of the Johnson case, *New York Times* legal reporter David Margolick called the will contest "the largest, costliest, ugliest, most spectacular, and most conspicuous in American history" (Margolick 1993: 12).[1]

A few weeks after Barbara ("Basia") Piasecka arrived from Poland, Seward Johnson's second wife, Esther Underwood "Essie" Johnson, hired her as a cook. Basia cooked so badly, however, that soon the Johnson's Polish maid (who had recruited her) switched jobs with her. Working as a chambermaid, Basia made $100 dollars a week. A year later, she quit her job with the Johnsons. But by that time she had caught Seward's eye. He offered Basia, who had studied art history in Poland, a $12,000-a-year job as curator for his new art

---

[1] See also Goldsmith 1987 for an account that differs from Margolick in some details.

collection. He also showered her with gifts: not only jewelry and furs, but also two Italian homes and a $500,000 trust fund.

By 1971, the now seventy-six-year-old Seward had divorced Essie and promptly married thirty-four-year-old Basia. Eight years later, in 1979, his health began to deteriorate. Off and on until his death in 1983, Basia nursed him and supervised his care. One of the attending professional nurses called Basia his "number one nurse" (Margolick 1993: 254). Indeed, during his final illness, Basia

> massaged Seward. She gave him ice packs and heating pads where he ached. She salted his broth and prepared him her special herbal tea. . . . She read to him, bathed him, cut his nails, combed his hair, trimmed his beard, put on his clothes, wiped his forehead. She helped him walk, and when he could no longer lift up his hand, she could almost telepathically pinpoint his pain. . . . She wiped his rectum, uncomplainingly. (Margolick 1993: 161)

Another nurse wondered "why she wanted an R.N. when she would always do everything for him" (Margolick 1993: 161).

Seward's will made Basia the principal beneficiary of his $400 million fortune. His six children from two previous marriages, however, objected to this arrangement. Their lawyers raised three complaints against the bequest: one, that Seward was not competent; two, that the will had not been executed in proper form; and three, that the will had been procured "by fraud, duress and undue influence on the part of Seward Johnson's widow" (Margolick 1993: 215). The children's attorneys portrayed Basia as domineering, even intimidating, thereby exerting undue influence on a debilitated old man. In response, Basia's witnesses and legal team portrayed her as attentive, loving, and lavish in her care for the dying man.

Note what the disappointed heirs did and did not claim. They did not challenge the validity of the marriage itself, the fact of Basia's energetic care, or even Seward's devotion to her. On the contrary, they argued that the care constituted an improper campaign to influence the inheritance, isolating Seward from other influences, and thus excluding his children from their rightful heritage. After a protracted three-year suit, including extensive courtroom hearings, the parties settled in 1986, leaving Basia a substantial share of the estate. In effect, the children's attorneys conceded that Basia retained substantial rights as a consequence of her relationship to Seward.

The legal doctrine of "undue influence" has remarkable implications for the purchase of intimacy. It assumes not only that certain kinds of intimate attention belong to some relations and those alone, but also that in those same relations too much intimate attention constitutes suspicious abuse of the relationship. Much more generally, in fact, both ordinary practice and legal doctrine match proper qualities and amounts of personal care to particular social relations, disapproving and sometimes penalizing mismatches. Claims of undue influence extend into professional relationships. Take the Mississippi case of Clarence Holland, Fannie Moses, and her sisters and brother (*In re Will of Moses*, 227 So. 2d 829 (Miss. 1969); see also Dobris and Sterk 1998: 394–401). At her death in 1967, Moses' will of 1964 (unlike an earlier will) turned out to leave the bulk of her $125,000 estate to her attorney and lover, Holland, who had visited and attended her almost daily during her declining years.

In Jackson, Mississippi, Fannie Moses managed four apartment buildings and a farm. According to a judge in her case, she had "a strong personality and pursued her own course, even though her manner of living did at times embarrass her sisters and estranged her from them" (*Moses*, 227 So. 2d 839). The already twice-widowed Fannie Moses became romantically involved with Clarence Holland some time after 1950, when she was in her forties and still married to her third husband, Walter Moses. After Walter's death, Fannie and Holland's relationship intensified. The court reports that he "was in almost daily attendance upon Mrs. Moses on terms of utmost intimacy." Indeed, Fannie had declared that Holland—fifteen years her junior—was not only her attorney but her boyfriend. And he continued his "constant and amorous attentions" (833), during Fannie's last years of alcoholism, heart trouble, and breast cancer. In a 1961 will, Fannie had bequeathed Holland her jewels but kept her sister as primary beneficiary. Three years later, she revised her will, leaving him with most of her estate.

When the will came to probate in 1967, the Chancellor turned it down, ruling that it was the product of undue influence. In this view, Fannie and Holland's double relationship, lawyer-client and intimate lovers, made Fannie vulnerable to illegitimate pressures. Holland appealed, but the Supreme Court of Mississippi rejected his claims. The court supported arguments that this "aging woman infatuated with a young lover . . . who was also her lawyer," was unable to make sound decisions. Worse still, the court noted, "There was testimony too indicating that she entertained the pathetic hope that he might marry her" (833, 835). It was not, the court agreed, that Fannie Moses was of unsound mind. Nor was the "sexual morality" of the relationship at issue: that was relevant, the court stated, only "to the extent that its existence . . . warranted an inference of undue influence, extending and augmenting that which flowed from the attorney-client relationship" (836). That concern superseded even Holland's claim that in drafting her will Fannie had the benefit of an independent counsel.

J. Robertson, the dissenting judge, disputed the finding of undue influence, insisting that the will had been properly executed. "The fact that she chose to leave most of her property to the man she loved in preference to her sisters and brother," the judge contended, "is not such an unnatural disposition of her property as to render it invalid" (840). Ultimately, however, the majority of the Mississippi court concluded that Clarence Holland had abused a professional relationship, thus producing undue influence over his client.

The Johnson and Moses undue influence cases might seem to justify the idea of hostile worlds. Mixing personal care and economic transactions, one might conclude from these court battles, inevitably produces double corruption: encouraging the exploitation of care giving by scheming opportunists, converting what should be strictly professional relationships into misbehavior. In fact, however, both ordinary practice and legal doctrine accept and even encourage the mingling of intimate care with economic transactions, just so long as the proper matching of relationship, transaction, and medium occurs. This chapter analyzes the matching process, examines distinctions among caring relations, and watches the subtle work of

separating approved from forbidden forms of care. Going well beyond the couples of the previous chapter, it looks closely at the relational work of caring.

What defines care? Caring relationships feature sustained and/or
intense personal attention that enhances the welfare of its recipients.
We might set the minimum for "sustained and/or intensive personal
attention" at a commercial backrub in a shopping center or a brief
telephone counseling session with a spiritual adviser. The maximum
might then take the form of lifetime mother-daughter bonds or the
devotion of a long-term personal servant. Clearly, care varies greatly
in its degree of intimacy, from quite impersonal to tightly inter-
locked. Caring relationships also qualify as intimate to the degree
that they involve trust: they entrust at least one of the parties with
information about, or attention to, another party that is not widely
available and that would be damaging if offered to third parties.

Caring relationships vary in duration, range, and type of attention. They overlap with some varieties of coupling (as we saw in
chapter 3) and often form one component of relationships within
households (as we will see in chapter 5). The task of the current
chapter, however, is to bring out how caring and economic transactions of production, consumption, distribution, and transfers of
assets intertwine. The topic deserves special attention because mingling of personal care with economic transactions frequently generates intense moral and legal controversies over proper and improper
matchings. The two undue influence cases of Barbara Piasecka
Johnson and Clarence Holland illustrate the high stakes and intense
hostilities sometimes produced by contestable mixes of caring and
economic transactions. But controversy also arises over a wide variety of other matchings between caring and economic transactions
than the sexual intimacy of the Johnson and Holland cases: proper
compensation for commercial child care, fees for medical treatment,
salaries for housewives, protection of elderly people in nursing
homes, responsibility of children for the health and welfare of their
aging parents, and much more.

What sorts of economic obligations does care generate or fulfill?
Answers to that crucial moral, legal, and political question actually

turn out to vary enormously by time, place, and social setting. Social and political changes such as aging of the general population, entry of women into paid employment, tightening of welfare eligibility, increases in schooling, and restrictions over children's work all affect the relative salience of different sorts of caring as well as their place in the economy as a whole.

Following the model set by chapter 3, this chapter sketches change and variation in the intersection of economic activity with caring relationships before examining the sorts of legal disputes that draw American courts into adjudicating appropriate matches between caring and economic transactions. In everyday practice and in the legal arena, it shows how much relational work goes into the provision of personal care. In both regards, it concentrates on the more intimate forms of caring—those in which trust and potentially damaging information figure significantly. To discipline the analysis of popular caring practices, it will help to lay out a continuum of sites for caring relationships: caring that takes place entirely within households at one end, caring that takes place mainly outside households at the other end, caring that crosses household boundaries in between. Let us proceed from within-household to cross-household to non-household relations.

HOUSEHOLD CARING

Almost by definition, households combine a wide range of caring attentions and economic transactions. Members provide each other with health care, child-care advice, information, and numerous other services. At the same time, they engage incessantly in production, consumption, distribution, and financial transfers. Feeding the family provides an obvious yet often forgotten intersection of caring and economic activity. As Marjorie DeVault (1991) has shown, the largely invisible, unpaid labor of planning, shopping, and preparing meals involves constant, often contested, negotiations of family relationships. Drawing from her interviews with a diverse set of thirty households in the Chicago area, DeVault reports that women—who do most of the feeding work within households—strive to match meals with expected definitions of husband-wife or mother-child relationships. For example, appropriate meals for husbands involved enactment of deference to a man's preoccupations and responsibilities outside the household. Meals, DeVault demonstrates, involved more than nutrition or economy: they routinely symbolized appropriately gendered ties.[2]

Food acquisition and preparation, however, inform a whole set of social relations beyond gender. DeVault provides a telling example of how Janice, a nurse living with her husband and two adult children, manages simultaneously to preserve both family cohesion and independence:

> Meals are often family events, prepared and eaten at home together. Janice or the children decide on the spur of the moment whether or not to cook, and "whoever is home sits down and eats it." Janice's shopping is what makes this kind of independence possible: "What I do is provide enough food in the house for anybody who wants to eat. And then whoever is home, makes that meal, if they want it." (DeVault 1991: 63)

As DeVault's account implies, behind the actual feeding of the family hides a whole complex of what she calls monitoring and provisioning; watching the changing demands and consumption patterns of household members in order to adjust the supply and production of household food and searching for appropriate and affordable food. In fact, DeVault points out how regularly the women in her study either negotiated purchases by other members of the household or drew those members into the act of shopping to acquire information about their preferences. Janice, for instance, reported how she occasionally encouraged her teenage children to food shop with her: "Then they get what they want, and not what I

---

[2] In another investigation, DeVault shows the same work of creating and sustaining family relations with "family outings" such as zoo visits; see DeVault 2002. For a comparison between DeVault's and lesbian/gay households, see Carrington 1999.

want. And I also get their idea of what they like. Would you rather this brand or that brand? . . . This kind of thing, where you've got to sort of get to know your kids, and the people you're working with" (62). Each of her respondents, DeVault observes, "through day-to-day activities . . . produces a version of 'family' in a particular local setting: adjusting, filling in, and repairing social relations to produce—quite literally—this form of household life" (91).

To be sure, as DeVault shows, not all household relations of consumption generate harmony and collaboration. Consider another well-documented study. In his account of Philadelphia's inner-city, poor, African-American children, Carl Nightingale reports acute rancor and conflict between parents and children in their negotiations over consumption. Parents exasperated by their kids' unreasonable and persistent demands for spending money are pitted against children disappointed by their parents' inability to provide them with material goods. Contest over how to spend limited family monies, including income tax refunds or welfare checks, Nightingale observes, severely strain household relations:

> All the kids whose families I knew well lived through similar incidents: yelling matches between Fahim and his mother on how she spent her welfare check, Theresa's disgust when she found out she was not going to get a dress because her mom's boyfriend had demanded some of the family's monthly money for crack, and Omar's decision to leave his mother's house altogether because "I hate her. She always be asking y'all [the Kids' Club] for money. That's going to get around, and people'll be talking." Also he felt that she never had enough money for his school clothes (Nightingale 1993: 159; see also Bourgois 1995).

Thus, the mixture of caring and economic activity within households takes place in a context of incessant negotiation, sometimes cooperative, other times full of conflict.

Feeding and purchasing clothes by no means exhaust the caring activity that goes on within households. As the story of Barbara Piasecka and J. Seward Johnson has already shown, health care sometimes becomes even more central to household caring relationships than the provision of food and clothing. Even when medical professionals provide instructions or medicine, family members regularly take part in supplying care. They assure hygiene, fetch drugs and other medical supplies, and learn medical technologies such as injections and monitoring of vital signs. Household members also manage sick persons' schedules and their transportation, as well as the special diets and other comforts appropriate for their condition. In Los Angeles, for instance, Guatemalan immigrant women relied heavily on their interpersonal networks to secure medical care for themselves and their family members. Through a variety of informal ties, the women gained knowledge and access to both American medicine and unofficial means of healing, such as herbs, rituals, and medicines regulated in the United States but available without prescription in the home country.

As a consequence, mothers involved themselves daily in the delivery of health care at home. Cecilia Menjívar reports on Aida, one of the Guatemalan women she interviewed in a study of such healing practices:

> Like almost all the women in this study, Aida feels fully responsible for her family's health needs. . . . She is always mindful of her family's health and is industrious in putting together whatever treatments she can find. There was a reminder to herself on the refrigerator door: *Darle las vitaminas a la beiby. Ponerle las pastillas en la lonchera a Luis.* (Give the vitamins to the baby. Put the pills in Luis's lunchbox.) (Menjívar 2002: 452–53)

Both in immigrant households and among the native born, a great deal of health care thus takes place within households. Even now, for example, the bulk of elder care still occurs in homes (Cancian and Oliker 2000: 65; Wolf 2004). Obviously, family caregiving extends to an even higher proportion of sick children (Lukemeyer, Meyers, and Smeeding 2000).

For a century or so, it is true, the growth of hospitals, clinics, and medical professions moved a significant share of health care from households to professional settings. Over recent decades, however, the development of health management organizations and the aging of the American population have combined to place an increasing burden of health care on households. In 2003, a clearinghouse for information about health care offered the following impressive observations:

- An estimated 22.4 million, or one out of four U.S. households engages in caring for a loved one age fifty or older.
- Between 5.8 million and 71 million family members, friends, and neighbors provide care to a person sixty-five or older who needs assistance with everyday activities.
- As many as 12.8 million Americans of all ages need assistance from others to carry out everyday activities.
- By the year 2007, the number of caregiving households in the United States for persons age fifty and above could reach 39 million.
- In California, 28 percent of residents 40 and older needed in-home care for themselves or a family member during 2002. Of those, more than half needed in-home help for more than six months.
- If the services provided by family, friends, and neighbors had to be replaced with paid services, it would cost an estimated $196 billion.[3]

Household health care is thus becoming one of America's most formidable economic activities. How does it work? In her landmark study of health care, Nona Glazer interviewed professional nurses, home health aides, nurse managers, and social service workers about what she calls "amateur" family caregiving for acutely ill patients. With American hospital policy encouraging early discharge of patients, family members, Glazer found, have taken on increasingly demanding caring tasks. She reports:

[3] Adapted from the "Family Caregiver Alliance Fact Sheets: Selected Long-Term Care Statistics," "Selected Caregiver Statistics," "Work and Eldercare." Family Caregiver Alliance, http://www.caregiver.org. Accessed May 24, 2003. See also Gray and Feinberg 2003.

> "Care" has come to encompass a new range of nursing-medical tasks. Family caregivers now monitor patients for a wide array of problems, everything from reactions to medicine to major crises. . . . The work that family caregivers learn may be fairly simple, such as supervising breathing exercises, or may be complex, such as keeping equipment from being a conduit for dangerous bacteria into the heart. (Glazer 1993: 193)

Nurses must therefore train unskilled family members and patients to follow technical, often delicate, and sometimes dangerous procedures. Even immigrant families with little knowledge of English learn to use medical techniques. Glazer cites a Vietnamese family, in which only the dying patient's husband knew English. Family members nevertheless managed to learn how to administer intravenous chemotherapy, give pain-control medication, and monitor the wife for any alarming symptoms. It took the husband, Glazer notes, ten visits to learn how to irrigate a Hickman catheter (for similar coping in lesbian/gay households, see Carrington 1999: 136–38).

To be sure, family caregiving does not always produce solidarity or result in competent attention. Family members often worry, for example, that dependent parents will outlive the resources available to pay for that care (see Abel 1990, 1991: 140–41). Glazer reports instances of antagonism, resistance, or sheer exhaustion from the stress involved in long-term demanding care work (Glazer 1993; see also Pyke 1999; Spragins 2002). Household health care taxes family resources.

Precisely because of the volume and difficulty of household health care, policy debates have intensified concerning the financial responsibilities of individuals, households, and government for the provision of care. At the same time, advice and advocacy have proliferated. At one extreme stands the idea that each individual should take care of himself or herself, at the other that the government should be providing for universal health care. In between, however, many combinations of proposed policy and advice appear.

Since 1990, in tune with an age of privatization, a number of programs have involved some form of publicly backed compensation for nonprofessional long-term provision of family care for the frail elderly and younger persons with disabilities. These so-called consumer-directed programs include caregiver "allowances" and attendant care payments. The first arrangement provides small stipends to family caregivers ($100 to $200 monthly stipends) to subsidize everyday purchases, such as continence pads or over-the-counter medications. The monies are not intended as payments for care work. In contrast, the second program pays wages to family members, treating the family caregiver-recipient relationship as that of employer-employee (Polivka 2001: 3–4).

As of 2001, the most extensive American programs of this kind operated in California. Clients, in this state's consumer-directed program were allowed to "hire and fire, schedule, train and supervise" their assistance providers, which could mean their spouses, parents, other family members, friends, or neighbors. A 1999 study of the California system, funded at UCLA by the U.S. Department of Health and Human Services, concluded that family members actually provided higher-quality service than unrelated workers. Specifically, the study found that clients employing family care workers "reported a greater sense of security, having more choice about how their aides performed various tasks, a stronger preference for directing their aides, and a closer rapport with their aides" (Doty et al. 1999: 5). Family care providers, the study noted, have a major advantage over nonfamily aides: they are legally allowed to perform paramedical or medically related tasks, such as bowel and bladder care and administering medicines.

In her study of San Francisco Bay Area Chinese immigrant families, Pei-Chia Lan (2002) describes how households negotiate their relations to the California plan. Immigrants who had elderly parents to care for in the Bay Area generally chose between two arrangements, both of which fulfilled their obligations of filial piety. Some lodged their parents in their own homes, sometimes hiring care workers who came in during the day when the younger couple were off at work. Others hired caregivers who helped the parents in separate dwellings. In either case, family members regularly arranged transfers of legally visible wealth away from parents so that the parents could qualify for U.S. governmental benefits. Between the generations, nevertheless, resources could flow in either direction, in the form of housing, food, money, and payments for household care work. In the latter case, lower-income households often relied on the California payment system, recruiting Taiwanese workers who took on the guise of fictive kin and frequently collaborated with the children in planning care. (In such circumstances, delicate negotiations took place over the responsibilities and moral performances of children and in-laws.) Although wealthy immigrants avoided state subsidies as a stigma, their lower-income counterparts treated the state payments as an entitlement, as a means of fulfilling filial obligations, and as a supplement to Social Security, Medicare, and other federal entitlements. (For details of how similar plans operate in Great Britain, see Ungerson 1997, 2000.)

Other experimental public programs have tried paying poor women for the care of their own sick or disabled children, thus, ironically, formalizing them as paid providers of care. Consider Tasha's case, as reported in a study of strategies used by welfare-reliant mothers caring for children with chronic health conditions or disabilities after the welfare reforms of the early 1990s. Tasha, a forty-five-year-old unmarried African-American living in Cleveland with her two children, had first dropped out of Ohio State University to care for her sick father. She then became primary caregiver for her daughter who had a severe seizure disorder. Pushed out of welfare, she managed to get hired by an agency that paid her a low hourly wage without medical benefits for thirty hours of weekly care work. The meager salary helped redefine Tasha's social standing:

> I feel good, good you know because like I said, I feel fortunate that I can still do things at home. I went to look at some living room furniture the other day and the guy said: "Are you employed?" And I said: "Yes, I'm employed." You know my social security number, you know, you check it out. So, that kinda thing, it makes you, it makes you feel good. . . . You know, you're in a different status [when] you're not considered unemployed. (London, Scott, and Hunter 2002: 109)

In this case, the entry of paid care into the household by no means undermined its moral economy; quite the contrary. (On paid kinship foster care for children, see Geen 2003.)

Nevertheless, as we might expect, such policies incite acute moral and political debates, often with hostile worlds warnings about the contamination and undermining of moral obligation (Olson 2003). The 1999 California report summarizes pros and cons of employing family caregivers. On the plus side, supporters argue that paying family members is sometimes preferable to involving strangers in what are often very intimate forms of assistance. This sort of payment, they contend, actually "reinforces natural caring relationships." On the minus side, critics worry that paying people "for meeting moral obligations within the family system" is both fiscally irresponsible and morally corrupting, escalating public expenses and at the same time "distorting family relationships." Equally alarming, critics contend, is the reverse contamination: "Emotional ties and complex family relationships can complicate and even undermine what should be a business-like service relationship. . . . Firing a family member (especially one who shares your household) in case of unsatisfactory job performance may be extremely difficult, if not impossible" (Doty et al. 1999: 11).

Note that opponents of state-paid family caregiving invoke the now-familiar dual ideas that the intrusion of the marketplace into the sacred space of the family inevitably brings corruption, while introducing sentiment into the workplace reduces efficiency. Even supporters remain wary. The 1999 report notes that California county case managers are trained to "identify and to subtract out the services (such as housekeeping and meal preparation) that family members living in the home who are not themselves disabled should be able and willing to provide without being paid" (39). By this policy, they thus displace but still protect the boundary between appropriately commercial and intrinsically noncommercial zones of care.

Despite these innovative government policies, the majority of household members remain responsible for unpaid provision of each other's health care. As a consequence, they regularly confront both routine and exceptional economic responsibilities. Recognizing such responsibilities, a number of advocacy organizations provide advice to family caregivers. For example, family consultants at the Family Caregiver Alliance urge adults who are deciding whether to move a dependent parent into their home to consider such issues as these:

- What will the financial arrangement be? Should I charge rent? Will I have expenses for her to cover?
- How will my siblings feel about the financial arrangement?
- Will my work situation have to change, and if so, how will I cover the bills?[4]

Here, as elsewhere, economic arrangements for the provision of care do not simply call up considerations of cost, convenience, and efficiency. They involve negotiation of the forms, representations, obligations, and rights attached to meaningful interpersonal ties.

CARING THAT CROSSES HOUSEHOLD BOUNDARIES

In the commercialized United States of the early twenty-first century, then, household members still remain the principal providers of care to other household members. No doubt that household concentration of caring services reinforces the supposition of a sharp division between the diffuse, sentimental, and noncommercial world of the family and the specialized, impersonal, and commercialized world of goods and services outside the family. We have already seen a major flaw in that division: the incessant buzz of economic production, consumption, distribution, and transfers of assets within households, not to mention in links between households and their kin elsewhere. But caring relations also regularly cross household

---

[4] "Changing Places: Should Your Parents Move in with You?" Family Caregiver Alliance, http://www.caregiver.org. Accessed May 24, 2003. See also advice to "kinship caregivers" by the Child Welfare League of America, http://www.cwla.org/programs/kinship/financial.htm. Accessed May 25, 2003. See also Copeland 1991; Fish and Kotzer 2002.

and kin boundaries, and just as regularly occasion the creation of differentiated ties involving well-defined economic transactions between providers and recipients of care. As Francesca Cancian has argued forcefully, the commercialization of caring services by no means blocks the provision of personalized, caring attention.[5]

In North America, some kinds of care provided within households by persons based outside date far back in history. Take the case of midwife and healer Martha Ballard. As professional caregiver, Ballard occupied a powerful position among the residents of eighteenth-century Hallowell, Maine. In Laurel Thatcher Ulrich's presentation of Ballard's diary we learn that within a twenty-one-day span in 1787, Ballard "performed four deliveries, answered one obstetrical false alarm, made sixteen medical calls, prepared three bodies for burial, dispensed pills to one neighbor, harvested and prepared herbs for another, and doctored her own husband's sore throat" (Ulrich 1991: 40). Thus, as Ulrich remarks, in modern terms Ballard "was simultaneously a midwife, nurse, physician, mortician, pharmacist, and attentive wife" (40).

As midwife, Ballard intervened repeatedly at crucial moments in household lives. In the 1790s, her typical fee of six shillings for managing a birth equaled her husband Ephraim Ballard's daily income in his professional activity as surveyor. It sometimes greatly exceeded it, when some affluent households doubled or quadrupled her standard pay. Ballard carefully recorded her various midwifery payments:

> Mr Lathrop paid me my fee for attending his wife the 19th of March last . . . received sugar Nov. 28

> Mr Parker gave me 18/ for attending his Lady in her illness with her Last Child . . . his Lady made me a present of 1½ yards ribbin

> Received a lb coffee, 1 yd ribbon, & a cap border as Extraordinary for waiting on her (197, 199)

---

[5] Cancian 2000; see also Crittenden 2001; England and Folbre 1999; Folbre and Nelson 2000; Geen 2003; Linsk et al. 1992; Macdonald and Merrill 2002; Rose 1994; Ungerson 2000; Uttal 2002a; Williams 2000.

As the standard six shilling–fee for childbirth suggests, Ballard generally gauged her fee by the task, not by the time and effort involved. For impoverished families, she reduced or eliminated fees. In one case she sent her husband Ephraim "to see that [Mrs. Welch] had wood, and made her a shovel" (198, 384). Ballard varied the required payment not only by the service and the social relationship but also in the actual form of compensation. She received three main forms of pay: cash, in kind, and store credit. (Sometimes, grateful neighbors also made her gifts in appreciation of her caring services). As Ulrich reports, Ballard received everything from "1m shingles" to "a pair flat irons." Most payments were in food, textiles, or household necessities: cheese, butter, wheat, rye, corn, baby pigs and turkeys, candles, a great wheel, unwashed wool, checked cloth, one-half quintal of cod, teapots, thimbles, a looking glass, handkerchiefs, and snuff (1991: 197). Merchants, however, were more likely to pay, often generously, with store credit. Martha Ballard's caring economy thus interwove subtly with the complex patterns of social relations in this eighteenth-century village.[6]

More than two centuries later, professional caregivers are usually more specialized than Martha Ballard. They range from physicians to morticians. One of the less rewarded professions is commercial home health aid. Studying how changes in Medicare and managed-care financing restructured home caring practices, Deborah Stone interviewed twenty-four caregivers, including nurses, physical therapists, occupational therapists, and home-care aides. She discovered a payment system that compensated caregivers exclusively for patients' bodily care, not for conversation or other forms of personal attention or assistance. She also discovered, however, that home-care workers did not transform themselves into unfeeling bureaucratic agents. They remained, Stone reports, "keenly aware that home health care is very intimate and very personal" (Stone 1999: 64).

---

[6] For the economy of seventeenth-century women healers, see Tannenbaum 2002; for nineteenth-century women caregivers, Abel 2000; for the overlap of healing and magic in English history, see Davis 2003.

Almost without exception, the care providers she interviewed reported visiting clients on their days off, often bringing some groceries, or helping out in other ways. The agency's warnings against becoming emotionally attached to their clients, aides and nurses told Stone, were unrealistic: "If you're human," or "if you have any human compassion, you just do" (66). To circumvent an inadequate payment system, home-care workers define their additional assistance as friendship or neighborliness. Furthermore, despite agencies' prohibitions against gift giving, caregivers and clients frequently exchange presents. Nurses, for example, Stone reports, "often bring flowers, home-baked food, or small items they know a client can use" (Stone 2000a: 109; see also Aronson and Neysmith 1996; Karner 1998: 79). Care workers also manipulate the rules by treating other than the officially approved problems and sometimes even attending to a patient's spouse's health. To be sure, as Stone remarks, inadequate payment structures exploit paid caregivers' concerns for patients. Her interviews conclusively demonstrate, however, that monetary payment systems do not obliterate caring relations. Instead, caregivers actually manipulate the payment system to make sure they can provide care appropriate to the relationship. Once again, we discover a correspondence of media, transactions, and meaningful social relations.

Similar processes occur in outsiders' care of a household's children. Historically, child-care workers have long been a part of American households as nurses, wet nurses, nannies, and governesses. During the later twentieth century, however, increasing employment of mothers away from home generated an urgent demand for paid child care. A great deal of that care now takes place outside of households, in day-care centers and schools. Still, a majority occurs within households (Center for the Childcare Workforce 2002: 6). Many of the in-household caregivers come from minority and immigrant populations. Some of the immigrants, furthermore, lack legal residence, which makes them vulnerable to exploitation.

Child care by outsiders within households poses a series of delicate relational problems. Workers are hired to care for children, but they get their employment, pay, and working conditions from parents. They thus have to satisfy two sets of often conflicting duties; pleasing the child may sometimes contradict parents' expectations. If, for instance, the caregiver forms strong bonds with a child, that can complicate relations with the child's parents. It often leads to competition between parents and caregivers for the child's affection and respect. What's more, although their caring labor is crucial to the family's welfare, the workers are typically underpaid and powerless.

In this context, child-care workers' economic transactions with their employers become delicate and often contentious. At issue is not only assessing hourly or weekly wages. Disagreements range over the household accommodations, the food provided, clothing standards, additional responsibilities such as cleaning and caring for pets, authority of the caregiver over the children's comportment, and time off from work. These matters go far beyond wages and hours; they symbolize the social standing of the caregiver within the household and the social relations between the caregiver and household members. Mary Romero explains from her own observations how this works:

> Before beginning a college teaching post in Texas, I stayed at the home of a colleague who employed a live-in domestic worker. Until then, I had been unaware of the practice of hiring teenage undocumented women as live-in household help. Nor had I had access to the social or "private" space of an employer. I was shocked at the way my colleague and his family treated the 16-year-old domestic whom I will call Juanita. Only recently hired, Juanita was still adjusting to her new environment; her shyness was reinforced by my colleague's constant flirting. I observed many encounters that served to remind Juanita of her subservient role. For example, one evening I walked into the kitchen as the employer's young sons were pointing to dirty dishes on the table and in the sink and yelling, "Wash! Clean!" Juanita stood frozen; she was angry and humiliated. (Romero 1996: 2; see also Romero 1992)

As a result of such complications, child-care relationships within households often end in bitterness on the part of employer and worker. To be sure, household child care divides into several rather different employment contracts; some of the more obvious are the live-in nanny, live-in nanny-housekeeper, the live-out nanny-housekeeper, babysitters, paid kin, plus friends and neighbors who provide child care under a variety of economic arrangements. In Los Angeles, Pierrette Hondagneu-Sotelo distinguishes three kinds of household employment among immigrant Latinas: live-in nanny-housekeepers, live-out nanny-housekeepers, and housecleaners. Her evidence concerning the first two groups comes from interviews of Latina workers and their employers conducted in the mid- to late 1990s, plus a survey questionnaire of the immigrant workers. Her findings show, counterintuitively, that living in provides less economic leverage to the workers than living elsewhere and coming in to provide child care. One might have thought that the accumulation of local knowledge and continuous presence in the household would build up a nanny's influence, but in fact it increased her vulnerability to exploitation and degradation.

Live-in nanny-housekeepers studied by Hondagneu-Sotelo worked an average of sixty-four hours a week, often earning less than the minimum hourly $5 wage. These payments, ordinarily in cash, were supplemented by lodging and meals. But the lodging was not always private; the caregivers often slept in the children's bedroom and were thus on call throughout the night. Food was an even more ambiguous benefit: workers often complained bitterly that employers either provided no adequate food for them, or begrudged them access to any available supplies. One nanny volunteered that a *señora* had not only complained when she took a bag of fruit but also tried to charge her for it (Hondagneu-Sotelo 2001: 252n). Many of the women ended up using their wages to buy their own food—which was sometimes eaten by their employer's family.

Clearly, the parties to such work contracts exert very unequal power. Employers of live-in nanny-housekeepers, according to Hondagneu-Sotelo, generally set wages by consulting with their own friends. Candace Ross, for instance, told her by what means she decided how much to pay her first live-in nanny-housekeeper: "I checked that [what neighbors were paying] out, and um, I found a real range. I found a range that went $125 a week on up to like

$200, so we started her at $150, which would have been, in my opinion, a very good deal" (82). In fact, high-paying parents reported
feeling pressure from their nanny-hiring neighbors to bring down
the wages they paid (84). At the same time that they relied on their
own networks to establish the "going rate," employers typically tried
to inhibit their nanny-housekeepers' consultation with their counterparts in other households. Indeed, Hondagneu-Sotelo found that
some employers forbade nannies' taking children to the park, for
fear that other nannies would tell them about better wages or work
opportunities.

Many immigrants who began as live-in nanny-housekeepers understandably moved out when they had a chance. Living out not
only gave the workers more control over their time and private lives,
but also brought them higher wages as well. In some cases, employers of live-out nannies also reimbursed them for out-of-pocket expenses. Twenty-four-year-old Ronalda Saavedra, for example, got
$50 per week for her gasoline expenses. Ronalda "spent a portion
of each afternoon driving on errands, such as going to the dry cleaners and ferrying the children [two six- and nine-year-old boys] home
from school and then to and from soccer practices, music lessons,
and so on" (38). For live-out nannies, feeding the children became a
more central activity. It sometimes involved their bringing in special
homemade treats, such as homemade flan or *pan con crema*. Not all
the nanny-housekeeper tasks, however, were so agreeable. Several of
Hondagneu-Sotelo's interviewees, for example, complained about
having to take care of the family's pets, including sick dogs, iguanas,
snakes, lizards, and various rodents.

The very unequal negotiations over the details of the nanny's job
recurrently led to what Hondagneu-Sotelo calls "blowups": "a
screaming match that terminates employment" (114). As might be
expected, however, some nannies and their employers develop more
reciprocal economic relations. In her interviews of upper-middle-
class parents and their children's caregivers in Los Angeles and New
York, Julia Wrigley heard from employers who provided a variety
of services to the workers. These included money loans, paying
medical and dental bills, taking workers to their own doctors, help-

ing them negotiate with landlords and creditors, or even getting a caregiver's relative out of jail. To be sure, some employers resented the additional economic burden. One Los Angeles mother complained about her Salvadoran caregiver: "She was only with us for four months, and in that four-month period she managed to borrow money to the amount of $600, and she had a color television that she took home so that her kids could use it" (Wrigley 1995: 90). Both Hondagneu-Sotelo and Wrigley, then, portray caring relations full of tension and negotiation over both their economic contents and their social meanings (see also Rollins 1985). The complexity of their relations increases because—as both Wrigley's respondents and a semifictional best-selling memoir by two former Manhattan nannies confirm—both caregivers and parents tend to avoid explicit discussions about the financial conditions of their contract (Wrigley 1995: 88; McLaughlin and Kraus 2002: 3).

Expert advice to parents hiring nannies confirms many of these observations. In their guide "to navigating the parent-caregiver relationship," psychoanalysts Joseph Cancelmo and Carol Bandini note the peculiar character of that relationship: "At one end of the continuum is the view that the caregiver is simply an employee. At the other end, she is viewed as a member of the family. Some days [people] feel one way, some days the other, with various gradations in between" (Cancelmo and Bandini 1999: 83).

Based on their interviews with mostly middle- and upper-middle class working professional parents and with in-home caregivers, who were primarily immigrant women, Cancelmo and Bandini note that even the employers' lexicons revealed the variety of relationships: "Is she the babysitter, someone sitting in, a day mother (as several mothers succinctly characterized the relationship), a nanny, a caregiver, a special friend?" (87). Caregivers and the children in their charge likewise differentiated among relationships. Sudha, who had cared for five-year-old Michael since birth noted: "That does not feel right inside of me [clasping her hand to her breast]. . . . In the beginning I was just a babysitter. Gradually, more than a babysitter I became. Like I was in the family and feeling close to Michael, and the new little boy. I love these kids so much" (91–92). Michael in turn called Sudha "Auntie" after hearing her own nieces and nephews using that term when they visited. Another seven-year-old boy, after hearing his parents' responses, offered his own critique of the term *caregiver*: "It doesn't make any sense to me. Who *is* she caring for, anyway—a "giver"? I like *babysitter*. It's like—she has really taken care of me since I was a baby—she is my babysitter, you know what I mean?" (93).

Payment systems, Cancelmo and Bandini found, likewise reflected the multiple relationships. Along with the "official" wages, for instance, they found an "unofficial" salary that sustained kin-like ties:

> Caregivers were given tickets to ballgames, new and nearly new clothing, museum memberships, and special trips and meals out with the family. Some families handed down outdated but usable computer equipment to their own children and to the children of the caregiver. Lawyers did free legal work for the caregiver and her family, doctors provided referrals to specialists, just as they would do for their own family. . . . Many parents would also provide money, ostensibly loans for things a caregiver might need but could never afford on her salary. This included airfare to visit a dying mother or father in another country, and help in paying for funeral costs. (102)

Even the availability and supervision of petty cash served to differentiate employer-caregiver relationships:

> Some [parents] . . . wanted exact documentation of all expenses. Several nannies and au pairs described it this way: "Like it's my allowance or something." Other parents were more flexible, providing a well-stocked jar with sufficient money for emergencies, without rigid rules for documentation or use. . . . But for some, there was . . . a depriving quality. . . . When expenses were incurred during the caregiver's daily management of the household, she was expected to submit receipts for reimbursement, as if in a business setting (104).

Children also created their own monetary markers. As one eight-year-old boy promised his caregiver who had been with him since infancy, "I'm going to be a baseball star for the Yankees. I'm going to make a lot of money and I'm going to give you a million dollars" (104).[7] In short, nannies, their employers, and children negotiate definitions of who they are, how they are related to each other, what sorts of economic transactions are proper for their relationship, and in what media those transactions should occur. Similar negotiations with different outcomes occur in a variety of other transecting relations: babysitters, paid and unpaid kin care, exchanges of child care among single mothers, and even the establishment of child-care services in local currency communities.[8]

Immigrant nannies themselves establish distinct personal and economic relations with family members or paid help who care for their own children. In these cases, the immigrant nannies regularly provide money and gifts to their children's caretakers.[9] When caregiving crosses household boundaries, it makes more salient and delicate the sort of mutual defining that occurs wherever intimacy, care, and economic activity intersect.

CARE OUTSIDE OF HOUSEHOLDS

When it comes to care outside of households, you might expect it to be steely, brisk, and efficient, thus a contradiction in terms. After

---

[7] On children's perceptions of how their parents negotiate with child-care providers, see Hochschild 2001.

[8] See Chaudry 2004; Formanek-Brunell 1998; Guzman 2004; Nelson 2002; Neus 1990; Sadvié and Cohen-Mitchell 1997: 5; Uttal 2002b; Zelizer 2004. For historical parallels, see Katzman 1978; Michel 1999; Palmer 1989; Rose 1999. "Local currency communities," such as Ithaca, New York's Ithaca HOURS, create a distinct currency for exchanges of goods and services among local residents; see, e.g., Raddon 2002.

[9] See Hochschild 2002; Hondagneu-Sotelo and Avila 2002; Romero 2001; Parreñas 2001: 112–13; Wrigley 1995: 152–53n.15.

all, care in this setting becomes formalized and commercialized. Providers themselves are often low-income workers who depend on caregiving wages for their own survival. These features call up images of baby farms and exploitative nursing homes. Available evidence, however, contradicts any such picture. To be sure, care outside households differs from the care we have observed within homes. Generally speaking, for instance, the relationship between the service provider and care recipient is more contingent on changes in the life circumstances of the parties; relations with grandparents rarely break off in an instant, but parents often yank their children from preschools abruptly. Nevertheless, people caring outside of households do establish warm personal ties, often involving extensive intimacy. The sites for nonhousehold caregiving vary from psychiatrists' offices to nursing homes to day-care centers, and each of the caring relationships establishes its own distinctive mix of economic media, transactions, and relations. Consider the diverse circumstances of family child-care providers, nurses, physicians, and hotel service workers.

Family day-care providers turn their homes into commercial work settings, attending unrelated children for a fee. An authoritative analysis of paid child-care workers in the United States during 2002 identified a total of 2.3 million individuals, distributed thus:

- 550,000 in center-based settings
- 650,000 providing family child care
- 804,000 paid relatives
- 298,000 other paid nonrelatives, for example, nannies

According to this estimate in 2002, 76 percent—1.75 million—of the people providing paid care to U.S. children ut to age five were working for their pay within households. But 24 percent—550,000—were doing their work in private and public child-care centers, Head Start programs, prekindergarten programs, and similar settings (Center for the Childcare Workforce 2002: 6).

Commercializing domestic child care raises standard hostile world concerns: will the payment downgrade the caring? Will the household setting undermine the caregiver's efficiency? What's more, paid family child-care providers confront three intersecting and often conflicting sets of demands: one, in their relation to the child; another, in their relation to the parent, and a third, in their involvement in generating income for their own families. Mary Tuominen's interviews with eighteen family child-care workers of diverse racial and ethnic backgrounds suggest how providers manage these multiple demands. They do so not by becoming unfeeling custodians, nor by denying that they are involved in a commercial enterprise. Instead, Tuominen shows how care workers negotiate distinctive sets of relationships, transactions, and media, without excluding intensive attachments to the children.

Repeatedly, the women told Tuominen of their close, affectionate relationship to the children they were paid to care for. Their relationship to parents was more ambivalent. On the one hand, the workers complained about parents exploiting their services by arriving late to pick up their children without paying overtime for the extra hours of work. On the other, they often adjusted their fees to accommodate a parent's financial situation. For instance, Anne Burns, herself subsisting below the poverty level, explained why, in the case of one boy, she had reduced by half her monthly rate from $300 to $150 without cutting down the hours of care: "His mom is trying to move. And she's trying to sell all the furniture and trying to get all the bills paid before she leaves, so . . ." Annie McManus reported similar considerations in setting her rates: "It was negotiated. . . . It fluctuated. Especially with the two single moms—depending on what was happening with them financially" (Tuominen 2000: 122).

Echoing Deborah Stone's findings concerning home-care workers, these women also reported going beyond strict contractual agreements, for instance, by picking up a child at the child's home when the mother was unable to drive, even if it caused the caregiver significant inconvenience. Tuominen's findings fully confirm Margaret Nelson's study of Vermont family day-care providers. Nelson's survey of 345 care workers plus 70 close interviews show her respondents conducting carefully run businesses: they set hourly or weekly rates, negotiate fee increases with their clients, specify the range of their services (for example, what sort of food they will provide for the child), and offer formal discounts for a second child in the family or when they take in a relative's child.

For all their commercial arrangements, Nelson still found providers troubled by the combination of monetary payment and loving care. As one woman put it, "It's so hard because you're dealing with their *child*. I mean you're supposed to have unconditional love with their child. Yet that's the hard part, you're getting money for that kind of love. How can you put a price on that?" (Nelson 1990: 61). Setting prices for their labor, however, was not the chief source of the care providers' conflicts. Instead, the women were especially upset at parents' disregard or disrespect for their underpaid efforts. One respondent complained about a mother who "would keep track of how much, you know, and pay me just so much, and that hurt me because I thought, here I am giving so much. How can she be so cheap with me?" (61). More generally, Nelson listened to providers' anger when parents "forget to pay on time, . . . haggle over every nickel and dime, . . . make a fuss about a slight increase in rates, and . . . assume that 'overtime' is free" (55). Parents' picking up children late often caused trouble. In all sorts of social relations, who makes the other person wait signals inequalities in the relationship, and thus becomes a matter of negotiation and resentment. Parents who arrive late for their children's return home, without paying extra, cause the triple harms of signaling their disregard for the care worker, keeping the care worker from other tasks, and costing the care worker money.

Care workers therefore appreciated any evidence of parents' recognition of their labor, including personal gifts. One explained, "[Jennifer's] mother is so good to me. . . . On the year anniversary of her being here I got this beautiful bouquet of flowers . . . and it had a real nice card. 'Thank you for all the love and care you've given me. To my second mom.' . . . When I feel [parents] appreciate me, that makes a big difference" (64). However, thanks alone did not keep their businesses going. Child-care workers had to manage their finances, charging enough to keep their own households afloat. Thus they constantly balanced among competing claims on their energies (see also Enarson 1990).

NURSING CARE

Surprisingly, for all the differences between themselves and other types of care providers, hospital nurses reveal many of the same tensions in their caring work. Nurses differ from the majority of care workers in belonging to a profession: with government backing, nurses exercise at least a modicum of collective control over recruitment, training, licensing, rights, duties, and compensation within their areas of competence. Like their fellow health professionals—pharmacists, psychologists, and physicians—they collectively guard the boundaries between their specialty and adjacent caregiving fields.[10]

Nurses divide into a variety of ranks and specialties: administrators, practical nurses, aides, nursing students, members of surgical teams, and more. The mainstay registered nurses qualify for their jobs through substantial college educations. Compared with other care workers (excluding physicians, of course), RNs receive relatively good pay. Indeed, in the contemporary United States intense competition for their services often includes a signing bonus. Nurses' technical and emotional caring services are multiple: they range from storage and administration of medicines to monitoring of life-sustaining machines, checking of vital signs, provision of bodily care, answering questions from patients and their families, advising and psychological counseling, and administering hospital wards from day to day—and night to night. As Daniel Chambliss found in his extensive field research within medical institutions, such multitasking requires efficient organization:

> The staff nurse dispenses hundreds of pills a day to dozens of patients, starts and maintains intravenous lines, gives bed baths, documents on paper virtually everything she does, monitors temperatures, blood pressures, and urine "outputs," delivers food trays, and responds more or less to all the miscellaneous patient and family requests. . . . Simply getting through an

[10] Abbott 1988; Cancian 2000: 146–48; Glenn 1992; Reverby 1987; Stevens 1989; Weinberg 2003.

eight-hour shift without mistakenly giving Mrs. Jones the pills for Ms. Smith, or forgetting to check Mr. Martin's IV line, or not helping Miss Garcia eat her lunch is challenge enough. And these are the everyday, non-emergency tasks. (Chambliss 1996: 34–35)

As distinguished from physicians, most nurses spend a great deal of their time providing bodily and emotional care. In that regard, they resemble many other caregivers, for example those we have already encountered within households. As Chambliss notes, "Close patient contact, with all five senses, is nursing's specialty. . . . Nurses are constantly talking with, listening to, and touching their patients in intimate ways; the prototypical, universal dirty work of nursing is 'wiping bottoms' " (64). Physicians do, of course, as Chambliss mentions, "perform major procedures (inserting tubes into the chest for bronchoscopies): but most of what is said and physically done to patients is said and done by bedside nurses" (64).

As in other varieties of paid care, nurses often find themselves pulled in three directions: toward their formal professional responsibilities, toward their personal advantage, and toward concern for their patients' welfare. Forty-year-old Karen Mitchell, a nurse at Mercy Hospital in suburban Minneapolis, specializes in tending patients who fall somewhere between intensive care and general medicine. According to a *New York Times* reporter, for Mitchell,

> the concerns of making money and the concerns of healing have never been easy companions. . . . Which is why Mitchell sometimes takes it upon herself to sacrifice one for the other. It's her small act of rebellion, a quiet vote cast for the future. Every once in a while, when Mitchell encounters a patient like Mr. Beaudry—a strong soul having a moment of true vulnerability—she will unclip the hospital phone from her hip and pull out its batteries. And then closing the door, she sits down beside her patient, just to be near. (Corbett 2003)

Nurses occupy conflicting positions. On one side, their daily attentions sustain lives and produce much of the healing that actually occurs in medical care. On the other, they lack the physician's authority to prescribe drugs, make significant changes in treatment, call for tests, transfer patients, and to make diagnoses, but still often take the blame when things go wrong. From the perspective of supervising physicians, nurses succeed when they perform their technical duties well, enforce the treatment regime, keep records adequately, respond effectively to life-threatening emergencies, and keep patients from complaining. But to accomplish these objectives, nurses establish close relations with their charges. Not only do they provide intimate bodily and emotional attention, but also they deploy the skilled practices of personal intimacy—joking, cajoling, consoling, and sympathetic listening. Yet they bear greater organizational responsibility for their patients' welfare than do the nurse's aides, attendants, food servers, and cleaners who also sometimes establish personal relations with patients. It is a taxing job, as conversations in the nurses' lounge always reveal.

PHYSICIANS AS CAREGIVERS

Patients rapidly detect the difference in the caring relations that connect them to nurses and to physicians. Nurses serving in American health care no longer usually wear the starched white uniforms, caps, and badges that once distinguished them. But they typically introduce themselves by their first (not their last) names and wear inconspicuously serviceable clothing. Physicians, in contrast, typically wear white coats or scrub suits, carry stethoscopes, and insist on being called "Doctor." (High-ranking nurses, it is true, sometimes blur the line by wearing white coats and carrying stethoscopes.) Dress and demeanor signal differences in what patients can expect from nurses and physicians.

As Danielle Ofri's vivid sketches of her experiences on the way from medical student to staff physician at New York's Bellevue Hospital indicate, junior physicians share many of nurses' responsibilities: taking vital signs, inserting intravenous taps, calming agitated patients, and more. One major difference, however, is precisely the physician's public responsibility for decisions concerning diagnosis, treatment, medication, tests, and patient management. "Contrary to the stereotype," comments Ofri,

> doctors do not lack for emotions. The medical student is too embarrassed to ask a patient to undress for a physical exam. The intern is sweating and cursing because the IV won't go in on the seventh try and she hasn't seen sunshine in three days. The resident is angry at the cocaine addict whose refusal of a CT scan will make him stay late again and miss, once again, putting his kids to bed. The attending [physician] is nervous on rounds because he's a bit "rusty" with his inpatient skills and the residents might get wind of his ignorance. (Ofri 2003: 238)

In some sense, physicians bear the stress of combining caring with responsibility for the outcome. The combination, Ofri points out, can create surprisingly powerful connections between doctor and patient:

> A unique bond is created, I learned, after you accompany someone through a lifesaving experience. Just by being near him and touching him during that near-death episode, I felt like I'd been privy to a singular intimacy. Mr. Wiszhinsky couldn't just recede into the multitudes of old men in the hospital, and I couldn't be just another medical student in the team. Not after we'd been so close to death together. (11)

Life-and-death responsibility weighs heavily on physicians, both in the midst of their training and later.

In addition to tending lives, however, physicians must also cope with complex changing organizational and financial environments. Within the health-care professions, physicians have long occupied the highest ranks. As compared with nurses and other health-care professionals, they have generally enjoyed greater discretion, higher compensation, and larger influence over the work of their fellow caregivers. Nevertheless, they share the problems of other paid caregivers outside of households in two crucial regards. First, massive changes in the financing and regulation of paid care in the

United States have deeply altered relationships among physicians, patients, and third parties. Second, like other health-care workers, physicians engage in delicate negotiations to match their provision of life-sustaining services, their compensation for those services, and the meaning of the physician-patient relationship: clearly intimate in some regards, but sharply bounded by technical, moral, ethical, and economic limits. Drawing distinctions between strictly business attention and personal concern therefore causes physicians great trouble. Like other caregivers, physicians face a dilemma. They consider themselves professionals, working above and beyond commercial considerations, and yet they draw their income from treating the sick.

Exactly how the dilemma operates, however, changes as the organization of health-care changes. David Rothman's historical account of physicians' compensation during the twentieth century reveals major shifts in the connection between medical services and payment (Rothman 2002; see also Starr 1982; Tomes 2003; Walsh 1977). Until recently, American physicians set their own fees, which often varied by the patient's ability to pay. Such discretion came at a cost, precisely because doctors collected directly from patients who often felt free to delay their payment (what physicians called "slow pay") or not pay at all. Indeed, in the 1920s and '30s, physicians (and their wives) forced to keep up respectable appearances, pay for their offices, and meet other expenses, repeatedly protested against a double standard. The public expected them to rise above monetary concerns, yet at the same time demanded they pay their own bills on time.

As Rothman reports, "Doctors were required to pay the baker, butcher, and candlestick maker immediately, but they, in turn, had to suffer slow pay." He quotes a physician's wife's complaint in a 1932 *Harper's Magazine* article: "I had to put the grocer off. What I meant but did not say, was that if any of several patients who owed my husband goodsized and overdue bills would only pay him we would pay our own bills with joy" (113). Yet if they complained too loudly about missed fees, physicians were accused of greed and avarice. In fact, during this time some physicians supplemented their comfortable but not spectacular middle-class incomes with more dubious strategies, such as kickbacks from referrals, selling drugs or eyeglasses to their patients, or owning their own hospitals where they sent their patients. Nevertheless, the profession as a whole distanced itself from money-grubbing practices. It promoted the image of the genial, patient, caring family doctor that graced magazine covers of the time.

After 1966, the commercial reorganization of health care boosted American physicians' income spectacularly, while at the same time transforming the physician-patient relationship. Three key changes made the difference: Medicare, new forms of billing, and benefits from pharmaceutical companies. Under Medicare, physicians' fees were not set by the government but by professional definitions of a customary and reasonable rate. As Rothman points out, that doctrine was "a give-away, an open invitation to doctors to bill at the highest possible level (for example, using the best-paid physicians in the community as the standard)" (115).

Physicians' income also rose as a result of the development of new surgical procedures for which physicians billed item by item rather than according to time spent. Rothman explains:

> If psychiatrists, pediatricians or internists had to set their fees with an eye to the clock—for example so much for 50 minutes—surgeons (or dermatologists or gastro-enterologists) could ignore the clock and bill for the procedure: a transplant (50 minutes but $15,000) or a wart removal (one minute $300) or a colonoscopy (10 minutes and $500). (116)

Finally, although less significantly, drug companies began providing physicians with in-kind benefits, such as dinners, free travel, vacations, and occasionally, honoraria for lectures.

Since the 1980s through the 1990s, increased surveillance by health maintenance organizations (HMOs), insurance companies, and hospital administrators further transformed physician-patient relations. Physicians confronted patients who themselves had little choice but to shop on the basis of price and service, an unprecedented shift in American medicine. Rothman reports physicians' complaints that patients "unceremoniously drop them as soon as their companies change plans, refusing to pay a full fee when they could pay a $10 co-pay fee" (119). More important for our purposes, the changed commercial aspects affect the actual quality and scope of treatment:

> The HMOs did something else as well: they subverted the trust between doctor and patient. Consumers, alert to all these changes and understanding the general rules of the managed care game—if not knowing the exact details of the contract with the physician sitting across from him—worried, appropriately, whether the physician was withholding treatment or a referral because his concern with own income was trumping his concern for his patient's welfare. (118)

On their side, physicians also sought to escape the limits set by bureaucratic control of health care. (Another escape from HMOs and insurance, but not bureaucracy, consisted of becoming a full-time doctor on a company staff, treating solely the company's employees; see Draper 2003). Most dramatically, during the late 1990s, physicians in the Pacific Northwest started organizing high-end medical practices; those practices soon drew the labels "boutique," "concierge," or "retainer" medicine. Patients paid a substantial entry fee (ranging from $1,500 for an individual to $20,000 for a family) in return for guaranteed rapid access to their physicians, longer office visits, and personalized care. The system offered doctors opportunities to withdraw from insurance plans, governmental fee-setting, and extensive paperwork while gaining access to a privileged clientele.

Critics, however, complained that boutique medicine compromised a crucial principle: provision of the same quality of medical service to every patient regardless of income or social standing. Although the American Medical Association Council on Medical and Judicial Affairs replied that this new sort of patient-physician contract might actually help patients "establish trust in a physician," clearly the new move separated well-heeled patients from other recipients of health care (quoted at Medical Rants 2003).

A closely related trend produced "boutique" hospitals, luxury settings in which patients can opt out of regular hospitals and receive extravagantly personalized care. In these for-profit hospitals, that typically specialize in high-revenue procedures, such as heart care, patients' perks include gourmet meals, spacious suites, and daily massage. At the Rancho Mirage, California Heart Hospital, for instance, "a gourmet chef visits patients individually to learn meal preferences. The staff aims to create a hotel or resortlike décor with [guest suites] painted in teal and fuchsia." (Stringer 2001: 3–4; see also Japenga 2000)

Boutique hospitals and medical practices highlight a significant pattern: caring labor generally increases in value to the extent that givers of care adapt its delivery to the recipient's identity and circumstances—when they recognize the recipient as a distinctive individual, take account of other persons in the recipient's life, and modulate the treatment according to the recipient's tastes or fears. That is true both of use value (the extent to which the effort actually enhances the recipient's welfare) and of commercial value (the price commanded by the service on the current market). On the whole, caring gains value through personalization.

To see the point even more clearly, we can draw an analogy to the world of health care from the world of luxury hotels. Anyone who has ever smiled at being recognized by a headwaiter will instantly understand why luxury hotels make great efforts to individualize their service and give signs of acknowledging their clients as distinct personalities. Indeed, in her study of luxury hotels, Rachel Sherman shows that "caring labor is one of the central features of hotel service" (Sherman 2002: 2). Here hotel workers' caregiving consists of personalized attention. She offers three striking examples of personalization:

- A housekeeper's noticing that a guest ate a peanut butter cookie provided for him in the evening, but left the chocolate chip one untouched; the next night she left him two peanut butter cookies.

- A housekeeper known for going through guests' garbage to see what kind of candy they ate and what magazines they read, in order to enter their preferences into the guest's database record.
- The staff had remembered not only [a traveler's] name and her husband's, but also the name of her two dogs. (5–6)

Sherman documents the luxury version of a very general phenomena. As our examination of child care shows clearly, however, personalization of intimacy also exists when prices run low. To be sure, many critics have thought that any commercialization of care eliminates the individual attention, the flexibility, the very intimacy of caring relations. Furthermore, ethical codes governing relations between clients and physicians, psychotherapists, clergy, lawyers, nannies, personal trainers, celebrity assistants, and others who professionally provide personalized care struggle to shield the provision of effective, personalized care from the dangers of excessive intimacy.[11] Yet our survey shows that even in settings of intense commercialization, the characteristic synthesis of localized media, particularized transactions, and meaningful relations continues to thrive.

When Caring Goes to Court

Sometimes, however, the provision of care—or its failure—becomes a matter of legal contention. When vital services, strong personal ties, rights, obligations, and financial stakes coincide, intense disputes concerning who owes what to whom often break out. Such disputes can easily go to court. If personal care forms the pivot of the questioned relationship, legal conflicts can easily become both tangled and fiery. They include such esoteric questions as the misuse

[11] See American Bar Association 2003; American Psychological Association 2003; Missouri Synod 1999; NALS of Missouri 2003; National Register of Personal Trainers 2003; New York Celebrity Assistants 2003; Reid 1999; Seattle Nanny Network 2003.

of confidential information by personal assistants or personal trainers, embezzlement or blackmail by private secretaries, or medical
malpractice. However, they also arise over the very same kinds of
everyday relations we have been reviewing: over compensation for
unpaid or underpaid personal or medical care; over expenditures for
child care as tax-deductible business expenses, over alimony, and
much more. The disputes become all the more intense because the
division of labor with respect to caring so regularly falls along the
lines of age, gender, race, ethnicity, and class. The outcomes of such
disputes have weighty economic and personal consequences for
those involved.

From the wide array of relevant disputes, let us select just a few
that exemplify legal conflicts arising from the mingling of economic
transactions and intimate personal care: disputes concerning a domestic worker's unpaid wages, the taxability of personal care, inheritance claims over care, legitimate compensation for family care, and
compensation for loss of care in accident cases.

When relations between unpaid or poorly paid live-in caregivers
and their employers go sour, for example, what had been private
blowups within the household sometimes become matters of bitter
contention in open court. The 1980 District of Columbia U.S. District Court case of Gabina Camacho Lopez illustrates the point dramatically (*Lopez v. Rodriguez*; 500 F. Supp. 79 (D.D.C. 1980)). Born
of a Bolivian Indian family around 1957, Gabina Lopez went to
school for five years but by the age of twelve was working full time
as a maid. In January 1976, she took a job with Felipe and Esther
Rodriguez in Cochabamba, Bolivia. In the Rodriguezes' house,
Gabina not only did housework but also took care of three Rodriguez grandchildren who were living in Cochabamba while their parents, Manuel and Mirtha, the Rodriguezes' son and daughter-in-
law, were working in the Washington, DC, area.

Later that year, Mirtha Rodriguez visited Bolivia. After consulting
with Gabina and her relatives, she recruited nineteen-year-old Gabina as her housekeeper and nanny, thus making it possible for the
Rodriguezes to take their three children back with them. In this
process, Gabina, an illegal immigrant to the United States, found

herself sequestered by the Rodriguezes' practices and her slight knowledge of English. For almost three years, Gabina cooked, cleaned, and took care of the Rodriguezes' children: "She worked seven (7) days per week, ten (10) to twelve (12) hours per day, without vacation or time off except occasional shopping trips or social visits with either or both of the [Rodriguezes] and usually with their children" (81).

During those years, Gabina never left the Rodriguez home alone. As compensation, the Rodriguezes provided her with room and board, "miscellaneous clothing and toiletries, medical expenses and minimal pocket money" (81). They told Gabina they were depositing her wages in the bank. In 1979, after the Rodriguezes refused Gabina's demands to obtain her money, while also preventing her from making friends or attending church, Gabina sued them under the Fair Labor Standards Act, claiming her unpaid wages.

Obviously, the Lopez case raised questions of justice and exploitation. But the court case pivoted on whether Gabina qualified as an employee under the Fair Labor Standards Act. The Rodriguezes denied she was their employee, but Lopez's attorneys insisted that she was precisely an underpaid, exploited employee. Indeed, they pointed out, the Rodriguezes had claimed a child-care credit of $900 on their 1976 income tax return for Gabina's household services. Gabina's lawyers claimed not only that the couple had violated the law by paying less than the minimum wage but also that they had illegally made Lopez work overtime and withheld the bulk of her wages to boot.

The court thus had to decide whether to treat Gabina Lopez's relationship to the Rodriguezes as a regular employment contract subject to the law governing all such contracts. Despite rebuffing the claims for overtime wages, the District Court ruled resoundingly in favor of Lopez. The Rodriguezes, the court declared, "failed to demonstrate a good faith effort to comply with the Fair Labor Standards Act. They exploited for their own purposes a young, poorly educated, native alien who was completely at their whim and mercy" (81). The various courts involved eventually awarded Gabina her minimum wage of $28,000 and an equal amount in damages plus court costs, less the amount that the Rodriguezes had actually spent on board and lodging. Hondagneu-Sotelo (2001) describes the settlement as: "perhaps the highest such court award to any live-in housekeeper in the United States" (237).

As our earlier review of practices indicates, young Latin American women often migrate illegally to work as nannies, housekeepers, cooks, or maids for prosperous families. Occasionally they hit the headlines, as in 2001 when President-elect George W. Bush withdrew the nomination of Linda Chavez as secretary of labor on the public outcry over Chavez's lodging of Marta Mercado, an illegal Guatemalan immigrant as a "house guest." Only incidentally, according to Chavez, did Mercado do laundry, perform housework, take care of children, and receive spending money (*New York Times* 2001). Most such relationships never surface. But now and then, as in the Gabina Lopez case, they become the subject of weighty legal proceedings (see Banks 1999; Lobel 2001; Hondagneu-Sotelo 2001: chap. 8).

Note two features of the legal dispute. First, no one denied that Lopez had actually provided care to the Rodriguezes and their children, or even that she received little monetary compensation for that care. The question was *in what relation to the Rodriguez family* she provided that care. Second, the court made an essentially dichotomous choice: either Gabina Lopez was a valued household member performing her duties free of charge and receiving the usual consideration and support due a family member or she was an employee in the commercial service sector and therefore subject to the laws governing wages and employer-worker relations. The courts accepted Lopez's lawyers' arguments that her relationship to the Rodriguezes fell into the second category. She and they collected.

QUALITIES AND CONDITIONS OF CARE
BEFORE THE COURTS

When confronted with disputes concerning the intersection of caring work and commercial transactions, American courts regularly adopt the three-part procedure we have seen operating in the court-room struggle between Gabina Lopez and the Rodriguez family. First, they locate the contested relationship within a larger grid of possible relationships. Second, within that grid they mark the line separating gratuitous provision of care from commercial provision—almost regardless of the care's content or effectiveness. Third, they search for appropriate matches among media, relations, and caring work. Finally, courts draw conclusions concerning both (a) the propriety of the caring work supplied, and (b) who owes what to whom as a consequence.

Legal disputes over caring characteristically erupt in four rather different situations: wrong care, exploitative care, missing care, and thankless care.

1. In cases of *wrong care*, at least one party claims that another party gave care that was inappropriate for the relationship. For example, authorities prosecute a herbalist who sells cures for practicing medicine without a license.

2. In cases of *exploitative care*, someone claims that someone else derived unfair economic advantages from his or her provision of care. For example, a priest offers counseling to a parishioner who disinherits his children and leaves all his money to the priest's church.

3. In cases of *missing care* someone fails to provide care that a recipient had a right to receive. For example, an accident at work caused by employer's negligence keeps the employee from supplying companionship and personal care to the employee's spouse.

4. In cases of *thankless care*, someone provides extensive care but then receives little or no economic reward despite previous promises to the contrary. For example, Gabina Lopez received little more than room and board for three years of housework and child care.

None of these four types of care are legal categories. They are typical complaints that people make, which legal practitioners then translate into their own idiom. In all four situations, what commonly happens is that someone who has no special knowledge of the law comes to a court, judge, or lawyer with a complaint about the economic treatment that he, she, or someone else has received. Legal specialists then translate the complaint into categories afforded by existing legal doctrines. How is that translation accomplished? In general, the doctrines depend partly on the definition of the personal relationship among the parties, on the economic transaction among the parties, on the nature of the care given and the services rendered, and on the classic distinction between gratuitous and commercial care.

Courts typically treat gratuitous care as its own reward, or at least as part of a reward system (for example, that of neighbors) in which the law should not be intervening. Commercial care, in contrast, calls up the market and therefore questions of fair or at least reasonable compensation. Courts often overlay this distinction between gratuitous and commercial care with other dichotomies. The familiar separate spheres division between the worlds of sentiment and of rationality certainly operates in many such disputes. But courts often draw on two other specifically legal distinctions: between confidential and nonconfidential relationships, and between professional and nonprofessional relationships. *Black's Law Dictionary* (1999) defines confidential, or fiduciary, relationships thus:

> A relationship in which one person is under a duty to act for the benefit of the other on matters within the scope of the relationship. Fiduciary relationships—such as trustee-beneficiary, guardian-ward, agent-principal, and attorney-client—require the highest duty of care. Fiduciary relationships usually arise in one of four situations: (1) when one person places trust in the faithful integrity of another, who as a result gains superiority or influence over the first, (2) when one person assumes control and responsibility over another, (3) when one person has a duty to act for or give advice to another on matters falling within the scope of the relationship, or (4) when there is a specific relationship that has traditionally been recognized as involving fiduciary duties, as with a lawyer and a client or a stockbroker and a customer. (640)

Nonconfidential relations, then, include all others. These days, ironically, in this dichotomy even husband-wife relationships typically qualify as nonconfidential. As we have seen repeatedly, courts also distinguish between the obligations and rights of licensed professionals, such as doctors, lawyers, and psychotherapists, and nonprofessionals who sometimes provide very similar services but without a license. In each case, classifying the caring relationship on the confidential or professional side of the boundary places the parties on the site of especially binding rights, privileges, and obligations. The placement thus identifies the portion of the law that will govern the justice of the economic transactions under contestation.

In all these regards, nevertheless, courts frequently reshape the distinctions so that they produce what legal specialists regard as justice. Sometimes these legal distinctions produce ironic consequences. Byrnece Green, a stockbroker, learned about these consequences the hard way (*Green v. Comm'r* 54 T.C.M. (CCH) 764 (1987)). For nine years, she and Maxwell Richmond had lived as husband and wife, following an earlier ten-month engagement, from which Richmond had "begged to be released . . . explaining that he had a 'mental problem about marriage,' " but assuring her that he would provide for her after his death. Green had relented and "made his life as comfortable as possible," watching his diet, taking care of him when he was ill, and advising him on business affairs (*3). But when Richmond died in 1971, his will left his estimated $7 million estate to his brother and sister. Green sued the estate for the value of her services to Richmond. A jury awarded her over a million dollars. They endorsed her claim of *thankless care*. The Supreme Judicial Court of Massachusetts turned down an appeal from the estate, but reduced her compensation to $900,000, payable during 1977 and 1978.

The trouble started because Green did not include these payments in her income tax returns, contending that the payments were gifts in return for her "wifely services," and therefore not taxable. But the Internal Revenue Service challenged her claims precisely on the grounds that the settlement payment had been allowed as restitution for her earned but unpaid compensation for services.

Green was ordered to pay income tax. If Richmond and Green had actually married, Green would unquestionably have had a right to her share of the estate, rather than a claim for unpaid compensation. Thus, apparently subtle legal distinctions have weighty economic consequences.

To observe this complex legal process in action we return to the class of legal disputes with which this chapter began: claims of undue influence. Such claims most often arise in disputes over bequests and inheritance. The question in general is whether someone who receives advantages from an inheritance earlier unfairly influenced the testator's judgment by means of coercion or care. Courts become particularly wary when the recipient of benefits has a confidential relationship to the donor. Did a psychotherapist improperly suggest that his patient donate to his clinic? Did a lawyer extract the client's investment in a business the lawyer controlled? Did a nurse who took care of a dying patient prejudice the patient against his children?

The undue influence doctrine is, however, a slippery legal instrument rather than a simple cookie cutter. It involves courts and lawyers in fine distinctions and difficult moral judgments. It requires, for example, judgments of when care that would be obligatory or at least acceptable for the relationship in question becomes excessive. It looks suspiciously at care given in confidential relationships, despite the presumption that the more powerful persons in such relationships will, indeed, provide professional care to the less powerful. It generally exempts spouses from that suspicion, but not members of cohabiting couples, whether heterosexual or homosexual.[12] To be sure, just such suspicions often arise when an old person marries a young one. The undue influence doctrine requires judgments of whether care given by close kin to the old or ill involved a deliberate effort to discredit the claims of other close kin. The doctrine of

---

[12] See DeFuria 1989; Merin 2002; Sherman 1981; Thornley 1996. Recognizing this reality, legal advisers to lesbian and gay couples strongly urge them to establish legal documents securing their economic contracts; see, for example, Curry, Clifford, and Hertz 2002.

undue influence, in short, draws courts into exquisitely complex classifications of relationships, interactions, and intentions (see, for example, Leslie 1996, 1999; Madoff 1997).

The 1945 Supreme Court of Wisconsin case of *In re Faulks' Will* illustrates these points extensively (17 N.W.2d 423 (Wis. 1945)). In July 1903, George and Mary Faulks, a childless couple living on a farm near Waupaca, Wisconsin, took in Will Jensen, an eleven-year-old boy from a nearby orphan's home. Sixteen years later, after Will married Pearl, a longtime neighbor, they both moved into the Faulks's farm home, while the Faulkses took up residence in Waupaca. The Jensens had one daughter, Lorraine. The Faulkses never legally adopted Will. Yet during all those years they treated him "as a son and he fulfilled the obligations of a good son to his foster parents":

> He assisted them in the conduct of their business affairs, looked after them during their illness, had access to their papers, looked after the repair of their residence, did odd chores for them, and in case of illness saw that they were properly cared for. His wife co-operated with her husband in the care of Will's foster parents and both were on excellent terms with George and Mary. . . . Mary was very fond of Lorraine, often referred to her as her granddaughter, and when Lorraine graduated from high school in 1941, Mary offered to pay for her attendance at the University of Wisconsin for one year. (425)

In 1934, 72-year-old George died. About the same time, Mary, who was two years younger than her husband, began having serious heart problems as a result of myocarditis. In 1932, the then twenty-eight-year-old Dr. L. G. Patterson had arrived from Ohio to start a medical practice in Waupaca. He began attending Mary in 1937 and three years later became her regular physician. At that time, Mary started loaning thousands of dollars to Dr. Patterson, first to help him out with his home mortgages, then to subsidize a hangar and an airplane. After she gave him $1,100 for the hangar, Dr. Patterson apparently made an oral agreement to provide Mary with lifetime medical care.

Mary's relationship with Patterson thrived during the early 1940s. The doctor and his wife lived three blocks away from Mary's home, and the two women often visited each other. On Mother's Day, May 11, 1941, while she was a patient in the hospital Patterson owned with a partner, the doctor sent her flowers and took her on two airplane rides. That summer, the Pattersons, their four-year-old son, and Mary drove to Yellowstone Park; Mary took care of all expenses. According to one of her old neighbors, their conversations now regularly concerned Patterson: "She was always telling how nice he was, how wonderful a doctor she had. . . . She was smiling all the time she talked about him." With Alice Faulks, her sister-in-law, Mary was more specific about the doctor's devotion:

> He would come up there every night when he was so tired. He would come to the house to see how she was and she always felt so sorry for him because he was overworked. She said one night she did not feel very well and he said, "Well, you get your things on," . . . and she said he was there in a few minutes. The way she spoke it was as though he picked her up and carried her out, and she said in a few minutes she was in the hospital and in bed. I said, "I am glad somebody takes care of you, because I can't." (430)

Meanwhile, Mary's relationship with Will and Pearl began to sour. The couple grew increasingly resentful of her favors to Dr. Patterson. In early January 1942, when Will and Pearl visited Mary at Dr. Patterson's hospital, Mary admonished them for being unpleasant to the doctor. Will retorted, "All he is after is your money." As he later explained, "I could not feel any different for someone that would take money from an old lady that way. I had heard quite a few people talk about her giving him money. It had become quite a subject of conversation in the community at that time" (426–27). The dispute terminated Mary's contact with Will and Pearl. Indeed, when Mary died in December 1942, the couple did not attend her funeral.

After several earlier testaments that had benefited Will; Pearl; their daughter, Lorraine; George's sister, Eliza Palmer; and her sister-in-law, Alice Faulks, on January 14, 1942, Mary signed what turned out to be her final will, making Dr. Patterson the main beneficiary. Will Jensen contested the bequest. In May 1944 the County Court for Waupaca County supported his demand to substitute an earlier testament for the later document. That court supported Will's claim of *wrong, exploitative* care. The following year, Dr. Patterson appealed. Against Will's claim of undue influence on the doctor's part, Patterson's attorney's argued that Mary was an independent, resolute soul, of sound mind, who had every right to choose her beneficiaries. The claim of undue influence rested on the allegations that Patterson not only "was disposed to influence her unduly for the purpose of procuring improper favors," but that he "had the opportunity to exercise such influence and to induce her to make a will in his favor." That opportunity was ample, since as her physician and her neighbor, the first court determined, "he was called frequently to her home to attend her as well as to attend her while she was in the hospital" (431, 441).

Patterson's rebuttal on appeal, however, insisted that none of this constituted evidence of undue influence. True, he "called upon her frequently, did little favors for her" (442), and Mary was indeed greatly attached to him. Stressing that the natural gratitude of a seriously ill, elderly patient for the care and attention of a competent physician fell within the bounds of expected doctor-patient relations, the appeals court ruled against the argument that Patterson had deliberately manipulated the relationship with Mary to his own advantage. His care was genuine, it was not excessive, it was not fraudulent, and finally it did not constitute undue influence. Thus, the court confirmed that Patterson had provided neither wrong nor exploitative care, and that to deprive him of the bequest would render his care thankless. If, of course, Faulks and Patterson had been lovers, there is a significant chance that Patterson would have lost his claim (Murthy 1997; Ross 1997). They were not, and he regained the bequest.

As for the long-suffering foster son, the appeals court vigorously rejected Will's claim of *thankless* care: that his faithful service and his earlier congenial relationship with the Faulkses entitled him to a substantial share of the estate. Although Will was like a son to the Faulkses, the court continued, in the last analysis he was a foster child, not their biological heir: "Long, pleasant and mutually intimate association is no substitute for blood relationship either in law or in fact" (442). (On the ambiguous legal status of foster children's household contributions see Draper 1979.)

BATTLES WITHIN FAMILIES

The Faulks case involves contestation over professional medical care, much of which took place outside the patient's home. It also involves competition between the claims of a foster son and those of the doctor that provided the care. What happens then when legal adversaries are members of the same family and when care occurs mainly within the household? Here care crosses the border from commercial to gratuitous, a difficult frontier for those seeking compensation, as courts ordinarily define any care rendered by family members as gratuitous.

In some cases, nevertheless, courts manipulate the boundary by defining care given by family members as sufficiently demanding and unexpected that it actually calls for compensation. In another variant, they examine whether the relations among kin were sufficiently distant to make the care given exceptional and therefore compensable (see Horsburgh 1992). Courts often do so by invoking the doctrine of implied contract, thus injecting legitimate commercial considerations into family transactions. Take for example, a 1985 Supreme Court of Minnesota decision, concerning Alice Ann Beecham's claim to a portion of her mother-in-law's $166,000 estate. The mother-in-law, Sara Edith Beecham, had cut Alice from the will in favor of her four grandchildren. Two years after marrying Edith's son, Alice had taken the elderly, sick woman into her home. For the last six and a half years of Edith's life, Alice cared for her full-time; not only cooking and cleaning but performing delicate nursing tasks. The court ruled that despite their family relation,

Alice Ann was entitled to a portion of the estate (*In re Estate of Beecham*, 378 N.W.2d 800 (Minn. 1985)).

When Alice had first contested the will, the trial court had ruled in her favor, finding an implied contract to pay for her personal services. The court noted that Edith had shown no reciprocity for Alice's strenuous care—except for an occasional $5 or $10 "tip" for transportation expenses. An appeals court reversed that decision, on the grounds that Alice's services, because they involved a family member, and in the absence of an oral or written contract, had to be gratuitous. The Supreme Court, however, reinstated the initial decision to award Alice compensation, supporting the trial's court finding of an implied contract. Alice's "around the clock care" of Edith, the Minnesota Supreme Court concluded, went "beyond services usually and ordinarily gratuitously rendered to family members" (804). In essence, the court declared Alice's care thankless. Based on experts' estimates of the commercial value of Alice's home-care services, the court set the compensation at $32,000, at the lower end of the estimated range.

For all their fascinating complexities, legal disputes over undue influence and extraordinary care provided by family members do not serve our inquiry as limiting cases or curiosities. On the contrary, they shine floodlights on questions that always arise where caring crosses the law, but usually lurk in the shadows: Who has the right or obligation to provide what sort of care to whom? How much? With what compensation, if any? As they confront these questions, lawyers and judges negotiate placement of the relationships in question within larger arrays of possible relationships among the parties, match proper and improper forms and extents of care with those relationships, and draw conclusions concerning the sorts of compensation, if any, the parties deserve.

To be sure, lawyers and judges resort to the comforting legal language of intent when they can; they pounce on apparent revelations of intentions in the form of private letters, overheard conversations, and preambles to wills. But much of the reasoning that enters the legal record consists precisely of describing interpersonal transactions, sorting out those that qualify as care, assigning them to appropriate categories of relations evaluating their propriety or worth, then assigning rewards and obligations accordingly. Attorneys and dissenting judges regularly argue over each of these elements: transactions, care, relations, value, rewards, and obligations. This same sort of reasoning pervades legal disputes over caring relations but becomes especially visible with allegations of undue influence and family-provided care beyond the call of duty. Eyes sharpened, we can see the reasoning at work more clearly in a wide variety of other caring disputes: over expenditures for child care as tax-deductible business expenses, over alimony, over compensation for unpaid or underpaid personal care, over medical malpractice, over damaging release of confidential information, and much more. It even shows up, surprisingly, in legal disputes over the consequences of industrial accidents. Unlike most of the cases we have reviewed, industrial accidents regularly involve third parties who themselves are not providing personal care.

In 1913, Avonia and Andrew S. Griffen learned how complex such legal decisions can become (*Griffen v. Cincinnati Realty Co.*, 27 Ohio Dec. 585 (Ohio Super. Ct. 1913)). After Andrew was injured at work, his wife Avonia, a seamstress, left her own job to nurse Andrew during a period of fifteen weeks. She then filed a suit against Andrew's former employers on two grounds: for her lost wages as a direct consequence of Andrew's injuries, and for loss of Andrew's consortium as a result of his injured condition. The Superior Court of Cincinnati split its decision. On the one hand, it denied that the Workmen's Compensation Act covered wives of employees who themselves could receive benefits under that act. It therefore turned down Avonia's request for that compensation. It also insisted that her nursing of Andrew fell into the category of gratuitous family care and therefore did not qualify for the $120 compensation Avonia demanded. The court allowed that if Avonia and Andrew had written a contract for her services, or if they had hired an outside nurse, Andrew could have collected for the value of the nursing care.

When it came to question of consortium, on the other hand, the Superior Court made a surprising judgment for its time. As chapter 2 pointed out, until the mid-twentieth century, when a husband was injured, courts rarely allowed his wife to collect damages for the loss of his companionship and services. Yet the Cincinnati court, recognizing women's increased legal entitlements, granted Avonia $500 for the loss of her husband's consortium. The court rejected the claim for *thankless care* but accepted the claim for *missing care*. It manipulated the available legal categories to fulfill a sense of justice.

CARE IN AND OUT OF THE LAW

Caring relations involve sustained and/or intense personal attention that enhances the welfare of its recipient. Care becomes intimate care to the extent that at least one party to the relationship acquires information not widely available to third parties, and whose dissemination could somehow hurt the information-giver. Intimate care involves strenuous relational work: establishing, matching, repairing, and sometimes terminating boundaries, media, transactions, and intimate interpersonal relations. Intimate care sentimentalizes easily, for it calls up all the familiar images of altruism, community, and unstinting, noncommercial commitment. From there it is only a step to a notion of separate spheres of sentiment and rationality, thence to the hostile worlds supposition that contact between the personal and economic spheres corrupts both of them.

Our close look at actual caring relations has once again revealed the difficulty in any such argument: in fact, personal care incessantly mingles economic transactions with the provision of sustained and/ or intense life-enhancing personal attention. Looking meticulously at caring relations reveals that participants themselves do not contend over whether those relations should involve economic transactions. They contend instead over appropriate matches among relations, media, and transactions, taking great pains to distinguish relations providing similar practical forms of care but having significantly different implications for longer-term connections among the people involved. In negotiating the economic conditions of care, participants are also defining meaningful social relations.

In that regard, the situation does not change much when care goes to court. Legal practitioners consult their own grids of possible relations and deploy such doctrines as undue influence, loss of consortium, and implicit contract as they adjudicate disputes over the proper and improper provision of care. They sometimes invoke hostile worlds reasoning to defend a judgment. They also introduce such exotic dichotomies as gratuitous-commercial, confidential-ordinary, and professional-nonprofessional. But legal practitioners, too, conduct analyses and arguments concerning the proper matching of relations, media, and transactions.

Because the law governing caring relations necessarily changes, however slowly and erratically, in response to alterations in the practical provision of care, we can look at the courtroom as a sort of shadow theater in which the actors improvise stylized versions of everyday struggles using the distinctive idioms of their craft. But beware of the metaphor! What happens on the legal stage affects the actual provision of care in everyday life; relations of doctors and patients, lawyers and clients, nannies and children, immigrants and their employers, children and their parents, cohabiting couples, even caring spouses depend in part on what lawyers argue and judges or juries decide. We will witness a similar interweaving of law and everyday practice as we turn to intimate relations within households.

CHAPTER 5

HOUSEHOLD COMMERCE

On February 28, 2004, the *San Diego Union-Tribune* published a
father's anguished query:

> *Question*: I find myself between a rock and a hard place. When
> I was divorced 14 years ago, my son was 3. I remarried and have
> three daughters with my second wife. I have always paid my
> child support in advance and have even agreed to increases over
> the years because I knew my son needed it and because I wanted
> to avoid a fight. Now my ex is demanding that I make arrange-
> ments for our son to attend a premier, out-of-state college with
> a price tag of more than $40,000 per year—plus travel, spend-
> ing money, etc. I don't know why I, as a divorced father, can be
> required to make these kinds of payments when, if my ex and I
> were still together as a family, I could tell my son—who has a
> B average—to attend a state-supported school.[1]

The newspaper's advice experts (one of them a lawyer) agreed
that the boy's father faced a problem. They strongly encouraged
him to negotiate a solution by discussing his financial constraints
with both his former wife and his son. If peaceful strategies failed,
the private dispute could end up in court: "depending on where you

---

[1] At http://www.signonsandiego.com/uniontrib/20040228/news_1c28solo.html.
Accessed May 8, 2004.

live, it may well be that both parents, as well as the child, are part of the equation by which [the courts determine] who pays what when it comes to financing post–high school education." If fortunate enough to live in Pennsylvania, however, the father could "take solace in the fact that the Supreme Court of that state has ruled that laws treating divorced parents differently than married parents when it comes to ordering them to pay for post–high school education violate the Equal Protection Clause of the Constitution."[2] The experts closed with their own judgment and final recommendation: "With all due respect to your ex-wife and son, a "B" average may not justify a $40,000 per year school under the circumstances you describe. But don't take it from us. With a $160,000 potential obligation staring you in the face, hire a good lawyer."

As the *San Diego Union-Tribune* advisers suggested, disputes over children's college tuition often bring divorced parents into court. Take the case of *Troha v. Troha* (663 N.E.2d 1319 (Ohio Ct. App. 1995)). When Hanna and William A. Troha divorced in 1992 after twenty-six years of marriage, their separation agreement stipulated payments for the college education of Kristofer and Shaye, two of their three children. The provisions were detailed: the monies would come from Mr. Troha's $3,850 savings bonds; two certificates of deposit in the names of Kristofer and Shaye, respectively; plus proceeds from the sale of three vacation properties owned by the couple. If additional funds were needed, Mr. Troha agreed to make up the difference.

[2] As of 2004, only a minority of states authorized courts to impose a legal obligation on separated or divorced parents to pay for their children's college education. In Pennsylvania, the Supreme Court in 1995 overruled the constitutionality of such an obligation. The court argued that imposing mandatory post-majority educational support discriminated against children in intact marriages who lacked similar legal claims and was therefore in violation of the Equal Protection Clause of the Fourteenth Amendment to the U.S. Constitution (*Curtis v. Kline* 666 A.2d 265 (Pa. 1995); see also Momjian and Momjian 2004). Still, divorcing parents in Pennsylvania and other states that oppose mandatory obligations for children's college support may include college support provisions in private property settlement agreements (see "Responsibility of Noncustodial Divorced Parent" 1980; Snearly 2003).

By 1994, Kristofer was studying at Clemson University while Shaye was still in high school. In March of that year, William Troha went to court. He accused his former wife of violating their separation agreement, among other things, by refusing to turn over Shaye's certificate of deposit. Since Kristofer's CD had already been spent for his education, Troha argued that before dipping into his own funds, Shaye's CD should be cashed to subsidize her brother's college expenses. Claiming it had no jurisdiction over either child's CDs, the court responded that it could not enforce the monetary transfer. Troha's appeal the following year again failed. The court acknowledged "the well-established principle in Ohio that parents generally have no duty to provide support, including payment for college expenses, for emancipated children" (1,324). But since the Trohas had agreed to insure both children's college education, the appeals court concluded it was unfair to subsidize one child's expenses by drawing from his sibling's fund. The fact that most of the funds in Shaye's CD had come to her as settlement for a dog-bite injury when she was a young child further dramatized her rights to the contested money. By rejecting Mr. Troha's claim, Ohio courts imposed their own legal frame on household obligations.

Disputes also arise over the educational expenses of married couples. What happens, for instance, when a couple divorces but still has outstanding student loans incurred by the husband or the wife during their marriage? Consider, for example, the Tennessee case of *Varner v. Varner* (2002 WL 3118327 (Tenn. Ct. App. 2002)). Both husband and wife, divorcing after less than two years of marriage, had significant student loans, the wife over $11,000; the husband more than $16,000. Rather than treating the total of $27,000 as shared household debt to be divided equally, the court ordered each of them to pay their own separate debts.

In similar cases, however, courts make distinctions based on the duration and character of the marriage. Note the Nebraska divorce case of *Schmid v. Schmid* (2003 WL 21397862 Neb. Ct. App. 2003)): during the couple's twenty-six years of marriage, the wife had taken out student loans over four years to subsidize her bachelor's degree. She testified not only that teaching was her vocation but that her work contributed to the household's economic welfare. The lower court ruled that the debt was indeed marital and divided the outstanding loans equally between the former spouses. An appeals court confirmed the fairness of the judgment (see M. Momjian 2004).

More surprisingly, children in some circumstances successfully bring legal action to extract payment for college expenses from parents. In 2004, for example, the Georgia Court of Appeals ruled that Ronald Houston had established a binding agreement with his daughter Allyson when he promised to pay half her tuition if she attended a historically African-American private college or university. Once Allyson had actually incurred the expense of enrolling at Clark Atlanta University, the court ruled, Ronald no longer had the right to renege on his repeated promises (*Houston v. Houston*, 600 S.E. 2d 395 (Ga. Ct. App. 2004)).

These conflicts over parental or marital responsibility to pay for educational expenses translate household disputes into legal cases. Most disagreements over similar matters never reach the courts. Members of households are constantly negotiating responsibility both for accumulated debt and for expenditures on such consequential matters as education for household members without resorting to the law. In the cases at hand, disputed issues include what claims household members have on other members' resources, who has an obligation to pay for what, and which of these obligations continue after a household breaks up. Family obligations, legal responsibilities, and routine household economic life intertwine. Their intersection calls up demanding, continuous, consequential relational work.

Households introduce new subtleties into our exploration of intimacy and economic activity. By simple virtue of inhabiting the same household, people share in production, consumption, distribution, and transfers of assets; acquire legally enforceable obligations; and fashion intimate relations with each other. Households do not simply combine couples and caring. Chapter 3 left couples at the threshold, about to establish households. Chapter 4 traced caring relations within households, across household boundaries, and well beyond them. As court disputes about educational expenses indicate, however, far more goes on in households than coupling and caring.

Living together produces shared economic problems, opportunities, rights, and obligations for everyone who takes part.

For several decades, intense debates with strong policy implications have swirled around the economic advantages, if any, enjoyed by married couples over single persons and unmarried couples, as well as the differential advantages and disadvantages imposed on men, women, and children by divorce. Competing explanations in these controversies pivot on the dynamics of household life.[3] Management of household assets, maintenance of the household economy, and dealing with departures, breakups, or new arrivals all present household members with serious interpersonal challenges. This chapter concentrates on relational work inside households.

Let us adopt a narrow definition of household: two or more people who share living quarters and daily subsistence over substantial periods of time. This excludes prisons, schools, hospitals, shelters, and military units, despite the fact that those institutions raise some of the same questions about intimacy and economic activity that this book is pursuing. I will examine larger kinship groups only to the extent that common residence at some point creates rights and obligations extending beyond household breakup or departure of its members. Households in this narrower sense still include paid caregivers, foster children, lovers, and relatives, just so long as they share bed and board. They also extend to family businesses in so far as household members work in them.

Whatever pains and pleasures it brings, living in a household almost always engages household members in intimacy. Household relations supply people with information and attention that, if widely shared, could damage the reputations and welfare of other people within the same household. By virtue of their shared living, people acquire understandings, rights, obligations, routines, and property that set household relations apart from those of couples or of parties to care. Once a household contains more than a couple,

---

[3] See Antonovics and Town 2004; McManus and DiPrete 2001; Gallagher 2003; McLanahan and Sandefur 1994; McLanahan et al. 2002; Waite and Gallagher 2000; Weitzman 1985.

furthermore, things get more complicated: relations to third parties such as children, care workers, or aging parents start influencing household dynamics significantly. Inside complex households, relational work never ends. Intersections of intimacy and economic activity within households therefore pose new questions about the purchase of intimacy.

As it happens, discussions of households have often involved extreme versions of the same mystifications concerning intimacy and economic activity we encountered earlier: ideas of hostile worlds and separate spheres, countered by nothing-but reductions that treat households as no more than little economies, distinctive cultures, or separate power structures. In particular, three mistaken ideas have bedeviled the analysis of household intimacy:

1. The vision of households as domains of sentiment and solidarity in which any intrusion of economic calculation threatens corruption of sustaining social relations
2. Dismissal of household economic activity, including women's and children's domestic work, as inconsequential for the economy as a whole, except perhaps when it comes to consumption
3. In reaction to the first two ideas, claims that self-conscious revamping of households as rational economic organizations would improve their efficiency and rectify unjust inequalities

We will never succeed in explaining the interplay of intimacy and economic activity in households without recognizing the distinctive patterns of interdependence and coordination produced by shared involvement in these communities of fate (Heimer and Stinchcombe 1980).

The mistaken ideas actually incorporate some correct intuitions but take them too far. As a consequence of shared living over substantial periods of time, for example, household members do commonly develop understandings, practices, rights, obligations, and sensitivities with regard to each other that surpass the complexity, intensity, and durability of most other social ties. Care and coupling do take place disproportionately within households. More so than in most other caring and coupling relationships, however, household interactions with third parties almost inevitably impinge on the quality of caring and coupling. Legally and morally, household members acquire obligations with regard to each other's behavior that no other settings entail.

Anglo-Saxon law, furthermore, literally fortifies the doctrine of separate spheres. Under the word *castle*, the *Oxford English Dictionary* offers references from 1567 onward in the vein of the great jurist Sir Edward Coke: "The house of every man is to him as his Castle and Fortresse, as well for his defence against injury and violence, as for his repose." Note the gendered principle! American law still insists on the distinction between transactions taking place within a household and otherwise similar transactions taking place elsewhere. Despite more than a century of feminist agitation, the law still bears residues of a time when, legally speaking, if by no means necessarily in practice, men ran their households and represented them in the outside world.

Has commercialization changed all that? Authorities, critics, and professional economic analysts often hold to an illusion: since the decline of family farms and domestic crafts, they say, households have lost their economic function. Households once did important economic work, goes the argument, but now they only consume. The illusion maintains a distinction between separate spheres but now portrays one of the spheres as seriously shrunken. Accordingly, household economic activity disappears from public discussions of inequality and productivity. As we will soon see, however, production and distribution remain alive and well within American households. Feminists may well be right to claim that equal pay for housework and outside wage work would benefit women as much as equal wages within commercial firms would. In that sense, "market standards" can serve as levers for equity. Nevertheless, the way to make such levers effective is not to deny that households have special properties but to identify those special properties and investigate how they work.

THE WORK AT HAND

Building on the earlier analyses of coupling and caring, this chapter therefore addresses four main questions:

1. How does shared participation in households affect people's management of economic activity, of intimacy, and of their intersection?
2. What sorts of rights and obligations does household membership entail, and how do those rights and obligations impinge on intersections of economic activity and intimacy?
3. How does the presence of third parties to intimate relationships—for example, children, parents, and live-in care workers—affect coupling and caring?
4. When disputes originating in households reach the legal arena, how does the law treat such disputes?

Rather than addressing these questions separately one by one, this chapter pursues them across a wide variety of household activities. Considering these questions across contemporary American settings will of course reveal substantial differences in household organization by class and ethnicity. Yet we will also continue to see Americans of different classes and ethnicities investing great effort in distinguishing different kinds of relationships from each other; marking their boundaries; negotiating their meanings, rights, and obligations; creating appropriate media for their economic reckoning; and matching economic transactions to intimate relationships. Every sort of household engages in extensive relational work.

Households teem with economic activity: production, distribution, consumption, and transfers of assets. No household survives for long without renewing its resources and sustaining its members. Households differ from other sites of economic activity, however, in four crucial regards. First, continuous cohabitation creates more extensive mutual knowledge, influence, rights, and obligations than usually develop in other economic settings. Second, negotiations within households take place in a longer time perspective and with greater consequences for long-term reciprocity than characteristically occur within other economic settings. Third, in American law, economic transactions within households occupy a substantially different position from those that take place among households, between households and other economic units, or entirely outside of households. Fourth, transfers of assets *among* households—for example, parents' contributions to their children's college expenses or to newlyweds' acquisition and furnishing of their new home—continue to loom large from practical, sentimental, economic, and legal standpoints.[4]

This chapter first examines the intersection of economic activity and intimacy in routine practices of household members. It groups those practices under three main headings: (1) control and transfer of assets, (2) consumption and distribution, (3) production. How, for instance, do members of households negotiate the reallocation of money that individual members earn outside the household? What happens when grandparents or other kin contribute to household income with gifts or loans? Who decides which household members do what kinds of housework? And in what ways do parents and children collaborate or compete in the spending of household monies? The disruption or breakdown of households raises an entirely new set of economic issues: how, for instance, do people renegotiate their economic rights and obligations when the household goes bankrupt? After reviewing household practices of control and transfer of assets, production, consumption, and distribution, the chapter therefore looks more closely at economic practices in shattered households.

Having reviewed a range of household practices, I then consider what happens when the same sort of issues become matters of legal dispute. Who, for instance, is responsible for paying taxes or honoring debts? Does household work establish legal claims to compensation in divorce cases? Legally speaking, how do agreements clearly established within households differ from commercial contracts?

[4] See Bengtson 2001; Eggebeen and Davey 1998; Furstenberg et al. 1995, 2004; Furstenberg and Cherlin 1986; Ingersoll-Dayton et al. 2001; Logan and Spitze 1996; Rossi and Rossi 1990; Rossi 2001.

What happens when the separate spheres doctrines still built into American law confront the nothing-but arguments of law's economic reductionists? In court, households provide a marvelous site for observation of intimacy's purchase.

Before taking this inquiry into American courtrooms, however, we need to organize our knowledge about household practices bearing on the intersection of intimacy and economic activity. I will do so by moving from an analysis of the control and transfer of household assets to household involvement in production to consumption and distribution within households. Earlier chapters on the law, coupling, and caring unsurprisingly gave little attention to intimate relations involving children. As a moment's thought about parent-child relations will indicate, however, children loom large in the world of intimacy. This chapter therefore gives more than perfunctory attention to children's places in household economic activity and intimacy. Discussion of disruptions in all these processes provides a transition to legal disputes over household intimacy and economic activity. As in earlier chapters, close study of household economic transactions and disputes will show that the interplay of intimacy and economic activity follows neither the laws of the market nor the requirements of tradition or sentiment, but a demanding logic of interpersonal negotiation over the meaning of household relations.

CONTROL AND TRANSFER OF HOUSEHOLD ASSETS

In chapter 4, we saw Vermont family day-care providers dealing with parents of the children they supervised (Nelson 1990). But the income they generated this way became crucial assets for their own household survival. For these providers, earnings from child care averaged more than a third of their total household income. According to Margaret Nelson, the presence of that income generally bolstered women's say in household affairs. However, those monies did not simply flow easily into household coffers. The women's income became a matter of continuous negotiation over whose money it was, how it would be spent, and how it defined relations among household members.

Husbands tended to protect their positions by labeling their wives' income from child care as supplementary, in contrast to the essential money brought in by the male wage earner. Even when the female provider's earnings were crucial to the household's survival, husbands and wives kept the monies gendered. Nelson discovered that "when *his* money pays for these [essential] things, they are necessary; when *her* money does, they are extras." As one husband put it, the wife provides "fun" money (Nelson 1990: 133). The wife in another household elaborated further: "What he makes there is mainly like insurance, taxes, and all that. What I make usually goes for food, clothing—whatever I find necessary to spend my baby-sitting money on or just to take the kids once a week to Middlebury and blow it" (132; see also Romero 1992: 64). Some husbands further marked the boundary between their income and their wives' by failing to report her earnings for tax purposes.

Ironically, Nelson found that if the spouses earmarked the two incomes by placing them into separate accounts, the husband more easily treated his wife's money as discretionary income that could be spent on gifts, entertainment, and other nonessentials. In an extreme case, one husband seized command over his wife's monies. The wife reported: "It bothered me a little bit [because] I thought the money was going one way and it wasn't. . . . I let him get control of the money. . . . It's my money but it's gone before you knew it. . . . At Christmas it was crazy. He went out and bought these things and I couldn't understand it—all these extravagant things" (131).

Nelson describes husbands and wives in these households as creating a "fiction"—a story defending the husband's sense of masculinity. "Predictably," comments Nelson, "women who actually make more money than their partners experience extreme tension in maintaining this fiction" (134). Where the household could not survive without the female provider's income, Nelson nevertheless found that husbands were more likely to recognize the seriousness of her efforts. In multiple ways, therefore, as these Vermont child-care providers managed their income, they were simultaneously defining relations within their households. The fictions people created played their own parts in defining husband-wife relationships.

Evelyn Nakano Glenn's close study of Japanese-American women's involvement in domestic service reveals some subtle variations on household financial negotiations. Glenn interviewed forty-eight women drawn from three generations of Japanese Americans on the West Coast: first-generation immigrants (*issei*), second-generation (*nisei*), and war brides, the post–World War II immigrants. All of them brought in income from domestic service, but an interesting difference from the Vermont families showed up in Glenn's study: these women were much more likely to keep their money separate and even secret from their husbands. The pattern was even more decisive among war brides than among the other generations; four of the twelve war brides Glenn interviewed concealed their actual earnings from their husbands while the rest kept their monies outside the family pool, "earmarked for special expenses or personal bills" (Glenn 1986 233). Mrs. Bentley, one of the war brides who hid the amount of her earnings from her husband, explained, "I can do with it what I want," and Glenn witnessed her determination to keep it that way: "I was asking her about her hourly rate just as her husband walked through the room. She glanced up conspiratorially and shook her head. After he left, she whispered the amount into the tape recorder" (140).

Another respondent, Kazuko Frankel, "also kept her husband in the dark about how much she earned and maintained her money in a separate account on the grounds that 'It's none of his business' " (140). The war brides' more extreme strategies, according to Glenn, resulted from the women's lack of social support from their kin, their arrival in an unfamiliar environment, and their more fragile relations with their spouses. Thus, once again, income does not remain simply income, but, in this case, becomes a tool with which vulnerable women negotiate relations to their husbands.

As the stories from Vermont day-care providers and the West Coast domestic workers imply, budgets are a crucial site of bargaining and conflict over the proper definition of household relations. A study of New York Dominican immigrants by Sherri Grasmuck and Patricia Pessar produced a series of striking findings regarding changing arrangements based on gender:

- Prior to migration, most Dominican couples' household budgets were male-controled, even when wives contributed income.
- Women's income in these households was usually earmarked for nonessential collective expenses, not their personal consumption.
- Pooling of income in premigration households was almost exclusively a female-headed household strategy.
- After migration, as Dominican wives increasingly took paid jobs, most Dominican couples transformed their budgetary practices, shifting to a pooled income system that blurred distinctions between essential and peripheral incomes.
- Democratization of budgetary practices increased women's autonomy and their determination to remain in the United States.
- New conflicts emerged over allocation of household monies: wives spent on homes, home furnishings, and other durable goods ensuring long-time residence; husbands opted to save funds destined for their eventual return to the Dominican Republic.

For Dominican couples, budgetary practices were one combustible site where they worked out transformations in gender relations. "Not infrequently," note Grasmuck and Pessar, "[the financial strategy] places the man at odds with his spouse, who has embarked on an opposing financial course" (Grasmuck and Pessar 1992: 158; for similar observations on Mexican immigrants, see Hirsch 2003). Sometimes negotiations failed: they report that a key precipitating factor in five of the eighteen cases of divorce they encountered was the husband's return to the Dominican Republic with his savings while the wife remained in the United States.

Controversies concerned not only short-term disposition of household income but also long-term relations of the household to kin and friends at the point of origin. Indeed, these Dominican immigrants devoted a significant part of their New York income to remittances going back to the Dominican Republic. Grasmuck and Pessar estimate that in the 1980s, about a third of Santiago de los Caballeros city residents received a significant share of their income from remittances. Remittance-receiving households in Santiago achieved a better standard of living than those that did not have relatives in the United States sending them monies. Some fifteen years later, in Miraflores, another Dominican Republic town, according to Peggy Levitt almost 40 percent of households reported that three-quarters or more of their income came from remittances (Levitt 2001b: 200). For the Dominican Republic as a whole, the 1996 official total of incoming remittances came to $1.14 billion.[5]

Remittances thus maintain long-distance household ties between the emigrants and people back home. We can therefore better understand conflict and bargaining within households by looking directly at these immigrant transactions. More visibly than husband-wife struggles, remittances involve a whole set of third parties—children, grandparents, siblings, and others. What is more, they transform households at both origin and destination. Levitt describes how this transnational economy operates. In her close observation of ties between Miraflores and the Boston suburb of Jamaica Plain, where many of the Dominican townspeoples' relatives migrated, Levitt notes that

> fashion, food, and forms of speech, as well as appliances and home decorating styles, attest to these strong connections. In Miraflores, villagers often dress in T-shirts emblazoned with the names of businesses in Massachusetts, although they do not know what these words or logos mean. They proudly serve their visitors coffee with Cremora and juice made from Tang. (Levitt 2001a: 2; see also Levitt 2004)

---

[5] Waller Meyers 1998; see also Durand, Parrado, and Massey 1996; de la Garza and Lindsay Lowell 2002; Pew Hispanic Center 2003. On how remittance systems connect to bargaining within households, see Curran and Saguy 2001; Georges 1990; Mahler 2001. On remittances and social ties more generally, see Mooney 2003; Roberts and Morris 2003.

Nonmigrant Dominicans, in turn, often provide their migrant relatives with care for the children they have left behind, supervise their local affairs, and treat them as "royal guests" during visits. Forty-year-old Cecilia, who has three siblings in Boston, for instance: "wants to give something back to her brothers and sisters, but she is exhausted when they leave" (Levitt 2001a: 90). Levitt points out that narrow economic interchange is only part of the remittance flow; she calls attention to what she calls "social remittances," the transfer of "ideas, behaviors, identities, and social capital that flow from host to sending-country communities" (54). Social and material remittances, however, do not constitute separate streams; in both cases people are fashioning and refashioning meaningful social relations, in some cases with consumer goods, in others with belief systems, social practices, or network connections.

Such connections between immigrant origins and destinations create households whose members move back and forth between continents. Interviewing Salvadoran immigrant children in San Francisco, Cecilia Menjívar heard their longing to reunite with their grandparents. She reports her conversation with nineteen-year-old Edwin M: "[He] told me that he misses his grandmother and often worries about her. He wants to get a job so that he can send remittances to her regularly and send her a plane ticket so that she can come to visit." So too, with Carolina and Ileana A., who "with their eyes watery . . . expressed the wish to have [their grandparents] close. . . . When they started earning an income, they saved money to send to their grandparents for airfare so that they could come to the United States for a visit" (Menjívar 2000: 268n.9).

A common pattern for Latin American immigrants is for children of U.S. residents to grow up largely in their community of origin, raised by grandparents, uncles, aunts, or other relatives. The remittance stream here goes partly to support the children and partly to maintain ties with their caretakers at home (Hondagneu-Sotelo and Avila 2002). This applies not only to Latin Americans but also to immigrant parents from the Philippines and other parts of the world (see for example Parreñas 2001). Transnational parenting does not always proceed smoothly. Levitt, for instance, reports children's occasional manipulation of their Dominican caretakers: "They know the grandparents need the money their parents send. They use this as a bargaining chip, threatening to tell their parents if their grandparents do something they do not like" (Levitt 2001a: 78). And a Miraflores resident complained to Levitt:

> The kids are just waiting, holding over the grandparents the envelope that comes every month. . . . You can't discipline them because it is their parents who are sending the money. They say, I will let my parents know what is happening here and they will stop sending so much money back to you. My sister sends $200 a month to support my nephew. When I was his age I was already working in the *conuco* (the fields) producing something. That kid does not do anything. He is a leech. (79)

These quick vignettes of arrangements for control and transfer of money illustrate the relational stakes of economic activity within households. Far from a Monopoly game in which people deploy stylized cash in pursuit of their own individual advantage, we find household members, children included, bargaining consequentially over their relations. The examples at hand, to be sure, fall far short of covering the great range of variation across American households. Interpersonal relations within households, monetary practices, and bargaining strategies vary significantly by class, income, ethnicity, and household composition.[6] Same-sex and unmarried cohabiting households behave differently in some of these regards from married heterosexuals with children (see Blumstein and Schwartz 1983; Carrington 1999; Kenney 2004). Commuter couples who work far apart create their own special syntheses of economic life and intimacy.

Transfer and control of assets, furthermore, includes inheritance, dowry, gifts, interhousehold loans, provision of personal services, lending of influence with outside authorities, and shifts in ownership or occupancy of family-controled dwellings. Through all these vari-

---

[6] See Edin and Lein 1997; Edin, Lein, and Nelson 2002; Gerson 1993; Hamer 2001; Henly 2002; Hertz 1986; Schwartz 1994; Treas 1993.

ations, nevertheless, we rediscover the same basic principle: once households are operating, transfer and control of assets to, from, or within them inevitably affect the structure and meaning of relations among household members. As a consequence, they frequently generate struggle not just over who gets what but also over structure and meaning.

HOUSEHOLD CONSUMPTION AND DISTRIBUTION

Students of contemporary America have often thought that households are nothing but sites of consumption, and have thought of consumption primarily as an expression of households' social position. But, alerted by the profusion of economic activity involved in the transfer and control of household assets, we can see immediately that neither of these assumptions will hold up to close scrutiny. Critics also often regard consumption as a light-headed, somewhat frivolous dimension of economic life, with potentially corrupting influence over households' moral fiber. While such concerns may of course be occasionally warranted, they fail to capture the consequentiality and meaningful involvement of consumption in households' most vital interactions.

Consumption's place in household social relations ranges from the purchase, preparation, and distribution of food to the acquisition of such status markers as luxury automobiles and swimming pools.[7] In earlier chapters, we have already seen how acts of consumption that might seem to be nothing but practical steps to survival—for example, purchase, preparation, and consumption of food—take on significance as definitions of interpersonal relations. Surprisingly, U.S. immigration inspectors build that insight into their screening procedures for green card applicants. Concerned to identify spurious commercially motivated marriages, inspectors regularly ask questions about the household's possessions as a gauge of the green

---

[7] See Berhau 2000; Cross 2000; DeVault 1991; DiMaggio and Louch 1998; Halle 1993; Horowitz 1985; Joselit 1994; Miller 1998; Pleck 2000; Zukin 2003.

card applicants' actual knowledge of his or her putative household's everyday interactions. Here are some sample interview questions:

- How many telephones are in your house? Where are they?
- How many televisions are in the house? In which rooms? Do you watch shows together, or separately?
- How many cars do you have?
- What is the color of your microwave oven? (Bray 2001: 13–14; Famuyide 2002: 56).

Far beyond this narrow focus, however, household consumption and distribution both broadcast and influence the members' public standing, their relations to other households, and their internal social relations. To illustrate that range without by any means exhausting it, let us review just three important areas of intersection between consumption and household life: housing, purchase of consumer durables, and children's connections to goods and services.

Consider the purchase of a home, the most significant investment for most households. In their challenging analysis of middle-class expenditures at the turn of the twenty-first century, Elizabeth Warren and Amelia Warren Tyagi dispute what they call the "over-consumption myth" of American spending. Families, they argue, are not frittering away their paychecks with useless purchases of brand-name clothing, unnecessary trips, or elaborate second homes. Instead, the bulk of the average middle-class American family's income goes toward the purchase of a home. Not a particularly elaborate home, either. According to their study, most husbands and wives pay skyrocketing real estate prices primarily to secure preferred safe neighborhoods with good schools for their children: "Families put Mom to work, used up the family's economic reserves, and took on crushing debt loads in sacrifice to these twin gods [safety and education], all in the hope of offering their children the best possible start in life" (Warren and Tyagi 2003: 23).

The acquisition and use of housing affects household life in three fundamental ways. First, whether rented or bought, for most households a home represents the largest single financial investment the household ever makes. For purchasers, furthermore, housing typically involves the most onerous single category of month-to-month household expenditure, the major store of wealth, the most momentous site of gifts and loans linking the household with outside relatives, and the major form of wealth for transmission to the next generation.[8] In the United States, wealth inequality outside of the very rich depends mainly on home ownership, and transmits from one generation to the next chiefly through home ownership (Conley 1999; Oliver and Shapiro 1997). Second, acquiring a particular kind of housing assumes a weighty set of commitments, conscious or unconscious. It announces a program for household identity and activity. It also deeply affects subsequent self-representation, social relations outside the household, and daily interactions within the household. By renting or buying a place to live in a particular location, household members are inserting themselves practically and symbolically into a web of social contacts. Third, actual management and use of housing involves day-to-day negotiation and conflict over rights and obligations, including such diverse questions as which activities go on in which spaces; who has rights to privacy; who must clean, repair, or maintain what features of the dwelling; and what decorations are appropriate or inappropriate where.

The housing that people actually purchase or rent therefore significantly affects their self-conceptions and their relations to others. Speaking especially of high school graduates from the early 1970s, Nicholas Townsend describes a "package deal" that seals membership of American men and their households in the middle class. The package contains four items: holding a steady job, being married, having children, and owning a home. Home ownership, according to Townsend, anchors the other three items by advertising respectable employment, providing a base for life inside and outside the household, and locating the household visibly in the American structure of class and race. The home matters so much, Townsend reports, that its acquisition often involves extraordinary efforts on the husband's part including "turning to kin, increasing their hours

---

[8] See Calder 1999; Chinoy 1955; Gans 1967; Halle 1984; Lynd and Lynd [1929]1956; Nicolaides 2002; Patillo-McCoy 1999.

of employment, commuting farther, and relying on their wives' income" (Townsend 2002: 139). Aid from kin, Townsend reports, includes various forms of assistance, such as "a father's mortgage, a loan from their parents, a gift of the down payment, subsidized rent" (150). The men also received nonfinancial help such as cosigning a mortgage, living with parents rent-free while saving for a down payment, and buying from a relative below market price (Townsend 1996). In addition, most men reported that they saw the likelihood of family assistance—especially their own parents'—in case of financial crisis as a crucial form of insurance.

Townsend's respondents were men in their late thirties, from varied social backgrounds, all of whom had graduated from the same San Francisco Bay Area high school. They typically acknowledged receiving substantial family help of one kind or another in their first home purchase: help included both direct financial assistance, guarantees such as cosigning a mortgage, and other nonfinancial support in finding or building the house. The men, however, downplayed that help in favor of self-portraits representing their own capacities to provide their households with adequate, appropriate shelter. Listen to Jack, a college graduate employed in an unskilled public service job, reporting how he had purchased the home he now lived in with his wife and two young children:

> I did not buy this house totally by myself. *I could have.* I put down the whole down payment myself. . . . I have a sister two years younger than me, and I think she was living in an apartment. So I said, "Why don't I help her? We'll buy the house together. She'll pay me back later, half the down payment." . . . We had a plan to keep the house for five years and I would buy her half of the equity out. She could buy herself a condominium or whatever. *She'd still be in an apartment if I didn't help her.* . . . My parents actually paid me back her half of the down payment on the house, which was fine. I just put that money in the bank. And I bought her out four years later. (Townsend 2002: 147).

This pride in home ownership takes a terrible blow when middle-class breadwinners lose their jobs and thus their ability to keep on paying their housing expenses. Katherine Newman watched this harsh process closely. She interviewed 150 Americans, who for different reasons had "fallen from grace," experiencing the sort of frightening downward mobility typically ignored by sunnier stories of Americans' social success. She spoke to divorced mothers, displaced managers, fired air traffic controllers, and blue-collar workers who had suffered a plant closing. As she heard from managers who had lost high-ranking jobs, Newman found that having to give up their family home represented the worst disgrace. It became "the watershed event in the life cycle of downward mobility," publicly announcing that the family had "truly lost their membership card in the middle class" (Newman 1988: 102).

But the loss reached farther than a decline in social status. It meant losing the family's crucial site for social activity, interaction, and security. John Steinberg, one of Newman's respondents, retained painful memories from that process. Eight years after his father lost his job, the family had to sell their three-story house: "Letting go of that house was one of the hardest things we ever had to do. We felt like we were pushed out of the place we had grown up in. None of the rental houses my family lived in after that ever felt like home. You know, we had a roof over our heads, but losing that house made us feel a little like gypsies" (102). That is why families clung to their homes, often making extraordinary sacrifices before finally putting the house for sale.

Divorced women had similar experiences when they lost the incomes of their husbands, but retained the houses. The house loomed even larger, Newman found, for women who had grown up during the Depression, at a time when a family's worst fear was eviction. For these women, the house represented a base for their shattered families, an investment in the family's future, a guarantee of stability in their children's friendships, and a setting for family celebrations. Women therefore hung on to their houses long past the point of economic prudence. Upkeep often suffered as a consequence. Jacqueline Johansen, a mother of three, divorced after twenty-five years of marriage to a northern California dentist, held on to an expensive large house she could no longer afford to maintain properly. She told Newman: "I have no money to fix up the house. Everything in it is destroyed now. The roof leaks and I can't afford to fix it. It was my dream house; now the image is being destroyed and I can't do anything to stop it" (213). Those mothers who sold their houses and moved to poorer neighborhoods did, as expected, face disruption, but unexpectedly, some of them reported that the downward skid produced greater solidarity between mother and children (227). Acquisition and loss of houses fundamentally affects relations within middle-class households.

BIG BUYS

American critics of conspicuous and wasteful consumption rarely single out housing. Most frequently they fix on consumer durables such as automobiles, electronic devices, household appliances, and furniture. Although we may deplore excesses in all those regards, the acquisition and use of such items neatly illustrates how consumption simultaneously activates household social relations, shapes those relations, involves negotiation among household members, and represents the household's social location to outsiders. Lizabeth Cohen, who has chronicled the great expansion of U.S. consumer activity after World War II, points to the close connections between purchase of homes and acquisition of other consumer durables:

> Buying homes, particularly new ones, motivated consumers to purchase things to put in them, and thereby helped stoke the crucial consumer durables market. Billions of dollars were transacted in the sale of household appliances and furnishings, as refrigerators, washing machines, televisions, and the like became standard features in postwar American homes. (Cohen 2003: 123)

House buying also led to automobile purchases, especially with the proliferation of suburbs, shopping malls, and long commutes. Between 1946 and 1955, in what Cohen calls the postwar "consumers' republic," sales of new cars quadrupled; by the end of the '50s, three-quarters of U.S. households owned at least one car (123). Much like household appliances such as vacuum cleaners, washing machines, and refrigerators, far from minimizing effort, the car paradoxically spawned a whole series of new, demanding domestic activities. For instance, as delivery services dwindled, housewives now drove to the grocery story, the butcher's shop, or the supermarket to purchase their families' foodstuffs. They also became resident chauffeurs, driving children to parties or other activities (Cowan 1983; Vanek 1974).

In rural areas, cars similarly became the object of new household strategies and division of labor. At first, as rural automobile use expanded after World War I, cars were mostly a man's possession, assimilated to rural work as another practical farm tool, much like a tractor. When farm wives wanted to shop, they waited for their husbands to take them (Barron 1997). But as women began to drive, the automobile, instead of easing their work, once again, often multiplied their tasks. Here's the experience of an Ohio farm wife in 1919. Before the family acquired a car, she had established a butter and egg route that took a great deal of her time. With the car, she expanded the business, but also increased her other household tasks:

> One morning [she] cooked that night's dinner in a "fireless cooker" [an insulated box in which a boiled dinner could cook all day], drove forty-one miles to visit her daughter in Cleveland, shopped in the city in the afternoon, then drove home in time to put a late supper on the table from the fireless cooker. . . . After the car was bought she could wash the breakfast dishes, sweep the kitchen, and then get to her customers [on the butter and egg route] as early as before, and generally get home in time to serve the dinner." (Kline 2000: 84, citing *Rural New Yorker*)

Three-quarters of a century later, in contemporary urban middle-class America, a second car has become a necessity for many households. Despite making some parts of life easier, the second car produces an even more complicated set of claims and counterclaims on transportation. "With Mom in the workforce and the family located even further from the city's center," note Warren and Tyagi (2003), "that second car became the only means for running errands, earning a second income, and getting by in the far-flung suburbs" (47). In rural, urban, and suburban America, people reshaped family life as they acquired automobiles. The house and the automobile dramatize a more general process: the interplay between household social relations and consumption. All households craft connections between the goods and services they use and the quality of their collective social lives.

Revealing results occur when households receive large sums of money all at once. This can happen through prizes, bonuses, lottery winnings, legal settlements, inheritances, or income tax refunds. Because the American government has experimented with the earned income tax credit and related programs as a way of encouraging families to exit from poverty and welfare, researchers have compiled an unusual amount of evidence concerning the effect of such windfalls on low-income households (for details, see, for example, Meyer and Holtz-Eakin 2002; Mayer 1997). How, they ask, do families use their tax credits? Far from treating lump-sum payments as simply more income of the same old kind, household members typically distinguish "tax money" from "paycheck money," often earmarking tax money for exceptional commitments, such as down payments on houses, buying cars, consumer durables, school tuition, children's wardrobes, family celebrations, and liquidation of major debts.

For example, Carlotta Saylor, a forty-one-year-old mother of five boys, worked two jobs: as part-time preschool aide during the school year and full-time summer day camp counselor. Interviewed at a rundown Louisville, Kentucky, public-housing project in 1997, Saylor reported how, besides taking care of some bills, she had spent the previous year's $2,000 earned income tax credit: "I bought a washer and paid cash for it. . . . It was the first time I ever paid cash for anything. I got a washer that was brand-new. . . . Then I went to the grocery store and made a big purchase. And I took each of

the kids shopping and got them new school clothes and supplies"
(Shirk, Bennet, and Aber 1999: 128). Saylor also indulged her children with a movie and the rare experience of a restaurant meal. She
had different plans for the current year's tax credit. Hoping to save
most of the money, she said:

> I want to buy me a house. . . . It doesn't have to be anything
> grand—just a little house, with four bedrooms and a basement,
> so the kids have some place to play when it's cold. . . . They are
> always talking on TV about how important it is to eat family
> dinners together. . . . Here, we don't have room for a table. It'd
> be nice to all sit down together at a table someday (Shirk, Ben-
> net, and Aber 1999: 128–29)

In a follow-up visit two years later, the interviewers found the Saylor
family living in a rent-subsidized Louisville two-story, four-bed-
room house, with a large kitchen and a backyard. But Saylor still
could not afford the kitchen table necessary for the dreamed family
gathering.

A systematic 1998 study reports earned income tax credit expenditures by 650 low-income Chicago-area taxpaying single parents
and two-parent families. The study looks at two categories of expenses: "making ends meet," or consumption use (utility, rent, food,
clothes, durables), and "improving economic and social mobility,"
or asset building. The latter include moving, car or transportation,
saving, and tuition or other schooling expenses. The authors found
that almost 70 percent of their respondents anticipated spending at
least some of their tax credit for economic and social mobility, with
cars and schooling heading the list. But 65 percent also planned to
spend part of the money for more immediate consumption, largely
on utility bills, rent, purchasing food and clothing. The distribution
of first priorities ran as follows:

Paying bills	50 percent
Purchase	13 percent
Saving	12 percent

Tuition	7 percent
Move	4 percent
Purchase or repair car	4 percent
Other	10 percent

Debts took priority over consumer expenditures, but household purchases loomed large (Smeeding, Phillips, and O'Connor 2002: 312).

A parallel ethnography of forty-two low-income Wisconsin families with young children who received payments from income tax refunds and/or tax credits produced similar findings. Households treated tax credits as something quite different from their routine income, as money they could spend on important improvements in their family lives. Furthermore, despite any skepticism we might feel about people's stated intentions, in fact, the families generally followed through and spent the lump-sum money on the same categories as we saw earlier. They did not simply pour the money into their weekly income stream. Instead, they paid bills, saved some, spent on children's tuition, bought household appliances, invested in cars, and so on. One woman "from a close-knit extended family," the authors report, "gave money to family members to make an insurance payment, knowing that they would help her if needed" (Romich and Weisner 2002: 383).

A significant share of the lump-sum tax income went to expenditures on children, especially clothing. The mother of two young children explained: "When my taxes come . . . I'll take the kids shopping because my kids really need to go shopping . . . especially [my older son]. . . . I can't send my son to school like this. Once I get the money, you know, send in all the papers—my W2 thing, [I] go to Wal-Mart and Kmart and just stock up" (382–83). After the fact, moreover, most families, the authors note, pointed to some household item purchased with their previous tax credit: a couch, a bed, tables, a refrigerator, a stove, a television, or a car. Some even pointed to the house itself.

Let me issue three warnings, however, against concluding that windfall money simply flows immediately to virtuous uses. First, some recipients of quick money go on binges, buy extravagant objects, or other indulgences. Second, other kin and friends frequently make claims on such found money, which therefore does not end up in the recipient's own household. Third, who gets the money makes a critical difference: for example, payments to women are much more likely to produce benefits for children (see Kenney 2002; Lundberg, Pollak, and Wales 1997).

These qualifications simply fortify the main point: within and across households, income catalyzes relational work. We can see this clearly in the case of same-sex couples. Dealing with a substantial sample of gay and lesbian households from the San Francisco Bay Area, Christopher Carrington underlines the importance of what he calls "consumption work." Through interviews and observation, Carrington identified a remarkably wide range of consumption activities, including browsing catalogs, magazines, and newspapers; consulting brochures, books, and etiquette manuals (for example, for instruction on gift-giving); listening to radio or television advertising; consulting other lesbian and gay families; comparison shopping in grocery stores or department stores; phoning goods and service providers; keeping files with instructional manuals and service information; commuting to megastores; waiting on the phone, in line at the store, at the post office, or at ATM machines; and determining the affordability of particular goods and services.

Carrington brings out three points of great importance for our inquiry: first, that the acquisition of a house and consumer durables represented the stability and long-term prospect of the couple's relationship; second, that within these couples, commonly a specialization in different kinds of consumption work emerged; and third, that consumption routinely involved negotiation with members of the household and other kin. "From purchasing their first futon to selecting a home for retirement," Carrington found, "lesbigay families conceive of these consumption work–laden acts as symbols of family and relational solidarity" (Carrington 1999: 173).

Listen to how Bill Fagan, one of Carrington's respondents, an artist and the household's "consumption worker," talks about shopping: "I find that I am thinking about all kinds of stuff about our

house when I go out to shop. Like I will be thinking of presents for
Rick's [his partner's] birthday, or gifts for my nephews for Christmas, when I go, or I will get ideas about how to improve things in
the house" (152). In another case, purchasing required subtle household diplomacy. Michael Herrera recounted his efforts to persuade
Federico Monterosa, his partner of four years, to purchase a fancy
coffee maker:

> It was quite an effort to convince Freddy that we should get it.
> He doesn't drink coffee too much. . . . Or if we got one, he only
> wanted a cheap one. . . . I had to come up with a good reason
> to get a nicer one and spend more money. So, it turned out
> that Freddy's parents were coming to San Francisco and were
> planning to stay with us. Freddy's mom likes coffee, and so I
> made the case that we should buy a nice coffee maker to make
> her feel at home . . . because it was kind of hard on her when
> Freddy came out to her and all. With that, he agreed and we
> went to Macy's and bought a decent coffee maker. (156)

In this vignette, we see Michael and Federico realigning their relations to each other and to their families.

KIDS' CONSUMPTION

If a household with children moves into a new house, buys a different kind of car, builds a swimming pool, purchases racing bicycles,
buys a used air conditioner, or acquires the latest computer system,
the children often play significant parts in the consumption decision
and almost always alter their own daily activities and relations as the
new possession becomes a routine resource for family life. But how
exactly does consumption engage relations of children to adults and
children to each other?

For those same-sex households Carrington studied who had children, consumption work, besides expanding as it would in any other
family, involved special concerns. Most notably, lesbian and gay
families tried to protect their children against stigma from intolerant

salespeople or service providers. They spent time and effort searching for "inclusionary" stores and providers. In this regard, they resembled heterosexual households, whose adults likewise seek stores and services that will treat their children civilly. All sorts of parents worry about their children's consumption and their contact with providers of goods and services. But to understand the relational side of consumption we must look not only at parents' efforts, but at children themselves as active agents in consumption.

Children's purchasing power is no trivial economic matter. Researcher James McNeal reports that as of the late 1990s, American children between the ages of four and twelve, with an annual income of over $27 billion, spent $23 billion and saved what was left. Over $7 billion a year of children's own money went for snacks, and a similar amount was expended on play items. What's more, they influenced about $188 billion of their parents' spending each year (McNeal 1999: 29). By 2002, kids' impact on parental purchases had climbed to $300 billion (McNeal cited in Schor 2004: 23). This influence had grown so great that a practical guide to home purchasing included the following advice to parents: "If you have children, you should give some thought about how best to include them in the home buying process. . . . Older children . . . can not only provide you with valuable input, but should rightly have a voice in the matter" (Perlis 1999 15).

As Juliet Schor reports, kids' influence extends to major consumer items: according to one industry estimate, for instance, children influence 67 percent of parents' car purchases (see also Sutherland and Thompson 2003: 118). One marketer told Schor: "When I was a kid I got to pick the color of the car. Kids nowadays get to pick the car" (Schor 2004: 24). American children have, indeed, been increasing their involvement in household consumption. An important study of American three to twelve-year-olds' time use in 1981 and 1997 indicates that among children of single parents, shopping time rose 65 percent, from 71 to 117 minutes. Trends in two-parent households were similar: shopping rose from 117 minutes to 188 minutes (Hofferth and Sandberg 2001: table 4). Judging from participation in shopping, American children's involvement in consumption is increasing not only in terms of dollar volume, but also in terms of time expended.

Child consumers are not simply indulging themselves. They are often performing relational work. Elizabeth Chin's ethnographic account of ten-year-old, poor and working-class black children's consumption practices in the Newhallville neighborhood of New Haven, Connecticut, documents the day-to-day relations activated in children's consumption. To understand Newhallville's children's practices better, Chin supplemented her two-year participant observation in homes, schools, and neighborhoods with shopping trips. She gave twenty-three children $20 each to spend entirely at their discretion (some of the children brought along other children— siblings, relatives, or classmates). With her money, ten-year-old Shaquita bought: two pairs of shoes at Payless—$6.99 denim mules for herself and $9.99 golden slip-ons as a birthday gift for her mother. She spent the remainder at Rite-Aid: $0.99 for a bag of bubble gum to share with her older sister and $2.09 for foam hair rollers to give her grandmother (Chin 2001: 126). As with most of the other children, Shaquita's shopping spree did not turn into a wild, self-indulgent experience. Instead, Chin identified two notable features of child shoppers' purchases: practicality and generosity. They bought useful items for themselves, such as shoes, socks, underwear, or school notebooks, and picked gift goods for family members. Both types of purchases cemented children's position in the household. They also established or confirmed their social ties with family members.

Lest these New Haven children appear to be impossibly reasonable and altruistic, Chin reminds us about the mixture of meanings that flowed from their purchases: obligation to share with other members of poor families, acting out of responsibility within the household, as well as the pleasure of giving. Chin sums this up:

> The deep sense of mutual obligation, and even debt, between family members played a central role. [For kids] these obligations and debts were often not only sustaining and joyful but

also painful, onerous, and highly charged. I sometimes suspected that the lesson imparted to children and imparted by them was at times a coercive generosity: share or else. (128)

As Chin suggests, household members often struggle over consumption. Recall Carl Nightingale's reporting on conflicts over children's clothing purchases in chapter 4. The same households got involved in other types of disputes over household expenditures. Nightingale tells the tale of eleven-year-old twins Andre and Georgie Wilkins:

> [Their] parents would occasionally succumb to a temptation that is surely hard for inner city parents to resist—promising their kids a new Nintendo or some sneakers when the "income tax" [refund] comes. The news would immediately earn Mr. and Ms. Wilkins the undying affection of their kids and a sense of family solidarity that would be written all over their faces, only to disappear when the appointed day arrived and there was no new Nintendo (Nightingale 1993: 159)

To the children, such disappointments were serious. Georgie, Nightingale reports, "bears a set of jagged scars on this forearm from the time shortly after one episode like this, when he took a broken bottle by the neck and ground the sharp end into the top of his wrist" (159).

In the course of his fieldwork, Philippe Bourgois heard similar stories coming from "El Barrio," New York City's crack-ridden East Harlem. Ten-year-old Angel complained about his mother's boyfriend:

> [He] had broken open his piggy bank and taken the twenty dollars' worth of tips he had saved from working as a delivery boy at the supermarket on our block. He blamed his mother for having provoked her boyfriend into beating her and robbing the apartment when she invited another man to visit her in her bedroom. "I keep telling my mother to only have one boyfriend at a time, but she won't listen to me." (Bourgois 1995: 264)

Likewise, the middle-class divorced mothers studied by Katherine Newman encountered serious resistance from their children to forced reductions in their standard of living. In the case of mothers who stayed within the same neighborhood, the conflict was often bitter: "My children don't seem to realize that we can't afford the kinds of things we had before. They are always asking me for money or clothes, and they sulk if I don't give it to them. . . . What can I do? We can't live the way we used to, and they can't seem to understand that" (Newman 1988: 225). Children's consumption within households thus takes place in a context of incessant negotiation, sometimes cooperative, other times full of conflict. Consumption, furthermore, demonstrates far more than individual acquisition. It reveals children as active, inventive, knowledgeable consumers. More important, it shows us dynamic, differentiated, social relations in action.

HOUSEHOLD PRODUCTION

If households have gained notoriety as sites of consumption—wasteful or otherwise—Americans commonly think of household production as a thing of the past. Perhaps Grandma and Grandpa ran a farm or a store, goes the thought, but now everyone travels elsewhere to produce. That idea rests on a mistaken equation of production with paid employment and/or sale of a product in outside markets. As we saw earlier, in fact, plenty of paid employment does occur within households; specialized care workers provide their services to household members, mothers take in other people's children for paid day care, and employed people work at home. But the bulk of household production takes place without direct monetary compensation. Unpaid personal care, food preparation, repair and maintenance of clothing, pet and plant care, home improvements, housecleaning, financial record keeping, automobile maintenance, yard work, children's school homework, parental supervision of that homework, sending out family news, and driving household members from one activity to another all belong to household production. Put together, they absorb a large share of contemporary Americans' efforts.

We have already encountered household production repeatedly, most obviously in the frenzied workdays of immigrant caregivers. We have seen plenty of evidence that household work divides along lines of gender and age, with substantial inequalities in both regards. Spouses often struggle over that division of labor, as do parents, children, and other household members. In working out household divisions of labor, indeed, people are defining their relations more generally—establishing rights, obligations, and definitions of relative worth that organize household life. Moreover, despite the absence of wages in the strict sense, households establish systems of reward and punishment for participation in household work. In the short run, gifts, loans, allowances, and household budgets build monetary transfers into those systems. In the longer run, households work out rules of reciprocity, including claims on household assets. In this way, households establish production economies as complex as those of many a commercial firm.

Many households, furthermore, build commercial activity directly into their daily operations. Spouses and children of executives and officials find themselves participating in the employed member's public activities. Parents organize the participation of their children in contests, competitions, and part-time jobs. People in sales, finance, editing, and various forms of writing sometimes work out of their home. And a surprising number of households—especially immigrant households—run family businesses. In all these cases, commercial relationships do not simply transect and influence household relationships; they *become* household relationships.[9]

Instead of surveying the whole complex range of household production, let us settle for two illustrations of these general points: age and gender differences in household work and children's participa-

[9] On family businesses, see Aldrich and Cliff 2003; Fletcher 2002; Gersick et al. 1997; Lansberg 1999; Light and Gold 2000; Portes and Rumbaut 1990; Portes 1996; Spector 2001.

tion in household production. In both cases, by now the main points should be recognizable:

- Households operate as small economies, with significant divisions of labor.
- Within households, intimate relations and economic relations coincide.
- Household members match meaningful relations with appropriate economic transactions and media.
- Because these relations significantly affect household members' individual and collective fates, members repeatedly negotiate with each other over the proper definitions of their rights and obligations, sometimes breaking into rancor and open struggle.
- The frequent presence of third parties to any such negotiation—children, parents, paid helpers, kin—makes the interplay among household members more complex and consequential than in ordinary paired relationships.

As anyone who has ever lived in a household knows, both age and gender mark the division of domestic production: helpful children clean their rooms; studious children prepare their homework; parents drive the kids to sports competitions or music lessons; grandparents babysit their grandchildren and also help their grown children with errands or housework; wives clean, plan and cook meals, shop for groceries, wash dishes, do laundry, and hire the nanny or the maid; husbands help out with some of the same activities but typically specialize in taking out the garbage, yard work, car care, and household repairs.

On the whole, gender differences in household production have attracted more attention than age, kinship, and generational differences. Feminist critics have observed, puzzled, and fumed over persistent inequities in the allocation of household labor between men and women. A wide variety of studies document what Arlie Hochschild identifies as the "second shift" (Hochschild 1989) and what Kathleen Gerson calls the "housework gap" (Gerson 1993). Women do a disproportionate share of the labor that goes into maintaining and reproducing a household's daily life: cleaning, cooking, repairing, caring, transporting, maintaining contact with kin and friends, and monitoring the household's means of existence (Daniels 1987; Di Leonardo 1987). For contemporary American households, a series of striking observations recur: the box on page 244 summarizes standard findings from household studies.

What accounts for such patterns? Analysts of these findings disagree sharply over their explanations: sexism, tradition, power struggles, labor market gender discrimination, economic efficiency, gender ideology, and sheer time available outside of work all compete for recognition as fundamental causes. Since similar struggles and inequalities often occur in same-sex households, however, some share of these patterns must result from household dynamics as such rather than from general features of male-female relations (Carrington 1999; Sullivan 2004). But for present purposes, findings and explanations converge on this book's basic point: in organizing their economic activities, household members are actually negotiating the significance of relations among themselves.

These debates, furthermore, are not just esoteric academic disputes. They correspond to day-by-day struggles within households. But when it comes to practical advice on how to handle domestic work equitably, commentators ordinarily minimize household dynamics and turn the problem into a question of personal and individual strategy. How do you get a husband to pitch in more often or more effectively? How much should you do around the house to satisfy your wife's requests? Often the solution hinges on negotiating skills and assertiveness. For Linda Babcock and Sara Laschever, a key obstacle to gender equality is women's reluctance to ask: "Women don't ask. They don't ask for raises and promotions and better job opportunities. They don't ask for recognition for the work they do. They don't ask for more help at home" (Babcock and Laschever 2003: ix). If women are to balance the increasing demands of the workplace and family, they urgently need to become skilled negotiators. "Seeing the home as an arena in which negotiation plays an important role," the authors conclude, "can enable both men and women to start thinking more creatively and more fairly

Standard Findings on the Division of Labor in Household Work

As women's share of work outside the household rises—as measured by time or income—men's absolute and proportionate contributions to housework increase.

However, even when women bring in all the household's outside income, men's contributions, on the average, do not equal women's; indeed, at that extreme, some studies suggest that men's contributions actually decline.

Looked at more closely, male and female contributions to household production almost always turn out to differ in kind, for example, with women concentrating their effort inside the dwelling and men doing yard work, house repairs, car maintenance, and similar more "masculine" activities.

The division extends to child care, where women do far more than half the work in most circumstances, and men are much more involved in children's play and homework.

For intact families, this sort of division extends to days of the week, with fathers concentrating their contributions to masculine versions of child care on weekends.

When it comes to children's participation in organized activities away from home, mothers contribute a disproportionate share of the effort.

The gender division also applies to help given by adult children to their aging parents, with daughters more likely to help with housekeeping and sons with repairs and yard work.

In two-job families, nonstandard work schedules tend to increase the share of husbands' household work and the likelihood that men will take over tasks traditionally defined as female.

Sources: Bittman, England, Folbre, and Matheson 2003; Brines 1994; Casper and Bianchi 2002; Coltrane 1996,1998; Gershuny 2000; Gjerdingen and Center 2005; Goldscheider and Waite 1991; Greenstein 2000; Jacobs and Gerson 2004; Lareau 2003; Logan and Spitze 1996; Presser 2003; Robinson and Godbey 1997; U.S. Department of Labor 2004; Yeung, Sandberg, Davis-Kean, and Hofferth 2001.

about ways to share their household responsibilities" (183). Individual negotiation matters more than political ideology or social scientific analysis.

How-to books of household management gesture in the same direction. For instance, in *Just Kiss Me and Tell Me You Did the Laundry*, Karen Bouris offers numerous guidelines for mediating couples' "chore wars" over which spouse is expected to perform what household task. To first determine the level of existing inequality, she provides a "housework quiz" that easily reveals the current "domestic dominator" by asking questions such as these: "Where are the mop, the children's Tylenol, and emergency numbers for the babysitter?" "Without looking, how much laundry detergent, dishwashing liquid, and milk do you have in the house?" "When is the car due for an oil change?" (Bouris 2004: 192). For Bouris, individual consciousness looms large in fair settlement of domestic chore wars. "Developing awareness and mental responsibility," she notes, "may require a major personality paradigm shift that takes years to fully develop" (198).

A return to the households of the Vermont family day-care providers discussed earlier displays concrete evidence of gender as well as age differences in domestic production. In these households, women's earnings bolstered their say within the home. At the same time, however, in order to protect masculine pride, husbands and wives minimized the significance of the women's income for household survival. Both points underscore the interplay of household economic activity and gender relations. When it came to the Vermont couples' division of housework, both husbands and wives treated the fact that women worked at home as opportunity and justification for the women to take on a disproportionate share of housework. Surprisingly, women themselves sometimes interpreted day care as something other than work. Meg Garber, one of Margaret Nelson's respondents, explained why she did all the housework: "Seven days out of the week, I'm the one who does it. . . . If I were working he would help" (Nelson 1990: 138). Furthermore, spouses usually maintained a traditional gender division of labor, most commonly women performed work inside the house while men took on the outside duties. As one woman noted: "I don't do anything outdoors. I never ever have. And he's the one that keeps the outside looking good so I basically do all the inside" (136).

Finally, in her conversations with providers, Nelson discovered an interesting distinction in gender relations between women who contributed relatively small and relatively large parts of household income. Modest contributors, she reports, had to request help from their husbands for any household work, whereas larger contributors could more confidently claim that help as an entitlement (for similar observations, see Grasmuck and Pessar 1992). Indeed, in the extreme cases, wives recruited their husbands to help with the care of their clients' children.

In the same households, mothers also established economic relations with their children. Many of the women, for instance, reported their children's household duties. Others, confident that work responsibilities taught children valuable skills, recruited their teenagers to assist with day-care duties, sometimes hiring them for pay. When the caregivers' children themselves had children, an interesting new set of negotiations often occurred. The grandmother and her adult children had to decide whether or not the children should pay for their children's care. Not all households ended up with the same arrangement; of the four grandmothers Nelson interviewed, one took care of her grandchild for free, two charged a lower rate, and the fourth collected the full amount.

PRODUCING KIDS

More generally, what part do children play in household production? The general idea that households have lost their economic functions, except for consumption displays, implies another misconception: that children no longer contribute to the household economy. Any household work children do perform, moreover, is expected to build the child's character or skills, but not seriously help their parents. True, child labor laws did push children out of most wage-earning occupations. True also that children, much like fathers, typically perform fewer household duties than their mothers. Yet household production is not just adult work, nor is it merely an educational device. As soon as we examine children's contributions closely, we discover their substantial economic relevance for the entire household. Here I concentrate on children age fourteen or younger.

The meaning, organization, contribution, and compensation of children's work varies systematically and dramatically from one social setting to another. Let us try to identify the principles of that variation. Here is how the overall argument runs:

- Children's work divides between immediate production of transferable use value and production of material, financial, human, social, and cultural capital. For example, children often work directly in household economic enterprises, but in so doing they acquire skills and social connections that will later serve them in enterprises of their own.
- Some of the capital production remains with the child itself for later transfer, but some of it immediately increases the capital of social relations and groups in which children participate, notably that of their families and households. For example, a child's stellar school performance enhances not only the child's own future, but also the standing of his or her family.
- Permissible and forbidden forms of children's work vary strikingly with the social relations to which they are attached. For example, many parents require their children to weed the family flower garden, but any teacher who required pupils to weed his or her own family's garden would risk job loss.
- Within each social relation, more precisely, participants and third parties promote proper matching of meanings, monetary media, and economic transactions, including the transactions we call work or production. For example, over a wide range of Western households, parents can reasonably tie allowances to their children's household work but could not

possibly hire outside children to do the same work for the same rewards.

- Participants also mark the boundaries between different social relations with labels, symbolic representations, and moral injunctions. For example, almost every household makes a sharp distinction between the rights and obligations of children that belong to their household and those of children who count as temporary visitors.

Within those limits, however, children and other persons involved in their work incessantly negotiate the precise matching of meanings, media, and transactions. For example, children across the world bargain with their parents about what clothing, toys, or forms of entertainment they can and cannot buy.

In the United States, children participate in a variety of productive domestic tasks, such as cleaning up their rooms, cooking, dusting, doing laundry, washing dishes, vacuuming, setting or clearing the table, cleaning the bathroom, sweeping floors, carrying out garbage, mowing the lawn, doing yard work, or caring for younger siblings and pets. In fact, recent studies report that American children are spending increasing amounts of their time in such household chores (see Lee, Schneider, and Waite 2003). Children's marketing specialist McNeal estimates that children in the United States perform 11 percent of total household work (McNeal 1999: 71; see also Goldscheider and Waite 1991).

In most cases, children expect some kind of domestic payment. Parents comply: according to a 2004 survey, a little over half of children in the United States between the ages of six and fourteen, receive a weekly allowance (Jordan 2004). McNeal itemizes five different sources of children's cash income. In the late 1990s, 16 percent of kids' income came from gifts from parents, 8 percent from others' gifts, 45 percent from allowances, 10 percent from work outside the home, and 21 percent from household work. Significantly, he notes that children's compensation from household work rose to 21 percent from 15 percent in the mid 1980s (McNeal 1999: 69, 71). However, since parents are not standard employers, negotiating suitable payment systems turns into a delicate and highly contested issue. At issue is not merely a wage bargain but a definition of proper relations between parents and their offspring. Indeed, the nature of children's allowances has excited debate for over a century, with some experts and parents strongly advocating compensation for children's household work, and others insisting on a separation between work effort and allowances (Jacobson 2004; Zelizer 1985). In the latter cases, allowances qualify not as compensation but as a parent's discretionary gift or the child's entitlement. Nevertheless, whether compensation, gift, or entitlement, allowances are subject to continuous bargaining between parents and children.

Negotiations occur over both allowances and other monetary transactions. Parents, for their part, often impose a set of terms, overseeing, and in some cases closely supervising, their children's expenditures, or else deciding which chores to compensate with money. Some parents give children extra money for outstanding school performance. In these transactions, however, children do not simply echo parents' preferences for household payments, but work out their own moral views and strategies. *The Kids' Allowance Book*, based on interviews with 166 children between the ages of nine and fourteen from eleven schools around the United States, reports a variety of such rationales and strategies. Children, for instance, repeatedly praise regular allowances as welcome sources of discretionary income. Before getting an allowance, Katie explains, "If I wanted a pair of special sneakers, [my parents] might say it's too expensive and not a necessity. Now that I get an allowance, it they don't want to pay, I can pay for it myself" (Nathan 1998: 6).

Children divide, however, over whether or not allowances should compensate for their domestic chores, some children insisting that helping out is an expected, fair, and therefore free, household contribution. Others forcefully defend their often elaborate monetized exchanges. Listen, for instance, to Amanda:

> On top of all the cleaning and garbage toting Amanda B. has
> to do for her allowance, she regularly does freebies like folding

the clothes or setting the table. "If I'm sitting around and my mom asks me to do something, I'll say sure and won't ask to get paid," she says, "I do it to help out." But if she is saving up for something special, she'll hunt for a big job that needs doing, such as basement cleaning. Ugh! She'll ask if her mom will pay extra for it. That's when the freebie pays off. "Since I'm not always working just for money, when I ask if she'll pay me to do something extra, she usually does."

Children report numerous, often intricate, negotiating tips, ranging from how to choose chores (pick your own: "if your mom chooses, she might give you a chore you can't even bear the thought of doing"); receive a fair wage (find out what other kids earn); make sure parents pay on time ("I remind my dad on the day before, to make sure he has the right change for my allowance the next day"), and get a raise ("no-no's" include whining, begging, asking for way too much, or not doing chores on time; among the "do's": "do lots of stuff to help out and be nice to your brother or sister [if you have one]," and "ask for a slightly bigger raise than you want so you can give in a little and still come out okay") (55, 52, 20, 46; for other kids' strategies, see also Consumer Reports for Kids Online and Kid's Money Web site).

We only have limited information on actual bargaining between parents and children over housework and allowances. The same is true about other categories of children's productive, money-earning efforts. McNeal reports that children's income from work outside the home, unlike their increasing pay for household work, has remained fairly stable at about 10 to 13 percent for children under twelve. Children earn by babysitting; raking leaves; mowing lawns; watering plants; shoveling snow; cleaning garages; selling cookies, candies, or lottery tickets to raise funds for school activities or charities; washing cars; taking care of pets; as runners or look-outs for drug dealers; watching cars; or as baggers at supermarkets. More recently, some eleven- and twelve-year-olds have been making money with investments and savings (McNeal 1999: 72; see also Lewis 2001).

In some cases children's earnings matter greatly for household survival. For instance, in their study of single low-income mothers' strategies for "making ends meet," Kathryn Edin and Laura Lein found one woman who, after having lost other sources of kin support, turned to her children: her teenage son's wages from an after-school McDonald's job, plus her thirteen-year-old daughter's money from baby-sitting neighbors' children on weekends. Sometimes, they note: "mothers were not sure where their children were getting the money but suspected involvement in petty crime and drug sales" (Edin and Lein (1997: 153). Once we shift our attention outside of households, it becomes clear how many of children's activities involve different kinds of production—not only household errands and part-time jobs but also volunteer efforts and school work. Most American children in all kinds of households spend a considerable share of their daily effort working.

In immigrant families, children play distinctive parts in household production. In a study of Mexican and Central American immigrants in the Pico Union area of central Los Angeles, Marjorie Orellana observed children involved in a variety of daily work, including "running errands; caring for siblings; cleaning; doing the laundry; taking siblings to school, the library, and other appointments; helping siblings with homework; . . . answering and making phone calls" (Orellana 2001: 374). Especially notable was the extent to which children served their families by caring for younger children (see also Valenzuela 1999: 728). Orellana also reports children's involvement in wage labor: "selling food, clothes, or other merchandise alongside adult street vendors; helping their parents to clean houses, care for children, or mow lawns; cleaning tables in a *pupuseria* (a Salvadoran restaurant); sweeping the floors of a beauty salon" (Orellana 2001: 374–75; see also Orellana, Thorne, Chee, and Lam 2001). In her study of Salvadoran immigrants, which likewise documents children's crucial contributions, Cecilia Menjívar tells the story of ten-year-old Sonia, who went along with her mother, Rosa María B. when she cleaned houses: "Sonia helped her clean, but the girl also baby-sat one of her bosses' children, for which she would get $5 for the six hours that it took Rosa María to clean this person's house"

(Menjívar 2000: 218). Meanwhile, in immigrant family-run businesses, children help operate the family's shop or small business (see, for example, Park 2001, 2004).

Next, let us look more closely at two other categories of children's productive contributions: translation services for immigrant households and provision of personal care in a wide variety of families. Both cases reveal an impressive variety of children's labor and illustrate the crucial contributions that children make to the maintenance of their households.

CHILDREN AS LINGUISTIC MEDIATORS

Consider the impact of children's linguistic skills for their immigrant parents. Even when young, children educated and brought up in the receiving country often have far greater skills in the new country's language than their parents (see Portes and Hao 2002). In one crucial way, this reverses the usual skill distribution within the household. Studying Mexican immigrant households in Los Angeles, Abel Valenzuela (1999) recognized that these families typically faced urgent problems with respect to social and cultural capital. They knew little of how U.S. institutions—schools, workplaces, churches, unions, courts, and banks—functioned. Of more immediate importance, they often lacked the English language skills to negotiate with such institutions.

Children became their parents' indispensable allies. In sixty-eight interviews, including forty-four adult heads of immigrant households and twenty-four of their now-grown children, Valenzuela drew from their recollections of past interactions. He found that children occupied three key household roles. They served first as their parents and siblings' tutors, translating, interpreting, and teaching. Besides straightforward translation of television news or government documents, the children mediated delicate transactions between their parents and physicians, teachers, bank officials, and other authorities. Children's second role was as advocate, intervening on behalf of their parents in complex or controversial interactions—for instance, when a public official or salesperson misunderstood or became impatient with their parents or siblings. Valenzuela's interviews revealed a strong gender pattern; daughters assisted their parents with financial, employment, legal, and political transactions more often than their brothers did.

Following up the Valenzuela study, Marjorie Orellana, Lisa Dorner, and Lucila Pulido (2003) went directly to observation of young children (see also Orellana, Reynolds, Dorner, and Meza. 2003). They studied bilingual fifth- and sixth-grade children of Mexican and Central American immigrants in four communities—one in central Los Angeles, two in Chicago, and a fourth in Engleville, Illinois. Drawing on extensive interviews, participant observation in children's homes and classrooms, and audiotaped data, Orellana and her collaborators closely documented the remarkable range of parental reliance on their children's linguistic skills. Children, they report, intervened as translators in seven different domains:

1. Educational: for example, translate at parent-teacher conferences for themselves and/or siblings, cousins, or friends; call schools to report their own or siblings' absences.
2. Medical/health: for example, translate at doctor's and dentist's offices during family visits; interpret instructions for medicine, vitamins, and other health-care products.
3. Commercial: for example, shop for or with parents; complete refund transactions, settle disputes, and check for mistakes in sales transactions.
4. Cultural/entertainment: for example, translate plot and dialogue at movies; read and translate stories, self-help guides, song lyrics, or instructional manuals.
5. Legal/state: for example, call insurance company regarding car damage or car accidents; obtain welfare or Social Security by accompanying parents to office, answering questions.
6. Financial/employment: for example, cash or deposit checks at the bank or currency exchange, or help parents fill out applications for work or for unemployment benefits.

7. Housing/residential: for example, translate between parents and landlords; talk to managers regarding things broken in the apartment. (Adapted from Orellana, Dorner, and Pulido 2003: 512–13, table 1).

Children experienced most of these linguistic encounters as no more than daily routines of family life. Some of their interventions, however, not only demanded skill but also produced considerable stress. Skill and stress coincided most often when the children mediated between their parents and formidable outsiders. Take the example of Jasmine in the medical arena:

> When I was about 8–9 years old we went to the doctor because my baby brother was 1 month or so. He had to go for a check up and a doctor told (asked) my mom if she was going to give my baby brother milk from he(r) breast, but I did not know what breast meant. So I told the doctor if she could explain what breast meant. She was nice and kind and said yes of course. She touched her breast and (I) told my mom what the doctor was saying. As far as I can remember this was the scariest translating thing I (had) ever done. I did not translate things that much this week but I did work long time ago translating stuff. Well, I felt so nervous to translate for the doctor because I thought I would not be able to understand the big words doctors use. (Orellana, Dorner, and Pulido 2003: 516)

In these circumstances, children of immigrants assume serious responsibility for their parents' and their household's welfare. In the process, they are not only performing fundamental services but adding to their family's capital. Orellana, Dorner, and Pulido note that children's knowledge of English and U.S. cultural practices enhance their families' household reproduction. Nevertheless, as Orellana and her collaborators warn, these children sometimes resist and negotiate their obligations, while parents sometimes impose them as family duties (see also Fernández-Kelly 2002: 198). In her study of Salvadoran immigrants in San Francisco, Menjívar often heard complaints that children had not performed as their elders expected. She recounts, for instance, Lolita Q.'s anger when her twelve-year-old nephew and translator took dangerous liberties during an interview with a legal caseworker:

> To her dismay, he had portrayed her as a felon who smuggled people across the border as her main occupation. He had mistaken her political imprisonment in El Salvador for U.S. criminal incarceration, and because he had heard that his aunt tried to enter the United States more than once, he concluded that it was a routine activity. (Menjívar 2000: 215)

Lolita was unsure whether her nephew's misinterpretation had been an innocent mistake or deliberate revenge. The day before the interview, Lolita had chided him for treating his parents disrespectfully.

CARING KIDS

Children are also involved in household caring work. In chapter 4, we saw the obstacles to recognizing personal care, including child care, as real work. Acknowledging children's own care work, however, turns out to be even more challenging than recognizing adults' efforts. Children, after all, are not supposed to be caregivers, but recipients of care. Yet, as a number of researchers have shown, children involve themselves in a great deal of caring work, ranging from babysitting their siblings to attending a sick grandparent. The kinds of caring work children engage in vary dramatically with social relations: for example, children provide very different kinds of caring services to neighbors and to siblings. The various caring efforts vary also in their moral legitimacy. Like adults, children mark very strong boundaries between what they define as appropriate and inappropriate relations for care work. For instance, a child who regularly cooks for or takes an ailing grandparent to the bathroom would not ordinarily do the same for a neighbor. Both adults and children typically mark such boundaries with invocations of hostile worlds, noting the dangers of providing intimate services to the wrong people. Children, and adults, also distinguish care work from other types of child work, such as housework or wage work. What is more, children's paid care work, such as babysitting for other families, differs practically and symbolically from unpaid help around the house.

Children's care work matters. It extends to such crucial activities as making sure that ailing family members receive their medicine, and thus at times involve children in collaboration with health-care professionals and social workers. In the course of such work, children not only produce goods and services directly, but also accumulate capital—such as the human capital gained by knowledge of medical treatment and the social capital gained with links to health-care workers. In addition, children's individual accumulation of capital commonly enhances the store of capital available to the household as a whole. By connecting households with powerful outside institutions, children's mediation sometimes greatly affects the family's social position. Immigrant families, as we saw earlier, often depend on their native-born children to establish a wide range of connections between the household's adults and the alien environment. Counterintuitively, this means that a household lacking children will in certain circumstances accumulate less capital than those with children.

Children's caring efforts take a wide variety of forms, each corresponding to a different bundle of social relations. In her ethnographic account of pickup time at an elementary school in a mixed-income, ethnically diverse area of Oakdale, California, Barrie Thorne reports:

> The pick-up scene offers glimpses of children actively constructing and negotiating everyday life, including divisions of labor within and extending beyond households. Kids take responsibility for locating younger siblings and getting them home; they organize themselves into groups to head for after-school destinations; they make phone calls to check up on adults who are late; they carry messages between school and home. In addition, kids sometimes help out on adult job sites—

for example, by sorting dry cleaning at an uncle's store or by helping a mother clear tables in a restaurant. Children also contribute to housework. (Thorne 2001: 364)

Ask the Children, Ellen Galinsky's national survey of a representative sample including more than one thousand U.S. children in grades 3 through 12, offers some revealing glimpses into the variety of children's care work. The survey, supplemented with interviews, reported children saying that they "take care" of their parents by findings strategies of reducing parents' stress and fatigue. One twelve-year-old girl used humor to help her mother: "I try and make her feel better. My friend can make people laugh so easy. And so usually I'm like, "Chris, my mom feels kind of bad right now—you wanna come over and cheer her up?" and in just at least five minutes my mom is laughing so hard" (Galinsky 1999: 240). Some of the children complained about their caring duties, feeling, says Galinsky, that "their parents had become their children and that they were parenting them" (240).

In a reversal of perspectives, Galinsky thus shows that children responded to their parents' work in interesting, unexpected ways. While most experts and parents worry that parents are not spending enough time with their children, children fretted less about the time deficit. They did worry a great deal about their parents, but mostly about the quality of their interchanges when parents were under a great deal of stress. Indeed, she points out, children often play detective, gathering "mood clues" from their parents. One child told about calling her parents at work "to get a reading on how they are feeling so she can determine whether she should clean up the house before they come home" (xvii).

Children actually provide a surprising range of services to their families. Yet the scope, variety, intensity, and value of children's caring labor clearly have not received the attention they deserve. With precisely that deficit in mind, British advocates have coined the term "young carers" to designate children who make crucial contributions to other people's welfare (on children's care work, see also Becker, Aldridge, and Dearden 1998; Boulding 1980; Olsen 2000;

Robson and Ansell 2000). Household caring work and immigrant enterprise illustrate the substantial contributions children make to household production. As in relations between spouses, furthermore, these close studies of children show them not performing their work like automata, but implementing and reshaping their relations to each other, to parents, and to other adults as they invest their effort.

HOUSEHOLD DISRUPTION

What happens when ongoing household relations break down? How do parents, children, siblings, and other household members realign their economic transactions? Two categories of disruption differ significantly in their impact on household relations: one breaks an existing connection between the household and the rest of the world, the other intervenes directly in household relations. In the first category, we find unemployment, bankruptcy, prison, natural disasters, and war; in the second category fall the arrival, departure, or death of a household member; severe illness; migration; retirement; and divorce. Of course the two types of disruption interact. Any household in which a crucial member, for instance, goes to prison, undergoes internal disruption as well, while internal struggles almost always translate into changed relations with the rest of the world. Nevertheless, the two types of disruption differ in the way in which they affect household relations and in the interpretation people construct of what is happening.

In the first category, let us look at what happens with job loss and bankruptcy.[10] As she interviewed downwardly mobile families, Katherine Newman observed radical changes in domestic economies after a father had lost his job. Most notably, the crisis reversed expected middle-class parent-child relations. As family funds dwin-

---

[10] On the impact of economic depression on households, see the classic studies by Bakke [1940] 1969; Elder 1974; Jahoda, Lazarsfeld, and Zeisel [1933] 1971; Komarovsky 1940. On bankruptcy see Sullivan, Warren, and Westbrook 1999.

dled, adolescents and college-age children took on increasing financial responsibilities. Teenagers relied on part-time jobs to subsidize their expenses, while older children became the family's
indispensable "sub" parents or "junior breadwinners" (Newman
1988: 107, 111). Sometimes it meant combining college with work;
other times it meant forgoing college altogether. In one case, a child
took out multiple student loans only to subsidize family bills. John
Steinberg, whom we met before, dropped out of college for one year
to work in construction jobs. His earnings helped support his parents and younger sisters. Steinberg also recalled his embarrassment
as his father took over domestic work from his mother, work that
young Steinberg saw as demeaning (118).

As their economic relations shifted, parents frequently drew their
children into the financial secrets of their households. This could be
intimidating for children who previously lived affluent lives without
worrying much about financial matters. Janet Wilson confided to
Newman: "Maybe it was because I was the oldest child or because
role reversals had already occurred, but my mother always used to
say you should know about our finances, how much the mortgage
is, where we keep our information on the bank account. . . . This
was kind of scary sometimes. You wonder what's so immediately
dangerous" (107).

Unemployment similarly tested former managers' husband-wife
relations as well as their ties to other kin, including siblings, parents,
and in-laws. Newman notes, for instance, the men's reluctance to
borrow money from family members. For many, accepting help or
even asking for financial assistance threatened established patterns
of relations. What exactly were they asking for posed dilemmas as
well: Was it a gift or a loan? Should they repay it? If so, how soon?
(124–28). At the extreme, loss of a job means loss of a home, which
in turn may cause households to double up with their kin or to accept assistance in the form of subsidized housing. Margaret Nelson
and Joan Smith's study of rural Vermont working-class families
demonstrates costs of such arrangements. Matt Dwire and his wife
Patty moved into a house owned by her father at reduced rent but
in exchange for Matt's part-time work for his father-in-law. Matt's

work consisted of doing a demanding range of chores at the family's exotic animal farm. Matt complained: "It was hard. They say never rent from a family member. They expected more than what they told us when we moved in as far as work that should have been done" (Nelson and Smith 1999: 115).

Bankruptcy produces parallel effects. According to Warren and Tyagi's analysis in *The Two-Income Trap*, bankruptcy has become more common and painful for American middle-class households in recent years precisely because of some of the changes discussed earlier: the purchase of more expensive houses and the assumption of larger debt loads on the premise that both spouses' wages will continue indefinitely. Bankruptcy strikes not only husbands and wives but also their children. Warren and Tyagi estimate that more children are involved in their parent's bankruptcy than parental divorce. They predict that in the United States, by 2010 one out every seven children will live through their parent's bankruptcy (Warren and Tyagi 2003: 177). Bankruptcy obviously disrupts the relationship of a household to the rest of the world, putting serious restrictions on people's ability to use their household money to solve external problems. But it also requires adjustment within the household, not merely because of reduced income, but also because the new arrangements demand complicated management.

Deborah Thorne interviewed bankrupt couples, as well as bankruptcy lawyers, judges, and others to find out how households actually cope. She found family members on their way to bankruptcy trying a number of strategies: pawning jewels, borrowing from kin, drawing from children's part-time wages, and more. As they slid into bankruptcy, a remarkable gender pattern emerged—husbands withdrew, while their wives assumed the household's financial dirty work. Many husbands, for example, refused to answer the telephone as bill collectors started hounding them, kept themselves ignorant of current finances, and left all the legal work to their wives. One husband told Thorne: "I'm so bad, I mean, I love my wife, but I have to admit I was bad. They'd [bill collectors] call and I'd say, 'Oh, I'm sorry, he's not here right now' or, "she's [his wife] right here' " (Thorne 2001: 178). Many wives, therefore, found themselves in charge of keeping careful records, juggling bills, holding off hostile bill collectors, taking the initiative to file for bankruptcy, and then dealing with the arduous legal paperwork. Such tasks were often daunting. One woman, who took care of her three children during the day and waited tables at night, described her financial acrobatics. Thorne reports:

> [the woman] allocates her tips, *down to the dollar*, to the most pressing bills. For example, the day we talked, she had received a call from the electric company: if she didn't get them at least a partial payment, they were going to shut off her lights. She told me: "OK, I made $50 [in tips] last night. I can put it in the checking account and write them a check." (173)

Bankrupt parents often try to shield their children from these difficulties. In the course of interviewing over two thousand families who had filed for bankruptcy, Warren and Tyagi heard about thirty-eight-year-old Sara Swerdling's efforts to protect her eleven-year-old son from the family's deteriorating finances: "She carefully hid the past-due notices, told him the telephone was shut off due to a 'mechanical difficulty,' and said the car was towed away because the transmission was broken" (Warren and Tyagi 2003: 177). The deception worked until her son's orthodontist, informed of the bankruptcy, refused to continue caring for the boy's braces. With great difficulty, Swerdling was able to finally locate a dentist willing to remove the braces, if paid cash in advance. Explaining what happened to her son was even harder. They report: "She had to explain to her eleven-year-old what had gone wrong in their lives, why a stranger would take off his braces while his teeth were still crooked, and how his life was about to change" (177). Thus, as households confront unemployment or bankruptcy, family members rework not only their finances but also their relationships. Children and parents, husbands and wives, as well as other family members, sometimes painfully, devise new ways of mingling their intimate relations and economic transactions.

This is even more obvious in the case of separation or divorce, when one member actually leaves the household. Any such departure, among other things, alters the relationship not only between the spouses but also between parents and children, grandparents and grandchildren, as well as between the sundered spouses and their own families of origin. Two vignettes from Kathleen Gerson's interviews with a varied group of fathers in the New York metropolitan area illustrate some of the changes. Considering the men's financial contributions to their families and their participation in household work, Gerson classifies them into three main categories: primary breadwinners, autonomous fathers, and involved fathers. If, for example, a father ranked relatively low on economic contributions and on participation in household work, he qualified as autonomous. She found that with divorce, some of the traditional breadwinners became involved fathers. Those men soon discovered major relational changes.

Take the case of Roger, a businessman and father of three sons, who took over custody of the children after his wife left him for another man. He discovered how much work, including relational work, went into running a household: "I went from having to do almost nothing except playtime to having to do virtually everything. . . . You sit down, and where do you start? From scratch. You start by writing a list of everything that comes to your mind that you need to do. You realize the list goes from the floor to the ceiling a half-dozen times" (Gerson 1993: 239).

After divorce, some breadwinners took an opposite route, distancing themselves from their families. These newly autonomous fathers encountered a different set of substantial changes in their relationships with their children. Alan, a property assessor, whose wife had also left him for another man, reported his increasingly contentious exchanges with his son and stepdaughter: "They turned hostile, sent the money back, tearing it up. So I figured, 'If that's the way they want it to be . . .' I could have forced the issue but who was going to suffer? I figured, 'They'll come back' but it never materialized" (136).

Households disrupted by job loss, bankruptcy, separation, or divorce reveal the interdependence between household economic activity and intimate interpersonal relations. Crises that begin in one relationship, especially between spouses, ramify rapidly through all other household relations. Crises such as job loss and bankruptcy that radically and quickly reduce external sources of support for household activity immediately alter social relations in both areas: inside the household and in connections between household members and the rest of the social world. Financial flows often reverse, with children, siblings, or other relatives starting to aid newly beleaguered couples. Readjustments of this kind become even more visible when household transactions become matters of legal contestation.

HOUSEHOLDS AT LAW

With all the complex intersection of intimacy and economic activity going on in households, one might think that lawyers would delight in bringing household disputes to court. In fact, American law sets important barriers between household struggles and litigation. Unlike commercial dealings, the law generally presumes that economic transactions among cohabiting family members are "gratuitous," not for sale. Courts are loath to enforce promises made within households, much less to judge the value of such matters as companionship, fidelity, and contributions to household upkeep. In short, American law approaches households hesitantly, with gloves on. Nevertheless, household relations do become matters of legal dispute. Here is a sample of questions that have come before American courts over the past few decades:[11]

- If a couple divorces, does a wife who supported her husband as he worked toward a professional degree have a claim on his future professional earnings?

[11] For cases bearing on these issues, see *In re Marriage of Graham*, 135 Cal. Rptr. 2d 685 (Cal. Ct. App. 2003); *Riggs v. Riggs*, 478 S.E.2d 211 (N.C. Ct. App. 1996); *Eller v. Comm'r*, 11 T.C. 934 (1981); *Ver Brycke v. Ver Brycke*, 843 A.2d 758 (Md. 2004); *In re Marriage of Morris*, 640 N.E.2d 344 (Ill. App. Ct. 1994); Gary Coleman suit against parents, http://www.minorcon.org/childrenaschattels.html;

- If, unbeknownst to other household members, a spouse runs up a large debt, is the other spouse liable?
- If parents pay their children for work in their family businesses, may the parents deduct the wages as business expenses on their income tax?
- If parents contribute the down payment on a house purchased by their son and daughter-in-law, but the couple later divorce, can the parents recover their contribution?
- If a household member buys a lottery ticket and wins the jackpot, what claims do other household members have on the money?
- If parents collect large sums of money for the performance of a child actor or athlete, how much can they legitimately spend on themselves?
- If a lesbian parent has children during her cohabitation, does her partner, who shares partial custody, owe child support in case of separation?
- Is a divorced father liable for his children's tutoring expenses?

Money obviously looms large in such disputes. Furthermore, legal settlements in court cases on these issues commonly take the form of forced monetary payments. In recent years, for example, payment for child support has become a dominant issue in divorce settlements (Carbone 2000; Elrod and Spector 2004). Yet the disputes go far beyond money as such. They center on the mutual rights and obligations of household members.

Instead of surveying this wide range of legal disputes, let us return to the three main areas of household practices already examined: control and transfer of household assets, consumption-distribution, and household production. In the legal arena, these three areas of household activity commonly reappear as (1) disputes over household finances, (2) claims on household property, and (3) valuation of economic contributions of household members. As we will see, the law is more likely to take up those aspects of households that

---

L.S.K. v. H.A.N., 813 A.2d 872 (Pa. Super. Ct. 2002); Bass p. Bass, 779 N.E.2d 582 (Ind. Ct. App. 2002). See also Spragins 2003.

most closely resemble nonhousehold legal matters—contracts, torts, crimes, and so on. Indeed, the law regularly reinterprets household transactions into the languages of contracts, torts, crimes, and the like. Furthermore, households disrupted by death, divorce, separation, imprisonment, or bankruptcy appear more frequently before the bar than do intact households. As a consequence, households take on different guises in courtrooms than in routine social life.

DISPUTES OVER HOUSEHOLD FINANCES

Every household works out some arrangements for receipt, storage, distribution, and expenditure of the household's financial assets. Most households stabilize those arrangements by such devices as budgets, allowances, pooled or separate bank accounts, and responsibility for payment of bills. So doing, members of households simultaneously represent and shape their shared understanding of relations within the household and the household's collective relations to others outside. Even when these arrangements smooth into routines that household members take for granted, changing circumstances produce controversies over finances. A new job, children growing into adolescence, a serious illness, and divorce all illustrate the sorts of adaptations most households make sooner or later. Most of the time, households deal with stressful changes by relying on their own resources or those of friends and family.

But some disputes over finances become occasions for legal action. As before, we can make a rough but useful distinction between struggles that develop out of the household's internal relations and conflicts that begin with relations between the household and others outside. In the first category, let us look especially at disputes centering on pooled household financial assets; in the second, legal controversies over responsibilities of household members for the dubious activities of one of them. Of course, routine household financial management—how much family members spend, for what, how much is saved, and how the money is invested—gives rise to recurrent domestic squabbles, but those disputes rarely go to court. Even

if they did, the law would refuse to intervene in such private disagreements (Hartog 2000; Siegel 1994; for exceptional nineteenth-
century cases in which courts did intervene, see Kahn 1996: 383).
When households break up, however, their most routine financial
practices often turn into bitter accounting disputes. Collective monies must be relabeled, as his, hers, or theirs.

Lawyers and courts regularly distinguish between marital and
nonmarital property: indissolubly mingled assets that belong to the
household as such, and those they can somehow separate as belonging to contracting individuals. For example, courts often invoke
the doctrine of transmutation, asking whether the couple undertook
deliberate actions that converted individual assets into collective
goods. Did a spouse, for instance, buy property with her funds but
title it in both spouses' names? Or did a husband deposit his separate
money into a joint bank account with his wife? By doing so, it is
usually assumed that separate funds convert into a marital asset (see
Hadden 1993–94; Weyrauch, Katz, and Olsen 1994: 140–56).

In the absence of deliberate action, courts often apply a "source of
funds" rule: they search the origins of the contested assets, seeking
evidence that they did in fact belong to only one of parties. Did a
husband acquire a property after the divorce? Did a wife get her
money as a personal gift or bequest? Were the funds compensation
for one spouse's personal injury? In such cases, and with, of course,
the usual, extensive state-to-state variation, the asset is often declared nonmarital. But not always. Tracking ownership is often a
daunting legal quest. Commingling funds, for instance, is not definitive proof of their joint ownership. If spouses' separate funds are
commingled into a joint checking account and also used for collective household expenses, the commingling does erase earlier traces
of earlier separate ownership. But if the court is able to trace the
separate monies in a joint account or investment fund, or show their
personally earmarked uses, then a spouse often retains individual
ownership rights.

That is what happened in the case of *Tolley v. Tolley* (592 N.W.2d
318 (Wis. Ct. App. 1999)). In 1988, Bertie Tolley had received some
$300,000 for compensation of a personal injury, while Barbara, his

wife, got about $21,000 for loss of consortium resulting from the injury. The couple deposited both awards in their joint names. When the Tolleys divorced, the court determined that the funds did not belong to the marital estate. Barbara appealed the decision, claiming that the commingling of awards in a joint account, compounded by the use of the monies for household expenditures had converted the funds into marital property. But the Wisconsin Court of Appeals rejected her claims, ruling that the source of the monies overrode their commingling. Citing an earlier case, the court underlined the specificity of a personal injury award in these terms: "Just as each spouse is entitled to leave the marriage with his or her body, so the presumption should be that each spouse is entitled to leave the marriage with that which is designed to replace or compensate for a healthy body" (318).

From a doctrinal point of view, source of funds overwhelmed transmutation. A reverse outcome occurred in the divorce case of *Spooner v. Spooner* (850 A.2d 354 (Me. 2004)) in Maine's Supreme Judicial Court. At stake here was an investment account with stocks worth about $60,000. A trust established by Deborah Spooner's mother had endowed Deborah with those securities, which Deborah placed in a joint account with her husband, Stephen Spooner. The Spooners used some of the money to pay off credit card debts, "down payments on vehicles for both Stephen and Deborah, repayment of a car loan, Deborah's dental work, and repayment of a college loan for Deborah's son" (357).

The district court trying the Spooner's divorce was persuaded by Deborah's claims—supported by a trust document establishing her as her mother's sole beneficiary—that the stocks were hers alone, not her husband's. Stephen disagreed and appealed the judgment. He argued that even if the assets had originated as Deborah's personal funds, the stocks had converted into marital property once his wife had placed them in their joint account and they had spent the money for mutual debts and purchases. Transmutation, by his argument, had occurred. The Supreme Court agreed with Stephen and reversed the district court's initial judgment. In so doing, the court made two crucial rulings in the case: first, that the doctrine of transmutation applies to securities, not just property; and second, that in the absence of strong evidence to the contrary, transmutation trumps source of funds. The court did not contest Barbara's claim that her mother's stocks had been a gift to her alone, but once she had placed them in a joint account, they ceased being her personal property.

In other cases, the legal dispute does not originate within the household, but in relations between the household and outside authorities. A striking case in point arises with tax obligations. Over the past half-century, U.S. households have usually filed joint tax returns and borne joint responsibility for any errors, misrepresentations, or fraud. Internal Revenue Service guidelines make clear the extent of married couples' joint liability: "Both taxpayers are jointly and individually responsible for the tax and any interest or penalty due on the joint return even if they later divorce. . . . One spouse may be held responsible for all the tax due even if all the income was earned by the other spouse" (Internal Revenue Service 2004).

What happens when a husband or a wife makes fraudulent claims of which the other spouse has little or no knowledge? Since often one spouse prepares the tax return and the other simply signs, the opportunity for serious trouble looms large. Indeed until 1971, under American tax law, the unwitting conspirator shared full liability for fraud, whether the couple was divorced or still married. Between 1971 and 1998, however, Congress introduced some protection for what it called an "innocent spouse." If a wife or a husband could prove she or he was unaware and had no reason to know of any tax understatement, the IRS would exempt that spouse from unfair liability.

In 1989, for instance, a U.S. Court of Appeals declared Patricia Price an "innocent spouse," reversing an earlier judgment by the U.S. Tax Court. In their 1981 joint federal income tax returns, Charles Price, her husband, had claimed a $90,000 deduction for expenses related to a Colombian gold mine investment. Patricia testified she "thought [it] was a bit much," yet reassured by her husband, she signed. When the IRS challenged the deduction some years later, Patricia pleaded innocence: she had trusted her husband's business expertise without suspecting foul play. Although the Tax Court rejected her claims, the U.S. Court of Appeals was persuaded, noting, among other factors, Patricia's subordinate involvement in the household's financial accounting system:

> [W]e note that Patricia had limited involvement in the financial affairs of her marriage with Charles in general and none whatsoever in the [gold mine] investment in particular. . . . Indeed, Charles held a separate checking account for his investments, while Patricia's participation in the couple's money matters apparently was limited to paying household expenses and the mortgage on their home. (*Price v. Comm'r* 887 F.2d 959, 965 (9th Cir. 1989))

Charles, concluded the Appeals Court, "had taken advantage of Patricia's lack of understanding of their financial affairs and misled her" (959). Nevertheless, under the legislation prevailing until 1998, few aggrieved spouses either filed for protection or won their cases (Willis 1998: 2).

In 1998, Congress responded to complaints by reducing joint liabilities further, but by no means eliminating them. In fact, Elizabeth Cockrell, who had agitated for tax reform, nevertheless lost her own case when it came to the U.S. Supreme Court. During their two-year marriage, John P. Crowley, Cockrell's then husband, a commodities broker who speculated in tax shelters, allegedly duped her into signing tax statements claiming fraudulent deductions for sham tax shelter losses. In 1990, nine years after their divorce, the IRS, unable to collect from Crowley, billed Cockrell, now a single mother of two, for $650,000. Cockrell's claim of innocence faced several difficulties: her college education; her training as a stockbroker; her involvement, however limited, in her husband's business; the couple's lavish living style; and the sheer size of the deductions for which the IRS was pursuing them. As a result, both the Tax Court and an Appeals Court rejected her defense (*Cockrell v. Comm'r*, 97–2 U.S. Tax Cas. (CCH) P50, 549 (2d Cir. 1997)).

Stung by her defeat, Cockrell became an outspoken advocate of legislative reform. She testified before the 1998 Senate Finance

Committee and created Women for IRS Financial Equity (WIFE) to defend vulnerable spouses. Congress did act on her group's proposal: after the 1998 tax reform, the number of innocent spouse claims multiplied. Between 1999 and 2001, for instance, the IRS received over 150,000 relief requests (Cozort 2003; see also U.S. General Accounting Office 2002). Cockrell, however, did not benefit personally. In 1999, the U.S. Supreme Court refused to hear her argument that she was an "innocent spouse." Yet concern about her plight continued: in December 2003, a *Daily News* gossip story reported that Hollywood movie producers were considering a movie about Cockrell's experience and that of another innocent spouse (Grove 2003).

CONTESTED CLAIMS ON HOUSEHOLD PROPERTY

Major household purchases, as we have seen, typically involve most or all household members and sometimes draw in other kin as well. When trouble starts, the nature of those purchases and payment for them often become acute matters of legal dispute. In divorce settlements, for example, whether a household automobile belonged to one spouse or both often hinges on whether they purchased it separately, whether they used it separately, or whether one spouse gave it to the other as a gift (see Hadden 1993–94).

Another recurrent form of property dispute is the attempt of parties in a legal case to decide whether a given person's collaboration in a purchase constituted a gift, a loan, an entitlement, or a co-purchase. When the legal action involves a divorce, a house is usually by far the largest single piece of property up for division. At that point, who paid for the house, how, and why becomes the crucial legal issue. When parents, for instance, gave their child and the child's spouse money for a down payment, did they expect repayment as they would of any loan, or was that money a gift? If a gift, was it a conditional gift, with the expectation that the child would eventually help out the donors? Did they and the children purchase the house jointly? If the child later divorces, what happens to the parents' investment? If the payment qualifies as a loan, the divorcing couple is equally responsible for repayment, but if a gift, much depends whether it was a joint or individual gift. In the absence of strong evidence concerning the donor's intentions, however, courts commonly rely on the doctrine of gratuity: the presumption that transfers of property between close relatives constitute gifts (see Marvel 1979). Thus, if parents buy a house for their married child, without further evidence of intentions, courts commonly decide that the house purchase was a gift.

Some of these issues come forth dramatically in an unusual dispute over home ownership decided in 2002 (*Hudak v. Procek*, 806 A.2d 140 (Del. 2002); see also *Hudak v. Procek*, 727 A.2d 841 (Del. 1999); *Elder Law* 2002). At issue was parents' investment in a house purchased by a child and surviving family members' claims on that house. Anna and John Procek, the parents, migrated from Czechoslovakia, settling in an ethnic New Jersey neighborhood with other fellow Czechs, where they raised three daughters. The Proceks never learned much English, nor how to drive a car. In 1978, when they were in their mid-seventies, the couple decided to sell their New Jersey home and move to Delaware near their eldest daughter Helen Hudak. Helen had promised to take care of them in their old age. Unfamiliar with complex financial transactions (they only used cash for their purchases), the Proceks delegated Helen to purchase their new home—one block away from her own—with the proceeds from the sale of the New Jersey property. The house was titled in daughter Helen's name alone, although she had been married to John Hudak Jr. for over two decades. After the Proceks moved in, they paid all the new house's expenses, but relied on Helen and John for various forms of routine help. Helen drove her parents "to stores and to medical appointments. . . . The Proceks gave cash to Helen who wrote checks to pay [their] bills" (*Hudak*, 806 A.2d 145), while John took care of occasional house repairs.

In April 1990, tragedy struck: after a short illness Helen died of cancer. Before she died, Helen had offered to transfer the house's ownership to her parents, but they declined. Therefore, after Helen's death, the house title passed to her surviving husband. A few months later, concerned that Hudak might remarry and evict them, John Procek persuaded his widowed son-in-law to sign an agreement guaranteeing that the older couple could remain in the house until their death. Procek died just three years later. Three years after that, the now ninety-two-year-old Anna decided to move out and live with Irene, another of her daughters. That's when the trouble started. Irene and Annie (the third daughter) asked Hudak to sell the house and divide the proceeds equally among the three of them. Hudak rejected the proposal and moved into the disputed property with his son. Anna went to court, claiming the house was hers, not Hudak's. She had not, Anna testified, purchased the house as an outright gift for her daughter: "See, I pay every penny for my house. She not pay nothing, just take care of me, you know." When the court asked her why she and her husband had put the house in Helen's name, Anna answered: "I think she needs to take care of me but she die so quick" (148). The Proceks would have gifted the house to their daughter as reward for her care, but after their own deaths, not hers.

Three court decisions sided with the older woman: first, the Delaware trial court in 1998, and twice, on appeal, Delaware's Supreme Court. Yet the odds had been against Anna: after all, she had to counter the strong legal presumption that when a parent transfers property to a child, that transfer is an outright gift, not a conditional donation. In reaching their decisions, the courts took into account the elderly Proceks' lack of familiarity with the American legal system to explain why they probably had not understood the legal implications of putting the house in Helen's name. Nor was there a record of a gift tax filing. In addition, the courts were skeptical that parents of three daughters would privilege only one of them to such an extent. The courts based a significant part of their decision on their reading of the Proceks' intentions and thus found themselves fitting a complex set of household transactions into the narrower niches supplied by the law.

VALUATION STRUGGLES

Everyday household disputes often turn on contributions of family members to the collective enterprise: spouses' participation in housework, children's responsibility for household tasks, negotiation with outside organizations, and so on. Such issues become matters of legal contestation when one member or another seeks compensation for services to the household after the fact or makes claims on household assets by virtue of contributions to their production. The most obvious cases result from injury, illness, death and divorce. Such disruptions often raise thorny questions concerning the valuation of household work. Unpaid contributions raise particularly delicate issues because courts must decide whether such services should be valued at all and if so, what value to assign.

The landmark divorce case of *Hartog v. Hartog* raises just such issues (647 N.E.2d 749 (N.Y. 1995)). Katherine and Albert Hartog divorced in 1991, after twenty-three years of marriage during which they had raised two sons, who were then in their twenties. During their time together, Katherine, who was fifty-one at the time of the divorce, had devoted herself to her activities as "spouse, parent, housekeeper and hostess" (752). From time to time, she had taken sporadic but low-earning jobs. Albert spent five or six days a week working in F. Staal, his family's jewelry business. He was also involved as director and shareholder in two other family businesses, Hartog Trading Corporation and Hartog Foods International. Albert, however, was not directly responsible for the management of those companies; his brother and others supervised those two enterprises. With the exception of one joint checking account, the couple kept separate banking and brokerage accounts. Along the way, the Hartogs had their share of serious medical problems. Katherine had undergone mastectomies for breast cancer in 1985 and 1986, while Albert was diagnosed with prostate cancer in the later stages of their divorce litigation.

When Katherine and Albert divorced, their case, as one judge put it, presented "a multifaceted puzzle of issues" (752). Indeed, *Hartog v. Hartog*, first decided by the Supreme Court of New York, was twice appealed, first in 1993 and again two years later. The contested issues included:

1. Did Katherine have a claim on the appreciation of value in F. Staal, where Albert worked many days a week?

2. Did she have an equivalent claim on the appreciation of the other two family business, in which Albert did not participate very actively?

3. Was Katherine entitled to a portion of a bonus earned by Albert prior to their divorce but paid him after the divorce proceedings began?

4. Were the stocks and bonds that Albert kept in a safe deposit box—some of which had been gifts to him from his parents—his personal property, or did they also belong to Katherine, since the stock and bonds had been commingled with marital assets?

5. Was Katherine entitled to an award that guaranteed her ability to maintain the couples' predivorce standard of living?

After an adverse 1993 judgment by the Appellate Division of the Supreme Court, in its final 1995 judgment, the Court of Appeals established the wife's right in almost all these regards. The court ruled most significantly that Katherine had a claim on the appreciation of Hartog Trading and Hartog Foods, despite Albert's argument that neither her effort nor his had caused the disputed appreciation. Albert's involvement in both family businesses, albeit limited, the court decided, sufficiently contributed to the appreciation of their value. As a result, a portion of that appreciation rightfully became marital property. But what precisely gave Katherine any claim to the appreciated value of two firms in which she had never worked directly? The court judged that her maintenance of the Hartog household sufficed to qualify her claims. Citing 1980 domestic equitable distribution principles and the 1986 precedent case of *Price v. Price* (593 N.E.2d 684 (N.Y. 1986)), the Court stated the law's intent: "to treat marriage in one respect as an economic partnership and, in so doing, to recognize the direct and indirect contributions of each spouse, including homemakers" (*Hartog*, 647 N.E.2d 755). Shortly after the case ended, Albert Hartog died of cancer. Katherine collected from his estate (Plesent 2004). *Hartog v. Hartog* became a landmark case precisely because of the principles on which the wife collected. The more general assumption that domestic work actually contributes to the economic welfare of the household by now has acquired visible standing in American law.

The monetary awards for deaths of 9/11 victims brought similar concerns into stark relief. How were those tragically lost lives to be justly valued? American law has, of course, long provided opportunity for suits alleging wrongful death. As we saw in chapter 2, the loss of the deceased person's income or practical services long dominated court awards of compensation. Nevertheless, by the early twentieth century, courts reluctantly moved toward also recognizing the economic value of sentimental loss, including companionship, affection, personal care, and sexual relations. Relatives of persons killed on September 11 could have filed standard wrongful death suits individually, and some of them did. But instead, for a number of reasons, most notably to spare airlines from unmanageable litigation, the U.S. government decided to minimize individual suits by creating a national Victim Compensation Fund, to be apportioned among certified claimants. Lawyer Kenneth Feinberg took on the delicate job of administering the fund and deciding how to allocate available monies among those physically injured in the attack and bereaved kin of those killed.

Feinberg received a great deal of discretion in deciding how to proceed. Thus, he could have simply awarded equal amounts to survivors of every single victim. Or he could have bargained individually with those survivors. Instead, Feinberg took on directly the daunting problem of evaluating the extent of each loss. That decision engaged him in a very complicated set of computations and negotiations. He had to gauge carefully who was an eligible claimant, who had the right to speak for a given victim's claimants, how much compensation eligible claimants should receive, and for what losses. For example, he relied on variable prospective economic loss to determine survivors' claims, but set a standard per-victim payment for the survivors' pain and suffering ($250,000 for each individual killed, plus $100,000 for each surviving spouse or child).

As compensation guidelines shaped up, one remarkable feature of discussions surrounding the fund was the salience of moral themes. Passionate debates broke out over why widows or parents of top-earning executives should receive more money than a janitor's or a firefighter's survivors, and over whether gay and lesbian partners should be allowed to collect. Did bereaved common-law partners and fiancés qualify for compensation? What about estranged spouses? Why the cap on pain and suffering losses? And why such prominence to economic loss? As one critic put it, "It is all too easy to do the math with work hours rather than with heartbreak" (Meyerson 2002).

Meanwhile, the families of victims killed in other disasters—the 1993 World Trade Center bombing, Oklahoma City, the U.S.S. *Cole*, embassies in East Africa—questioned the moral legitimacy of a fund that compensated for the September 11 losses, but not theirs. For instance, Kathleen Treamor, who lost her four-year-old daughter in the Oklahoma City attack asked, "Why is it right for a New York stockbroker's widow to be given millions of dollars and not a poor farmer's family in Oklahoma? . . . Why is my daughter worth less than these people?" (Belkin 2002: 95; see also U.S. Department of Justice 2002).

The fund closed on June 15, 2004. How did Feinberg apportion almost $7 billion to settle 2,900 claims for death and 4,400 claims for personal injury? Following wrongful death litigation precedent, Feinberg relied largely on the economic loss created by each death. But two other issues drew him even more directly into household affairs. The first was determining which bereaved claimant was entitled to receive monetary compensation; the second, deciding what precisely constituted a household's economic loss. Specifying legitimate claimants involved Feinberg in drawing difficult distinctions. Members of the same household as the deceased—spouses and children—were obvious candidates. But Feinberg had to contend with multiple other claims, most notably unmarried cohabitants and same-sex partners. To make matters more complicated, in many cases relatives and companions of victims bitterly contested which of them had the right to compensation. For example, Feinberg finally decided that only if the same-sex partner and the victim's family agreed on the claims, would the same-sex partner qualify (Boston 2004; Gross 2002).

Estranged spouses presented equally tangled problems. Consider the case of Mandy Chang, employed at the First Commercial Bank of Taiwan, who died on the seventy-eighth floor of the World Trade Center's south tower. Her surviving estranged husband, James C. Burke, and her mother, Feng-yu Wu, battled over their rights to compensation from the fund. Because Burke and Chang never divorced, he claimed to be her legal heir. According to her friends, however, the only reason the couple had not yet divorced was Chang's reluctance to engage in a legal and financial struggle. Chang's mother, who lived with her in Manhattan and was declared as a tax dependent, challenged her son-in-law's moral claims to compensation. Her attorney, Michael Cervini, tried voiding the marriage (Chen 2002). As it happened, however, Burke could not make a credible claim for his own financial loss. After hard bargaining by Cervini, the estranged husband accepted a smaller award and conceded the bulk of the payment to his mother-in-law (Cervini 2004).

Determining what constituted economic loss was an equally challenging task. Initially, the fund made no provision for compensating unpaid household work—which as we have seen constitutes a crucial part of household economic activity. Organized feminists raised complaints and lobbied Feinberg intensively on this issue. In January 2002, New York Congresswoman Carolyn Maloney and eleven other members of Congress protested in writing against Feinberg's failure to "take into account household services performed by the working person for the family, such as child care and household upkeep" (Maloney 2002). Martha Davis, vice president and legal director of the National Organization of Women's Legal Defense and Education Fund joined Joan Williams, director of the Program on Gender, Work and Family at the Washington College of Law, American University, in making a detailed appeal. They argued that "ignoring the unpaid work performed by full-time workers raises sex discrimination concerns. . . . Women victims," they continued, "especially mothers, are much more likely to have expended significant time on unpaid work" (Davis 2002: 220).

Feminists succeeded: Feinberg changed the policy. The Victim Compensation Fund Final Rule in March 2002 allowed for a case-by-case consideration of claims for "replacement services loss": bereaved survivors could now claim compensation for the economic value of household services provided by the decedent (U.S. Department of Justice 2002). The unpaid labor included that of both women and men. Feinberg's case-by-case approach allowed a detailed calculation of such household contributions. The fund typically took evidence of the survivors' actual expenditures after 9/11 on unpaid household tasks the victim would have performed, then extrapolated the proven expenditures to the victim's normally expected lifetime. For example, in the case of a forty-year-old unmarried firefighter who earned $71,000 a year, the "initial estimated gross award" amounted to $1.5 million. The fund included in its compensation calculations the fact that he had assisted his parents, who were in frail health, with multiple chores and other services. The computation of the fireman's parents' award used as a basis the $3,300 the parents spent on roof repairs after 9/11, on the ground that, if alive, the fireman would have done the job himself. The fund treated this expense as "labor component of supplemental purchased services," and awarded the parents a $40,000 supplement to the wage-based compensation for the fireman's death (Dreher 2004).

A married fireman's survivors received supplemental compensation based on actual expenses incurred during 2002 and 2003, extended through his normal life expectancy. The reported items included:

Interior house painting	$700
Stain windows	400
Lawn care	800
Tree removal	1,200
Roof replacement	15,240

Snowplowing	180
Exterior house painting	600
Plumbing	125
Total	$19,245

Clearly, the items featured men's unpaid household work (Dreher 2004). In the case of a twenty-six-year-old accountant who had worked in the World Trade Center for a financial services company earning $50,000 annually, the fund increased the award by considering the economic value of the woman's assistance to her disabled immigrant mother, who spoke no English. According to the family's lawyer: "She was her mom's go-between with the outside world. It was sort of a reverse parental role" (Chen 2004: 4).

HOUSEHOLD LAW MEETS HOUSEHOLD PRACTICE

Go to your local bookstore. The average general bookstore has a full shelf of advice books, which frequently stand high on best-seller lists. Amid the advice on making a billion dollars, losing a hundred pounds, and transforming your psyche, you will find plenty of legal advice, sometimes on how to take a problem before the courts, but more often on how to protect your interests and avoid trouble with the law. When it comes to management of household finances, here, for instance, are some samples of the advice Shelby White gives to women in her book *What Every Woman Should Know about Her Husband's Money*. "If you have separate property," White warns, "think very carefully about whether you want to put it in a joint account. It's easy to give up control to show that you trust somebody. But you may regret it in the future" (White 1992: 29). She illustrates some of the "terrible mistakes" women make with money:

> *Using her money for expenses while her husband's investments increased.* For nine of the thirteen years of her marriage, Linda outearned her husband. They split expenses and used her extra earnings to pay taxes. Sounds reasonable. But all the time they

were using her money, his separate investment account, which he had before they married, continued to grow. (45)

Using her separate money to buy something in joint name while her husband holds on to his separate investments. When they split, Abby's husband got half the joint property, Abby got nothing of his separate investments. (46)

But the "biggest mistake of all" White stresses, is "thinking that talking about money is not romantic. The very precautions that would help you at the time of a divorce or the death of your husband—prenuptial agreements, accurate records about property, knowing the value of stock options—are viewed as unromantic" (46–47).

When it comes to family loans, advice experts are equally emphatic. One money expert, for instance, characteristically agrees that parents should help a hard-working child buy a new home or start a business. But "keep it business-like" she counsels: "If you don't document the transaction you risk not getting paid back and have little recourse legally. . . . If you loan money to your child and his or her spouse, a written agreement insures that each party has an obligation to you in the event of premature death or divorce" (Sahadi 2000).

A Legal Guide for Lesbian and Gay Couples also provides advice for its constituency. It counsels members of same-sex households on a broad range of financial concerns. When it comes to household work, the book offers a specific set of injunctions to make the division of labor equitable:

A person who spends all weekend fixing up a jointly owned house or a home solely owned by the other partner can be paid an agreed-upon hourly rate, with the compensation either paid in cash by the other or added to the carpenter's equity in the house. A stay-at-home mate can be given a weekly salary or can trade services (you fix the car while your love does the laundry). You should also think about the homemaker's future if you split up. You can agree on a period of support payments for the homemaker, thereby creating your own alimony-like arrangement by contract. (Curry, Clifford, and Hertz 2002: chap. 6, p. 22)

In the area of household life, legal advice books (plus their equivalents in newspapers, magazines, Web sites, and television broadcasts) make a subtle point of great importance for our understanding of households and the law. Despite the peculiarities of each single case, lawyers, judges, and juries follow principles that are sufficiently visible and uniform for dispensers of advice to tell wary household members which practices will have adverse legal consequences. In this way, interpretations of the law influence household practices

Another, even subtler, kind of feedback links legal routines to household practices. Despite general respect for statutes and precedents, lawyers, judges, juries, and legal scholars regularly call attention to perverse consequences of existing statutes and precedents—consequences for life outside the courtroom. For instance, as we saw earlier, having discovered how collective liability for income tax fraud penalized households in which one spouse had cheated on its income tax return, American courts and legislatures worked out a distinctive doctrine to protect truly innocent spouses and other household members. Now advice experts regularly warn spouses to check on income tax returns before signing, to qualify themselves for innocence in the event of a later claim by the IRS. A *Washington Post* columnist put it bluntly:

> Girlfriends, if I've told you once, I've told you a thousand times, look at what you sign. But you are hardheaded. Each year thousands of women find themselves liable for tax debts incurred by their ex-husbands. In most cases these women had let their husbands do the taxes and then had simply signed the tax form presented to them. (Singletary 1999: HO2)

Thus the law and household practice intertwine like vine and tree, each one operating on partly independent principles, each one responding to the other's life.

Relations between imprisoned felons and their households cast an unexpected light on this interplay between households and the law.[12] In this case, the law of crime and punishment occupies center stage. At a time when the United States ranks second only to Russia among Western countries in its ratio of prisoners to general population, the issue is pressing (Mauer 1999: 19). Looking at the District of Columbia, Donald Braman reports that "about one out of every ten adult black men . . . is in prison, and, at last count, over half of the black men between the ages of eighteen and thirty-five were under some type of correctional supervision." The United States, Braman notes, "at a cost of over $40 billion a year . . . now holds one out of every four of the world's prisoners" (Braman 2004: 3).

Although some convicted felons are solitary men, most of them maintain regular connections, however troubled, with households—their households of origin as well as households they themselves had formed. Members of those households who maintain contact with prisoners bear a serious burden. To document those burdens, Braman spent three years interviewing more than two hundred inmates and their families within the District of Columbia. Economic interactions between households and prisoners included (extremely expensive) collect phone calls by prisoners to their families, sending of portions of the miserable wages earned in prison to destitute families, families sending money for prisoners' purchases in the prison canteen, and repeated negotiations between prisoners and their relatives over means of coping with the economic hardships imposed on families by the prisoner's absence.

One of Braman's families illustrates the wrenching difficulties faced by all the rest. Edwina and her son Kenny were at the core of this household's travails. Years earlier, the now sixty-two-year-old Edwina had moved from Alabama to D.C. She had separated from her husband and raised her two children alone, working her way up to a supervisory position in an Army division. By 1998, she was planning to retire on a small pension, sell her house, and return to

---

[12] Clayton and Moore 2003; Edin, Nelson, and Paranel 2004; Martin 2001; Mumola 2000; Western, Patillo, and Weiman 2004.

Alabama with the proceeds from that sale to help her sister care for their mother, who was in the early stages of Alzheimer's disease. At that point, Edwina shared her house with the forty-two-year-old Kenny and his two sons. Kenny, who worked as a computer technician, helped his mother by paying for routine expenses and the mortgage, as well as taking care of house and car repairs. He also contributed to a niece's college expenses at Howard University. Edwina, meanwhile, helped Kenny with child care.

One violent incident undid their household arrangements. As Kenny returned home one day, he was assaulted by a neighborhood crack addict. He fought back, stabbing the man with a knife he carried for self-protection. The man died and Kenny went to prison. Meanwhile Tasha, Kenny's daughter from a previous relationship, moved in with Edwina bringing along her newborn baby. Edwina had to make up for Kenny's lost income and household assistance, as well as to manage the additional costs of occasional babysitters for the children, plus Kenny's prison expenses. She therefore cancelled her plans to return to Alabama, took a second mortgage on her home, and returned to work part-time. Kenny knew how badly his absence hurt the household. He told Braman: "By me being the only man—I'm from the South, and you know, you're the man, and you're supposed to take care of all the females—and there's just a lot of things around the house that goes wrong. . . . I fix the car, and I fix all the plumbing and . . . it becomes a strain when you have to find money to fix things" (Braman 2004: 110). Kenny's contributions, comments Braman, are "typical in that he not only drew from but also contributed to a number of familial resources, benefiting both himself and others" (109).

HOUSEHOLDS IN AND OUT OF THE LAW

As we have seen, household commerce presents the law with even greater challenges than do the complex issues raised by coupling and relations of care. Why is that? Household economic relations involve an intricate mix of intimacy and economic activity. They interweave long-term commitment, continuous demands of coordination and reciprocity, relations to kin, friends, and others outside the household. They impose shared vulnerability to the failures, mistakes, and malfeasance of other household members. These multiple concerns surface in the routine management of household finances, in both major and ordinary domestic purchases, and in negotiations over household work. When households get into financial trouble or break up, economic interactions of family members add yet another layer of complexity: kin help the unemployed, and financial roles often reverse, with children, for instance, now supporting their parents. Intimacy and economic activity continue to intersect, but they take on new configurations.

The law faces two difficulties in dealing with this formidable set of household transactions. First, it lacks sufficiently subtle templates to represent the multiple relations and transactions that occur in households. Second, legal templates operate on different principles, relying on a distinct set of procedures and distinctions when household members bring their economic disputes to court. Transactions among household members, for example, vary enormously in meaning and consequences, from the coins a mother gives her child to buy an ice cream bar to the money parents later commit to the same child's college education. But for most purposes the law compresses monetary transfers among household members into just three categories: gifts, bargained exchanges, and thefts (Baron 1988–89; Rose 1992). Furthermore, while household members and their kin put great energy into distinguishing different relations from each other, legal proceedings commonly lump relations together by setting: an arena of legally enforceable contracts, and another arena in which commitments, although operating on moral principles, have no claims to legal enforcement.

From a nonlegal viewpoint, some of these distinctions look strange. The law regularly treats transactions that would qualify as contracts outside of households—for example, performance of housework—as gifts. The gift-bargain distinction also cuts the other way, however; in high-stakes divorce settlements and compensation for wrongful death, as we have seen, courts frequently start counting up unpaid contributions to household welfare as if they resembled wage work. The law continues to distinguish between a "gratuitous" and a "commercial" sphere, but it draws the line differently from that prevailing in everyday practice.

The imposition of such a distinction tilts the angle of reflection as household practices appear in their legal mirrors. Most obviously, children play prominent, influential parts in household life, but child-child and child-adult relations rarely figure in legal contests. To be sure, people go to court over claims concerning child custody, child abuse, paternity, and occasionally even a child's education. But for the most part, courts place children on the gratuitous side of the legal boundary, declining to intervene in what they define as family matters. The distinctions make a difference. Recall that courts generally refuse to enforce a child's claim on financial support for a college education, yet a few states make a dramatic exception in the case of divorce. Then the obligation of one or both parents to pay for college can become an enforceable contract. More generally, in the legal world divorce moves many a relation from the gratuitous to the commercial sphere. Similar adjustments of the boundary often occur in the legal treatment of inheritance. Contestation over the legal rights of same-sex households pivots on just such distinctions: on which side of the line between gratuity and commerce do relations within those households belong? When same-sex couples with children break up, does one of the adults have a right to alimony? To child support? To recovery of household assets?

In these ways and more, contests and decisions in the legal arena shape household life. Influence obviously runs in the other direction as well: lawyers, judges, and juries deploy their own knowledge of changing household structure and practices as they make binding decisions. Cohabitation, divorce, and separation become more common, and present new problems to the law. More women go into wage work, and courts have no choice but to notice the changing division of household labor that results from women's employment. Shifts in caring, coupling, and household practices all eventually affect the law, its interpretation, and its application to concrete cases.

In the law or outside, households absorb some of the most intense relational work that people ever carry on. That work intertwines intimacy and economic activity so closely that one often becomes indistinguishable from the other. Household members feed each other, contribute their labor to the household's collective enterprises, and transfer goods, services, and assets as a matter of course. While conducting the household as an intimate economic enterprise, adults and children pursue two activities we have observed repeatedly in our exploration of coupling, caring, and household life: marking boundaries among different relations that transect the household, and within each boundary matching media and transactions to each relation's distinctive meaning. In their own versions of household intervention, courts do the same. Doctrines of hostile worlds, separate spheres, and nothing-but, we see once more, fall lamentably short of catching the intimate complexity of household interactions.

CHAPTER 6

INTIMATE REVELATIONS

Hildegard Lee Borelli and Michael J. Borelli were married in 1980. Three years later, as Michael's health began to falter, he went to the hospital repeatedly with heart trouble. In 1988, after he suffered a stroke, Michael's doctors recommended round-the-clock institutional care. But Michael resisted the move. Instead, he promised his wife that if she cared for him at home, at his death he would leave her a large share of his estate. He did not keep the promise. The following year, after Michael's death, Hildegard discovered he had bequeathed the bulk of his estate to Grace Brusseau, his daughter by an earlier marriage. Her legal appeals for enforcement of the marital promise failed.

In a 1993 decision, the California Court of Appeals turned down Hildegard's claims. The decision became notorious among feminist legal scholars (see, for example, Siegel 1994; Williams 2000). Severely condemning the Borellis' "sickbed bargaining," the court ruled that, as Michael's wife, Hildegard owed him nursing care free of charge and therefore had no right to ask compensation for her efforts (*Borelli v. Brusseau* 16 Cal. Rptr. 2d 16, 20 (Cal. Ct. App. 1993)). A dissenting judge vigorously disagreed with the implication that Hildegard "had a preexisting . . . nondelegable duty to clean the bedpans herself" (20). The judge commented that in this day and age spouses should have every right to contract with each other for services and their compensation. After all, Hildegard could easily have hired commercial help for the day-to-day drudgery of caring for an invalid, but responded to her husband's promise by doing it herself. The court's majority, however, rejected that view:

> The dissent maintains that mores have changed to the point that spouses can be treated just like any other parties haggling at arm's length. Whether or not the modern marriage has become like a business . . . it continues to be defined by statute as a personal relationship of mutual support. Thus, even if few things are left that cannot command a price, marital support remains one of them. (16)

Both sides of the *Borelli v. Brusseau* court decision impale themselves on the horns of hostile worlds/nothing-but reasoning. One horn declares that marriage must remain sacred, insulated from commercial transactions; the other horn announces that marriage *is* a commercial transaction. Both sides thus fail to recognize one of this book's most important revelations: that every relationship of coupling, caring, and household membership repeatedly mingles economic transactions and intimacy, usually without contamination, yet relations of coupling, caring, and household membership operate differently from other relationships. As long as we cling to the idea of hostile worlds we will never recognize, much less explain, the pervasive intertwining of economic activity and intimacy. Yet nothing-but reductionism fails to allow for the distinctive properties of coupling, caring, and households. The prominence of intimacy in those social relations transforms the character and consequences of economic activity within them. The question, therefore, is not whether intimate partners can or should engage in economic transactions but what sorts of economic transactions match which intimate relations. In contrast to hostile worlds and nothing-but understandings, this book has forwarded a connected lives view: in all social settings, intimate and impersonal alike, social ties and economic transactions mingle, as human beings perform relational work by matching their personal ties and economic activity.

By no means do all matches work well. Some properly excite indignation, or at least generate surprise. Guy de Maupassant invented a story illustrating precisely this point. His nineteenth-century fiction *In the Bedroom (Au bord du lit)* tells the tale of the Comte de Sallure, who once had dallied with various mistresses, offering the women "money, jewels, suppers, dinners, theatres." After ignoring his wife for some time, Sallure suddenly developed a renewed and powerful infatuation for the Comtesse. The newly smitten Sallure became jealous of his estranged wife's many admirers. One evening, returning home from a reception, Sallure resolved to seduce her by declaring his reborn passion. After reminding her husband of his infidelities and his earlier claims that "marriage between two intelligent people was just a partnership," the Countess agreed to rekindle their relationship, but at a price. Sallure would have to pay her five thousand monthly francs, approximately what he had spent on each of his mistresses. When the husband protested "that the idea of a man paying for his wife is stupid," the Countess explained the bargain: "Well, you want me. You can't marry me because we are already married. So why shouldn't you buy me? . . . Instead of going to some slut who would just squander it, your money will stay here, in your own home. . . . By putting a price on our lawful love you'll give it a new value . . . the spice of wickedness" (Maupassant [1883] 1971: 215–16).

Sallure relented, tossing her his wallet with the francs inside, asking only that his wife "not make a habit of it." The Comtesse insisted on her terms, adding that "if you're satisfied . . . I'll ask for a raise" (216). Maupassant caught the incongruity of a quid pro quo contract—sex for money—in the marriage of his time. The point was not that spouses never passed money from hand to hand in nineteenth-century French households. It was that the terms of the proposed contract blurred existing boundaries between prostitution and marriage. By negotiating medium, transaction, and boundary, the aristocratic couple were defining the content and conditions of their relationship.

As this book's complicated journey began, we set out to seek answers for three big questions:

1. Under what conditions, how, and with what consequences do people combine economic transactions with intimate relations?

2. Why and how do they erect complicated stories and practices for different situations that mingle economic transactions and intimacy?

3. How does the American legal system—attorneys, courts, judges, juries, and legal theorists—negotiate the coexistence of economic claims and intimate relations?

The pursuit of the answers through an analysis of coupling, caring, and households has taken us into worlds full of adventure. We have seen, for example, men and women announcing themselves as committed to marriage by purchasing an expensive ring, and have then observed courts facing a complex problem when those engaged couples break up and go to law. Of assets transferred during the engagement, including the ring, which now belongs to whom? (In this instance the courts commonly deploy the exotic doctrine of "conditional gifts.") With regard to caring relations, we have noted family members delivering medical care to ailing kin but have also watched courts adjudicate whether that care qualified the caregiver for compensation after the ailing person's death. And—even more surprising—whether the care constituted "undue influence" over the bequest of the recently departed. Households have presented even greater complexity. For example, awards to survivors of 9/11 victims raised the knotty question of compensation for the victim's unpaid household work, just as within intact households who owes what unpaid services recurrently becomes a matter of negotiation and dispute. (In the victim compensation cases, we see lawyers debating the "labor component of supplemental purchased services.")

Our first question—how, when, and with what consequences people mingle intimacy and economic activity—therefore receives a double answer: economic activity is integral and essential to a wide range of intimate relations, but the presence of intimacy endows the economic activity with special significance. Economic practices such as major purchases, household budgets, provision of health care, and ceremonial gifts engage participants in selecting appropriate media for payment, matching that media with transactions, assigning meaning to their relationships, and marking boundaries that separate intimate relationships from other relationships with which they might easily and dangerously be confused.

Why, then, do participants in intimate relationships create elaborate stories and practices for situations that mingle economic activity and intimacy? For essentially the same reasons. Within households, for example, every bargain struck has significance both for the transaction at hand and for longer-term relations among household members. To the extent that household members have spun a web of reciprocity, a community of fate, and a set of obligations to mutual, collective protection, confusing household interaction with routine market transactions would, indeed, signal a threat to household viability. There lies the truth in the otherwise defective doctrines of separate spheres and hostile worlds: although they teem with economic activity and often involve their members extensively in market transactions, zones of intimacy operate according to different rules from other sorts of organization.

Different rules? What exactly have we learned about the distinctive properties of intimate settings? First, a resounding *negative* conclusion: intimate settings do *not* stand out from others by the absence of economic activity. Nor do they lack connection with the commercial world. On the contrary, coupling, caring, and households entail extensive production, consumption, distribution, and transfer of assets. None of these intimate interactions would long survive without their economic component. We must, however, maintain the distinction between intimate *ties* and intimate *settings*. Intimate ties include all those in which at least one party obtains information or attention that if widely available would damage one or both of the parties. Intimate ties occur in a wide range of settings, including some that are predominantly impersonal in character. We have seen intimate ties appearing in professional-client relations and within commercial firms. Indeed, the reverse hostile worlds doctrine—that intimacy corrupts rationality—arises especially in just such settings. But in some settings intimate ties prevail.

Intimate settings turn out to have distinctive characteristics that mark them apart from impersonal settings. How do we recognize an intimate setting? It is one in which a high proportion of social interactions belong to ties in which at least one person gains access to information and/or attention that, if widely spread, could damage one of those participating in the interaction. Such settings create "communities of fate" in two regards. First, participants are making decisions and commitments that assume the continuing availability of shared resources and mutual guarantees. Second, by their very interactions they are transforming shared resources and mutual guarantees—degrading or improving the collective fortune such as a family house, creating or destroying means of internal coordination such as household budgets, expanding or contracting trust, such as the probability that one person will repay money borrowed from another, and so on.

Where we find a high density of intimate ties, we have seen, other crucial conditions prevail as well:

- Most interactions have implications for third parties who are intimately connected with at least one of the interacting persons, and often with both.
- Members of intimate settings are engaged not only in short-term quid pro quo exchanges but also in longer-term reciprocity—commitments to provide help and attention when need arrives.
- Because of these conditions, each transaction matters not only for the instant but also for future interactions, third parties, and the community of fate.
- That is why confusing relations belonging to an intimate setting with those—intimate or impersonal—attached to other, nonintimate settings, introduces conflict and reduces mutual commitments.
- That is also why seemingly minor failures take on major significance to the parties: they cast doubt on membership's meaning and future.

- Reacting to such threats of conflict and weakened allegiances, defenders of intimate settings introduce doctrines and practices of separate spheres and hostile worlds.

How does the American legal system deal with these intimate settings and relations? Answers to this third question have brought some of this book's greatest surprises. For we have seen legislators, lawyers, judges, and juries creating matrices of relationships within which distinctions, meanings, and operating rules often look quite different from those prevailing in everyday practice. Legal theorist Thane Rosenbaum notices the differences between legal proceedings and everyday practice, but deplores that difference (see also Noonan 1976). Taking the example of compensation for 9/11 survivors, he condemns a legal system that assigns monetary values to moral and emotional losses. What victims of such losses need, Rosenbaum argues, is a chance to tell their stories, to grieve with others, to receive moral counsel from the law. "People look to the law," he declares, "to provide remedies for their grievances and relief from their hurts, to receive moral lessons about life. . . . What most people don't realize is that judges and lawyers are motivated by entirely different agendas and mindsets" (Rosenbaum 2004: 5).[1] In this regard, Rosenbaum wants to erase the distinction between legal proceedings and everyday practice, at least the practice of moral discourse.

Rosenbaum's proposal, however, ignores the fact that legal specialists and everyday practitioners of intimacy are pursuing quite different objectives. Legal specialists are usually seeking ways to apply available rules to contested problems, while most of the time participants in intimate relations are simply trying to pursue their lives more or less satisfactorily. Precisely because the overlap is small but crucial and contested, translation between the two worlds requires delicacy, sophistication, and negotiation. To be sure, the law changes as general practices of intimacy change, legal decisions affect intimate practices, and participants in legal processes bring their

[1] For a contrasting view of stories and the law, see Brooks and Gewirtz 1996. For a far different evaluation of the 9/11 awards, see Shapo 2002.

own experiences and understandings of intimacy to bear on legal decisions (Ewick and Silbey 1998, 2003; Lazarus-Black and Hirsch 1994). Legislators and courts also change the law in response to political shifts and popular mobilization. Yet doctrines such as consortium, innocent spouse, and undue influence reveal a legal world that describes and prescribes intimate relations according to principles requiring a dramatic reinterpretation of those relations.

HOW FAR DO THESE LESSONS GO?

Is this book's account of how intimacy and economic transactions mingle an American contemporary story, the peculiar outcome of a money-driven U.S. culture? After all, it does focus on U.S. practices and law, most often during the past half-century. Certainly, the modern monetization of economic life has marked profound differences in our experiences of intimacy. Yet this book is most emphatically not just about the United States and not just about the recent past.[2] Its broadest arguments apply across the world, wherever and whenever intimacy and economic transactions intersect. There has never been the sort of time that separate spheres enthusiasts dream about, where intimacy's purity thrived uncontaminated by economic concerns.

Along the way, we have glimpsed the relevant American past, in such episodes as the caregiving experiences of Martha Ballard in eighteenth-century Maine, the domestic arrangements of Patsy and Samuel Miller in nineteenth-century Louisiana, and Leo Rosten's flirtation with New York taxi dancer Mona during the 1930s. The relations, transactions, media, boundaries, and overall meanings of

---

[2] For outstanding examples of non-American studies concerning similar phenomena, see Altman 2001; Castle and Konate 2003; Collier 1997; Cohen, Pepin, Lamontagne, and Duquette 2002; Comaroff 1980; Cresson 1995; Day 1994; Evers, Pijl, and Ungerson 1994; Fehlberg 1997; Gowing 1996; Guérin 2003; Gillis 1996; Howell 1998; Leonard 1980; Miller 1994; Moodie and Ndatshe 1994; Moors 1998; Pahl 1999; Saguy 2003; Scambler and Scambler 1997; Singh 1997; Song 1999; Wilson 2004.

intimacy have changed through history and continue to change. But from the very start, couples, caring, and household organization have brought together economic activity and intimacy.

What about non-American experiences? We could reach out very widely, as far back as classical Athens. Athenians adopted a strangely familiar set of distinctions separating the women they called *hetaera* from other sex workers. Hetaeras were capricious, felt free to refuse prospective lovers, offered sexual liaisons to those suitors who pleased them, expecting seduction rather than bargaining. They also insisted on receiving gifts rather than quid pro quo payment: "Hetaeras had a powerful interest in this game. Upon the fragile status of the gift depended their fragile status as 'companions' rather than common prostitutes" (Davidson 1998: 125). Clearly, the hetaeras distinguished themselves from other women who supplied Athenians with sex for money: "women who worked in brothels were registered and had to pay the *pornikon telos*, the whore-tax. Flute girls could charge no more than two drachmas a night and were forced to go with whomever the Astynomos [a public order board] allotted them" (124). For more than two millennia, then, people have been employing elaborate matrices of intimate relationships, taking great care to distinguish them, often using distinctive sorts of payment to mark crucial boundaries.

The lessons of this book also call up comparisons with the rest of the world in our own time. Just one example to make the point: French social scientist Florence Weber (2003) takes up the case of agricultural households, a well-studied site of intricate interaction between economic activity and family relations. Consider the legal arrangements of "deferred income" in which a child of an agricultural family eventually receives compensation for unpaid labor contributed to the farm's increase in value. In France, agricultural deferred income has served as a model for the creation of similar arrangements in retail trade, crafts, and wives' unpaid contributions to their husband's professional success.

This sort of mingling likewise promoted the invention of the doctrine of "undue enrichment." Much like undue influence, this French doctrine raises the question of whether the unpaid contributions of a child to the care of elderly parents establishes rightful claims to compensation from the parents' estate. While some courts rejected such claims, declaring filial help a moral duty, in 1994 the country's highest appeals court (Cour de Cassation) ruled in favor of compensating unpaid assistance that exceeded filial duty. The court reviewed the case of a man who took complete charge of his aging and ailing parents at the cost of his own career, thus enriching the family by saving the expense of a nursing home but impoverishing himself. The lower courts tried to defend something like a doctrine of separate spheres, but the higher court clearly ruled in favor of an appropriate match between compensation and intimacy. What is more, they actually set legal limits on the obligations of filial piety.

Both in the United States and elsewhere, the analysis of the law provides a triple lesson. First, systems of law have their own inbuilt conventions, doctrines, and traditions. We have just seen that France, as a civil law country, treats the purchase of intimacy in somewhat different terms from the United States, a country of common law. Second, the law evolves through contestation and adaptation. Weber displays the adaptation of French civil law through expansion of the agricultural model. In the U.S. case, earlier chapters have traced the remarkable evolution of coverture and consortium as doctrines applying to coupling and household intimacy. Third, all legal systems interact with ordinary practices in their areas of application. Weber, for instance, analyzes the response of French courts to changes in French household economies. On the American side, of course, we have seen this sort of interaction abundantly.

As much as it has explored legal territory, this book has not attempted to survey, much less to exhaust, the full range of legal debates in its area. For example, a legal scholar crossing the same terrain might very well take up questions of child support, alimony, foster care and adoption, or surrogacy and the sale of female eggs for reproduction. Others might analyze the practical impact of law on intimate economic practices, such as legalization of gay marriage or the parental rights of unwed fathers. Only occasionally, furthermore, has this study moved into the large adjacent territory in which both practices and the law limit the unwanted presence of intimacy in settings that are presumably impersonal, such as corporations, schools, and professional services. In these settings, indeed, we often see what we might call reverse hostile worlds reasoning: the presence of intimacy, in this view, corrupts proper standards, as exemplified by cronyism, nepotism, insider trading, and sexual harassment. Nor does the book provide analyses of the legal profession or legal institutions as social phenomena. It does, however, treat legal action—in this case especially litigation—as a social process, focusing on its interaction with routine practices outside the legal arena. Some of our most impressive findings concern that interaction, for example, in the ways that legal actors must recast practices they advocate in order to make them fit existing law.

WHAT ABOUT POLICY?

One final disclaimer: despite its occasional forays into normative questions, this book by no means takes up a systematic exposition of normative principles that ought to govern intimate relations either in ordinary practice or in the law. Instead, the book clarifies the stakes of a number of consequential policy questions. It does so by overturning statements of fact, of possibility, and of cause-effect relations that frequently appear in normative discussions. The most obvious case concerns the now familiar separate spheres and hostile worlds arguments. Certainly hostile worlds guardians care deeply about issues of injustice, inequality, and protection. Indeed, those concerns underlie their insistence on insulating spheres of intimacy to protect relations of trust and reciprocity. Yet paradoxically, by perpetuating the myth of inescapable divisions and battles between the worlds of sentiment and rationality, of market and domesticity, hostile worlds arguments divert us from real solutions. Such misunderstandings therefore not only create theoretical confusions but have serious practical implications. We have seen repeatedly how hostile worlds arguments shape legal decisions. Indeed, they often underpin unjust policies, such as the following:

- Denial of compensation to women for household work in a range of areas
- Low pay for caregivers, such as nannies and home-health aides
- Condemnation of welfare to unmarried mothers, as a spur to dependency
- Prohibitions on child labor that actually harm households or hinder children's acquisition of valuable skills

To the extent that normative discussions assume the existence of separate spheres and their mutual corruption at point of contact, those normative programs will fail to accomplish their announced objectives.

It therefore matters to get the interaction of intimacy and economic activity right. This book has put forth a connected lives approach, showing the continuous crossing of our intimate relations and economic transactions. Looking at coupling, care, and households we did not find separate worlds of economy and sentiment, nor did we see markets everywhere. Instead we have observed crosscutting, differentiated ties that connect people with each other. We witnessed people investing energy and ingenuity in marking differences among their relations to each other and regularly including economic transactions in those intimate relations. None of us, we have seen, lives in segregated spheres with unbreachable barriers between our personal relations and our economic ties.

What are the practical implications of such an approach? To direct our search toward just, noncoercive sets of economic transactions for different types of intimate relations. The goal is not therefore to cleanse intimacy from economic concerns: the challenge is to create fair mixtures. We should stop agonizing over whether or not money corrupts, but instead analyze what combinations of economic activity and intimate relations produce happier, more just, and more productive lives. It is not the mingling that should concern us, but how the mingling works. If we get the causal connections wrong, we will obscure the origins of injustice, damage, and danger. Certainly, this book does not confer an unqualified seal of approval on the reconciliation of all forms of intimacy and all kinds of economic transactions. Commercialization can and often does create injustice and corruption of intimate ties. But the book strongly rejects existing explanations of how, when, and why this happens.

A LAST LOOK AT CARE

For a concrete application, let us return to the contested topic of paid care, which has emerged as a crucial issue on the national political agenda. With the aging of the baby-boom generation, and as most mothers in the United States participate in paid work, the care of children, the elderly, and the sick is being seriously reassessed. We are confronting, Arlie Hochschild argues, a "care deficit" crisis (Hochschild 1995: 342). As Deborah Stone declared in a *Nation* editorial, "We have the Bill of Rights and we have civil rights. Now we need a Right to Care, and it's going to take a movement to get it." Noting both the emotional strains and professional constraints of informal caregivers, as well as systematic economic exploitation of underpaid formal caregivers, Stone insists, "We need a movement to demonstrate that caring is not a free resource, that caring is hard and skilled work, that it takes time and devotion, and that people who do it are making sacrifices" (Stone 2000b: 13).

Paying for care encounters the same difficulties and concerns that come up each time people try to think through the relationships between market activity and social obligations. What will happen, many worry, if paid care substitutes for informal assistance? Would the generalization of payment for such care destroy caring itself? Would its subjection to monetary calculation rationalize away its essential intimacy? Will recognizing the economic contributions of housewives turn households into impersonal minimarkets? Or, on the other hand, will subsidies to housewives increase the ghetto barriers separating them from other workers? Should grandmothers receive compensation when they care for grandchildren while their daughters work elsewhere? In any case, how can we possibly arrive at an appropriate financial evaluation of caretakers' contributions?

Payment for care thus raises all the questions of possible corruption and disruption that so concern critics of commercialization.

Increasingly impatient with standard hostile world and nothing-but answers to such questions, a group of imaginative feminist thinkers are moving toward an alternative approach very much in the spirit of connected lives. They identify multiple forms of connection between interpersonal relations and different spheres of economic life. Questioning the idealization of unpaid care, these analysts ponder possibilities and explore actual practices where payments and care fruitfully coexist. They thus shift away from rigid certainties about money's corruption to a clear-eyed investigation of both paid and unpaid caring. They also raise pointed questions about the equity and propriety surrounding the reward and recognition of care as a critical contribution to social well-being, arousing concerns about proper compensation for paid care workers; adequate provision for care of children, the sick, and the elderly; and economic security for unpaid caregivers.

Implicitly these thinkers are recognizing the distinctiveness and value of relational work. In the process, they are building a new economics of care. Consider, for instance, the challenge laid down by economists Nancy Folbre and Julie Nelson: "An a priori judgment that markets must improve caregiving by increasing efficiency puts the brakes on intelligent research, rather than encourages it. Likewise, an a priori judgment that markets must severely degrade caring work by replacing motivations of altruism with self-interest is also a research stopper." Instead, they insist, "the increasing intertwining of 'love' and 'money' brings us the necessity—and the opportunity—for innovative research and action" (Folbre and Nelson 2000: 123–24; see also England and Folbre 2003).[3]

Pointing to the child-care market as thickly social and relational, Julie Nelson argues that parents or caregivers seldom define that

---

[3] See also Crittenden 2001; Folbre 2001; Held 2002; Himmelweit 1999; Nelson 1999; Ruddick 1998. For an introduction to selected social science approaches to caring, see Cancian and Oliker 2000; Tronto 1994. For related views on regard as an incentive for reciprocity, see Offer 1997.

market "as purely an impersonal exchange of money for services. . . .
The parties involved engage in extensive personal contact, trust,
and interpersonal interaction. . . . The specter of the all-corrupting
market denies that people—such as many child-care providers—
can do work they love, among people they love, and get paid at
the same time." Paid care, she insists, should not be treated as
"relationally second rate" (Nelson 1998: 1470). Similarly Carol
Sanger makes the point that surrogate childbearing deserves recognition as serious women's work deserving full rewards (Sanger
1996). This book has repeatedly and amply confirmed Nelson's and
Sanger's claims.

What's more, these challengers note that hostile worlds assumptions portraying love and care as demeaned by monetization may in
fact lead to economic discrimination against those allegedly intangi-
ble caring activities. A group of legal specialists reviewing labor arbitration decisions in cases involving employees' use of work time for
caring duties discovered concrete evidence of such discrimination
(Malin et al. 2004). Their study focused on unionized workplaces,
which tend to be friendlier to families than nonunion shops. Although the record of decisions was mixed, the study nevertheless
found frequent disciplinary action, including firing, against employees who missed work to take care of family obligations to children,
spouses, grandchildren, and parents. Employees defended by their
unions in the arbitration hearings experienced a wide range of such
obligations: the cases included a janitor who had missed one day of
work to take care of a disabled child, a mechanic who stayed home
attending to his cancer-stricken wife, and a worker at a psychiatric
center who refused to work mandatory overtime because she was
unable to find child care for her two young children. The unions'
intervention subverted a too-rigid division between market work
and caring work that produced damage on both sides.

Legal intervention likewise combats discrimination against caregivers. In a review of legal cases where plaintiffs challenged the
"maternal wall" that discriminates against parental caregivers, Joan
Williams and Nancy Segal provide ample proof of continuing
stereotyping and unequal workplace treatment for parents, both

women and men. In fact, they discovered startling evidence of blatant bias, with some employers openly declaring mothers to be unfit workers and others deriding fathers' requests for parental leave. More surprisingly, however, they found an increase in litigation, as more employees file suits against unfair dismissals or penalties connected to their care work. What's more, Williams and Segal report that courts seem increasingly likely to recognize such employee claims. As a result, although the trend is recent, more plaintiffs are winning their cases, sometimes with substantial monetary awards and settlements. Williams and Segal strongly endorse such legal action as one mechanism to end workplace discrimination against parental care work. Breaking down the pernicious "maternal wall" by recognizing the rights of caregivers, they further argue, will produce better and more productive workplaces (Williams and Segal 2003).

On a closely related matter, as Paula England and Nancy Folbre point out, "the principle that money cannot buy love may have the unintended and perverse consequence of perpetuating low pay for face-to-face service work" (England and Folbre 1999: 46). Noting that typically it is women who are expected to provide caring labor, we should suspect, they warn, "any argument that decent pay demeans a noble calling" (48). Indeed, the first study focusing on the relative pay of care work documents a significant "wage penalty" for face-to-face service providers, such as teachers, counselors, healthcare aides, and child-care workers (England, Budig, and Folbre 2002). Although both men and women involved in care work pay this penalty, women do so more often, since they are more likely to be involved in this type of work (see also Budig and England 2001).

Allowing for the social and moral legitimacy of paid care, the feminist agenda stops fretting over whether or not to pay for caring labor, turning instead its attention to the amount and form of payment and to the investigation of actual caring relationships. The problem is not, they discover, whether money is involved but whether the type of payment system matches the caring relationship. In the process, these analysts join efforts in breaking down the traditional hostile worlds dichotomies that erroneously split economic transactions and intimate personal relations into separate

spheres, one antiseptically market-driven, the other cozily sentimental. To bring caring labor out of its economically marginal
ghetto, they forcefully establish its fundamental economic significance and its variable economic content.

Only after we recognize that caring labor has always involved economic transactions, can we construct democratic, compassionate
caring economies, supplying care workers with greater resources,
legal standing, and respect than they have previously enjoyed. To be
sure, recent feminist critics are not the first to identify these challenges. Historians have long since documented the nineteenth-century ideology of separate spheres segregating domestic from market
worlds (see Boydston 1990; Cott 1977), nineteenth-century move-
ments advocating wages for housework moved the issue into practical politics, and developmental psychologists (see Chodorow 1978;
Gilligan 1982) have debated extensively the cognitive gendering of
such worlds. Focusing on the economics of care, however, feminist
critics of hostile worlds ideology bring out even more clearly than
their predecessors the specific political and moral consequences of
separate spheres.

In this book's terms, the feminist rethinking of care concerns the
nature and valuation of relational work. As we have discovered
throughout our discussions of coupling, care, and household economies, intimate relations require extensive effort; people match particular relations with specific transactions and media, and distinguish them punctiliously from other relations with which they might
become confused. Caring relations, as we have seen, not only consist
of those between caregiver and recipient of care but also commonly
involve other kin, friends, and neighbors. Firing a nanny, for instance, not only disrupts relations between nanny and child but also
provokes changes in relations between parent and child, and often
between the nanny and her own household as well. Today's caring
interactions, moreover, always have implications for tomorrow's relations of those involved. In some cases, as with the estate claims
of caretakers, these long-term connections receive concrete legal
recognition.

A simple analogy with the market equivalent of a care service thus falls far short of exhausting that relationship's weight and complexity. For that reason, policies that reckon care within households on the basis of what is currently available in the market or as a two-party contractual matter, neither capture the likely impact of a policy intervention nor evaluate the service properly. Furthermore, the very medium and modality of payment have an impact on the caring relations: they signify to the participants what kind of relation they are carrying on. That is why, beyond a broad agreement that care work is currently underpaid and undervalued, we have to understand that the form and conditions of payment themselves matter. A daily payment in cash signifies a very different relationship from a monthly check. Although they matter in specific ways for intimate settings, taking notice of the form of payment is not a trivial sentimental consideration. We have extensive evidence of how much the form of compensation matters even to CEOs of large companies, who ordinarily receive a wide range of perquisites in addition to straight monetary payments. Take away the company car, the executive washroom, or the luxury travel, and you take away some of the CEO's distinction.

MONEY, MONEY

Such principles shed unexpected light on controversies about the moral standing of monetary compensation for accidental death (Borneman 2002; Lascher and Powers 2004.). In the case of 9/11 payments, critics often accused victims' families of simple, distasteful greed. However, 9/11 recipients of compensation repeatedly declared that it was "not about the money." Fund administrator Kenneth Feinberg backed them up:

> I have received . . . and have read in the newspapers, comments
> from a few American citizens expressing the opinion that the
> victims and their families are "greedy" in seeking additional
> compensation. As I have repeatedly stated . . . I believe that

characterization is unfair. This Fund, and the comments of dis-
tressed family members, are not about "greed" but, rather, re-
flect both the horror of September 11 and the determination
of family members to value the life of loved ones suddenly lost
on that tragic day. (U.S. Department of Justice 2002: 11,234).

Properly understood, indeed, recipients were mostly right to say
it was not *just* about the money. As Herbert Nass, a lawyer representing a 9/11 victim's family commented, "This is not about the
money for them, because it's such sad money" (Chen 2003: sec. B1).
On the whole, victims' families were seeking not only financial advantage but also public recognition of their loss and of their special
relationship to the victim. As we saw earlier, some payments directly
recognized the unpaid contributions that the victims had been making to their households. Once again, we see that the medium and
modality of compensation represents not simply quid pro quo cash
value but the meaning of the relationships involved. Yet in a very
different sense it *was* about the money. As in medical malpractice,
wrongful death settlements, and compensation for disabling on-the-
job injuries, the payment of large sums simultaneously announces
the seriousness of the loss involved and the responsibility of someone else for that loss. Large penalties may even impel the authors
of dangerous conditions to clean them up.

For our purposes, the most important feature of 9/11 compensation was its assignment of significant value to relational work. With
such valuation, courts and policymakers enter the world we have
been exploring. In this world, a simple search for the closest market
equivalent of the relational work at hand will almost always miscon-
strue and undervalue that work. Consider the analogy of ecological
intervention, where straightforward compensation of users for the
commercial value of forests or streams they have lost fails to reckon
the overall effect of depleted forests and streams on the environment
at large.

When policies assign value to relational work within intimate settings, they will distort what they are doing, and the intervention's
likely effects, unless they recognize the impact of proposed policies

on third parties, diffuse reciprocity, longer-term security, and communities of fate. Both in the short term and the long, superior policies will ask which arrangements for paid personal care of children, the elderly, the disabled, and the sick damage the recipients, the caregivers, and the households involved. Which arrangements actually enrich participants' lives? This book's intimate revelations thus bear on policy discussions.

Leaving aside questions of policy, this analysis also requires us to rethink more generally how intimate relations work. We have established the multiplex mingling of intimacy and economic transactions. We have seen that intimate relations not only incorporate economic activity, but depend on it and organize it. Beyond that discovery, in the process of documenting how people couple, care, and participate in household economies, we have traversed a profoundly relational world. A world in which courting teenagers, lovers, husbands and wives, partners, children, grandparents, caretakers, and the many other intimate partners we have encountered are continually involved in maintaining, reinforcing, testing, and sometimes challenging their relations to each other. In fact, their sense of themselves intertwines closely with the meanings of their relationships to others.

This world of intimacy is not, as some theories of social behavior imply, peopled with characters playing out fixed roles based on gender, sexual orientation, religion, or ethnicity. Nor is it a world, as other theorists would argue, in which each single individual is busily strategizing how to maximize his or her own self-interest. Yes, we do find continuous bargaining and negotiation between couples, caregivers, and care recipients, as well as among household members, but not one strategic actor moving against another. Instead, we find people locating themselves within webs of social relations, working out their places by means of interaction with others, and constantly taking into account the repercussions of any particular relation for third parties.

Intimate relations matter. Because of their importance, intimate relations become vulnerable to misunderstandings, moral outrage, mismatches, falsification, and betrayal. Intimacy creates all sorts of dilemmas: is this person a gold digger or an intimate friend? Is this a caring relation or exploitation? When should care be paid for? Why should it be acceptable to pay a babysitter but not to pay a sister to watch her baby brother? Over what kinds of children's and teenagers' expenditures should parents hold vetoes? Determining which kind of economic activity matches which kind of intimacy matters enormously to the participants. We have seen this in couples, caring, and households. People invest a great deal of energy in marking the right economic transactions for the relationship and distinguishing them sharply from the wrong economic transactions. We see this both in practices and legal arena. Which is an acceptable economic transaction for which family member?

Even more generally, we have discovered a relational world. The same people behave quite differently in different relations, as well they should. In this book's longer perspective, the old continuum from intimate to impersonal does not disappear but takes on new meaning. First, we find that it is, indeed, a continuum rather than a dichotomy into separate spheres. Second, we recognize that both individual relations and social settings vary significantly along the continuum. Third, we notice economic activity at every step along the continuum, instead of concentrated at one end. Fourth, we see that the economic activity actually supports and reproduces the relations and settings all along the continuum. Fifth, we observe throughout the range that people are constantly negotiating and renegotiating matches among relations, media, transactions, and boundaries. Sixth, we understand that some negotiated matches involve injustice, cruelty, damage, or confusion, not because they mix personal relations with economic activity but because they result from improper exercises of power. Finally, in a high proportion of cases we witness consequences for third parties: how people interact affects other relations in which those people are involved.

We could obviously follow these insights into other intimate settings this book has neglected: larger kinship groups, friendship, neighborhoods, family businesses, combat units, hospital wards, and more. In those settings, we would expect the same general lessons to apply. With appropriate changes in perspective, we could likewise follow them into other settings that are not predominantly intimate, but in which intimate relations nevertheless appear: corporations, schools, college dormitories, prisons, retail trade, soup kitchens, welfare offices, and the creative arts. The basic lessons would remain the same. Far from constituting a fragile separate sphere, intimate relations ramify across an enormous range of social settings and activities, beyond spouses, lovers, children, and kin.

If this book has done its job well, it will help readers recognize what is happening to them in everyday social life. All of us are, after all, constantly negotiating appropriate matches between our intimate relations and crucial economic activities. Choices people make in these regards carry great moral weight and have serious consequences for the viability of their intimate lives. Intimacy, we have seen, has great value for its participants, and therefore involves serious risks. No single model of intimacy will serve for all its uses. Intimacy takes many forms. So does its purchase.

REFERENCES

Abbott, Andrew. 1988. *The System of Professions*. Chicago: University of Chicago Press.

Abel, Emily K. 1990. "Family Care of the Frail Elderly." In Emily K. Abel and Margaret K. Nelson, eds., *Circles of Care*, 65–91. Albany: State University of New York Press.

———. 1991. *Who Cares for the Elderly?* Philadelphia: Temple University Press.

———. 2000. *Hearts of Wisdom: American Women Caring for Kin 1850–1940*. Cambridge, MA: Harvard University Press.

Abolafia, Mitchel Y. 2001. *Making Markets: Opportunism and Restraint on Wall Street*. Cambridge, MA: Harvard University Press.

The Abrams Report. 2002. MSNBC TV, September 27.

Adams, Rebecca G., and Graham Allan. 1998. *Placing Friendship in Context*. Cambridge: Cambridge University Press.

Aggleton, Peter, ed. 1999. *Men Who Sell Sex*. Philadelphia: Temple University Press.

Aldrich, Howard E., and Jennifer E. Cliff. 2003. "The Pervasive Effects of Family on Entrepreneurship: Toward a Family Embeddedness Perspective." *Journal of Business Venturing* 18:573–96.

Allan, Graham. 1989. *Friendship: Developing a Sociological Perspective*. Boulder, CO: Westview.

Altman, Dennis. 2001. *Global Sex*. Chicago: University of Chicago Press.

American Bar Association. 1996. *The American Bar Association Guide to Family Law*. New York: Three Rivers Press.

———. 2003. *Model Code of Professional Responsibility*. http://www.manupatra.com/downloads/code%20of%20professional%20conduct/ethics.pdf. Accessed August 9, 2003.

American Psychological Association. 2003. "Ethical Principles of Psychology and Code of Conduct." http://www.apa.org/ethics/ Accessed August 9, 2003.

Anderson, Elizabeth. 1993. *Value in Ethics and Economics*. Cambridge, MA: Harvard University Press.

Antonovics, Kate, and Robert Town. 2004. "Are All the Good Men Married? Uncovering the Sources of the Marital Wage Premium." *American Economic Review* 94 (May):317–21.

Aronson, Jane, and Sheila M. Neysmith. 1996. " 'You're Not Just in There to Do the Work': Depersonalizing Policies and the Exploitation of Home Care Workers' Labor." *Gender & Society* 10:59–77.

Babcock, Linda, and Sara Laschever. 2003. *Women Don't Ask: Negotiation and the Gender Divide*. Princeton, NJ: Princeton University Press.

Bailey, Beth. 1988. *From Front Porch to Back Seat: Courtship in Twentieth-Century America*. Baltimore: Johns Hopkins University Press.

———. 1999. *Sex in the Heartland*. Cambridge, MA: Harvard University Press.

Bakke, E. Wight. [1940] 1969. *The Unemployed Worker: A Study of the Task of Making a Living without a Job*. Hamden, CT: Archon Books.

Banks, Taunya Lovell. 1999. "Toward a Global Critical Feminist Vision: Domestic Work and the Nanny Tax Debate." *Journal of Gender, Race & Justice* 3:1–44.

Barber, Bernard. 1983. *The Logic and Limits of Trust*. New Brunswick, NJ: Rutgers University Press.

Baron, Jane B. 1988–89. "Gifts, Bargains, and Form." 64 *Indiana Law Journal* 155.

Barron, Hal S. 1997. *Mixed Harvest: The Second Great Transformation in the Rural North 1870–1930*. Chapel Hill: University of North Carolina Press.

Barry, Kathleen. 1995. *The Prostitution of Sexuality*. New York: New York University Press.

Bawin, Bernadette, and Renée Dandurand, eds. 2003. "De l'intimité." Special issue of *Sociologie et Sociétés* 35 (Autumn).

Becker, Gary S. 1996. *Accounting for Tastes*. Cambridge, MA: Harvard University Press.

Becker, Saul, Jo Aldridge, and Chris Dearden. 1998. *Young Carers and Their Families*. Oxford: Blackwell Science.

Belkin, Lisa. 2002. "Just Money." *New York Times Magazine*, December 8, 92–97, 122, 148, 156.

Bengtson, Vern L. 2001. "Beyond the Nuclear Family: The Increasing Importance of Multigenerational Bonds." *Journal of Marriage and the Family* 63 (February):1–16.

Berhau, Patricia. 2000. "Class and the Experiences of Consumers: A Study of the Practices of Acquisition." Ph.D. diss. Temple University.

Bernstein, Elizabeth. 1999. "What's Wrong with Prostitution? What's Right with Sex Work? Comparing Markets in Female Sexual Labor." 10 *Hastings Women's Law Journal* 91–119.

———. 2001. "The Meaning of the Purchase: Desire, Demand and the Commerce of Sex." *Ethnography* 2:389–420.

Biggart, Nicole Woolsey. 1989. *Charismatic Capitalism*. Chicago: University of Chicago Press.

Bittker, Boris I. 1983. *Fundamentals of Federal Income Taxation*. Boston: Warren, Gorham, and Lamont.

Bittman, Michael, Paula England, Nancy Folbre, and George Matheson. 2003. "When Does Gender Trump Money? Bargaining and Time in Household Work." *American Journal of Sociology* 109:186–214.

Black's Law Dictionary. 1999. Edited by Bryan A. Garner. 7th ed. St. Paul, MN: West Group.

Blumstein, Philip, and Pepper Schwartz. 1983. *American Couples*. New York: William Morrow.

Boag, Peter. 2003. *Same-Sex Affairs*. Berkeley: University of California Press.

Boase, Jeffrey, and Barry Wellman. 2004. "Personal Relationships: On and off the Internet." In Daniel Perlman and Anita L. Vangelisti, eds., *Handbook of Personal Relations*. Cambridge: Cambridge University Press.

Bohmer, Carol. 2000. *The Wages of Seeking Help*. Westport, CT: Praeger.

Borneman, John. 2002. "On Money and the Memory of Loss." *Etnográfica* 6(2):281–302.

Boston, Nicholas. 2004. "The Tough Fight for Compensation." *Gay City News* 3 (June 24–30). http://www.gaycitynews.com/gcn_326/thetough fightfor.html. Accessed December 2004.

Boulding, Elise. 1980. "The Nurture of Adults by Children in Family Settings." In Helena Lopata, ed., *Research in the Interweave of Social Roles: Women and Men*, 1:167–89. Greenwich, CT: JAI.

Bourgois, Philippe. 1995. *In Search of Respect*. New York: Cambridge University Press.

Bouris, Karen. 2004. *Just Kiss Me and Tell Me You Did the Laundry: How to Negotiate Equal Roles for Husband and Wife in Parenting, Career, and Home Life*. New York: Rodale.

Boydston, Jeanne. 1990. *Home and Work*. New York: Oxford University Press.

Braman, Donald. 2004. *Doing Time on the Outside: Incarceration and Family Life in Urban America*. Ann Arbor: University of Michigan Press.

Bray, Ilona M. 2001. *Fiancé and Marriage Visas*. Berkeley, CA: Nolo Press.

Brewis, Joanna, and Stephen Linstead. 2000. *Sex, Work and Sex Work*. London: Routledge.

Brines, Julie. 1994. "Economic Dependency, Gender, and the Division of Labor at Home." *American Journal of Sociology* 100 (November):652–88.

Brinig, Margaret F. 2000. *From Contract to Covenant: Beyond the Law and Economics of the Family*. Cambridge, MA: Harvard University Press.

Brooks, David. 2002. "Making It." *Weekly Standard*, December 23.

Brooks, Peter, and Paul Gewirtz. 1996. *Law's Stories: Narrative and Rhetoric in the Law*. New Haven, CT: Yale University Press.

Brown, Robert C. 1934. "The Action for Alienation of Affections." *University of Pennsylvania Law Review* 82 (March) 472.

Budig, Michelle J., and Paula England. 2001. "The Wage Penalty for Motherhood." *American Sociological Review* 66:204–25.

Butler, Judith. 1990. *Gender Trouble*. New York: Routledge.

———1993. *Bodies That Matter*. New York: Routledge.

Calder, Lendol. 1999. *Financing the American Dream*. Princeton, NJ: Princeton University Press.

Cancelmo, Joseph A., and Carol Bandini. 1999. *Childcare for Love or Money? A Guide to Navigating the Parent-Caregiver Relationship*. Northvale, NJ: Jason Aronson.

Cancian, Francesca. 1987. *Love in America: Gender and Self-Development*. New York: Cambridge University Press.

———. 2000. "Paid Emotional Care." In Madonna Harrington Meyer, ed., *Care Work: Gender Labor and the Welfare State*, 136–48. New York: Routledge.

Cancian, Francesca and Stacey J. Oliker. 2000. *Caring and Gender*. Thousand Oaks, CA: Pine Forge Press.

Carbone, June. 2000. *From Partners to Parents*. New York: Columbia University Press.

Carrington, Christopher. 1999. *No Place like Home: Relationships and Family Life among Lesbians and Gay Men*. Chicago: University of Chicago Press.

Casper, Lynne M., and Suzanne M. Bianchi. 2002. *Continuity and Change in the American Family*. Thousand Oaks, CA: Sage.

Castle, Sarah, and Mamadou Kani Konate. 2003. "Economic Transactions Associated with Sexual Intercourse among Malian Adolescents: Implications for Sexual Health." In *Reproduction and Social Context in Sub-Saharan Africa*, 161–85. Westport, CT: Greenwood Press.

Center for the Childcare Workforce. 2002. "Estimating the Size and Components of the U.S. Childcare Workforce and Caregiving Population." Washington, DC: Center for the Childcare Workforce; Seattle: Human Services Policy Center, Evans School of Public Affairs, University of Washington. http://www.ccw.org/pubs/workforceestimatereport.pdf. Accessed June 29, 2003.

Cervini, Michael. 2004. Personal communication, July 13.

Chamallas, Martha. 1998. "The Architecture of Bias: Deep Structures in Tort Law." 146 *University of Pennsylvania Law Review* 463.

Chambliss, Daniel F. 1996. *Beyond Caring: Hospitals, Nurses, and the Social Organization of Ethics*. Chicago: University of Chicago Press.

Chapkis, Wendy. 1997. *Live Sex Acts*. New York: Routledge.

———. 2000. "Power and Control in the Commercial Sex Trade." In Ronald Weitzer, ed., *Sex for Sale: Prostitution, Pornography, and the Sex Industry*, 181–201. New York: Routledge.

Chaudry, Ajay. 2004. *Putting Children First*. New York: Russell Sage Foundation.

Chauncey, George. 1985. "Christian Brotherhood or Sexual Perversion? Homosexual Identities and the Construction of Sexual Boundaries in the World War One Era." *Journal of Social History* 19 (Winter):189–211.

———. 1994. *Gay New York*. New York: Basic Books.

Chayko, Mary. 2002. *Connecting*. Albany: State University of New York Press.

Chen, David W. 2002. "Lure of Millions Fuels 9/11 Families' Feuding." *New York Times*, June 17, sec. A1.

———. 2003. "A Slow, Deliberate Process of Weighing 9/11 Awards." *New York Times*, February 18, sec. B1.

———. 2004. "What's a Life Worth?" Week in Review, *New York Times*, June 20.

Chin, Elizabeth. 2001. *Purchasing Power: Black Kids and American Consumer Culture*. Minneapolis: University of Minnesota Press.

Chinoy, Ely. 1955. *Automobile Workers and the American Dream*. Boston: Beacon Press.

Chodorow, Nancy. 1978. *The Reproduction of Mothering: Psychoanalysis and the Sociology of Gender*. Berkeley: University of California Press.

Clark, Homer, H., Jr. 1968. *The Law of Domestic Relations in the United States*. St. Paul, MN: West Publishing Co.

Clayton, Obie, and Joan Moore. 2003. "The Effects of Crime and Imprisonment on Family Formation." In *Black Fathers in Contemporary American Society*, 84–102. New York: Russell Sage Foundation.

Clement, Elizabeth A. 1998a. "Trick or Treat: Prostitution and Working-Class Women's Sexuality in New York City, 1900–1932." Ph.D. diss., University of Pennsylvania.

———. 1998b. "Prostitution and Community in Turn-of-the-Century New York City." In James E. Elias et al., eds., *Prostitution: On Whores, Hustlers, and Johns*, 47–60. New York: Prometheus Books.

Cohen, Jean. 2002. *Regulating Intimacy*. Princeton, NJ: Princeton University Press.

Cohen, Lizabeth. 2003. *A Consumers' Republic: The Politics of Mass Consumption in Postwar America*. New York: Alfred A. Knopf.

Cohen, Patricia Cline. 1998. *The Murder of Helen Jewett*. New York: Knopf.

Cohen, Yolande, Jacinthe Pepin, Esther Lamontagne, and André Duquette. 2002. *Les sciences infirmières: Genèse d'une discipline*. Montreal: Presses de l'Université de Montréal.

Cole, Steven A., and Julian Bird. 2000. *The Medical Interview*. St. Louis: Mosby.

Collier, Jane Fishburne. 1997. *From Duty to Desire: Remaking Families in a Spanish Village*. Princeton, NJ: Princeton University Press.

Collins, Randall. 2004. *Interaction Ritual Chains*. Princeton, NJ: Princeton University Press.

Coltrane, Scott. 1996. *Family Man*. New York: Oxford University Press.

———. 1998. *Gender and Families*. Thousand Oaks, CA: Pine Forge Press.

Comaroff, John L. 1980. "Bridewealth and the Control of Ambiguity in a Tswana Chiefdom." In John L. Comaroff, ed., *The Meaning of Marriage Payments*, 161–96. London: Academic Press.

Conley, Dalton. 1999. *Being Black, Living in the Red: Race, Wealth, and Social Policy in America*. Berkeley: University of California Press.

Constable, Nicole. 2003. *Romance on a Global Stage*. Berkeley: University of California Press.

Consumer Report for Kids. http://www.zillions.org/. Accessed August 3, 2004.

Cooke, Maud. 1896. *Social Etiquette*. Boston.

Coombs, Mary. 1989. "Agency and Partnership." 2 *Yale Journal of Law and Feminism*: 1.

Copeland, Tom. 1991. *Contracts and Policies: How to Be Businesslike in a Caring Profession*. St. Paul, MN: Redleaf Press.

Corbett, Sara. 2003. "The Last Shift." *New York Times Magazine*, March 16.

Cott, Nancy. 1977. *The Bonds of Womanhood*. New Haven, CT: Yale University Press.

———. 2000. *Public Vows*. Cambridge, MA: Harvard University Press.

Cowan, Ruth Schwartz. 1983. *More Work for Mother*. New York: Basic Books.

Cozort, Larry A. 2003. "Is the Tax Court Becoming a Divorce Court? The Answer Could Change How the Innocent Spouse Rules Are Interpreted." *Journal of Accountancy* 195 (February). http://www.aicpa.org/pubs/jofa/feb2003/index.htm. Accessed November 2004.

Cressey, Paul G. 1932. *The Taxi-Dance Hall*. Chicago: University of Chicago Press.

Cresson, Geneviève. 1995. *Le travail domestique de santé*. Paris: L'Harmattan.

Crittenden, Ann. 2001. *The Price of Motherhood*. New York: Metropolitan Books.

Cross, Gary. 2000. *An All-Consuming Century: Why Commercialism Won in America*. New York: Columbia University Press.

Culhane, John G. 2000–2001. "A 'Clanging Silence': Same-Sex Couples and Tort Law." 89 *Kentucky Law Journal* 911.

Curran, Sara R., and Abigail Cope Saguy. 2001. "Migration and Cultural Change: A Role for Gender and Social Networks?" *Journal for International Women's Studies* 2:54–77.

Curry, Hayden, Denis Clifford, and Frederick Hertz. 2002. *A Legal Guide for Lesbian and Gay Couples*. 11th ed. Berkeley, CA: Nolo Press.

Cushing, Ethel Frey. 1926. *Culture and Good Manners*. Memphis: Students Educational Publishing Co.

Daniels, Arlene Kaplan. 1987. "Invisible Work." *Social Problems* 34: 403–15.

Davidson, James. 1998. *Courtesans and Fishcakes*. New York: Harper-Perennial.

Davis, Adrienne D. 1999. "The Private Law of Race and Sex: An Antebellum Perspective." 51 *Stanford Law Review* 221.

Davis, Martha F. 2002. "Valuing Women: A Case Study." 23 *Women's Rights Law Reporter* 219.

Davis, Murray S. 1973. *Intimate Relations*. New York: Free Press.

———. 1983. *Smut*. Chicago: University of Chicago Press.

Davis, Owen. 2003. *Cunning-Folk: Popular Magic in English History*. London: Hambledon and London.

Day, Sophie. 1994. "L'argent et l'esprit d'entreprise chez les prostituées à Londres." In Maurice Bloch, ed. "Les usages de l'argent." Special issue of *Terrain* 23:99–114.

DeFuria, Joseph W., Jr. 1989. "Testamentary Gifts Resulting from Meretricious Relationships: Undue Influence or Natural Beneficence?" 64 *Notre Dame Law Review* 200.

D'Emilio, John, and Estelle B. Freedman. 1988. *Intimate Matters: A History of Sexuality in America*. New York: Harper and Row.

DeVault, Marjorie L. 1991. *Feeding the Family*. Chicago: University of Chicago Press.

———. 2002. "Producing Family Time: Practices of Leisure Activity beyond the Home." In Naomi Gerstel, Dan Clawson, and Robert Zussman, eds., *Families at Work: Expanding the Boundaries*, 266–83. Nashville: Vanderbilt University Press.

Di Leonardo, Micaela. 1987. "The Female World of Cards and Holidays: Women, Families, and the Work of Kinship." *Signs* 12 (Spring):440–53.

DiMaggio, Paul, 2001. "Introduction: Making Sense of the Contemporary Firm and Prefiguring Its Future." In Paul DiMaggio, ed., *The Twenty-First-Century Firm: Changing Economic Organization in International Perspective*, 3–33. Princeton, NJ: Princeton University Press.

DiMaggio, Paul, and Hugh Louch. 1998. "Socially Embedded Consumer Transactions: For What Kinds of Purchases Do People Most Often Use Networks?" *American Sociological Review* 63 (October):619–37.

Dobbs, Dan B., Robert E. Keeton, David G. Owen, and W. Page Keeton. 1988. *Prosser and Keeton on the Law of Torts* (Pocket Part). St. Paul, MN: West Publishing Co.

Dobris, Joel, C., and Stewart E. Sterk. 1998. *Estates and Trusts: Cases and Materials*. New York: Foundation Press.

Doty, Pamela, A. E. Benjamin, Ruth E. Matthias, and Todd M. Franke. 1999. "In-Home Supportive Services for the Elderly and Disabled: A Comparison of Client-Directed and Professional Management Models of Service Delivery." U.S. Department of Health and Human Services and the University of California, Los Angeles. http://aspe.os.dhhs.gov/daltcp/reports/ihss.htm#secI.B. Accessed May 24, 2003.

Draper, Elaine. 2003. *The Company Doctor*. New York: Russell Sage Foundation.

Draper, Jane Massey. 1979. "Establishment of 'Family' Relationship to Raise Presumption That Services Were Rendered Gratuitously, as between Persons Living in Same Household but Not Related by Blood or Affinity." 92 *American Law Reports* 726.

Dreher, William A. 2004. Personal communication from William A. Dreher, managing director of Compensation Strategies, Inc., July 23.

Dubler, Ariela R. 1998. "Governing through Contract: Common Law Marriage in the Nineteenth Century." 107 *Yale Law Journal* 1885.

———. 2000. "Wifely Behavior: A Legal History of Acting Married." 100 *Columbia Law Review* 957.

———. 2003. "In the Shadow of Marriage: Single Women and the Legal Construction of the Family and the State." 112 *Yale Law Journal* 1641.

Durand, Jorge, Emilio A. Parrado, and Douglas S. Massey. 1996. "Migradollars and Development: A Reconsideration of the Mexican Case." *International Migration Review* 30:423–44.

Eaton, Leslie. 2004. "In Nation's Courtrooms, Wounds from 9/11 Attacks Persist." *New York Times*, September 9, sec. B.

Edin, Kathryn, and Laura Lein. 1997. *Making Ends Meet: How Single Mothers Survive Welfare and Low-Wage Work*. New York: Russell Sage Foundation.

Edin, Kathryn, Laura Lein, and Timothy Nelson. 2002. "Taking Care of Business: The Economic Survival Strategies of Low-Income Fathers." In Frank Munger, ed., *Laboring below the Line*, 125–47. New York: Russell Sage Foundation.

Edin, Kathryn, Timothy J. Nelson, and Rechelle Paranel. 2004. "Fatherhood and Incarceration as Potential Turning Points in the Criminal Careers of Unskilled Men." In Mary Patillo, David Weiman, and Bruce Western, eds., *Imprisoning America: The Social Effects of Mass Incarceration*, 46–75. New York: Russell Sage Foundation.

Eggebeen, David J., and Adam Davey. 1998. "Do Safety Nets Work? The Role of Anticipated Help in Times of Need." *Journal of Marriage and the Family* 60 (November):939–50.

Elder, Glen, Jr. 1974. *Children of the Great Depression: Social Change in Life Experiences*. Chicago: University of Chicago Press.

Elder Law FAX. 2002. "Parents Never Meant to Gift Home to Daughter." August 26. http://www.tn-elderlaw.com/prior/020826.html. Accessed July 11, 2004.

Elrod, Linda D., and Robert G. Spector. 2004. "A Review of the Year in Family Law: Children's Issues Remain the Focus." 37 *Family Law Quarterly* 527.

Elshtain, Jean Bethke. 2000. *Who Are We?* Grand Rapids, MI: William B. Erdmans.

Enarson, Elaine. 1990. "Experts and Caregivers: Perspectives on Underground Day Care." In Emily K. Abel and Margaret K. Nelson, eds., *Circles of Care*, 233–45. Albany: State University of New York Press.

England, Paula, Michelle Budig, and Nancy Folbre. 2002. "Wages of Virtue: The Relative Pay of Care Work." *Social Problems* 49:455–73.

England, Paula, and Nancy Folbre. 1999. "The Cost of Caring." In Ronnie J. Steinberg and Deborah M. Figart, eds. "Emotional Labor in the Service Economy." Special issue of *Annals of the American Academy of Political and Social Science* 561 (January):39–51.

———. 2003. "Contracting for Care." In Marianne A. Ferber and Julie A. Nelson, eds., *Feminist Economics Today. Beyond Economic Man*, 61–79. Chicago: University of Chicago Press.

Ertman, Martha M. 1998. "Commercializing Marriage: A Proposal for Valuing Women's Work through Premarital Security Agreements." 77 *Texas Law Review* 17.

———. 2001. "Marriage as a Trade: Bridging the Private/Private Distinction." 36 *Harvard Civil Rights–Civil Liberties Law Review* 79.

———. 2003. "What's Wrong with a Parenthood Market? A New and Improved Theory of Commodification." 82 *North Carolina Law Review* 1.

Espeland, Wendy Nelson, and Mitchell L. Stevens. 1998. "Commensuration as a Social Process." *Annual Review of Sociology* 24:13–43.

Evans, David R., and Margaret T. Hearn. 1997. "Sexual and Non-Sexual Dual Relationships: Managing the Boundaries." In David R. Evans, ed., *The Law, Standards of Practice, and Ethics in the Practice of Psychology*, 53–78. Toronto: Edmond Montgomery.

Evers, Adalbert, Marja Pijl, and Clare Ungerson. 1994. *Payments for Care: A Comparative Overview*. London: Avebury.

Ewick, Patricia, and Susan S. Silbey. 1998. *The Common Place of Law: Stories from Everyday Life*. Chicago: University of Chicago Press.

———. 2003. "The Double Life of Reason and Law." 57 *University of Miami Law Review* 497.

Famuyide, Joseph Rotimi. 2002. *Green Card Interview Questions and Answers*. Brooklyn, NY: Law office of Joseph Famuyide.

Fass, Paula S. 1977. *The Damned and the Beautiful: American Youth in the 1920s*. Oxford: Oxford University Press.

Fehlberg, Belinda. 1997. *Sexually Transmitted Debt*. Oxford: Clarendon Press.

Fellows, Mary Louise. 1998. "Rocking the Tax Code: A Case Study of Employment-Related Child-Care Expenditures." 10 *Yale Journal of Law and Feminism* 307.

Felstiner, William L. F., Richard L. Abel, and Austin Sarat. 1980–81. "The Emergence and Transformation of Disputes: Naming, Blaming, Claiming." 15 *Law and Society Review* 1631.

Fernández-Kelly, Patricia. 2002. "Ethnic Transitions: Nicaraguans in the United States." In Berndt Ostendorf, ed., *Transnational America: The Fading of Borders in the Western Hemisphere*, 177–203. Heidelberg: C. Winter.

Finley, Lucinda. 1989. "A Break in the Silence: Including Women's Issues in a Tort Course." 1 *Yale Journal of Law and Feminism* 41.

Fish, Barry, and Les Kotzer. 2002. *The Family Fight*. Washington, DC: Continental Atlantic Publications.

Fletcher, Denise E., ed. 2002. *Understanding the Small Family Business*. London: Routledge.

Flowers, Amy. 1998. *The Fantasy Factory: An Insider's View of the Phone Sex Industry*. Philadelphia: University of Pennsylvania Press.

Folbre, Nancy. 2001. *The Invisible Heart: Economics and Family Values*. New York: New Press.

Folbre, Nancy, and Julie A. Nelson. 2000. "For Love or Money—or Both?" *Journal of Economic Perspectives* 14(4) (Fall):123–40.

Formanek-Brunell, Miriam. 1998. "Truculent and Tractable: The Gendering of Babysitting in Postwar America." In Sherrie A. Inness, ed., *Delinquents and Debutantes: Twentieth-Century American Girls' Cultures*, 61–82. New York: New York University Press.

Foster, Henry H. 1962. "Relational Interests of the Family." 4 *University of Illinois Law Review* 493.

Fox, Richard Wightman. 1999. *Trials of Intimacy: Love and Loss in the Beecher-Tilton Scandal*. Chicago: University of Chicago Press.

Frank, Katherine. 1998. "The Production of Identity and the Negotiation of Intimacy in a 'Gentleman's Club.' " *Sexualities* 1:175–201.

———. 2002. *G-Strings and Sympathy*. Durham, NC: Duke University Press.

Friedman, David D. 2000. *Law's Order*. Princeton, NJ: Princeton University Press.

Furstenberg, Frank F., Jr., and Andrew Cherlin. 1986. *The New American Grandparent*. New York: Basic Books.

Furstenberg, Frank F., Jr., Saul D. Hoffman, and Laura Shrestha. 1995. "The Effect of Divorce on Intergenerational Transfers: New Evidence." *Demography* 32:319–33.

Furstenberg, Frank F., Jr., Sheela Kennedy, Vonnie C. Mcloyd, Rubén G. Rumbaut, and Richard A. Settersten Jr. 2004. "Growing Up Is Harder to Do." *Contexts* 3 (Summer):33–41.

Gal, Susan. 1989. "Language and Political Economy." *Annual Review of Anthropology* 18:345–69.

Galinsky, Ellen. 1999. *Ask the Children*. New York: Morrow.

Gallagher, Maggie. 2003. "The Marriage Gap: How and Why Marriage Creates Wealth and Boosts the Well-Being of Adults." In Obie Clayton, Ronald B. Macy, and David Blankenhorn, eds., *Black Fathers in Contemporary American Society*, 71–83. New York: Russell Sage Foundation.

Gans, Herbert J. 1967. *The Levittowners*. New York: Vintage.

Garb, Sarah H. 1995. "Sex for Money Is Sex for Money: The Illegality of Pornographic Film as Prostitution." 13 *Law and Inequality* 281.

de la Garza, Rodolfo O., and Briant Lindsay Lowell. 2002. *Sending Money Home. Hispanic Remittances and Community Development*. Lanham, MD: Rowman and Littlefield.

Geen, Rob, ed. 2003. *Kinship Care*. Washington, DC: Urban Institute Press.

Georges, Eugenia. 1990. *The Making of a Transnational Community*. New York: Columbia University Press.

Gershuny, Jonathan. 2000. *Changing Times*. New York: Oxford University Press.

Gersick, Kelin E., John A. Davis, Marion McCollom Hampton, and Ivan Lansberg. 1997. *Generation to Generation*. Boston: Harvard Business School Press.

Gerson, Kathleen. 1993. *No Man's Land: Changing Commitments to Family and Work*. New York: Basic Books.

Giddens, Anthony. 1992. *The Transformation of Intimacy*. Stanford, CA: Stanford University Press.

Gilfoyle, Timothy J. 1992. *City of Eros*. New York: Norton.

———. 1999. "Review Essay: Prostitutes in History; From Parables of Pornography to Metaphors of Modernity." *American Historical Review* 104 (February):117–41.

Gilligan, Carol. 1982. *In a Different Voice: Psychological Theory and Women's Development*. Cambridge, MA: Harvard University Press.

Gillis, John R. 1996. *A World of Their Own Making: Myth, Ritual, and the Quest for Family Values.* Cambridge, MA: Harvard University Press.

Gjerdingen, Dwenda K., and Bruce A. Center. 2005. "First-time Parents' Postpartum Changes in Employment, Childcare, and Housework Responsibilities." *Social Science Research* 34:103–16.

Glazer, Nona Y. 1993. *Women's Paid and Unpaid Labor.* Philadelphia: Temple University Press.

Glenn, Evelyn Nakano. 1986. *Issei, Nisei, War Bride: Three Generations of Japanese Women in Domestic Service.* Philadelphia: Temple University Press.

———. 1992. "From Servitude to Service Work: Historical Continuities in the Racial Division of Paid Reproductive Labor." *Signs* 18:1–43.

Glenn, Norval, and Elizabeth Marquardt. 2001. *Hooking Up, Hanging Out, and Hoping for Mr. Right.* New York: Institute for American Values.

Godbeer, Richard. 2002. *Sexual Revolution in Early America.* Baltimore: Johns Hopkins University Press.

Goldscheider, Frances K., and Linda J. Waite. 1991. *New Families, No Families?* Berkeley: University of California Press.

Goldsmith, Barbara. 1987. *Johnson v. Johnson.* New York. Knopf.

Goodman, Jane, Elizabeth F. Loftus, Marin Miller, and Edith Greene. 1991. "Money, Sex, and Death: Gender Bias in Wrongful Death Damage Awards." 25 *Law and Society Review* 263.

Gowing, Laura. 1996. *Domestic Dangers: Women, Words, and Sex in Early Modern London.* Oxford: Clarendon Press.

Grasmuck, Sherri, and Patricia R. Pessar. 1992. *Between Two Islands: Dominican International Migration.* Berkeley: University of California Press.

Gray, Leslie, and Lynn Friss Feinberg. 2003. "Survey of Californians about In-Home Care Services." National Center on Caregiving, Family Caregiver Alliance. http://www.caregiver.org. Accessed May 23, 2003.

Green, Leon. 1934. "Relational Interests." 29 *Illinois Law Review* 460.

Greenstein, Theodore N. 2000. "Economic Dependence, Gender, and the Division of Labor in the Home: A Replication and Extension." *Journal of Marriage and the Family* 62:322–35.

Gross, Jane. 2002. "U.S. Fund for Tower Victims Will Aid Some Gay Partners." *New York Times*, May 30, sec. A1.

Grossberg, Michael. 1985. *Governing the Hearth: Law and the Family in Nineteenth-Century America.* Chapel Hill: University of North Carolina Press.

Grove, Lloyd. 2003. "It's a Taxing Double Feature." *Daily News Daily Dish*. December 8. http://www.nydailynews.com/news/gossip/story/143673p-127165c.html. Accessed July 11, 2004.

Guérin, Isabelle. 2003. *Femmes et économie solidaire*. Paris: La Découverte.

Guzman, Lina. 2004. "Grandma and Grandpa Taking Care of the Kids: Patterns of Involvement." Child Trends Research Brief (July), publication # 2004–17. Washington, DC: Child Trends.

Hadden, Cathy C. 1993–94. "Interspousal Gifts: Separate or Marital Property?" 32 *University of Louisville Journal of Family Law* 635.

Halle, David. 1984. *America's Working Man*. Chicago: University of Chicago Press.

———. 1993. *Inside Culture: Art and Class in the American Home*. Chicago: University of Chicago Press.

Hamer, Jennifer. 2001. *What It Means to Be Daddy*. New York: Columbia University Press.

Hansen, Karen V. 1994. *A Very Social Time: Crafting Community in Antebellum New England*. Berkeley: University of California Press.

Hareven, K. Tamara, and Randolph Langenbach. 1978. *Amoskeag: Life and Work in an American Factory-City*. New York: Pantheon.

Harmon, Amy. 2003. "Online Dating Sheds Its Stigma as Losers.com." *New York Times*, June 29, sec. 1.

Hartog, Hendrik. 2000. *Man and Wife in America: A History*. Cambridge, MA: Harvard University Press.

Hasday, Jill Elaine. 2004. "The Canon of Family Law." 57 *Stanford Law Review* 825.

Hausbeck, Kathryn, and Barbara G. Brents. 2000. "Inside Nevada's Brothel Industry." In Ronald Weitzer, ed., *Sex for Sale: Prostitution, Pornography, and the Sex Industry*, 217–43. New York: Routledge.

Heimer, Carol A., and Arthur L. Stinchcombe. 1980. "Love and Irrationality: It's Got to Be Rational to Love You Because It Makes Me So Happy." *Social Science Information* 19:697–754.

Heinze, Andrew R. 1990. *Adapting to Abundance*. New York: Columbia University Press.

Held, Virginia. 2002. "Care and the Extension of Markets." *Hypatia* 17: 34–51.

Henly, Julia R. 2002. "Informal Support Networks and the Maintenance of Low-Wage Jobs." In Frank Munger, ed., *Laboring below the Line*, 179–203. New York: Russell Sage Foundation.

Hertz, Rosanna. 1986. *More Equal Than Others: Women and Men in Dual-Career Marriages*. Berkeley: University of California Press.

Heyl, Barbara. 1979. "Prostitution: An Extreme Case of Sex Stratification." In Freda Adler and Rita James Simon, eds., *The Criminology of Deviant Women*, 196–210. Boston: Houghton Mifflin.

Himmelweit, Susan. 1999. "Caring Labor." In Ronnie J. Steinberg, and Deborah M. Figart, eds., "Emotional Labor in the Service Economy." Special issue of *Annals of the American Academy of Political and Social Science* 561 (January):27–38.

Hirsch, Fred. 1976. *Social Limits to Growth*. Cambridge, MA: Harvard University Press.

Hirsch, Jennifer S. 2003. *A Courtship after Marriage*. Berkeley: University of California Press.

Hirschman, Albert. 1977. *The Passions and the Interests: Political Arguments for Capitalism before Its Triumph*. Princeton, NJ: Princeton University Press.

Hirshman, Linda R., and Jane E. Larson. 1998. *Hard Bargains: The Politics of Sex*. New York: Oxford University Press.

Hochschild, Arlie Russell. 1983. *The Managed Heart*. Berkeley: University of California Press.

———. 1995. "The Culture of Politics: Traditional, Postmodern, Cold-Modern, and Warm-Modern Ideas of Care." *Social Politics* 2:331–46.

———. 2001. "Eavesdropping Children, Adult Deals, and Cultures of Care." In Rosanna Hertz and Nancy L. Marshall, eds., *Working Families*, 340–53. Berkeley: University of California Press.

———. 2002. "Love and Gold." In Barbara Ehrenreich and Arlie Russell Hoschild, eds., *Global Woman*, 15–30. New York: Metropolitan Books.

———. 2003. *The Commercialization of Intimate Life*. Berkeley: University of California Press.

Hochschild, Arlie Russell, with Anne Machung. 1989. *The Second Shift: Working Parents and the Revolution at Home*. New York: Viking.

Hofferth, Sandra L., and Jack Sandberg. 2001. "Changes in American Children's Time, 1981–1997." In Timothy Owens and Sandra L. Hofferth, eds., *Children at the Millennium: Where Have We Come From, Where Are We Going?* 193–229. New York: Elsevier Science.

Holbrook, Evans. 1923. "The Change in the Meaning of Consortium." 22 *Michigan Law Review* 1.

Holland, Dorothy C., and Margaret A. Eisenhart. 1990. *Educated in Romance*. Chicago: University of Chicago Press.

Holson, Laura M. 2003. "For $38,000, Get the Cake, and Mickey, Too." *New York Times*, May 24.

Hondagneu-Sotelo, Pierrette. 2001. *Domestica*. Berkeley: University of California Press.

Hondagneu-Sotelo, Pierrette and Ernestine Avila. 2002. "I'm Here but I'm There: The Meanings of Transnational Motherhood." In Naomi Gerstel, Dan Clawson, and Robert Zussman, eds., *Families at Work: Expanding the Boundaries*, 139–61. Nashville: Vanderbilt University Press.

Horowitz, Daniel. 1985. *The Morality of Spending*. Baltimore: Johns Hopkins University Press.

Horowitz, Helen Lefkowitz. 1987. *Campus Life*. New York: Knopf.

Horsburgh, Beverly. 1992. "Redefining the Family: Recognizing the Altruistic Caretaker and the Importance of Relational Needs." 25 *University of Michigan Journal of Law Reform* 423.

Howard, Vicki Jo. 2000. "American Weddings: Gender, Consumption, and the Business of Brides." Ph.D. diss., University of Texas at Austin.

Howell, Martha C. 1998. *The Marriage Exchange: Property, Social Place, and Gender in Cities of the Low Countries, 1300–1550*. Chicago: University of Chicago Press.

Humphreys, Laud. 1975. *Tearoom Trade*. Chicago: Aldine.

Hunter, Howard O. 1978. "An Essay on Contract and Status: Race, Marriage, and the Meretricious Spouse." 64 *Virginia Law Review* 1039.

Illouz, Eva. 1997. *Consuming the Romantic Utopia*. Berkeley: University of California Press.

Ingersoll-Dayton, Berit, Margaret B. Neal, and Leslie B. Hammer. 2001. "Aging Parents Helping Adult Children: The Experience of the Sandwiched Generation." *Family Relations* 50:262–71.

Ingraham, Chrys. 1999. *White Weddings*. New York: Routledge.

Ingram, Paul, and Peter W. Roberts. 2000. "Friendships among Competitors in the Sydney Hotel Industry." *American Journal of Sociology* 106:387–423.

Internal Revenue Service, Department of the Treasury. 2004.

Izzo, Kim, and Ceri Marsh. 2001. *The Fabulous Girl's Guide to Decorum*. New York: Broadway Books.

Jacobs, Jerry A., and Kathleen Gerson. 2004. *The Time Divide*. Cambridge, MA: Harvard University Press.

Jacobson, Lisa. 2004. "Allowances." In Paula Fass, ed., *Encyclopedia of Children and Childhood in History and Society*, 50–51. New York: Macmillan Reference.

Jahoda, Marie, Paul F. Lazarsfeld, and Hans Zeisel [1933] 1971. *Marienthal: The Sociography of an Unemployed Community.* New York: Aldine-Atherton.

Japenga, Ann. 2000. "Is a Luxury Hospital in Your Future?" USA Weekend.com, October 29. http://www.usaweekend.com/00_issues/001029/001029hospitals.html. Accessed June 15, 2003.

Jones, Carolyn C. 1988. "Split Income and Separate Spheres: Tax Law and Gender Roles in the 1940s." *Law and History Review* 6 (Fall):259–310.

Jordan, Miriam. 2004. "Ethnic Diversity Doesn't Blend in Kids' Lives." *Wall Street Journal,* June 18.

Joselit, Jenna Weissman. 1994. *The Wonders of America.* New York: Hill and Wang.

Kahan, Dan M. 1999. Unpublished memo, Yale Law School, October 1.

Kahan, Dan M., and Martha C. Nussbaum. 1996. "Two Conceptions of Emotion in Criminal Law." 96 *Columbia Law Review* 269.

Kahn, Zorina B. 1996. "Married Women's Property Laws and Female Commercial Activity: Evidence from United States Patent Records, 1790–1895." *Journal of Economic History* 56:356–88.

Kahn, Zorina B. and Kenneth L. Sokoloff. 2004. "Institutions and Democratic Invention in Nineteenth-Century America: Evidence from 'Great Inventors,' 1790–1930." *American Economic Review* 94 (May):395–401.

Karner, Tracy X. 1998. "Professional Caring: Homecare Workers as Fictive Kin." *Journal of Aging Studies* 12:69–82.

Karst, Kenneth L. 1980. "The Freedom of Intimate Association." 89 *Yale Law Journal* 624–92.

Katz, Jack. 1999. *How Emotions Work.* Chicago: University of Chicago Press.

Katzman, David. M. 1978. *Seven Days a Week.* New York: Oxford University Press.

Keeton, Page W. ed. 1984. *Prosser and Keeton on the Law of Torts.* St. Paul, MN: West Publishing Co.

Keister, Lisa A. 2002. "Financial Markets, Money, and Banking." *Annual Review of Sociology* 28:39–61.

Kemper, Theodore D., ed. 1990. *Research Agendas in the Sociology of Emotions.* Albany: State University of New York Press.

Kendall, Lori. 2002. *Hanging Out in the Virtual Pub.* Berkeley: University of California Press.

Kenney, Catherine. 2002. "Household Economies: Money Management and Resource Allocation among Married and Cohabiting Couples." Ph.D. diss., Woodrow Wilson School, Princeton University.

Kenney, Catherine. 2004. "Cohabiting Couple, Filing Jointly? Resource Pooling and U.S. Poverty Policies." *Family Relations* 53:237–47.

Kerber, Linda. 1998. *No Constitutional Right to Be Ladies*. New York: Hill and Wang.

Kids' Money. 2004. http://kidsmoney.org. Accessed August 3.

Klein, William A., and Joseph Bankman. 1994. *Federal Income Taxation*. 10th ed. Boston: Little, Brown and Co.

Kline, Ronald R. 2000. *Consumers in the Country: Technology and Social Change in Rural America*. Baltimore: Johns Hopkins University Press.

Knorr Cetina, Karin, and Urs Bruegger. 2002. "Global Microstructures: The Virtual Societies of Financial Markets." *American Journal of Sociology* 107:905–50.

Komarovsky, Mirra. 1940. *The Unemployed Man and His Family*. New York: Dryden Press.

———. 1985. *Women in College: Shaping New Feminine Identities*. New York: Basic Books.

Kornhauser, Marjorie E. 1996. "Theory versus Reality: The Partnership Model of Marriage in Family and Income Tax Law." 69 *Temple Law Review* 1413.

Korobkin, Laura Hanft. 1998. *Criminal Conversations*. New York: Columbia University Press.

Korzenowski, Scott. 1996. "Valuable in Life, Valuable in Death, Why Not Valuable When Severely Injured? The Need to Recognize a Parent's Loss of a Child's Consortium in Minnesota." 80 *Minnesota Law Review* 677.

Kuttner, Robert. 1997. *Everything for Sale: The Virtues and Limits of Markets*. New York: Knopf.

Lan, Pei-Chia. 2002. "Subcontracting Filial Piety: Elder Care in Dual-Earner Chinese Immigrant Households in the Bay Area." *Journal of Family Issues* 23:812–35.

Lansberg, Ivan. 1999. *Succeeding Generations: Realizing the Dream of Families in Business*. Boston, MA: Harvard Business School Press.

Laqueur, Thomas. 1990. *Making Sex: Body and Gender from the Greeks to Freud*. Cambridge: Harvard University Press.

Lareau, Annette. 2003. *Unequal Childhoods*. Berkeley: University of California Press.

Larson, Jane. 1993. "Women Understand So Little, They Call My Good Nature 'Deceit': A Feminist Rethinking of Seduction." 93 *Columbia Law Review* 374.

Lascher, Edward L., Jr., and Michael R. Powers. 2004. "September 11 Victims, Random Events, and the Ethics of Compensation." *American Behavioral Scientist* 48 (November):281–94.

Laumann, Edward O., Stephen Ellingson, Jenna Mahay, Anthony Paik, and Yoosik Youm. 2004. *The Sexual Organization of the City.* Chicago: University of Chicago Press.

Lazarus-Black, and Susan F. Hirsch. 1994. *Contested States: Law, Hegemony, and Resistance.* New York: Routledge.

Lee, Yun-Suk, Barbara Schneider, and Linda J. Waite. 2003. "Children and Housework: Some Unanswered Questions." In Katherine Brown Rosier, ed. *Sociological Studies of Children and Youth* 9:105–25. Oxford: Elsevier Science.

Leonard, Arthur S. 2004. "Lesbian Partner Wins in 9/11 Fund Suit." *Downtown Express* 17 (July 16–22). http://www.downtownexpress.com/de_62/lesbianpartnerwins.html. Accessed November 6, 2004.

Leonard, Diana. 1980. *Sex and Generation: A Study of Courtship and Weddings.* London: Tavistock.

Leslie, Melanie. 1996. "The Myth of Testamentary Freedom." 38 *Arizona Law Review* 235.

———. 1999. "Enforcing Family Promises: Reliance, Reciprocity, and Relational Contract." 77 *North Carolina Law Review* 551.

Lessig, Lawrence. 1995. "The Regulation of Social Meaning." 62 *University of Chicago Law Review* 943.

———. 1996. "Social Meaning and Social Norms." 144 *University of Pennsylvania Law Review* 2181.

———. 1998. "The New Chicago School." *Journal of Legal Studies* 27 (pt. 2):661–91.

Lever, Janet, and Deanne Dolnick. 2000. "Clients and Call Girls: Seeking Sex and Intimacy." In Ronald Weitzer, ed., *Sex for Sale: Prostitution, Pornography, and the Sex Industry,* 85–100. New York: Routledge.

Levitt, Peggy. 2001a. *The Transnational Villagers.* Berkeley: University of California Press.

———. 2001b. "Transnational Migration: Taking Stock and Future Directions." In Alejandro Portes, ed., "New Research on Immigrant Transnationalism." Special Issue of *Global Networks: A Journal of Transnational Affairs* 1:195–216.

———. 2004. "Salsa and Ketchup: Transnational Migrants Straddle Two Worlds." *Contexts* 3:20–26.

Lewis, Jacqueline. 2000. "Controlling Lap Dancing: Law, Morality, and Sex Work." In Ronald Weitzer, ed., *Sex for Sale: Prostitution, Pornography, and the Sex Industry*, 203–16. New York: Routledge.

Lewis, Michael. 2001. "Jonathan Lebed's Extracurricular Activities." *New York Times Magazine*, February 25.

Light, Ivan, and Steven J. Gold. 2000. *Ethnic Economies*. San Diego: Academic Press.

Linsk, Nathan L., Sharon M. Keigher, Lori Simon-Rusinowitz, and Suzanne E. England. 1992. *Wages for Caring: Compensating Family Care of the Elderly*. New York: Praeger.

Lippman, Jacob. 1930. "The Breakdown of Consortium." 30 *Columbia Law Review* 651.

Litwak, Eugene. 1969. "Primary Group Structures and Their Functions: Kin, Neighbors and Friends." *American Sociological Review* 34:465–81.

Litwin, Jack L. 1976. "Annotation: Measure and Elements of Damages in Wife's Action for Loss of Consortium." 74 *American Law Reports* 3d.805.

Lobel, Orly. 2001. "Class and Care: The Roles of Private Intermediaries in the In-Home Care Industry in the United States and Israel." 24 *Harvard Women's Law Journal* 89.

Logan, John R., and Glenna D. Spitze. 1996. *Family Ties: Enduring Relations between Parents and Their Grown Children*. Philadelphia: Temple University Press.

London, Andrew S., Ellen K. Scott, and Vicki Hunter. 2002. "Children and Chronic Health Conditions: Welfare Reform and Health-Related Carework." In Francesca M. Cancian, Demie Kurz, Andrew S. London, Rebecca Reviere, and Mary C. Tuominen, eds., *Childcare and Inequality: Rethinking Carework for Children and Youth*, 99–112. New York: Routledge.

Ludington, J. P. 1960. "Measure and Elements of Damages for Breach of Contract to Marry." 73 *American Law Reports* 2d.553.

Lukemeyer Anna, Marcia K. Meyers, and Timothy Smeeding. 2000. "Expensive Children in Poor Families: Out-of-Pocket Expenditures for the Care of Disabled and Chronically Ill Children in Welfare Families." *Journal of Marriage and the Family* 62:399–415.

Lundberg, Shelly J., Robert A. Pollak, and Terence J. Wales. 1997. "Do Husbands and Wives Pool Their Resources?" *Journal of Human Resources* 32:463–80.

Lynd, Robert S., and Helen Merrell Lynd [1929] 1956. *Middletown*. New York: Harcourt Brace Jovanovich.

Macdonald, Cameron Lynne, and David A. Merrill. 2002. " 'It Shouldn't Have to Be a Trade': Recognition and Redistribution in Care Work Advocacy." In Julie A. Nelson and Paula England, eds., "Feminist Philosophies of Love and Work." Special issue of *Hypatia* 17 (Spring):67–83.

Macneil, Ian R. 1980. *The New Social Contract.* New Haven, CT: Yale University Press.

Madoff, Ray. 1997. "Unmasking Undue Influence." 81 *University of Minnesota Law Review* 571.

Mahler, Sarah J. 2001. "Transnational Relationships: The Struggle to Communicate across Borders." *Identities: Global Studies in Culture and Power* 7(4):583–619.

Malin, Martin H., Maureen K. Milligan, Mary C. Still, and Joan C. Williams. 2004. *Work/Family Conflict: Labor Arbitrations Involving Family Care.* Washington, DC: Program on WorkLife Law, Washington College of Law, American University, June 14.

Maloney, Carolyn B. 2002. "Women Victims of 9/11 and Their Families Deserve Fair Compensation." Press release, January 14. http://www.house.gov/maloney/press/107th/20020114compensation.html. Accessed July 14, 2004.

Margolick, David. 1993. *Undue Influence.* New York: Morrow.

Markowitz, Deborah L. 2000. *The Vermont Guide to Civil Unions.* Vermont: Office of the Secretary of State. http://www.sec.state.vt.us/otherprg/civilunions/civilunions.html. Accessed August 10, 2004.

Martin, Jamie, S. 2001. *Inside Looking Out: Jailed Fathers' Perceptions about Separation from Their Children.* New York: LFB Scholarly Publishing.

Martin, R. F. 1952. "Rights in Respect of Engagement and Courtship Presents when Marriage Does Not Ensue." 24 *American Law Reports* 2d.579.

Marvel, Charles C. 1979. "Unexplained Gratuitous Transfer of Property from One Relative to Another as Raising Presumption of Gift." 94 *American Law Reports* 3d.608.

Mauer, Marc. 1999. *Race to Incarcerate: The Sentencing Project.* New York: New Press.

Maull, Samuel. 2002. "Businessman Must Pay Ex-girlfriend's Rent, She Sues for $3.5 Million." Associated Press State and Local Wire, September 26. Lexis Nexis Academic.

Maupassant, Guy de. [1883] 1971. *Selected Short Stories.* London: Penguin Books.

Mayer, Susan E. 1997. *What Money Can't Buy*. Cambridge, MA: Harvard University Press.

McBee, Randy D. 2000. *Dance Hall Days*. New York: New York University Press.

McCaffery, Edward J. 1997. *Taxing Women*. Chicago: University of Chicago Press.

McComb, Mary C. 1998. "Rate Your Date: Young Women and the Commodification of Depression Era Courtship." In Sherrie A. Inness, ed., *Delinquents and Debutantes: Twentieth-Century American Girls' Cultures*, 40–60. New York: New York University Press.

McDaniel, Paul R., Hugh J. Ault, Martin J. McMahon Jr., and Daniel L. Simmons. 1994. *Federal Income Taxation: Cases and Materials*. Westbury, NY: Foundation Press.

McKinley, Jesse. 2003. "Vows: Sharon Decker and Rick Davidman." *New York Times*, March 9.

McLanahan, Sara, Irwin Garfinkel, Nancy Reichman, and Julien Teitler. 2002. "Unwed Parents or Fragile Families? Implications for Welfare and Child Support Policy." In Lawrence L. Wu and Barbara L. Wolfe, eds., *Out of Wedlock: Trends, Causes, and Consequences of Nonmarital Fertility*, 202–28. New York: Russell Sage Foundation.

McLanahan, Sara, and Gary Sanderfur. 1994. *Growing Up with a Single Parent*. Cambridge, MA: Harvard University Press.

McLaren, Angus. 2002. *Sexual Blackmail*. Cambridge, MA: Harvard University Press.

McLaughlin, Emma, and Nicola Kraus. 2002. *The Nanny Diaries*. New York: St. Martin's Press.

McManus, Patricia A., and Thomas A. DiPrete. 2001. "Losers and Winners: The Financial Consequences of Separation and Divorce for Men." *American Sociological Review* 66:246–68.

McNeal, James U. 1999. *The Kids Market*. Ithaca, NY: Paramount.

Mead, Rebecca. 2001. "American Pimp." *New Yorker*, April 23 and 30, 74–86.

———. 2003. "You're Getting Married: The Wal-Martization of the Bridal Business." *New Yorker*, April 21, 1–13. http://www.rebeccamead.com/2003/2003_04_21_art_wedding.htm. Accessed August 28, 2004.

Meckel, Mary V. 1995. *A Sociological Analysis of the California Taxi-Dancer: The Hidden Halls*. Lewiston, NY: Edwin Mellen Press.

Medical Rants. 2003 "AMA on 'Boutique Medicine.'" June 19. http://www.medrants.com/archives.00178.html. Accessed July 15, 2003.

Menjívar, Cecilia. 2000. *Fragmented Ties: Salvadoran Immigrant Networks in America*. Berkeley: University of California Press.

———. 2002. "The Ties That Heal: Guatemalan Immigrant Women's Networks and Medical Treatment." *International Migration Review* 36:437–66.

Merin, Yuval. 2002. *Equality for Same-Sex Couples*. Chicago: University of Chicago Press.

Meyer, Bruce D., and Douglas Holtz-Eakin, eds. 2002. *Making Work Pay: The Earned Income Tax Credit and Its Impact on America's Families*. New York: Russell Sage.

Meyerson, Michael I. 2002. "Losses of Equal Value." *New York Times*, March 24, sec. 4.

Michel, Sonya. 1999. *Children's Interests/Mothers' Rights*. New Haven, CT: Yale University Press.

Miller, Daniel. 1994. *Modernity: An Ethnographic Approach*. Oxford: Oxford University Press.

———. 1998. *A Theory of Shopping*. Ithaca, NY: Cornell University Press.

Miller, Eleanor M. 1986. *Street Woman*. Philadelphia: Temple University Press.

Mills, C. Wright. 1963. *Power, Politics, and People: The Collected Essays of C. Wright Mills*. New York: Bantam.

Mischler, Linda Fitts. 1996. "Reconciling Rapture, Representation, and Responsibility: An Argument against per se Bans on Attorney-Client Sex." 10 *Georgetown Journal of Legal Ethics* 209.

———. 2000. "Personal Morals Masquerading as Professional Ethics: Regulations Banning Sex between Domestic Relations Attorneys and Their Clients." 23 *Harvard Women's Law Journal* 1.

Missouri Synod. 1999. *The Pastor-Penitent Relationship: Privileged Communications*. St. Louis: The Lutheran Church–Missouri Synod.

Modell, John. 1989. *Into One's Own: From Youth to Adulthood in the United States 1920–1975*. Berkeley: University of California Press.

Mogill, Michael A. 1992. "And Justice for Some: Assessing the Need to Recognize the Child's Action for Loss of Parental Consortium." 24 *Arizona State Law Journal* 1321.

Momjian, Albert, and Mark Momjian. 2004. *Pennsylvania Family Law Annotated*. St. Paul, MN: Thomson-West.

Momjian, Mark. 1997. "Limited Engagement: Suits over Rings and Things under Pennsylvania Law." *Pennsylvania Bar Association Quarterly* 68 (October):140–43.

Momjian, Mark. 2004. "Debts, Divorce, and Student Loans: Case Update on Division of Student Loans and Claims for Equitable Reimbursement." *Matrimonial Strategist* 22 (March):1–2, 4.

Moodie, T. Dunbar, with Vivienne Ndatshe. 1994. *Going for Gold: Men, Mines, and Migration.* Berkeley: University of California Press.

Mooney, Margarita. 2003. "Migrants' Social Ties in the U.S. and Investment in Mexico." *Social Forces* 81:1147–70.

Moors, Annelies. 1998. "Wearing Gold." In Patricia Spyer, ed., *Border Fetishisms*, 208–23. New York: Routledge.

Moran, Rachel F. 2001. *Interracial Intimacy.* Chicago: University of Chicago Press.

Mumola, Christopher J. 2000. "Incarcerated Parents and Their Children." *Bureau of Justice Statistics Special Report.* Washington, DC: U.S. Department of Justice.

Murthy, Veena K. 1997. "Undue Influence and Gender Stereotypes: Legal Doctrine or Indoctrination?" 4 *Cardozo Women's Law Journal* 105.

NALS of Missouri. 2003. Missouri association of legal secretaries. http://www.show-me-lsa.org/membership.htm. Accessed August 9, 2003.

Nathan, Amy. 1998. *The Kids' Allowance Book.* New York: Walker.

National Register of Personal Trainers. 2003. "Code of Ethics." http://www.nrpt.co.uk/find/nrpt/code-of-ethics.htm. Accessed August 9, 2003.

Neiburg, Federico. 2003. "Intimacy and the Public Sphere: Politics and Culture in the Argentinian National Space, 1946–55." *Social Anthropology* 11:63–78.

Nelson, Julie A. 1998. "One Sphere or Two?" In Viviana A. Zelizer, ed., "Changing Forms of Payment." Special issue of *American Behavioral Scientist* 41:1467–71.

———. 1999. "Of Markets and Martyrs: Is It OK to Pay Well for Care?" *Feminist Economics* 5:43–59.

Nelson, Margaret K. 1990. *Negotiated Care: The Experience of Day Care Providers.* Philadelphia: Temple University Press.

———. 2002. "Single Mothers and Social Support: The Commitment to, and Retreat from, Reciprocity." In Naomi Gerstel, Dan Clawson, and Robert Zussman, eds., *Families at Work: Expanding the Boundaries,* 225–50. Nashville: Vanderbilt University Press.

Nelson, Margaret K., and Joan Smith. 1999. *Working Hard and Making Do: Surviving in Small Town America.* Berkeley: University of California Press.

Neus, Margaret Marie. 1990. "The Insider's Guide to Babysitting: Anecdotes and Advice from Babysitters for Babysitters." M.A. project, Emerson College, Boston.

Newman, Katherine S. 1988. *Falling from Grace: The Experience of Downward Mobility in the American Middle Class.* New York: Vintage.

New York Celebrity Assistants. 2003. http://www.nycelebrityassistants. org/joinnyca.htm. Accessed August 9, 2003.

New York Daily News. 2002. "True Love or Just Lust?" September 27.

New York Law Journal. 2004. "Domestic Partner's Suit to Win Portion of 9/11 Fund Award Goes Forward." *New York Law Journal,* online edition, July 16, 1–7.

New York Times. 2001. "A Speedy Exit for Linda Chavez." January 10.

Nicolaides, Becky M. 2002. *My Blue Heaven.* Chicago: University of Chicago Press.

Nightingale, Carl H. 1993. *On the Edge.* New York: Basic Books.

Noonan, John T., Jr. 1976. *Persons and Masks of the Law: Cardozo, Holmes, Jefferson and Wythe as Makers of the Masks.* Berkeley: University of California Press.

Nussbaum, Martha C. 1998. " 'Whether from Reason or Prejudice': Taking Money for Bodily Services." 27(2)(pt. 2) *Journal of Legal Studies* 693.

———. 1999. *Sex and Social Justice.* New York: Oxford University Press.

Obscenity Law Bulletin. 2000. "A Review of Municipal Controls on Lap Dancing." New York: National Obscenity Law Center. http://www. moralityinmedia.org. Accessed: March 15, 2003.

Offer, Avner. 1997. "Between the Gift and the Market: The Economy of Regard." *Economic History Review,* 2nd. ser., 50:450–76.

Ofri, Danielle. 2003. *Singular Intimacies: Becoming a Doctor at Bellevue.* Boston: Beacon.

Ohio General Assembly. 2002. http://www.legislature.state.oh.us/bills. Accessed March 16, 2003.

Oliver, Melvin L., and Thomas M. Shapiro. 1997. *Black Wealth, White Wealth: A New Perspective on Racial Inequality.* New York: Routledge.

Olsen, Richard. 2000. "Families under the Microscope: Parallels between the Young Carers Debate of the 1990s and the Transformation of Childhood in the Late Nineteenth Century." *Children and Society* 14:384–94.

Olson, Laura Katz. 2003. *The Not-So-Golden Years.* Lanham, MD: Rowman & Littlefield.

Orellana, Marjorie Faulstich. 2001. "The Work Kids Do: Mexican and Central American Immigrant Children's Contributions to Households and Schools in California." *Harvard Educational Review* 71:366–89.

Orellana, Marjorie Faulstich, Lisa Dorner, and Lucila Pulido. 2003. "Accessing Assets: Immigrant Youth's Work as Family Translators or 'Para-Phrasers.' " Social Problems 50:505–24.

Orellana, Marjorie Faulstich, Jennifer Reynolds, Lisa Dorner, and Maria Meza. 2003. "In Other Words: Translating or 'Para-phrasing' as a Family Literacy Practice in Immigrant Households." *Reading Research Quarterly* 38 :12–34.

Orellana, Marjorie Faulstich, Barrie Thorne, Anna Chee, and Wan Shun Eva Lam. 2001. "Transnational Childhoods: The Participation of Children in Processes of Family Migration." Social Problems 48:572–91.

Otnes, Cece C., and Elizabeth H. Pleck. 2003. *Cinderella Dreams*. Berkeley: University of California Press.

Pahl, Jan. 1999. *Invisible Money: Family Finances in the Electronic Economy*. Bristol, Eng.: Policy Press.

Pahl, R. E., and Ray Pahl. 2000. *On Friendship*. Cambridge, Eng.: Polity Press.

Palladino, Grace. 1996. *Teen-agers: An American History*. New York: Basic Books.

Palmer, Phyllis. 1989. *Domesticity and Dirt*. Philadelphia: Temple University Press.

Park, Lisa Sun-Hee. 2001. "Between Adulthood and Childhood: The Boundary Work of Immigrant Entrepreneurial Children." *Berkeley Journal of Sociology* 45:114–35.

———. 2004. "Ensuring Upward Mobility: Obligations of Children of Immigrant Entrepreneurs." In Benson Tong, ed., *Asian American Children: A Historical Handbook and Guide*, 123–35. Westport, CT: Greenwood Press.

Parreñas, Rhacel Salazar. 2001. *Servants of Globalization*. Stanford, CA: Stanford University Press.

Parsons, Talcott. 1978. "The Changing Economy of the Family." In *The Changing Economy of the Family: Report of an Interdisciplinary Seminar*. Washington, DC: American Council of Life Insurance.

Pascoe, Peggy. 1999. "Race, Gender, and the Privileges of Property: On the Significance of Miscegenation Law in the U.S. West." In Valerie Matsumoto and Blake Allmendinger, eds., *Over the Edge: Remapping the American West*, 215–30. Berkeley: University of California Press.

Patillo-McCoy, Mary. 1999. *Black Picket Fences*. Chicago: University of Chicago Press.

Peiss, Kathy. 1983. " 'Charity Girls' and City Pleasures: Historical Notes on Working-Class Sexuality, 1880–1920." In Ann Snitow, Christine Stansell, and Sharon Thompson, eds., *Powers of Desire: The Politics of Sexuality*, 74–87. New York: Monthly Review Press.

———. 1986. *Cheap Amusements*. Philadelphia: Temple University Press.

Perlis, Alan, with Beth Bradley. 1999. *The Unofficial Guide to Buying a Home*. New York: Wiley.

Perovich, John D. 1972. "Rights in Respect of Engagement and Courtship Presents When Marriage Does Not Ensue." 46 *American Law Reports* 3d. 578.

Pew Hispanic Center and the Multilateral Investment Fund. 2003. "Billions in Motion: Latino Immigrants, Remittances, and Banking." http://www.pewhispanic.org/site/docs/pdf/billions_in_motion.pdf. Accessed September 26, 2003.

Pleck, Elizabeth H. 2000. *Celebrating the Family: Ethnicity, Consumer Culture, and Family Rituals*. Cambridge, MA: Harvard University Press.

Plesent, Stanley. 2004. Personal communication from Stanley Plesent, former attorney for Katherine Hartog, June 30.

Polivka, Larry. 2001. "Paying Family Members to Provide Care: Policy Considerations for States." Policy Brief no. 7. National Caregiver Alliance. http://www.caregiver.org. Accessed May 23, 2003.

Portes, Alejandro, ed. 1996. *The New Second Generation*. New York: Russell Sage Foundation.

Portes, Alejandro, and Lingxin Hao. 2002. "The Price of Uniformity: Language, Family and Personality Adjustment in the Immigrant Second Generation." *Ethnic and Racial Studies* 25:889–912.

Portes, Alejandro, and Rubén Rumbaut. 1990. *Immigrant America: A Portrait*. Berkeley: University of California Press.

Posner, Richard A. [1992] 1997. *Sex and Reason*. Cambridge, MA: Harvard University Press.

Posner, Richard A., and Katharine B. Silbaugh. 1996. *A Guide to America's Sex Laws*. Chicago: University of Chicago Press.

Post, Emily. 1922. *Etiquette*. New York: Funk and Wagnalls Co.

Post, Peggy. 1997. *Emily Post's Etiquette*. 16th ed. New York: HarperCollins.

Pound, Roscoe. 1916. "Individual Interests in the Domestic Relation." 14 *Michigan Law Review* 177.

Presser, Harriet B. 2003. *Working in a 24/7 Economy*. New York: Russell Sage.

Prosser, William L. 1971. *Law of Torts*. St. Paul, MN: West Publishing Co.

Pyke, Karen. 1999. "The Micropolitics of Care in Relationships between Aging Parents and Adult Children: Individualism, Collectivism, and Power." *Journal of Marriage and the Family* 61:661–72.

Raddon, Mary-Beth. 2002. *Community and Money: Caring, Gift-Giving, and Women in a Social Economy*. Montreal: Black Rose Books.

Radin, Margaret Jane. 1996. *Contested Commodities*. Cambridge, MA: Harvard University Press.

Rasmussen, Paul Keith. 1979. "Massage Parlors: Sex-for-Money." Ph.D. diss., University of California at San Diego.

Reid, William H. 1999. *A Clinician's Guide to Legal Issues in Psychotherapy, or Proceed with Caution*. Phoenix: Zeig, Tucker and Co.

Reiss, Albert J., Jr. 1961. "The Social Integration of Queers and Peers." *Social Problems* 9 (Fall):102–19.

"Responsibility of Noncustodial Divorced Parent to Pay for, or Contribute to, Costs of Child's College Education." 1980. 99 *American Law Reports* 3d. 322.

Reverby, Susan M. 1987. *Ordered to Care: The Dilemma of American Nursing, 1850–1945*. Cambridge: Cambridge University Press.

Rich, Grant Jewell, and Kathleen Guidroz. 2000. "Smart Girls Who Like Sex: Telephone Sex Workers." In Ronald Weitzer, ed., *Sex for Sale: Prostitution, Pornography, and the Sex Industry*, 35–48. New York: Routledge.

Ridgeway, Susan G. 1989. "Loss of Consortium and Loss of Services Actions: A Legacy of Separate Spheres." 50 *Montana Law Review* 349.

Rifkin, Jeremy. 2000. *The Age of Access: The New Culture of Hypercapitalism Where All of Life is a Paid-up Experience*. New York: Jeremy P. Tarcher/Putnam.

Roberts, Kenneth D., and Michael D. S. Morris. 2003. "Fortune, Risk, and Remittances: An Application of Option Theory to Participation in Village-Based Migration Networks." *International Migration Review* 37:1252–81.

Robinson, John P., and Geoffrey Godbey. 1997. *Time for Life*. University Park: Pennsylvania State University Press.

Robson, Elsbeth, and Nicola Ansell. 2000. "Young Carers in Southern Africa: Exploring Stories from Zimbabwean Secondary School Students." In Sarah L. Holloway and Gill Valentine, eds., *Children's Geographies*, 174–93. London: Routledge.

Rollins, Judith. 1985. *Between Women: Domestics and Their Employers.* Philadelphia: Temple University Press.

Romano, Renee C. 2003. *Race Mixing: Black-White Marriage in Postwar America.* Cambridge, MA: Harvard University Press.

Romero, Mary. 1992. *Maid in America.* New York: Routledge.

———. 1996. "Maid in the U.S.A.: Women Domestic Workers, the Service Economy, and Labor." Comparative Labor History Series, Working Paper no. 7, Center for Labor Studies, University of Washington, Seattle.

———. 2001. "Unraveling Privilege: Workers' Children and the Hidden Costs of Paid Childcare." In Katharine B. Silbaugh, ed., "Symposium on the Structures of Care Work." 76 *Chicago-Kent Law Review* 1651.

Romich, Jennifer L., and Thomas S. Weisner. 2002. "How Families View and Use the Earned Income Tax Credit: Advance Payment versus Lump-Sum Delivery." In Bruce D. Meyer and Douglas Holtz-Eakin, eds., *Making Work Pay: The Earned Income Tax Credit and Its Impact on America's Families*, 366–91. New York: Russell Sage.

Rose, Carol. 1992. "Giving, Trading, Thieving, and Trusting: How and Why Gifts Become Exchanges, and (More Importantly) Vice Versa." 44 *Florida Law Review* 295.

———. 1994. "Rhetoric and Romance: A Comment on Spouses and Strangers." 82 *Georgetown Law Journal* 2409.

Rose, Elizabeth. 1999. *A Mother's Job: The History of Day Care 1890–1960.* New York: Oxford University Press.

Rosen, Ruth. 1982. *The Lost Sisterhood: Prostitution in America, 1900–1918.* Baltimore: Johns Hopkins University Press.

Rosenbaum, Thane. 2004. *The Myth of Moral Justice.* New York: HarperCollins.

Ross, Brian Alan. 1997. "Undue Influence and Gender Inequity." 19 *Women's Rights Law Reporter* 97.

Rossi, Alice S., ed. 2001. *Caring and Doing for Others.* Chicago: University of Chicago Press.

Rossi, Alice S., and Peter H. Rossi. 1990. *Of Human Bonding.* New York: Aldine de Gruyter.

Rosten, Leo. 1970. *People I Have Loved, Known, or Admired.* New York: McGraw-Hill.

Rothman, David J. 2002. "Money and Medicine: What Should Physicians Earn/Be Paid?" In Irving Lous Horowitz ed., *Eli Ginzberg: The Economist as a Public Intellectual*, 107–120. New Brunswick, NJ: Transaction.

Rothman, Ellen K. 1984. *Hands and Hearts: A History of Courtship in America*. New York: Basic Books.

Rotman, Edgardo. 1995. "The Inherent Problems of Legal Translation: Theoretical Aspects." 6 *Indiana International and Comparative Law Review* 1.

Rubin, Lillian B. 1985. *Just Friends: The Role of Friendship in Our Lives*. New York: HarperCollins.

Ruddick, Sara. 1998. "Care as Labor and Relationship." In *Norms and Values*, 3–25. Lanham, MD: Rowman and Littlefield.

Sadvié, Tony, and Tim Cohen-Mitchell. 1997. *Local Currencies in Community Development*. Amherst: Center for International Education, University of Massachusetts at Amherst.

Saguy, Abigail Cope. 2003. *What Is Sexual Harassment? From Capitol Hill to the Sorbonne*. Berkeley: University of California Press.

Sahadi, Jeanne. 2000. " 'Can I Have a Loan, Mom?' " *CNNMoney*, August 7. http://money.cnn.com/2000/08/07/strategies/q_retire_lending/. Accessed July 14, 2004.

Salmon, Marylynn. 1986. *Women and the Law of Property*. Chapel Hill: University of North Carolina Press.

Salzinger, Leslie. 2003. *Genders in Production: Making Workers in Mexico's Global Factories*. Berkeley: University of California Press.

Sanchez, Lisa E. 1997. "Boundaries of Legitimacy: Sex, Violence, Citizenship, and Community in a Local Sexual Economy." *Law and Social Inquiry* 22 (Summer):543–80.

Sanger, Carol. 1996. "Separating from Children." 96 *Columbia Law Review* 401.

Sanger, Margaret. [1926] 1993. *Happiness in Marriage*. Old Saybrook, CT: Applewood Books.

Scambler, Graham, and Annette Scambler. 1997. *Rethinking Prostitution*. London: Routledge.

Schlanger, Margo. 1998. "Injured Women before Common Law Courts, 1860–1930." 21 *Harvard Women's Law Journal* 79.

Schlosser, Eric. 2003. "Empire of the Obscene." *New Yorker*, March 10, 61–71.

Schneider, Barbara, and David Stevenson. 1999. *The Ambitious Generation: America's Teenagers Motivated but Directionless*. New Haven, CT: Yale University Press.

Schor, Juliet B. 2004. *Born to Buy*. New York: Scribner.

Schrum, Kelly. 2004. *Some Wore Bobby Sox*. New York: Palgrave Macmillan.

Schulhofer, Stephen J. 1998. *Unwanted Sex: The Culture of Intimidation and the Failure of Law*. Cambridge, MA: Harvard University Press.

Schultz, Vicki. 1998. "Reconceptualizing Sexual Harassment." 107 *Yale Law Journal* 1683.

———. 2000. "Life's Work." 100 *Columbia Law Review* 1881.

Schwartz, Pepper. 1994. *Peer Marriage*. New York: Free Press.

Seattle Nanny Network. 2003. "Privacy Policy," http://www.seattlenanny.com/docs/privacy.html. Accessed August 9, 2003.

Shapo, Marshall S. 2002. "Compensation for Victims of Terror: A Specialized Jurisprudence of Injury." 30 *Hofstra Law Review*, 1245.

Sherman, Jeffrey G. 1981. "Undue Influence and the Homosexual Testator." 42 *University of Pittsburgh Law Review* 225.

Sherman, Rachel. 2002. " 'Better Than Your Mother': Caring Labor in Luxury Hotels." Berkeley: Center for Working Families, University of California, working paper no. 53.

Shirk, Martha, Neil G. Bennet, and J. Lawrence Aber. 1999. *Lives on the Line: American Families and the Struggle to Make Ends Meet*. Boulder, CO: Westview.

Siegel, Reva B. 1994. "The Modernization of Marital Status Law: Adjudicating Wives' Rights to Earnings, 1860–1930." 82 *Georgetown Law Journal* 2127.

Silbaugh, Katharine. 1996. "Turning Labor into Love: Housework and the Law." 91 *Northwestern University Law Review* 1.

———. 1997. "Commodification and Women's Household Labor." 9 *Yale Journal of Law and Feminism* 81.

Silver, Allan. 1990. "Friendship in Commercial Society: Eighteenth-Century Social Theory and Modern Sociology." *American Journal of Sociology* 95 (May):1,474–1,504.

———. 2003. "Friendship and Sincerity." *Sozialer Sinn* 1:123–30.

Simmel, Georg. 1988. *Philosophie de l'amour*. Paris: Rivages Poche Petite Bibliotèque.

Singh, Supriya. 1997. *Marriage Money: The Social Shaping of Money in Marriage and BAnking*. St. Leonards, Australia: Allen & Unwin.

Singletary, Michelle. 1999. "A Break for 'Innocent Spouses': Wives Should Watch What They Sign." Tax Time, *Washington Post*, January 17. http://www.washingtonpost.com/wp-srv/business/longterm/tax/jan99/columnists.htm. Accessed July 14, 2004.

Slater, Lauren. 2003. "Full Disclosure." *New York Times Magazine*, January 26.

Smeeding, Timothy M., Katherin Ross Phillips, and Michael A. O'Connor. 2002. "The Earned Income Tax Credit: Expectation, Use, and Economic and Social Mobility." In Bruce D. Meyer and Douglas Holtz-Eakin, eds., *Making Work Pay: The Earned Income Tax Credit and Its Impact on America's Families*, 301–28. New York: Russell Sage.

Smith, Charles W. 1989. *Auctions: The Social Construction of Value*, NY: Free Press.

Snearly, D. Susanne. 2003. "Drafting College Payment Provisions in Separation Agreements." 17 *American Journal of Family Law* 66.

Soehnel, Sonja A. 1985. "Action for Loss of Consortium Based on Nonmarital Cohabitation." 40 *American Law Reports* 4th 553.

Song, Miri. 1999. *Helping Out: Children's Labor in Ethnic Businesses*. Philadelphia: Temple University Press.

Spector, Barbara, ed. 2001. *The Family Business Compensation Handbook*. Philadelphia: Family Business Publishing Co.

Spragins, Ellyn. 2002. "Help for Elderly Parent Can Fray Family Ties." *New York Times*, November 3.

———. 2003. "When a Windfall Frays Family Ties." *New York Times*, September 7.

Stack, Carol B. 1997. *All Our Kin*. New York: Basic Books.

Stanley, Amy Dru. 1998. *From Bondage to Contract: Wage Labor, Marriage, and the Market in the Age of Slave Emancipation*. Cambridge: Cambridge University Press.

Stansell, Christine. 1986. *City of Women: Sex and Class in New York*. New York: Knopf.

Starr, Paul. 1982. *The Social Transformation of American Medicine*. New York: Basic Books.

Stevens, Rosemary. 1989. *In Sickness and in Wealth: American Hospitals in the Twentieth Century*. New York: Basic Books.

Stinchcombe, Arthur L. 1994. "Prostitution, Kinship, and Illegitimate Work." *Contemporary Sociology* 23 (November):856–59.

Stone, Deborah. 1999. "Care and Trembling." *The American Prospect* 43:61–67.

———. 2000a. "Caring by the Book." In Madonna Harrington Meyer, ed. *Care Work: Gender Labor and the Welfare State*, 89–111. New York: Routledge.

———. 2000b. "Why We Need a Care Movement." *Nation*, March 13.

Stringer, Heather. 2001. "Change of Heart." *NurseWeek*, January 22. http://www.nurseweek.com/news/features/01–01/luxury.asp. Accessed June 15, 2003.

Sullivan, Maureen. 2004. *The Family of Woman*. Berkeley: University of California Press.

Sullivan, Teresa A., Elizabeth Warren, and Jay Lawrence Westbrook. 1999. *As We Forgive Our Debtors*. Washington, DC: BeardBooks.

Sunstein, Cass. 1997. *Free Markets and Social Justice*. New York: Oxford University Press.

Sutherland, Anne, and Beth Thompson. 2003. *Kidfluence*. New York: McGraw-Hill.

Swidler, Ann. 2001. *Talk of Love*. Chicago: University of Chicago Press.

Szarwark, Ernest J. 2003. "Recovery for Loss of Parental Consortium in Non-Wrongful Death Cases." 25 *Whittier Law Review* 3.

Tannenbaum, Michelle. 2003. Personal communication, February 12. Staff member of *Bride's* magazine, citing Condé Nast Bridal Infobank American Wedding Study, 2002.

Tannenbaum, Rebecca J. 2002. *The Healer's Calling: Women and Medicine in Early New England*. Ithaca, NY: Cornell University Press.

Thorne, Barrie. 2001. "Pick-up Time at Oakdale Elementary School: Work and Family from the Vantage Points of Children." In Rosanna Hertz and Nancy L. Marshall, eds., *Working Families: The Transformation of the American Home*, 354–76. Berkeley: University of California Press.

Thorne, Deborah K. 2001. "Personal Bankruptcy through the Eyes of the Stigmatized: Insights into Issues of Shame, Gender, and Marital Discord." Ph.D. diss., Washington State University, Pullman.

Thornley, Trent. J. 1996. "The Caring Influence: Beyond Autonomy as the Foundation of Undue Influence." 71 *Indiana Law Journal* 513.

Tilly, Charles. 1984. *Big Structures, Large Processes, Huge Comparisons*. New York: Russell Sage Foundation.

Tilly, Charles, and Chris Tilly. 1998. *Work under Capitalism*. Boulder, CO: Westview.

Tomes, Nancy. 2003. "An Undesired Necessity: The Commodification of Medical Service in the Interwar United States." In Susan Strasser, ed., *Commodifying Everything*, 97–118. New York: Routledge.

Tomko, Elaine Marie. 1996. "Rights in Respect to Engagement and Courtship Presents When Marriage Does Not Ensue." 44 *American Law Reports* 5th 1.

Townsend, Nicholas W. 1996. "Family Formation and Men's Transition to Adulthood: The Role of Intergenerational Assistance in Buying a Home among Men from the American Middle-Class." Unpublished paper presented at the annual meeting of the Population Association of America.

———. 2002. *The Package Deal: Marriage, Work and Fatherhood in Men's Lives*. Philadelphia: Temple University Press.

Treas, Judith. 1993. "Transaction Costs and the Economic Organization of Marriage." *American Sociological Review* 58:723–34.

Tronto, Joan C. 1994. *Moral Boundaries*. New York: Routledge.

Tuominen, Mary. 2000. "The Conflicts of Caring." In Madonna Harrington Meyer, ed. *Care Work: Gender Labor and the Welfare State*, 112–35. New York: Routledge.

Tushnet, Rebecca. 1998. "Rules of Engagement." 107 *Yale Law Journal* 2583.

Ulrich, Laurel Thatcher. 1991. *A Midwife's Tale*. New York: Vintage.

Ungerson, Clare. 1997. "Social Politics and the Commodification of Care." *Social Politics* 4:362–81.

———. 2000. "Cash for Care." In Madonna Harrington Meyer, ed., *Care Work: Gender Labor and the Welfare State*, 68–88. New York: Routledge.

U.S. Department of Justice. 2002. "September 11th Victim Compensation Fund of 2001: Final Rule." Office of the Attorney General, 28 CFR, part 104. Reported in *Federal Register* 67, no. 49, March 13, Rules and Regulations, 11,233–47. http://www.usdoj.gov/victimcompensation/finalrule.pdf. Accessed July 14, 2004.

U.S. Department of Labor, Bureau of Labor Statistics. 2004. "American Time-Use Survey." Washington, DC.

U.S. General Accounting Office. 2002. "Tax Administration: IRS's Innocent Spouse Program Performance Improved; Balanced Performance Measures Needed." Report to the Chairman and Ranking Minority Member, Committee on Finance, U.S. Senate, April.

Uttal, Lynet. 2002a. *Making Care Work*. New Brunswick, NJ: Rutgers University Press.

———. 2002b. "Using Kin for Childcare: Embedment in the Socioeconomic Networks of Extended Families." In Naomi Gerstel, Dan Clawson, and Robert Zussman, eds., *Families at Work: Expanding the Boundaries*, 162–80. Nashville: Vanderbilt University Press.

Uzzi, Brian, and Ryon Lancaster. 2004. "Embeddedness and the Price of Legal Services." *American Sociological Review* 69:319–44.

Valenzuela, Abel, Jr. 1999. "Gender Roles and Settlement Activities among Children and Their Immigrant Families." *American Behavioral Scientist* 42:720–42.

VanderVelde, Lea. 1996. "The Legal Ways of Seduction." 48 *Stanford Law Review* 817.

Vanek, Joanne. 1974. "Time Spent in Housework." *Scientific American* 11:116–20.

Van Tassel, Emily Field. 1995. " 'Only the Law Would Rule between Us': Anti-miscegenation, the Moral Economy of Dependency, and the Debate over Rights after the Civil War." 70 *Chicago-Kent Law Review* 873.

Vedder, Clyde Bennett. 1947. *An Analysis of the Taxi-Dance Hall as a Social Institution with Special Reference to Los Angeles and Detroit.* Ph.D. diss., University of Southern California.

Velthuis, Olav. 2003. "Symbolic Meaning of Prices: Constructing the Value of Contemporary Art in Amsterdam and New York Galleries." *Theory and Society* 32:181–215.

Wacquant, Loïc. 1998. "A Fleshpeddler at Work: Power, Pain, and Profit in the Prizefighting Economy." *Theory and Society* 27 (1) (February): 1–42.

Wagner, Angie. 2002. "No Lap Dances outside Las Vegas." *Adult Entertainment News,* August 1. http://www.ainews.com. Accessed March 8, 2003.

Waite, Linda J., and Maggie Gallagher. 2000. *The Case for Marriage.* New York: Broadway Books.

Waller Meyers, Deborah. 1998. "Migrant Remittances to Latin America: Reviewing the Literature." The Tomás Rivera Policy Institute, University of Southern California, Los Angeles, working paper, May. http://www.thedialogue.org/publications/meyers.html. Accessed February 5, 2002.

Waller, Willard. 1937. "The Rating and Dating Complex." *American Sociological Review* 2:727–37.

Walsh, Mary Roth. 1977. *Doctors Wanted: No Women Need Apply.* New Haven, CT: Yale University Press.

Walzer, Michael. 1983. *Spheres of Justice.* New York: Basic Books.

Warren, Elizabeth, and Amelia Warren Tyagi. 2003. *The Two-Income Trap.* New York: Basic Books.

W.A.S. 1922. "Charge It to My Husband," 26 *Law Notes* 26–28.

Weber, Florence. 2003. "Peut-on rémunérer l'aide familiale?" In Florence Weber, Séverine Gojard, and Agnès Gramain, eds., *Charges de Famille,* 45–67. Paris: La Découverte.

Weinberg, Dana Beth. 2003. *Code Green.* Ithaca, NY: Cornell University Press.

Weitman, Sasha. 1998. "On the Elementary Forms of the Socioerotic Life." *Theory, Culture and Society* 15:71–110.

Weitzer, Ronald. 2000. "Why We Need More Research on Sex Work." In Ronald Weitzer, ed. *Sex for Sale: Prostitution, Pornography, and the Sex Industry*, 1–17. New York: Routledge.

Weitzman, Lenore J. 1985. *The Divorce Revolution*. New York: Free Press.

Welter, Barbara. 1966. "The Cult of True Womanhood: 1820–1860." *American Quarterly* 18:151–74.

Western, Bruce, Leonard M. Lopoo, and Sara McLanahan. 2004. "Incarceration and the Bonds among Parents in Fragile Families." In Mary Patillo, David Weiman, and Bruce Western, eds., *Imprisoning America: The Social Effects of Mass Incarceration*, 21–45. New York: Russell Sage Foundation.

Western, Bruce, Mary Patillo, and David Weiman. 2004. "Introduction." In Mary Patillo, David Weiman, and Bruce Western, eds., *Imprisoning America: The Social Effects of Mass Incarceration*, 1–18. New York: Russell Sage Foundation.

Weyrauch, Walter O., Sanford Katz, and Frances Olsen. 1994. *Cases and Materials on Family Law: Legal Concepts and Changing Human Relationships*. St. Paul, MN: West Publishing Co.

White, Harrison. 1988. "Varieties of Markets." In Barry Wellman and S. D. Berkowitz, eds., *Social Structure: A Network Approach*, 226–60. New York: Cambridge University Press.

———. 2001. *Markets from Networks: Socioeconomic Models of Production*. Princeton, NJ: Princeton University Press.

White, Shelby. 1992. *What Every Woman Should Know about Her Husband's Money*. New York: Turtle Bay Books.

Whyte, Martin King. 1990. *Dating, Mating, and Marriage*. New York: Aldine.

Williams, Christine L., Patti A. Giuffre, and Kirsten Dellinger. 1999. "Sexuality in the Workplace: Organizational Control, Sexual Harassment, and the Pursuit of Pleasure." *Annual Review of Sociology* 25:73–93.

Williams, Joan. 2000. *Unbending Gender: Why Family and Work Conflict and What to Do about It*. New York: Oxford University Press.

Williams, Joan, and Nancy Segal. 2003. "Beyond the Maternal Wall: Relief for Family Caregivers Who Are Discriminated against on the Job." 26 *Harvard Women's Law Journal* 77.

Willis, Lynda D. 1998. "Innocent Spouse: Alternatives for Improving Innocent Spouse Relief." Testimony before the Subcommittee on Oversight, House Committee on Ways and Means. Washington, DC: United States General Accounting Office.

Wilson, Ara. 2004. *The Intimate Economies of Bangkok.* Berkeley: University of California Press.

Witt, John Fabian. 2000. "From Loss of Services to Loss of Support: The Wrongful Death Statutes, the Origins of Modern Tort Law, and the Making of the Nineteenth-Century Family." *Law and Social Inquiry* 25:717–55.

———. 2004. *The Accidental Republic: Crippled Workingmen, Destitute Widows, and the Remaking of American Law.* Cambridge, MA: Harvard University Press.

Wolf, Douglas A. 2004. "Valuing Informal Elder Care." In Nancy Folbre and Michael Bittman, eds., *Family Time: The Social Organization of Care,* 110–29. London: Routledge.

Wolfe, Tom. 2000. *Hooking Up.* New York: Farrar, Straus and Giroux.

Wood Hill, Marilynn. 1993. *Their Sisters' Keepers.* Berkeley: University of California Press.

Woods, James D., with Jay H. Lucas. 1993. *The Corporate Closet.* New York: Free Press.

Wrigley, Julia. 1995. *Other People's Children.* New York: Basic Books.

Yeung, W. Jean, John F. Sandberg, Pamela E. Davis-Kean, Sandra L. Hofferth. 2001. "Children's Time with Father in Intact Families." *Journal of Marriage and the Family* 63:136–54.

Zatz, Noah D. 1997. "Sex Work/Sex Act: Law, Labor, and Desire in Constructions of Prostitution." *Signs* 22 (Winter):277–308.

Zelizer, Viviana A. 1985. *Pricing the Priceless Child: The Changing Social Value of Children.* New York: Basic Books.

———. 1994. *The Social Meaning of Money.* New York: Basic Books.

———. 2001. "Sociology of Money." In Neil J. Smelser and Paul B. Baltes, eds., *International Encyclopedia of the Social and Behavioral Sciences* 15:9991–94. Amsterdam: Elsevier.

———. 2004. "Circuits of Commerce." In Jeffrey C. Alexander, Gary T. Marx, and Christine Williams, eds., *Self, Social Structure, and Beliefs: Explorations in Sociology,* 122–44. Berkeley: University of California Press.

Zukin, Sharon. 2003. *Point of Purchase: How Shopping Changed American Culture.* London: Routledge.

Index